UNIVERSITY OF NORTH CAROLINA AT CHAPEL HILL
DEPARTMENT OF ROMANCE STUDIES

NORTH CAROLINA STUDIES
IN THE ROMANCE LANGUAGES AND LITERATURES

Founder: URBAN TIGNER HOLMES

Editor: JUAN CARLOS GONZÁLEZ ESPITIA

Distributed by:

UNIVERSITY OF NORTH CAROLINA PRESS

CHAPEL HILL
North Carolina 27515-2288
U.S.A.

NORTH CAROLINA STUDIES IN THE
ROMANCE LANGUAGES AND LITERATURES
Number 317

NARRATING DESIRE:

Moral Consolation and Sentimental Fiction in Fifteenth-Century Spain

NARRATING DESIRE:

MORAL CONSOLATION AND SENTIMENTAL FICTION IN FIFTEENTH-CENTURY SPAIN

BY

SOL MIGUEL-PRENDES

CHAPEL HILL

NORTH CAROLINA STUDIES IN THE ROMANCE
LANGUAGES AND LITERATURES
U.N.C. DEPARTMENT OF ROMANCE STUDIES

2019

Library of Congress Cataloging-in-Publication Data

Names: Miguel-Prendes, Sol, author. | University of North Carolina at
Chapel Hill. Department of Romance Studies, issuing body.
Title: Narrating desire : moral consolation and sentimental fiction in
fifteenth-century Spain / Sol Miguel-Prendes.
Other titles: North Carolina studies in the Romance languages and
literatures ; no. 317.
Description: Chapel Hill : North Carolina Studies in the Romance Languages
and Literatures, U.N.C. Department of Romance Studies, 2019. | Series:
North Carolina studies in the Romance languages and literatures; number
317 | Includes bibliographical references and index.
Identifiers: LCCN 2019041115 | ISBN 9781469651958 (paperback)
Subjects: LCSH: Spanish literature--To 1500--History and criticism. |
Sentimentalism in literature.
Classification: LCC PQ6060 .M54 2019 | DDC 863/.209353--dc23
LC record available at https://lccn.loc.gov/2019041115

Cover design: Ana Cristina Juan Gómez

Cover image: Adaptation of *Breviary.* Biblioteca Nacional de España,
Mss/9694, fol. 64v.

© 2019. Department of Romance Studies. The University of North Carolina
at Chapel Hill.

ISBN 978-1-4696-5195-8

Layout and copyediting by CJV Publicidad y Edición de Libros
claudialibros3@gmail.com, Cel.: (57) 3045698330

CONTENTS

ILLUSTRATIONS

INTRODUCTION

" ¿SOYS novelero?" the Dominican preacher Pedro de Covarrubias asked in his 1515 *Memorial de pecados y aviso de la vida cristiana, copioso, muy complido e provechoso assí para los confessores como
para los penitentes*, addressed to the duchess of Frías.[1] This short but
popular octavo handbook —a mere hundred pages reprinted at least
seven times between 1515 and 1545— aimed to help both priest and
penitent recall sins during the examination of conscience that precedes confession. It ranks *novelero* among the regular transgressions
of courtiers, along with bribing, procuring, and gossiping.

In the *Tesoro de la lengua castellana* (Madrid, 1611), Sebastián de
Covarrubias —no relation— applied the term *novelero* to rumor-mon-
gers who spread *nuevas* or *novelas* (news),[2] yet the same entry defines *novela* as "vn cuento bien compuesto, o patraña para entretener
los oyentes, como las nouelas de Bocacio" [a well-crafted tale, a tall
story meant to entertain, like Boccaccio's novellas]. This meaning is
supported by Richard Percival's translation of a *novelero* as "teller of
tales, fabulator" in his *Bibliothecae Hispanicae pars altera: Containing
a Dictionarie in Spanish, English and Latine* (1591). The Dominican
preacher was most likely referring to the ugly vice of defamatory talk,
but since the question comes shortly after the penitent is asked if he
is often at leisure and how he occupies his time —"¿Acostumbráys

---

[1] On this penitential, see Framiñán, who transcribed it for the CORDE database.
[2] "El que es amigo de traer nueuas" (565 *s.v.* novela). In the same entry, *novela*
is defined as "nueua que viene de alguna parte, que comunmente llamamos nueuas."

estar ocioso? ¿En qué os ocupáys?" Does *novelero* imply the crafting
of more sophisticated stories as a courtly pastime?

Diego de San Pedro's introduction to his *Tractado de amores de
Arnalte y Lucenda* (Treatise on the Love of Arnalte and Lucenda),
first published in 1491 but most likely circulated previously in manuscript form, calls the work "mis nuevas" (*Obras completas I. Tractado* 88). The character *el auctor,* who narrates his later *Cárcel de
Amor* [Prison of Love], the first best-selling romance produced by
the new medium of the printing press, seems driven by the three sins
the *Memorial* ascribes to courtiers —bribing, procuring, and gossiping. Was leisure time at court —the time for *ocio*— spent reading
and writing and relishing those *nuevas?*

This book is about *Cárcel de Amor* and other love tales labeled
sentimental fictions, sentimental romances, or even *novelas senti-
mentales,* a generic status fraught with controversy. Debating the
pleasures and dangers of love, the *materia de amore*, was undeniably
the most distinctive and persistent mode of literary creation in late
medieval Spain (Cátedra, *Poesía de Pasión* 277), and in spite of their
obvious formal differences, the texts critics classify as sentimental
family are only increasing. I propose a different taxonomy and conceptual frame. I single out a group of Catalan and Castilian moral
consolations whose interpretive and compositional practices sired
the sentimental genre. I examine their distortions of the rhetoric of
consolation and the moral therapy of conversion to stress the rhetorical energy of erotic appetite.

The *materia de amore* enjoyed widespread fame in Catalan and
Castilian courts prior to their international diffusion in print in the
sixteenth century, but their enthusiastic readers did not appear out of
nowhere.[3] A significant lay reading public emerged in the Christian
kingdoms of the Iberian peninsula in the later Middle Ages. Round
considers this development, closely analyzed by Lawrance, part of
a general "Europeanization" of the region (*Libro llamado Fedron*
69). Readers were noble or bourgeois and interpreted the works
in private, rather than debating them in public, as the schools did.
Noble patronage supported both translation of the classics and the
exhaustive vernacular apparatus, borrowed from the scholarly *lectio*
—the reading and interpretation of juridical or theological texts—
here intended for the entertainment and instruction of lay readers.

---

[3] On *Cárcel*'s international circulation, see Francomano's *The Prison of Love*.

Lawrance termed this complex cultural transformation "vernacular humanism," also called "prerrenacimiento" (Lida de Malkiel, Maravall), "atmósfera prehumanista" (Di Camillo), and "incipiente humanismo" (Gascón Vera), to distinguish it from the Italian Renaissance.[4] These formulations all underline traditional Castilian belatedness, but, in spite of certain parallels and overlaps with the Renaissance, "the input of intellectual models and influences into the Castilian process was differently made up," as Round notes (*Libro llamado Fedron* 66). These distinctions may safely be extended to the Crown of Aragon, even after accounting for its sociocultural diferences with Castile.[5]

Gómez Moreno accepted the challenge implicit in Round's statement. His extensive knowledge of Spanish archives allowed him to put the actual impact of Italian humanistic trends on Iberia in context. His 1994 *España y la Italia de los humanistas: primeros ecos* proves that fifteenth-century private libraries contained the same titles read by Francesco Petrarca (40). Their owners developed close friendships with prominent Italian humanists, and contacts among writers at the court of Alfons V, the Magnanimous, King of Aragon, who reigned in Naples from 1442–1458, and his son Ferrante (reigned 1458–1494) were even more frequent. The Spanish college at the University of Bologna, established in 1369, and the ecumenical councils celebrated in Pisa (1409), Constanza (1414–1418), and Basil (1431) provided further opportunities for interaction. In the past two decades, articles and monographs have completed the panorama outlined by Lawrance, Round, and Gómez Moreno; they are reviewed in two critical clusters published in *La corónica*: "Salió buen latino: los ideales de la cultura medieval española tardomedieval y protorrenacentista," guest-edited by Cortijo Ocaña and Jiménez Calvente (2008), and "Ottavio di Camillo's *El humanismo castellano del siglo XV*: Thirty-Five Years Later," guest-edited by Juan-Carlos Conde (2010). Cifuentes summarizes the role of translations and translators in the spread of lay literacy in the Crown of Aragon ("Traduccions i traductors").

---

[4] See Di Camillo (*El humanismo castellano del siglo XV*); and, above all, Lawrance ("Nuño de Guzmán;" "The Spread of Lay Literacy;" "On Fifteenth-Century;" "Humanism in the Iberian Peninsula;" "La autoridad de la letra").

[5] In the Crown of Aragon, a circle of Catalan bureaucrats in the chanceries of Joan I (1387–1395) and Martí I (1395–1410), "zealous followers of Petrarch and Boccaccio, began to write Latin epistles in which they strove for a purer style" (Lawrance, "Humanism in the Iberian Peninsula" 232).

These studies note that the same circles cultivated both Latin and vernacular literatures. Butiñá points to the royal courts of Juan II, King of Castile (1406–1454), and Alfons V in Naples, where writers of similar sensibilities composed with equal ease in Castilian, Catalan, and Latin ("El humanismo catalán" 29). Iberian writers were also avid readers of the new classics coming from Italy. To name just a few, Antoni Canals's *Scipió e Aníbal,* composed after 1395, is a partial translation of Petrarch's *Africa.* Aeneas Sylvius Piccolomini's *Historia de duobus amantibus* circulated both in Latin and Castilian. Dante's *Comedy* was translated into Catalan by Andreu Febrer in 1429 and Castilian by Enrique de Villena between 1427 and 1434. Bernat Metge's *Història de Valter e Griselda* (1388) rendered into Catalan Petrarch's third letter in book XVII of *Rerum senilium,* addressed to Boccaccio, which included a Latin version of "Griseldis," the last story in the *Decameron.*[6] The full *Decameron* was translated into Catalan in 1429 as *Novelas de Juan Bocacio* and possibly into Castilian at around the same time.[7] In *Lo somni* (1398), Metge avers that "Griseldis's" subject was well known —"old wives recite the tale to amuse themselves in winter evenings while spinning around the fire"— clearly quoting Boccaccio's defense of the "lowest kind of fiction" in the *Genealogia deorum gentilium* (book XIV, chap. IX–X).[8]

---

[6] For an analysis that contrasts Boccaccio and Petrarch's versions, see Butiñá ("De Metge a Petrarca"). However, Lluís Cabré demonstrates that Metge's version is also indebted to the French translation by Philippe de Mézières (1387), while the classical *exempla* of conjugal love that he appends to the translation are taken from Valerius Maximus ("Petrarch's *Griseldis*").

[7] The work's first known translation into Castilian, only partial, is housed in the Biblioteca de San Lorenzo del Escorial with the signature Esc J-II-21. It belonged to Queen Isabel. See Valvassori ("Observaciones"). The bibliography on translation of the classics is extensive; for an introduction, the reader should consult Russell (*Traducciones y traductores*); Serés ("La traducción en su contexto; "La autoridad literaria"); Alvar and Lucía Mejías ("Repertorio de traductores"); González Rolán and Saquero Suárez-Somonte (*La tradición clásica en España*); Conde ("Ensayo bibliográfico"); Avenoza (Traducciones, público"). Numerous studies focus on individual authors. See, for instance, Keightley ("Boethius in Spain"); González Rolán and Saquero Suárez-Somonte ("Boecio en el medievo hispánico"); Briesemeister ("The *Consolatio Philosophiae*").

[8] Metge says, "La paciència, fortitut e amor conjugal de Griselda, la istòria de la qual fou per mi de latí en nostre vulgar transportada, callaré, car tant és notòria, que ja la reciten les velles per enganar les nits, en les vetles, com filen en ivern entorn del foch" (*'The Dream' of Bernat Metge* 170). The mention of *aniles fabulae* told by the fire appears in Cicero and Seneca to indicate superstitious stories and tall tales, but Boccaccio defends them: under their humble cover, they may scare children, delight maidens, amuse old men, or at least show Fortune's power ("per quem velit aut terrorem incutere parvulis, aut oblectare puellas, aut senes ludere, aut saltem Fortune vires ostendere"), even if they have little to do with real poetry.

Petrarch echoes in many citations that omit his name —for example, *Celestina*— and *Flors de remeys de cascuna Fortuna*, a compendium of quotes from *De remediis utriusque Fortuna* circulated throughout the fifteenth century (Impey, "*Contraria* en la *Triste deleytación* 161).[9] By 1438, Boccaccio's popularity was so widespread that the Archpriest of Talavera blamed him for teaching women all there is to know about sex and complained that poems, love letters, and Boccaccio had replaced devotional works in respectable ladies' libraries.[10]

Lawrance considered Spanish humanism less professional and scholarly than its Italian counterpart ("On Fifteenth-Century" 78) but acknowledged that the rise of lay literacy meant "not only the triumph of the vernacular ... but the beginnings of modern literature as whole" ("The Spread of Lay Literacy" 80). If these *amateurs* threw together Italian innovations on medieval *auctores* and techniques with different degrees of understanding of the vast intellectual program implied in the *studia humanitatis,* their efforts still defined the horizon of expectations for much of fifteenth-century Iberian vernacular literary creation (Rico, "Imágenes del Prerrenacimiento" 15–16).[11]

Butiñá maintains that the contact with Italian humanism invigorated the genres of dialogue, narrative, and poetry in Catalan literature ("El humanismo catalán" 31). While I hold a different view of the nature and evolution of these genres in the Crowns of Castile and Aragon, the vast vernacular production on love with a taste for allegory and the *visio* is undeniable; although its main topic and techniques were medieval, it was galvanized by the arrival of Italian innovations. The translations of Dante, Petrarch, and Boccaccio sparked a widespread craze. In *Tragèdia de Lançalot*, a fragmentary work by *Mossén* Grass, a Catalan knight and perhaps the ambassador of Alfons the Magnanimous in Tunis, he abridged and adapted the French *Mort Artu* to cure "la plaga" that was wounding "la enamorada generació" (Riquer, Martín de "La *Tragèdia de Lançalot*"

---

[9] See Recio (*Petrarca y Alvar Gómez*; "El humanismo italiano;" "Intertextuality in Carroç Pardo;" *Los Trionfi de Petrarca*) for detailed studies of Petrarch's influence on Catalan and Castilian humanism.

[10] The anecdote is quoted by Lawrance ("The Spread of Lay Literacy" 79).

[11] See also Butiñá: "en el conjunto peninsular no se da ese entendimiento y discusión que de modo generalizado se dio en Italia ... sino que prepondera ese conglomerado de figuras mixtas, con rasgos confusos o mezclados" ("El humanismo catalán" 52).

131).[12] His version spurns glorious battles, knightly virtues, and the Arthurian legend's spiritual background in favor of an analysis of love passion. One chapter's truncated rubric summarizes the new content, now regrettably lost: an "exclamació que fa lo actor" on the dangers and misery that erotic desire inflicts on lovers.[13] The *Tragèdia de Lançalot* resembled the sentimental literature that was all the rage more than it did the Arthurian tradition (Riquer, Martín de "La *Tragèdia de Lançalot*").

The early formation of this *enamorada generació* was strongly influenced by the literary preferences of Violante de Bar (1365–1431), niece of Charles V of France, who married the Duke of Girone in 1380 and became Queen of Aragon when he ascended to the throne as Joan I in 1387. Among the titles that entered the Aragonese court at her request were a *Roman de la Rose* sent by her uncle, the Duke of Berry; Ovidian works —the "letres d'Ovidi en pla" and a copy of the "Ovidi mathamorphoseos moralisat;" and Arthurian titles of the Grail cycle. Vice-chancellor Domenec Mascó or an unknown translator rendered Andreas Capellanus's *De arte honeste amandi* into Catalan at the request of *Na* Canosa, wife of Antoni Vilaragut, King's Chamberlain and translator of Seneca's tragedies.[14] Violante's entourage imitated French literary *courts d'amour* in their refinement, literary tastes, and the creation of a "cercle de senyors lletraferits i de dames al qual pertanyen, entre molt altres, Bernat Metge, Domenec Mascó, Antoni Vilaragut i Na Canosa de Vilaragut" [a circle of *lletraferits* lords and ladies to which belongs, among others, Bernat Metge, Domenec Mascó, Antoni Vilaragut, and Lady Canosa de Vilaragut].[15] No English translation conveys all the nuances of the Catalan *lletraferit* that Pagès, first modern editor of Mascó's translation, applies to these aristocrats. The *Gran diccionari de*

---

[12] The *Tragèdia* survives in a 1496 fragmentary incunable; Martín de Riquer speculates that it was composed between 1444–1445, when a Luis Gras was ambassador in Tunis, and in 1485, the assets inventory of Joan Fuster, notary of Perpignan, lists "algunes obres de Lluis Gras, de poca valor." Perhaps *Mossén* Grass is the same person ("La *Tragèdia de Lançalot*" 117–18).

[13] "Exclamació que fa lo actor dolent-se dans, perills e congoxes que amor se procura per causa de aquests desdenys e mal tractes que als enamo ..." (Riquer, Martín de "La *Tragèdia de Lançalot*" 136).

[14] According to Cifuentes, the translation of *De amore* was attributed to Mascó without any reason. Its author is unknown but still within the circle of Queen Violante ("Traduccions i traductors" 147).

[15] My translation of a quote by Pagès in Cortijo Ocaña (*La evolución genérica*); all the information on Violante's court is abridged from that source (20–27).

la llengua catalana defines the word, first documented in 1916, as "amant de conrear les lletres," part bibliophile, part amateur writer, but the term's linkage of *lletra* (letters) and *ferit* (wounded) implies a much deeper and emotional connection with literature that accurately defines these Catalan dilettantes. They experienced love's wounds through literature and were enthralled by Ovid because, like them, he was an author in love, as Bernat Metge's *Ovidi enamorat* attested.[16]

Readers and translators of the classics, old and new, *lletraferits* and *letraheridos*, wrote in astonishing numbers for courtly audiences from the mid-fourteenth century for the following 150 years. Hundreds of noblemen and the emerging class of courtly clerks produced thousands of poems. Gómez-Bravo's important study focuses on the more than 7,000 extant poems that circulated in variant copies —more than all the poetry of France, Britain, and Germany combined, as Gerli proudly notes in his book review— to demonstrate poetry's "place of privilege as the ultimate mark of social legitimation and socio-economic inclusion" (*Textual Agencies* 47). Following work initiated by Weiss (*The Poet's Art*; "¿Qué demandamos?"; What Every Noblewoman"), she illustrates how textual production was a key strategy of conscious self-generation in the context of courtly and urban socio-professional networks.

Most of these poems survive in songbooks or collections of lyrics (Castilian *cancioneros*; Catalan *cançoners*), chapbooks, and printed anthologies; some are included in short prose narratives.[17] They address a broad range of topics in different genres, yet *cancioneros* are generally identified as "love" poetry, perhaps because, as Weiss argues ("La *Affección Poetal*;" "¿Qué demandamos?"), "woman" —her virtues, flaws, and effect on men as an index of Fortune's unpredictability— was reified as "a component in a peculiarly aristo-

---

[16] The full title, according to the only manuscript witness, is *Com se comportà Ovidi essent enamorat*. It is a prose translation of the Latin poem *De vetula*, which Metge believed was composed by Ovid (Butiñá, "De Metge a Petrarca" 225–26). Metge was not alone in this error; Antoni Canals disparaged "libres d'amors, libres d'art d'amar, Ovidi *De vetula*." Enrique de Villena included *De vetula* among works by Ovid that could be found in Spain (Rico, "Sobre el origen" 312).

[17] Over five hundred poets are documented for the Crown of Castile, although, as Whetnall remarks, they may be just a small fraction ("Cancioneros"). See Severin's *An Electronic Corpus of 15th Century Castilian Cancionero Manuscripts*. The Universities of Girona, Barcelona, and Autònoma de Barcelona are working on *Cançoners* DB, a database of facsimile editions of Catalan *cançoners* with diplomatic transcriptions, bibliographies, and other materials (www.narpan.net/).

cratic cultural field, and as a means of demonstrating their intellectual mastering of new learned forms of writing" ("¿Qué demandamos?" 250). Originally influenced by French and Provençal traditions, *cancionero* courtly poetry, like narrative, progressively incorporated Italian forms and themes.[18]

Along with lyric poetry, Catalan and Castilian songbooks included long narrative poems, a distinct Iberian phenomenon alien to the French and Provençal manuscript tradition (Cabré and Martí 175). In "La transmissió manuscrita," Pellisa Prades demonstrates that, in the Catalan tradition, the short prose narratives known as sentimental fictions also circulated in this form, with few exceptions. Martín de Riquer labeled Catalan narrative poems "poemes cortesans amorosos i allegòrics" (*Història* 1: 332–48).[19] Composed between the second half of the fourteenth and the first years of the fifteenth centuries, they dramatize the themes, abstractions, and metaphors of lyric poetry, which may explain their inclusion in *cançoners* (*Història* 2: 42–43). Some of them, such as the anonymous *Requesta que féu un frare a una monja* and *Stòria de l'amat Frondino e de Brisona,* were composed in epistolary form. Others, like the French *lais* that inspire them, set wondrous episodes in courtly milieux; the protagonist is sometimes transported from a magical garden to a fabulous, allegorical realm. Two examples cited by Martín de Riquer, the anonymous *Salut d'amor* and *Una ventura* by Vicenç Comes, who belonged to Metge's circle, exhibit the visionary setting and manipulation of French and Italian sources that will become the trademark of the sentimental *materia. Salut d'amor,* based on a troubadour genre of the same name, aims to convince a lady to accept a lover's request. He argues his case using two examples, the second of which is a love allegory based partly on Boccaccio's tale of Nastagio degli Onesti and an episode from Andreas Capellanus's *De amore* (*Història* 2: 54–59). In Vicenç Comes's *Una ventura,* the author, anguished by love, lounges by a garden fountain in the early morning, engaging in a long *planctus,* until he sees two richly clad ladies who turn out to be Hope and Mercy; they advise and console

---

[18] Francisco Imperial (died ca. 1409) introduced Dantean allegory and hendecasyllable verse; Íñigo López de Mendoza, Marqués de Santillana (1398–1458), wrote Petrarchan sonnets and experimented with Petrarchan motifs that were fully assimilated by his contemporary, the great Valencian poet Ausiàs March, in his songs to a "Plena de seny" and a "Lir entre cards."

[19] See also Annicchiarico ('*Narracions en vers*'); Riquer, Isabel de ("Les poèmes narratifs").

him (64–65). Santillana's narrative *dezires*, particularly the *Infierno*, *Triumphete de amor*, and *El sueño*, are distinct examples of Castilian love allegories that combine French and Italian sources with an imitation of Bernat Metge.

Deyermond ("El hombre salvaje," "On the Frontier") and Cortijo Ocaña (*La evolución genérica*) place these amorous narrative poems on the frontier of the literary genre called sentimental fiction. Since Menéndez Pelayo (1905–1915) defined it as a uniquely Spanish genre that conflates chivalresque adventures and solipsistic eroticism, a combination of *Amadís* and *Fiammetta* (482), critics have been unable to agree on its name, the number of works that constitute it, its defining features, and even whether it is a literary genre at all or just a modern fabrication from Castilian samples (Pellisa Prades *La ficció sentimental* 15)[20] by patriarchal critics (Weissberger, "The Gendered Taxonomy"). As a consequence, an impressive critical bibliography has grown over the last sixty years. Helpful reviews of generic questions appear in Aybar Ramírez (*La ficción sentimental*), Deyermond ("Estudio de la ficción"), and Cortijo Ocaña (*La evolución genérica*). The latter's introduction to the 2000 critical cluster that he guest-edited for *La corónica*, "La ficción sentimental: ¿un género imposible?," is particularly relevant. It generated a lively debate that he cleverly anticipated in his bellicose title. If the sentimental genre were dead, as some in the cluster maintained, its champions were alive and ready to fight. Rohland de Langbehn gallantly led the charge in 2002 with "Una lanza por el género sentimental ... ¿ficción o novela?," which provoked a forum the following year. The latest review appears in Pellisa Prades's remarkable dissertation on *La ficció sentimental catalana de la segona meitat del s. XV* (2013), where she demonstrates the vitality of Catalan fiction supported by a substantial bibliography.

While all sentimental works scrutinize the emotional aspects of love affairs, their formal disparity is such that Deyermond struggled to define them as short pieces on love with an unhappy ending ("La ficción sentimental" xxix). The solution to this impasse has been to highlight formal ambiguity and experimentation as the genre's main features. Gerli, for instance, claims that the genre "is best defined by mood and interest rather than by form" ("Metafiction" 475), and Gómez speaks of a certain ideological mood in the mixed Ovidi-

---

[20] "[U]na construcció mental que la crítica elabora inicialment, al voltant de la tradició literària castellana" (*La ficció sentimental* 15).

an genre called *artes de amores* ("Las 'artes de amores'" 13). Pellisa Prades casts aside the idea of genre as sterile, proposing instead an all-encompassing sentimental vogue or taste, "a moda o gust literari," that she considers a supra-generic entity ["una entitat supragenèrica"].[21] She acknowledges in "La transmissió manuscrita" that her goal is not so much defining a genre as compiling all the possible Catalan works that engage the *materia de amore*. Including narrative poems, letters, and translations, her methodology has the advantage of generating a substantial list of Catalan samples where earlier critics found few.

Other scholars, like Sharrer ("La fusión") and Brandenberger (*La muerte*) highlight the chivalresque stories included in some sentimental narratives and the later amalgamation of sentimental works into chivalry novels. In that tendency, however, Weissberger sees the death of an ersatz genre based on patriarchal ideas that oppose masculine chivalry to the sentimental and feminine ("The Gendered Taxonomy").

The genre's temporal, linguistic, and geographical boundaries appear to expand or contract, depending on the critic's approach. Deyermond accepts the undeniable influence of Ovid's *Heroides* and Boccaccio's *Fiammetta* that earlier scholars detected but suspects the indirect influence of Augustine's *Confessions*, Boethius's *Consolation of Philosophy*, and the correspondence of Abelard and Heloise ("La ficción sentimental" xi–xv).[22] Sentimental production, he concludes, was an Iberian phenomenon with notable similarities to works like *The Kingis Quair*, a poem in 197 stanzas attributed to James I of Scotland composed around 1423–1437 ("La ficción sentimental" xiv; "On the Frontier"). Cortijo Ocaña studied the genre's Catalan origins in the last two decades of the fourteenth century at the court of Violante de Bar and included among its precedents the Portuguese prose version of Gower's *Confessio amantis* and its subsequent translation into Castilian (*La evolución genérica*). Like Brandenberger, he places the last instances of the sentimental genre in mid-sixteenth century Portugal, also noticing some cross-pollination of the sentimental and Byzantine trends.

---

[21] In understanding the genre as a vogue, she acknowledges her debt to Rubió i Balaguer, who indicated in 1949 that those works "reflecteixen una moda en la manera de pensar i de decorar els sentiments" (*La ficció sentimental* 21).

[22] Following Deyermond, Aybar Ramírez (1994) developed an analysis of sixteenth-century sentimental titles.

After more than sixty years of spirited debate, another attempt to resolve the generic impasse may seem futile and perhaps unproductive because, as Casas Rigall points out, methodology is destiny ("la perspectiva metodológica cambia la percepción del objeto de estudio." "'Género literario'" 246). Early on, Michael illustrated some of the problems and dangers in imposing modern generic divisions on medieval literature; while convenient for the critic, they can be misleading ("Epic to Romance to Novel"). On the other hand, genre enables a comparative literary analysis (Blay Manzanera, "La conciencia genérica") that comprehends a work's worldview and discursive environment (Brownlee, "Genre, History").

What to name these works raises other significant methodological questions. Menéndez Pelayo first applied the term *novela* to works he found stylistically similar to Boccaccio's *Fiammetta*, perhaps motivated by Santillana's use of *novella* in his *Comedieta de Ponza* as "work being listened to by royal ladies in a garden" (Michael, "Epic to Romance to Novel" 519). In Rodríguez del Padrón's *Siervo libre de amor*, the term describes just one section, a short fiction like one of Boccaccio's tales.[23] However, although staunchly defended by critics like Rohland de Langbehn (*La unidad genérica*; "Una lanza"), Walde Moheno ("La novela sentimental"), and Brownlee ("Genre, History"), the term *novela* was unknown to medieval *artes poetriae*. Medieval writers of sentimental works called them *tractado, oración*, or *fábula*.[24] Hence, Krause proposed *tractado* to indicate that sentimental narratives were not novels but expository tracts with a didactic intent ("El 'tractado'"). Unfortunately, Whinnom demonstrated that for medieval authors, *tractado* was a polysemic word that might indicate a treatise, in the sense of a written exposition, or a fiction, as a synonym of *estoria*, but not a genre ("*Autor* and *Tratado*"). Dagenais confirmed this conclusion ("Juan Rodríguez").

The difficulty in finding a name that accommodates both Spanish and English linguistic and critical practices poses another challenge.

---

[23] Santillana's definition may be an echo of Boccaccio's epilogue to the *Decameron*, where he defends it from accusations of licentiousness by resorting to the notion of *decorum*: the stories are not meant to be told in church or school, where virtue is required, but "ne' giardini, in luogo di sollazzo, tra persone giovani benché mature e non pieghevoli per novelle" [in gardens, in places of pleasant diversion, among people young but mature and not easily led astray by stories]. Haywood believes that Santillana and Rodríguez del Padrón's contemporaries understood *novella* or *novela* to designate a translation of short prose narrative ("On the Frontiers" 83).

[24] Blay Manzanera gives a complete list ("La conciencia genérica" 219).

Spanish-speaking critics reject *romance* because it designates either a ballad or a language derived from Latin.[25] English-speaking scholars object that when *novel* is attached to the adjective *sentimental,* the genre is confused with a type of eighteenth-century English narrative. Casas Rigall also rejects *novela* for being a technical term that Spanish-speaking literary critics apply exclusively to realistic narratives, distinct from the English use of *novella* to describe shorter, more fantastic works than the "realist" novel. He finds *narrativa* and *relato* too broad and imprecise and favors *ficción sentimental* because the adjective *sentimental* restricts the semantic range of the more ambiguous *ficción* ("'Género literario'" 248–49). Rohland de Langbehn objects to *fiction,* or *ficción,* as favored by critics who stretch generic and geographical boundaries to the point of distortion ("Una lanza" 138), but Deyermond counters that those who defend or oppose generic unity use it equally ("Sentimental Romance" 268). Cátedra solves the problem by stressing the scholarly backdrop of all texts related to the *materia de amore* with the tag *tratados de amor,* regardless of their formal disparity (*Amor y pedagogía*; *Poesía de Pasión*). His choice of terminology in certain instances —*tratadismo* instead of *tratado*— reveals a fine intuition, although he never articulates it; to wit, that *tratado* designates, not a specific work or genre, but a compositional practice (*tractandum est*) that allowed students and scholars alike to mine literary treasures to create their own work.[26]

I favor the label *fiction* to describe both the consolations and their sentimental distortions analyzed in this study. The term's indeterminacy, the fact that it does not conflict with the names of other genres, and its effortless English-Spanish equivalence recommend it as the name for a unique late-medieval Iberian production. I agree with Rohland de Langbehn (*La unidad genérica*; "Una lanza") and Walde Moheno ("La novela sentimental") that concentrating solely on subject matter stretches the genre into a useless, misshapen bag. The sentimental component, Brownlee points out, does not denote a

---

[25] Michael adds contemporary Spanish use of the Anglicism *romance* to mean love affair, as in the expression "tener un romance" ("Epic to Romance to Novel" 511).

[26] Dagenais analyzed the use of *tractatus* in Juan Rodríguez del Padrón's translation of Ovid's *Heroides* in the *Bursario.* He concludes that the term is never used as a translation of the Latin *tractatus* but either renders specific names (*opus, liber, scripta*) or refers to Ovid's works; in one case, it is a translation of the verbal form *tractandum est* ("Juan Rodríguez" 133). I assume that Cátedra has this practice in mind when he speaks of *tratadismo amoroso* (*Amor y pedagogía*; *Poesía de Pasión*).

particular genre. On the contrary, the discursive context, "the imaginary universe constructed by a text," grounds the world it represents and, hence, its genre. In other words —Brownlee elaborates, quoting Jauss— a fairy-tale princess clearly differs from a princess in a novel; likewise, the chivalric hero "Amadís cannot die of despair any more than [sentimental lovers] Leriano or Grisel can live happily ever after, with perfect spouses and delightful progeny" ("Genre, History" 240–41).

Critics who view the *materia de amore* as the only identifiable connection among such disparate texts muddle discourse —"a systematically organized set of statements which give expression to the meanings and values of an institution" (Kress 11)— and genre —a conventionalized form of a social occasion with a specific purpose in the context of an institution. According to Kress, on whose theoretical insights I rely, the close link between an institution's nature and the kinds of occasions that characterize it makes genre and discourse seem identical, but they are not. Christian moral discourse not only provides the descriptions, rules, permissions, and prohibitions of social and individual actions related to erotic passion; it also determines literary interpretation and composition. As Irving notes, Christianity "alone has made love the dominant principle in all areas of dogma" (159). The *materia de amore* would seem to define the genre, if we dismiss the social conventions and interactions from which the texts draw meaning. Riffing on Jauss *via* Brownlee, a clerk in love at school clearly differs from a clerk in love at court, and an allegorical woman instructing a man on Stoic imperturbability has little in common with a woman writing a letter to her suitor, even if they all lament Fortune's vagaries.

Critics who study sentimental fiction's sociohistorical and cultural conditions tend to privilege the courtly setting over religious tradition. Similarly, scholars intent on rebuffing the notion of Catalan and Castilian belatedness lay disproportionate emphasis on the influence of Italian humanism. However, Rodríguez del Padrón, whose *Siervo libre de amor* was long considered the genre's first monument, was fully acquainted with Ovid's moral exegesis —in his *Bursario,* he translated and adapted William of Orléans's *Bursarii Ovidianorum,* a thirteenth-century commentary on the *Heroides* (Dagenais, "Juan Rodríguez"), perhaps via a Catalan translation— but he did not know Boccaccio's *Fiammetta.*[27] In fact, *Fiammetta*'s acclaim in Cas-

---

[27] Even if Rodríguez del Padrón translated directly from Latin, note that Guillem Nicolau also translated the *Heroides* into Catalan in 1390 from a Latin manu-

tile sprang from the popularity of sentimental fiction (Deyermond, "La ficción sentimental" xi–xiv).

Rico's caution regarding the different degrees of understanding of Italian humanism in Spain is an apt corrective. What made Italian *auctores* so enthralling was the old practice of reading as thinking that Augustine outlined in his *Confessions*.[28] Medieval monasticism contributed the visualizing techniques of affective meditation to it, a practice that all Christian scholars had in common and that Franciscans disseminated among the laity. Dante, Boccaccio, and Petrarch were articulating a new way of thinking about poetry, vernacular languages, and the classics, but their Iberian readers related to the aspects of their work that were familiar from their rhetorical training and spiritual practice. I am just extending to sentimental production Weiss's caveat about the Italian origins of Santillana's definition of poetry: "we should look on them not as sources ... so much as a group of writers who helped Santillana to assimilate, clarify and ultimately give concrete expression to ideas with which he and his contemporaries were already familiar" ("La *Affección Poetal Virtuosa*" 200). Bernat Metge, considered one of the earliest humanists in the Iberian Peninsula, displays a similar admixture of classical and Christian sources.

The fascination with allegory and dream vision required no break with late medieval tradition. Contrary to critical trends that trace the visionary structure and motifs in *Siervo* to Dante, Gerli identified a French religious influence ("*Siervo libre de amor*," "The Old French Source").[29] He demonstrated that Rodríguez del Padrón incorporated the rhetoric of confession and well-known allegorical images from the *Rommant des trois pèlerinages* by the Cistercian Guillaume de Deguileville. As we shall see, Bernat Metge's *Lo somni* is clearly indebted to Boethius's *Consolation,* even if Petrarch's *Secretum* is the intermediary. My 2004 article on *Cárcel de Amor*'s readership connected its compositional and readerly practices to the scholarly craft of contemplation; its readers' way of thinking, I contend, can be best described as a "prayer-book mentality" fostered by Franciscan reform.

---

script containing William of Orléans's *accessus* and glosses (Pujol "Les glosses;" The Hispanic Vernacular"). See also the considerations by Saquero Suárez-Somonte and González Rolán in the introduction to the *Bursario's* edition (Rodríguez del Padrón, *Bursario* 45–52).

[28] See Stock ("Reading, Writing;" "Reading, Ethics").

[29] Gómez Redondo supports Boccaccio's unquestionable influence on Rodríguez del Padrón ("De Boccaccio a Caviceo").

This study extends that connection to a larger group comprised of moral consolations and their sentimental distortions and develops ideas roughly sketched in subsequent articles ("La retórica del margen;" "Tratar de amores;" "Otra frontera"). Sections of those earlier approaches are interwoven here in the hope that better contextualization and an abundance of examples will make my argument more persuasive. In exploring the origin and boundaries of the sentimental genre, I follow Deyermond's suggestion to consider the impact of Augustine and Boethius; I look no further than the Catalan translations of *The Consolation of Philosophy*. Like Cortijo Ocaña (*La evolución*), I believe that any analysis of sentimental fiction is incomplete without setting Catalan and Castilian texts side by side.[30] I share his interest (especially in "Hacia la ficción;" "Notas;" "'De amicitia'") in sentimental fiction's connection with the *ars dictaminis*, the discipline that teaches, not only letter writing, but literary composition *sensu lato*.[31] Like him, I presume that sentimental authors took a course of study, but I associate it with, not only Salamanca, but Montpellier and the more general late-medieval educational training in virtuous living that Delgado Criado terms *pietas litterata* (*Historia de la Educación*). This phrase is often used to describe the Erasmian blend of piety and classical learning that traces its roots to the Augustinian Christian orator. I use it to refer to the program of the *ars dictaminis* in the wider context of grammatical *enarratio poetarum* —the adaptation of classical authors, particularly Ovid, to Christian ethics— and the rhetorical exercises that constituted what Carruthers (*The Craft*) calls "the craft of thought," drilled in the homosocial school setting.[32]

---

[30] For an earlier study of the interrelation of Catalan and Castilian literatures, see Cocozzella ("Pere Torroella").

[31] *Ars dictaminis* specifically refers to the art of letter writing, but in its earliest and widest sense, *dictamen* merely indicates the art of composition, both in poetry and prose (Paetow 560). Camargo translates it as "the art of written discourse" that, "throughout its history stood in an equivocal and shifting relationship to the canonical art of rhetoric that gave it birth and probably never ceased to nourish it. Most *dictatores* were quite comfortable in calling their subject rhetoric" ("Toward a Comprehensive" 168). Martín Baños includes a similar definition (129).

[32] For an introduction to "ethical poetics of the later Middle Ages," see Allen (*The Ethical Poetic*). On *pietas litterata*, see Bolgar, who points out that Erasmus "refused explicitly to restrict classical learning to stylistic analysis" and "was prepared to state that all ancient poetry and a good deal of ancient philosophy was 'allegorical'" (339). For a more medieval outlook on *sapientia christiana*, see Franco and Costa's analysis of a sermon by Vincent Ferrer on the moral utility of the liberal arts ("A *sapientia christiana*"). Ferrer, however, opposed pagan culture as an attack on Christian order.

My analysis does not contradict Cátedra's claim in his ground-breaking *Amor y pedagogía* (1989) that Alonso Fernández de Madrigal's Aristotelian views on love and friendship exerted a decisive influence on fictional works and scholarly treatises on the *materia de amore*. He and Folger (*Images in Mind*) studied the philosophical and medical theories that shaped late-medieval Christian moral discourse. Building on their work, I focus on the expression of those ideas in two rhetorical contexts fostered by school training: the young poet in love vs. the aged moralist. Those two contexts found their most lyrical expression in Dante's *translatio* of the human love described in his vernacular poetry into allegorical *caritas*.[33] Dante's impact is more pervasive than direct quotations and uneven imitations suggest: his role as a vernacular Ovid provided the standard for an "author in love," to use Minnis's clever phrase; literary authority was measured against it.

My redefinition of sentimental fiction draws inspiration from Astell's study on Boethian lovers (*Job, Boethius*) and Heinrichs's studies on lovers' consolations and classical myths ("'Lovers' Consolations;'" *The Myths of Love*). According to Astell, *The Consolation*'s initial triangle of prisoner, muses, and Lady Philosophy inspired "two distinct but closely related traditions of amatory romance: the first, parodic and reductive; the second, religious and expansive" (*Job, Boethius* 128). As part of the second tradition, Astell names Peter Abelard's *Historia calamitatum*, which Deyermond considered an indirect stimulus of sentimental fiction, and Dante's *Comedy*. In the parodic and reductive tradition, the lover complains about the instability of love and fortune's fickleness, and Lady Philosophy, as a go-between, offers instruction in Ovidian amatory remedies and manipulates Boethian arguments. Heinrichs points out that these parodies are not simply borrowings, "but adaptations of the *Consolation* by lovers or partisans of love who employ Boethian doctrine perversely in the service of false conclusions" ("'Lovers' Consolations" 93n3). *Roman de la Rose* and Boccaccio's *Elegia di madonna Fiammetta,* customarily cited as catalysts of the sentimental genre, fall into this category (Astell, *Job, Boethius* 127–58).

Instead of grouping all texts relating to the *materia de amore* into a loose, "supra-generic entity," as many critics do, I restrict the genre to prose or prosimetrum works in which moral consolations —or

---

[33] See Minnis ("Authors in Love").

penitential fictions— follow the scholarly exercise of the *enarratio poetarum*. I then characterize the unique genre of sentimental fictions as a distortion of the consolatory aim. The list of fictions that I analyze does not aim to be exhaustive. I am not so much proposing a new canon but a different framework for understanding the context, texture, techniques, and intent of the *materia de amore* and a series of readings that encourage further exploration.

While the meanings and values of penitential consolations and sentimental fictions stem from Christian moral discourse, each genre is the product of social interactions whose features clearly differ as do the purposes and goals of their participants. The rhetorical notion of *decorum* implies these distinctions, but also, as Weiss rightly notes, citing Berger's influential work, form is a "way of seeing" and has social meaning ("Medieval Vernacular" 173). Deyermond perceived that in the allegorical tradition, the only women with a voice are personifications, while in works based on Ovid's epistolary exchanges in *Heroides*, a heroine "speaks at some length and with some frequency" ("On the Frontier" 104–05). As a product of the classroom, clerical parlor, or locutorium, female characters in penitential consolations are problematic personifications that reveal clerical anxiety about the flesh.[34] They offer a soothing therapy to counteract the unhealthy effects of erotic desire and literary fiction.

Sentimental fictions, on the other hand, attempt to meet the demands of the mixed public in the great halls and seigniorial courtyards. Their authors exploit the dissonance of moral allegory to construct and perform their masculine courtly self. The products are contrafacta, my shorthand for what Bakhtin (1981) calls "intentional dialogized hybrids," prenovelistic forms in which many voices and discourses respond to, and engage with, each other.[35] Wardropper proposed the musical term *contrafacta* to categorize religious lyric poems that imitated and transmuted secular lyrics *a lo divino* (*Historia de la poesía lírica*). However, as Crosbie points out, contrafaction was a two-way process —religious verse was often recruited for secular purposes (61n1)— and it was not limited to poetry; a common school practice consisted in distorting dictaminal rhetorical and moral methods. Boncompagno da Signa's *Rota Venus*, Jean de

---

[34] Francomano studies the rhetorical tradition of personifying wisdom as a woman and the dissonances it produces (*Wisdom and Her Lovers*). See also Teskey (*Allegory and Violence*) and Quilligan ("Allegory and Female Agency").

[35] See Bakhtin's chapter "From the Prehistory of Novelistic Discourse" (41–83).

Meun's *Roman de la Rose*, and Juan Ruiz's *Libro de buen amor* are good examples.

Francomano and Haywood analyzed the material context of the sole extant manuscript of *Siervo libre de amor* to demonstrate a similar practice among late-medieval lay readers.[36] Manuscript compilations like BNE Ms. 6052 that were gathered according to thematic content more than form, Francomano claims, encouraged readers to associate very different texts generically or mnemonically ("Manuscript Matrix").[37] While I disagree with her quick dismissal of generic formal traits, I agree that *Siervo*'s placement in a codex with other consolatory texts on the topic of Fortune's vagaries further proves its close connection to the Boethian consolatory tradition. Haywood expands her argument in reconstructing the manuscript's second stage of transmission, when it contained BNE Ms. 6052 plus 128 missing folios of unknown content and Ms. 21549, comprised of burlesque parodies of epistolary rhetoric, falconry manuals, and apocalyptic prophecy ("On the Frontiers"). In a compilation whose contents "jostle against one another in earnest and jest" ("On the Frontiers" 87), *Siervo* confirms my generic taxonomy of the *materia de amore* in moral consolations and their contrafacta. A similar jarring admixture of love poetry and misogynistic compositions that put love passion on trial appears in Ms. 151 of the Biblioteca Universitària de Barcelona, a *cançoner* known as *Jardinet d'orats* (lunatics' garden) copied by a notary named Narcís Gual in 1486.[38] His grouping of mythological and hagiographical prose narratives reveals a similar rhetorical aim.[39] Both compilations point to a readerly interest in pitting various voices and discourses against each other, which sentimental contrafacta exploit.

Other critics have pointed out sentimental fiction's mixed registers. Grieve speaks of "textual multiplicity" (*Desire and Death*). Rohland de Langbehn's meticulous defense of the sentimental genre

---

[36] Francomano presented the argument in a 2006 MLA talk, "Manuscript Matrix and the Meaning of *Siervo libre de amor*." I would like to thank her for sharing a copy. Further remarks on practical and editorial genres appear in her 2018 study.

[37] Dolz's introduction to his edition of *Siervo* asserts the importance of the manuscript's material context in determining its readership and popularity in the last quarter of the fifteenth century (Rodríguez del Padrón 2004).

[38] The translation of the title *jardinet d'orats* is by Pellisa Prades (*La ficció sentimental*).

[39] Two mythological prose narratives —*Lamentacions, Biblis*— exhibit the same *ductus* as the hagiography *Vida de sancta Anna*, while the second hagiography —*Istòria de Josep*— is related to a pair of mythographies —*Leànder y Hero* and *Lo johí de Paris* (Martos, "La 'Vida de Sancta Bàrbara'" 1271).

calls attention to its Bakhtinian plurilingualism (*La unidad genéri-ca*); these accounts of unrequited love, she claims, began to absorb but failed to integrate complex themes and registers.[40] Neither critic explains the reason. My assessment of sentimental fictions as contra-faction of moral consolations also differs from other analyses of late medieval religious parody (Casas Rigall, *Agudeza y retórica*; Gernert; Severin *Religious Parody, Electronic Corpus*). Inspired by Vasvári's Bakhtinian analysis of the *Libro de buen amor* ("The Novelness"), I consider sentimental fictions not quite novels but place them in the context of the novel's prehistory and argue that their *novelness* lies in their distortion of the rhetoric of consolation. Vasvári appropriately emphasizes the subversiveness of the *Libro*'s parody, but I approach sentimental fictions from a more general understanding of hetero-glossia. They cross the languages, points of view, and speaking sub-jects of static allegory with those of narrative, moving from the social register of the school to the court. Penitential consolations progress from sensory chaos to symbol through moral allegory, transmuting love passion into love of God. Sentimental authors embrace chaotic transience and develop their narrative point of view and plot —their *fabula*— away from moral focus in what monastic writers call *curio-sitas*, a type of ethical laziness and weakness of rhetorical *memoria*.[41]

Exegetical performance on a text or textual motif, as Copeland shows, is a type of rhetorical *inventio* (*Rhetoric, Hermeneutics*). Penitential and sentimental authors were scholarly in approaching classical myths "as allegories of the struggle between reason and the passions" and *exempla* of "successful or unsuccessful government of the passions" (Heinrichs, *The Myths of Love* 50). They also exercised their creative chops using humanist best-sellers and contemporary vernacular works as warehouses of themes and motifs, which partly explains their hunger for translations.[42]

---

[40] "Esta narración absorbe complejos temáticos que haste ese momento sólo ocasionalmente formaban parte de la literatura narrativa y que, aplicando criterios estéticos modernos, no aparecen como artísticamente integrados. Se trata de los tex-tos insertos de que habla Segre (1984, 68), con los que se integran registros nuevos y una intertextualidad programática, fenómenos a los que Bajtin se había referido con el nombre de 'plurilingüismo,' pero que en la novela sentimental son 'fagocitados,' igual como en la novela de caballería en prosa, adaptando su estilo al nivel elevado que caracteriza a este grupo" (*La unidad genérica* 68).

[41] On the monastic vocabulary of mental laziness, see Carruthers (*The Craft of Thought* 210).

[42] Serés posited a close connection between the widespread appetite for transla-tions in Castile and Aragon and the emergence of the sentimental genre ("La lla-

Gerli called the convention of the author in love at work *metafic-tion* in his influential 1989 article "Metafiction in Spanish Sentimental Romance." It is the generic marker that distinguishes penitential consolations and their sentimental contrafacta from other texts that engage the *materia de amore*; for example, *cancionero* poetry, epistolary works in verse (*Frondino e Brisona*) or prose (Segura's *Proceso de cartas de amores*), and *disputationes*, such as Juan de Flores's *Grisel y Mirabella*. They are all speech genres that stress difference in power and knowledge. In contrast, penitential fictions attempt to bridge or to eliminate discrepancies and contradictions, a challenge that in sentimental contrafacta can only be solved by their protagonists' ultimate isolation or death.

The authors of penitential and sentimental fictions were also accomplished poets, and their works share with *cancionero* poetry certain compositional mechanisms of the dream vision —first-person voice, allegory, and the *disputatio* of Reason and Will. However, these features are framed by a letter correspondence, friendly exchange, or a patron-author relationship that demands silent reading, not public performance. Cortijo Ocaña demonstrates that letter writing was a popular pastime at the court of Violante de Bar, where Capellanus's *De amore* was translated (*La evolución genérica* 23). Pellisa Prades points out that the epistles Catalan poets exchanged appear in manuscript compilations as theoretical frameworks for the love passion depicted in poems and sentimental narratives ("La transmissió manuscrita" 73–74). Epistolary exchanges and debates are displays of male learning motivated by contrast, which is Weiss's reading of the correspondence between Alfonso de la Torre and an unknown lady on the topic of Fortune ("What Every Noblewoman"). Other displays of learning are the consolatory letters *in morte*, on turns of Fortune, illness, or wounds catalogued by Cátedra ("Prospección;" "Creación y lectura"). They were based on the classroom exercises of *suasoriae* and *controversiae* in which students recited their compo-

mada"). In the Catalan area, Pellisa Prades cites the translation of Chartier's *Belle dame sans merci* (as *Requesta d'amor de Madama Sense Mercè*) as a stylistic model for sentimental authors (*La ficció sentimental*; "La transmissió manuscrita"). Other Catalan translations that circulated in both manuscript and print form, which testifies to their popularity, were Ovid's *Lletres and Transformacions*; Andreas Capellanus's *Regles d'amor*; Boccaccio's *Fiammetta* and *Corbatxo, Paris e Viana*; Leon Battista Alberti's *Deifira* and *Ecatonfila*; Ilicino's *Commentari dels Trionfi de Petrarca*; and Diego de San Pedro's *Càrcer d'amor* (Pellisa Prades, "La transmissió manuscrita" 70). For a complete description of manuscripts and bibliography, see Pellisa Prades (*La ficció sentimental* 73–80).

sitions aloud to a student panel presided over by the teacher (Camargo, "Were Medieval" 183). Young *dictatores* were trained to argue opposite points of view using the same Ovidian characters they first encountered while learning Latin. Fine examples are Capellanus's *De amore*, for the most part a pseudo-scholarly dialogue in the style of rhetorical *declamationes*; Boncompagno da Signa's love letters in his dictaminal manual *Rota Veneris*; and Rodríguez del Padrón's *Bursario*, which translates Ovid's *Heroides* and draws on their themes and techniques to create three fictional letters.[43] The letters' passionate arguments, illusion of immediacy, and distinct female voice must have had the same appeal for courtly audiences as it did for school boys.

Grisel y Mirabella is a very courtly admixture of letter writing and *disputatio*. The letter exchange does not frame the narrative but is part of the plot; it consists of the surprising missive that women-hater Torrellas sends to Braçaida, declaring his love, and her reply immediately after they debate at length their respective positions on whom to blame for love transgressions during the trial of Princess Mirabella and her lover Grisel. Both the debate and correspondence bring onto a courtly stage *la querella de las mugeres*, the "Woman Question," and the contradictions implicit in moral discourse.[44] Its ending, which has perplexed critics, merely indicates that Flores conceives of *Grisel and Mirabella* as a speech genre. As in any *disputatio*, the goal is to demonstrate the author's rhetorical command in articulating both sides of *la querella*. Its sarcastic conclusion, a take on the Orpheus myth, makes plain what every clerk knew: man's reason overpowers women's beastliness.

Sentimental fictions cannot belong to the same consolatory genre they refract, which explains their tendency toward experimentation. Rohland de Langbehn (*La unidad genérica*; "Una lanza") and Brandenberger (*La muerte de la ficción*) rely almost exclusively on the *fabula* to define sentimental fiction's generic traits systematically throughout all its stages. I consider the initial dream vision as a defining formal feature through which sentimental authors read literary tradition and counterfeited its moral interpretation. Hence, I exclude, not only *Grisel y Mirabella,* but also sixteenth-century

---

[43] On the move from translation to creation in the *Bursario*, see Impey ("The Literary Emancipation").

[44] On the "woman question," see Archer (*The Problem of Woman*) and Weiss ("¿Qué demandamos de las mujeres?;" "What Every Noblewoman").

sentimental texts that completely lack an allegorical dream vision or drain it of all rhetorical energy. On the frontier remain some of the "poemes cortesans amorosos i allegòrics" and narrative *dezires* dramatizing lyric abstractions that Martín de Riquer noted. These poems may be narrative, but they do not assign the impulse for literary creation to volition or use reversal to envision the world —what Rohland de Langbehn perceptively saw as "el mundo degradado," a reformulation of Tolstoi's much-quoted dictum about happy and unhappy families applied to ill-fated lovers' narrative potential.

Penitential consolations and sentimental fictions are meant for, not public performance, but the meditative silent reading —"the privacy of the psychic space and soulful place" (Cocozzella, "Fra Francesc Moner" 74–75)— implied in the ethical interpretation of fiction, the *enarratio poetarum* prescribed for all *auctores*.[45] Haywood ("Lyric and Other Verse"), Blay Manzanera ("Espectáculos cortesanos;" "Las cualidades dramáticas"), and Severin ("Audience and Interpretation") might argue that sentimental fictions lend themselves to both individual silent reading and choral performances.[46] The groups of friends who gathered to read *Celestina*, as its paratexts mention, and the friendly after-dinner congregations recorded by Roís de Corella in his *Parlament* would appear to support such practices (see chapter 2). However, *Parlament* and *Celestina* do not present an author at work, which excludes them from my analysis. *Parlament*'s proem makes clear that the friends' speeches take place after the *delitós studi* and *reposat silenci*, the delightful study and peaceful silence, of meditation.

Inevitably, we must face the prickly problem of audiences and their experience of a text *mise en page*. Commenting on Rabinowitz's fourfold typology —actual, authorial, narrator's, and ideal narrative audiences— de Looze reminds us of the obvious fact that "for any medieval work the actual audience of readers over time most likely

---

[45] Gómez Redondo argues that Jacopo Caviceo, author of *Il Peregrino* (1508), dedicated to Lucrezia Borgia, adds to the "dominio sentimental," a variation in which "passion may be defeated if reason prevails over sensuality" ("De Boccaccio a Caviceo" 123). While his reading of *Il Peregrino* is correct, its *variation* cannot be considered an innovation, much less be delayed to the sixteenth century

[46] Gómez Redondo speaks of an ambiguous "realidad sentimental," a narrative model in which fiction must be "sometida a exégesis por los receptores conforme a los medios interpretativos con que los personajes recitan *novellae* en los medios cortesanos en que se mueven" ("De Boccaccio a Caviceo" 123).

includes centuries of readers who were not conceived of in the author's audience" ("Text, Author" 141). This problem is particularly vexing since some penitential and sentimental fictions survive exclusively in manuscript form; others from a printed version. Mazzocchi argues, after Cátedra (*Poesía de Pasión*), that the sentimental genre is closely associated with manuscript compilations that favor epistolary and oratorial genres composed by the scholastic circles of Salamanca ("I manoscritti" 372). Indeed, Severin noted in 1984 that Flores's *Grimalte y Gradisa* was revised no less than three times, the last time for the printing press. It circulated first among an exclusively male readership at Salamanca before it was adapted for courtly tastes. Pellisa Prades asserts that Catalan sentimental works are characterized by a "gran riquesa retòrica" and circulated predominantly in manuscript form ("La transmissió manuscrita" 60, 74). Such manuscript compilations fit well within the "textbook" genre since they contain rhetorical models and should be studied in the context of the *Ad Herennium*'s notoriety, as Woods does ("Rhetoric, Gender;" "Performing Dido"). The success enjoyed by bilingual and multilingual editions of Diego de San Pedro's *Cárcel de Amor* and *Arnalte y Lucenda* and Juan de Flores's *Grisel y Mirabella*, which served as manuals of style in sixteenth-century England, Italy, and France, points in that direction.[47] Boro notes that the paratextual materials of these vernacular polyglot texts show that "they were marketed and intended to be read as foreign-language manuals and that they participate in the twinned didactic traditions of linguistic and moral pedagogy" ("Multilingualism, Romance" 18). That is, they are a prime example of the *ars dictaminis* educational program adapted for courtly needs. The much-quoted anecdote about a lady who rejected a suitor's letter because "no viene a mi sino a Laureola" [it is not intended for me but for Laureola], *Cárcel de Amor*'s heroine, reveals the same practice in Castile.

The reading *locus* constructed by a text may also differ greatly from contemporary practice. Readers may assume the rhetorical role encoded by the text to coincide with the authorial audience or reject it, as did the resisting female readers Weissberger analyzed ("Au-

---

[47] According to Boro, "23 multilingual editions of *Grisel y Mirabella* were issued, including 15 Italian-French, 4 Spanish-French, and 4 Spanish-French-Italian-English; *Cárcel de Amor* boasts 18 bilingual French-Spanish editions; and *Arnalte y Lucenda* was printed in 5 French-Italian and 3 English-Italian texts" ("Multilingualism, Romance" 18).

thors, Characters;" "Resisting Readers"). Regarding Flores's pieces, Severin points out that men wrote with one intention, "but the message was probably received rather differently by an accidental audience of women" ("Audience and Interpretation" 70). Furthermore, actual women among the female audiences intended by the author may have resisted his imputations.

Nothing prevents readers from acting out segments or even complete texts, adapting them to a different purpose and medium. Indeed, the training in the *ars dictaminis* fostered vocal and written amplification of rhetorical models in the process of *inventio*, a practice that we can see at work in Nicolás Núñez's continuation of *Cárcel de Amor*. Whinnom, Cátedra, and Mazzochi consider Núñez's continuation a misreading (Mazzocchi 380), and I agree but only in the sense that, as DeVries notes, by the fifteenth century, allegorical dream vision had become a way of reading the poetic tradition. *The Prison of Love* (2018), Francomano's study of sixteenth-century translations and multimedia adaptations of *Cárcel de Amor* illuminates its transformation into a different cultural product, in a process not unlike the Disney factory's inflation of a fairy tale. Textual and readerly agencies interact to create practical genres.

Still, regardless of whether the work appears in manuscript or print form, textual clues signal its dictaminal reading practices. Penitential and sentimental fictions consider the physical and psychological effects of silent private reading on the imagination, particularly of young men, and rely on *memoria* to access individual inner libraries. In that sense, Mazzocchi contends, the printing press did not drive the sentimental genre but was the external projection of certain private, introspective reading habits that coincide with the process of dictaminal *inventio* and the meditative reading of small prayer books that proliferated among lay readers in the later Middle Ages ("I manoscritti" 379). At the same time, Mazzocchi aptly points out, once a text was in the hands of printers who largely favored highly fictional texts and toned down their scholastic content, transmission became less personal and readership less predictable (379–90). Editorial interventions may have reflected personal needs; Francesc Moner's works were published after his death by his nephew Miguel Barutell, who perhaps hoped to capitalize on *Cárcel de Amor*'s popularity, as Badia suspects.[48] In spite of these challenges, we can still outline the

---

[48] See chapter 2: 167–68.

rhetorical categories that construct the "textual space" and broader contexts of penitential and sentimental fictions.[49]

Chapter 1 begins by considering the discourses on passionate love associated with the rituals of becoming a man in the clerical world of medieval schools, a process that Minnis terms "masculation" (*Magister amoris*). It constructed a model of masculinity that rejected the uncontrolled, animal lasciviousness associated with femininity. The rational man did not reject sex but had power over his sexual impulses (Karras 108), as Juan Ruiz's *loco amor* [foolish love] proves. The kinds of social occasions that characterized the single-sex university environment —solitary study, bonding rituals that explicitly rejected the feminine— give form to the genre of the lover's consolation, based on Boethius's *Consolation of Philosophy* and Ovid's conversion in his old age as narrated in pseudo-Ovid's *De vetula*. A work widely read by young students, *The Consolation* relegates human desire to a fetter the soul must shed on its ascent toward the supreme good. The moral allegories it inspired taught rejection of temporal things, and medieval universities presented *contemptus mundi* as the purpose of liberal arts study (Bultot). Studying the classics would lead students to love God. The task was not easy. Ovid's *Ars amatoria*, the pseudo-Ovid *De vetula*, and the elegiac comedy *Pamphilus de amore* were set texts to instruct boys and young men in grammar. Juan Ruiz's *Libro de buen amor* shows that these "rape narratives," in Wood's words, were well known among Iberian clerics and clerks; it adapted full episodes of the Ovidian and pseudo-Ovidian corpus, and Metge's Catalan *Ovidi enamorat* translated *De vetula*.[50]

Moral consolations taught another lesson: how to use the intellect and free will to effectively control sexual fever and the symptoms of its attending mental illness, *amor hereos*. In Alain de Lille's *De planctu Naturae*, for instance, sexual perversion is a metaphor for moral confusion, and, as in its Boethian model, Reason plays physician (Lynch *The High Medieval*). Memory work and silent prayer —when

---

[49] Blay Manzanera defines "textual space" as the way an author invents a text's formal design in the process of writing it: "el modo en que el autor inventa el diseño formal del texto, a la par que lo escribe; ello se logra mediante la adecuación de unos recursos estilísticos, asegurados por la tradición, a unas intenciones temáticas, canalizadas de informaciones genéricas, que, al pasar el tiempo, podrán o no constituirse en grupos diferenciados" ("La conciencia genérica" 206n2).

[50] On the influence of *Pamphilus* on the *Libro*, see Seidenspinner-Núñez's *The Allegory of Good Love*.

the intellect, through moral allegory, helps free will to convert errant memory into moral reprobation of sin— were a therapy particularly appropriate for men at an age when their bodily heat was at its peak.

Scholarly consolations were either translations of Boethius that incorporated lengthy commentaries or took more creative forms like Lille's *De planctu naturae*. Late-medieval examples of these two trends are, respectively, the Catalan commentaries on *The Consolation* and Petrus Compostellanus's *De consolatione Rationis*, composed at the University of Montpellier. We can see some of the motifs at work in Enrique de Villena's *Doce trabajos de Hércules* [Twelve Labors of Hercules] and Santillana's *El sueño*.

Chapter 1 draws heavily on the work of Carruthers (*The Craft of Thought*) to outline the clerical art of thinking and Minnis (*Medieval Theory*; *Magister amoris*) to discuss medieval theories of authorship and the process of "masculation." Weiss provides background on the culture wars that sparked Iberian lay literacy ("La *Affección Poetal Virtuosa*;" "What Every Noblewoman"). At the crossroads of literary, penitential, and medical discourses on erotic passion, the *caballero sçiente* —Villena's term for the lettered nobleman— emerges as the vernacular author.

Chapter 2 deals with a group of consolations written in Catalan or Castilian almost exclusively by Catalan authors: Bernat Metge's last two books of *Lo somni*; Romeu Llull's *Lo despropriament d'amor*; and Francesc Moner's *La noche* and *L'Ánima d'Oliver*. A Valencian knight, Francesc Carrós Pardo de la Casta, uses the same style to recant the follies of his youth in his *Regoneixença o moral consideració*. I also include a Castilian work, Rodríguez del Padrón's *Siervo libre de amor*, to oppose the critical tradition that places it firmly among the most esteemed monuments of the sentimental genre; its treatment of the *materia de amore* conforms to French penitential tradition, as Gerli ("The Old French Source") and Conde ("De las fuentes") have shown.

Highly conventional in structure and content, these dream visions use narrative material to enact a moral allegory. Critics tend to analyze them almost exclusively in the context of French and Italian humanist trends that entered the Iberian peninsula through the Crown of Aragon. Without denying the obvious French and Italian sources, I stress the shared rhetorical tradition of translation as *inventio*. Dream vision is the tool to read literary tradition ethically as a therapy against sexual desire's immediate and ravaging psychological effects. I term these vernacular consolations *penitential fictions* to stress their links to both confessional and dictaminal narrative practices, the background against which sentimental fictions define themselves. I place Santillana's narrative poem *El sueño* on the border between penitential and sentimental fictions, as Deyermond did, along with Roís de Corella's *Parlament*.

Chapter 3 examines sentimental fictions as counter-presentations of the moral therapy of conversion. They were written by young courtiers, whose age situated them as poets in love, the rhetorical stance of an author in the company of ladies. These works include titles from Whinnom's sentimental canon (*The Spanish Sentimental Romance*) but only those that have a visionary frame or clearly distort the rhetoric of consolation: Pedro de Portugal's *Sátira de infelice e felice vida*; the anonymous *Triste deleytación*; Francesc Alegre's *Somni* and *Rehonament*; Juan de Flores's *Grimalte y Gradisa*; and Diego de San Pedro's *Arnalte y Lucenda* and *Cárcel de Amor*. I discuss Pere Torroella's correspondence on the subject of hope that, with Aristotelian naturalism, shaped courtly love in Aragon and Castile and eroded the triangular dynamics that sustained moral allegory.

Following the Augustinian discourse on *caritas*, penitential consolations use erotic desire's energy to attain ethical conversion. The will of the flesh is a phenomenon closely related to volition, and, as Blay Manzanera noted following Vitz's "Desire and Causality in Medieval Narrative," it becomes a decisive structural element by incapacitating a character's agency ("La conciencia genérica" 225n40). More important, it is first and foremost the deliberate rhetorical option of a first-person narrator, often described as rowing his literary boat into dangerous waves and storms. It moves the text away from the vertical axis of allegory —in the opposite direction from Dante's beatific vision— and right into the chaotic transience of material life. Desire becomes, not a mere expression of carnal impulses, but a longing for imaginative and narrative freedom.

A final warning: critics familiar with the sentimental corpus may object to my detailed plot descriptions, but I hope to interest a wider readership, unfamiliar with many of the texts, especially those in Catalan, and provide a point of entry into their intriguing worlds.

I wish to thank colleagues who at different stages generously shared their expertise, asked questions, and took the time to comment on drafts; most notably and in alphabetical order, Linde Brocato, Antonio Cortijo, Frank Domínguez, Robert Folger, Emily Francomano, George Greenia, Nancy Marino, Ana M. Montero, Sanda Munjic, Gemma Pellisa Prades, Isidro Rivera, Núria Silleras Fernández, and Barbara Weissberger. I cannot overlook the impact that the companionship and encouragement provided by the Medieval Studies Group has had over the years: many thanks to Gillian Overing and Gale Sigal. July Edelson's wisdom and friendship worked hard to tame my worst rhetorical instincts. Juan Carlos González Espitia and Heather Minchew, at the North Carolina Studies in the Romance Languages and Literatures, have answered all my queries with grace and patience while steering the manuscript into print.

I am grateful to Wake Forest University for granting me a J. R. Reynolds Research Leave to finish the manuscript and contributing partial subsidies from the Provost Fund and the Publications Fund. The Ministerio de Cultura y Deporte del Gobierno de España made publication possible with an Hispanex Grant. My gratitude goes also to the librarians at the Z. Smith Reynolds Library, especially Lauren Corbett, for their steady support; and to the Museo del Prado and the Biblioteca Nacional de España, which gave me permission to reproduce images from their collections.

Martin's unconditional love is always my anchor but this book is for Natalia, in loving memory.

CHAPTER 1

THE CONSOLATION OF SCHOOLMEN

L ATE-MEDIEVAL clerics and clerks who filled the royal chanceries were trained in the *artes dictaminales* but so were jurists, notaries, town clerks, and doctors of the urban merchant and ruling classes. In the Crowns of Aragon and Castile the study of the law was considered indispensable for the lesser nobility and the younger sons of the urban oligarchies to find bureaucratic posts at court or in the local governments. Royal preceptors were often masters of theology, like Lope Barrientos, confessor of Juan II of Castile in charge of instructing the future Enrique IV on grammar and writing. Beceiro Pita gives notice of a school at Juan II's court where the Count of Haro, his father, and his grandfather received their education, although it lacked the consistency of scholastic training ("La educación" 198). There is little information on the specific content, particularly during infancy and adolescence but some insights may be gathered from passing mentions.[1] For instance, the fictional character Curial, eponymous hero of a fifteenth-century Catalan story, "as a boy learnt grammar, logic, rhetoric and philosophy, and became a 'poeta molt gran'," an ideal that powerful Castilian and Aragonese knights either inspired or followed (Lawrance, "On Fifteenth-Century" 64–65). What that process entailed for the student and even the patient teacher is the subject in Villena's moralization of the twelve deeds of Hercules analized at the end of this chapter.

---

[1] For general overviews of aristocratic education, mostly in Castile, see Beceiro Pita's invaluable ("Educación y cultura;" "Entre el ámbito privado;" "La educación;" "De las peregrinaciones").

Before learning to compose and to speak in public, students followed a centuries-old normative curriculum of medieval authors and
Roman classics.[2] Elementary Latin grammar texts and readers for *pueri*
between the ages of seven and ten included easy texts on ethics, such as
the *Ars minor*, attributed to Donatus; a collection of maxims entitled
Disticha Catonis; Aesop's moral fables; and the *Ecloga Theoduli*, a didactic debate on the representative virtues of paganism and Christianity.

At the next level, those between the ages of fourteen and twen-
ty-eight labored over metric verse grammars (*Doctrinale, Graecismus*)
and glossaries, such as the *Catholicon*. They practiced their Latin
with texts that continued to instruct them in morals, such as the verse
treatise *De contemptu mundi*, which counseled rejection of transient
worldly delights, also known by its first word, *Chartula,* and selected
classical *auctores*: Virgil, Ovid, Statius, Lucan, and Boethius. These
textbooks were still in use in 1440 according to a letter from Alonso de
Cartagena, Bishop of Burgos, to Pedro Fernández de Velasco, Count
of Haro. The bishop presented his old friend with a codex containing
the *Cathoniana confectio*, a verse adaptation of two of the *libri meno-
res*, the *Disticha Catonis* and the *Contemptus mundi*, "vulgares illos
duos tractatus ... qui ad rudimenta gramaticalis artis pueris adules-
centulisque tradenda legi solent" [those two treatises used to teach
children and adolescents the basics of grammar]. The count, a real-life
Curial praised by his contemporaries for his knowledge of Latin, had
asked Cartagena for "aliqua scripta scolastici exercicii" [some samples
of written school exercises], and the bishop, protective of his professional turf, replied with what Lawrance deems a condescending gift
meant to put the layman in his place ("La autoridad de la letra").[3]

TEACHING THE YOUNG

Ovid's early work, *Ars amatoria*, was considered particularly apt
in the classroom. Its anonymous French translator states in his intro-

---

[2] On the medieval curriculum, see Garin; Bultot; Grendler. Relevant information can be also found in Rico ("Sobre el origen;" "Las letras latinas;" "*Por aver
mantenencia*") and Lawrance ("The Audience). On the teaching of rhetoric in Spain,
see Faulhaber (*Latin Rhetorical Theory*; "Rhetoric in Medieval Catalonia"). On the
homosocial world of medieval universities, see Woods ("Rape and the Pedagogical")
and Karras.

[3] See Lawrance for a study and edition of Cartagena's epistle to the count (*Un
tratado*).

duction to *L'Art d'amours* (c. 1214–1215) that Ovid wrote his treatise to "remove despair from the hearts of the young," and its invitation to promiscuity expresses Ovid's hope "to reveal the fickleness of his youth" (Minnis, *Magister amoris* 55). Some were more skeptical about the ethical intent of the Ovidian *corpus eroticum*, which included numerous apocrypha and such Ovid-inspired tales as the twelfth-century elegiac comedy *Pamphilus*.[4] For instance, the *Libro de confesiones* (c. 1316) warned against its harmful effects: "they instill in students' hearts evil carnal desires as it is the case with Ovid's major work *De arte amandi* and the *Pamphilus* ("ca meten en el coraçon de los escolares amores malos e carnales con ellos asi como Ovidio mayor *De arte amandi* e *Panfilio*," qtd. in Giles 7).[5] Later Ovidian works restored belief in his righteous purposes; his *Remedia amoris* provided the lovesick practical advice on overcoming its melancholy and Pseudo-Ovid *De vetula* —a thirteenth-century French work probably composed by Richard de Fournival, also called *De mutatione vitae*— narrated Ovid's conversion to Christianity in his old age.[6]

In any case, schoolrooms were not the places of depravity and licentiousness that their preferred repertoires may suggest. True, by our modern standards, these texts, selected for their potential interest to students, were of dubious moral value and abound in rape narratives (Woods, "Rape and the Pedagogical"), but as staples of the Latin grammar curriculum, translators and commentators secured their place through a method of moral and allegorical exegesis explicated in their academic prologues, the *accessus ad auctores*.[7] While answering the question "cui parte philosophiae subponitur," they ascribed the Ovidian corpus to moral philosophy ("ethice subponitur") as a matter of course since its underlying aim was instruction on the *contemptus mundi*. In particular, the utility of Ovid's *Meta-*

---

[4] As part of the Ovidian corpus, Rico mentions a long narrative poem that manuscripts entitle *Ovidius puellarum* and *De nuncio sagaci*; five of the manuscripts and incunabula also contain the *Pamphilus* ("Sobre el origen" 310).

[5] Further information on Ovid in the schools in Schevill with particular attention to *Libro de Aleixandre's* injunction against women (20–22).

[6] In the introduction to her edition of *De vetula*, Robathan mentions that an intellectual figure of the stature of Roger Bacon expressed satisfaction that the pagan Ovid had become a Christian (1). In his *Opus maius*, Bacon marvels: "Ovid is said to have predicted the birth of Christ from an extraordinary conjunction of Saturn and Jupiter" (Alton and Wormells 69).

[7] See Quain; Minnis (*Medieval Theory*). In *Magister amoris* Minnis explores the implications of the medieval theory of authorship in the *Roman de la Rose*.

morphoses —a repository of mythological knowledge for medieval students known as *Ovidius maior*— resided in providing knowledge of spiritual matters from temporal change (Bultot 816).

A case in point is John of Garland's *Integumenta Ovidii* (c. 1234), a condensed verse allegorization of the *Metamorphoses* used for the moral instruction of male adolescents and as a memory aid. Its inherited gendered readings of Ovid's myths equate women with the flesh, while *vir* is synonymous with reason. In the exegesis of myth 10, *vir* is also likened to a lion "for his indulgence in sexual excess" (McKinley 69–73), stressing schoolboys' double nature as rational but sexual beings. Indeed, students laboring on their Ovid were at the age when their bodily heat was thought to be highest, and medieval schools, while praising a life of celibacy and chastity, did not or could not enforce Church teachings on the matter. Much to the contrary, in the process of becoming men, which Minnis terms "masculation" (*Magister amoris*), students learned that masculinity involved aggressive sexual performance. Latin schooltexts were filled with sexual imagery, and rape was a common narrative: "In the homosocial world of the classroom ... heterosexual desire was, paradoxically enough, actively encouraged as preparing boys and male adolescents for adulthood. Texts like the *Ars amatoria* and *Pamphilus* served this purpose well" (Minnis, *Magister amoris* 202).[8] No wonder, then, the routine incidents in which schoolmen harassed and raped university townswomen (Karras 79). Schoolmen were as sexually active and violent as their peers in the knightly estates and trades; what differentiated them from other men —and women and beasts— was not their sexual drive but their rationality (82).

THE RHETORIC OF RATIONALITY

The questionable content of Latin primers and the ardors of youth that moral exegesis sought to alleviate were also mitigated by the teachings and commentaries on another classical *auctor* included in the canon. By the sheer force of its philosophical argumentation and exquisitely moving personifications, Boethius's *Consolation of Philosophy* led students to reject *temporalia* and to attain knowledge

---

[8] See Woods ("Rape and the Pedagogical") for the pedagogical value of sexual violence.

of the highest good.[9] More important, it introduced students to the rhetorical genre of the dream vision as a disciplined cognitive method for thinking and composing by making mental images, what Carruthers calls "the craft of thought."[10]

The craft was a direct heir of classical rhetoric adapted to the needs and circumstances of monastic rule. Its goals and principles were set forth in the works of Augustine of Hippo and Boethius; they taught the practitioner to create his own meditational material by searching the inventory of his memory. A monk's memorial depository contained all kinds of mental phenomena, from likenesses of things seen to cognitive skills and emotional experiences. All these contents could be accessed by resorting to individually-crafted mnemonic pictures, each with two elements: a "likeness" that served as a token of the matter remembered and *intentio*, a coloration, inclination, or emotional attitude toward the remembered experience, which, in the case of the sacred text, was necessarily charity. When creating their own thinking images, early monks spurned the dangers of using material artifacts as mnemonic aids, which might have encouraged mental laziness. However, as Stock remarks, by the time of Petrarch, "the meditative ideal of earlier monastic thought [was] transformed into a type of literary subjectivity ... the self no longer resonates with its own inwardness but with the inner meaning of the texts read, written, and mentally recreated" and the interiority that Augustine associated with the mind became "the interior meaning of the text ... a *secretum* that is something sequestered and hidden away" ("Reading, Writing" 727).

The texts that populated schoolboys' memories and inner world were adapted to Christian ethics by reorienting the emotional reactions the licentious stories undoubtedly triggered toward the intention of charity; that is, sexual desire was morphed into love for God. This drastic move at work in the search for a Christian utility in pagan *auctores* effects a conversion that is both moral and rhetorical. It implies a mental journey through the content of memories before "converting" them. The first step, the *compunctio cordis*, is an

---

[9] According to Bultot, Conrad of Hirsau's *Dialogus super auctores* lists Boethius's work as *De consolatione et de mundi contemptu*; therefore, *ethice subponitur* because it affirms that we should not desire temporal things and teaches good morals (813).

[10] My analysis on the implications of the craft of thought is heavily indebted to Carruthers's *The Craft of Thought*. In the following paragraphs, I summarize the points relevant to my argument.

anxious, chaotic state of remembering. The initial panic and copious tears are meant, not to induce forgetfulness, but to adapt old memories and carnal readings to Christian thought. The emotional turmoil reorients the will to color them with an ethical attitude. This rhetorical realignment operates in the sacrament of confession, where personal willpower channels remembrance of sins toward virtue and salvation with the help of God's grace. As Carruthers remarks:

> What forgiveness changes is that *intentio*, the emotional direction (the root metaphor in *converto*) towards the memory images that still exist in one's mind, including those personal memories that make up "my life." The key, as usual, is the moral use that one makes of them: no longer producer of guilt or fear or *confusio*, they can "cooperate in our good," if we "take care" to use them well. (*The Craft of Thought* 97)

In *De doctrina christiana*, Augustine describes charity as the movement of the mind toward fruitfully enjoying God for His own sake. Ramon Llull's appropriately titled *Llibre d'intenció* [Book on Intention] explains it in more matter-of-fact terms.[11] He composed it in Montpellier between 1276 and 1283 for his adolescent son, whom he addresses as "amable fill," worthy of love, and its five chapters lovingly remember Christ's five wounds, a memory cue that betrays its contemplative origins. Ramon Llull elucidates the concept of intention and patiently illustrates it with straightforward examples suitable for a young adult progressing from "les obres sensuals e artificials" to cogitation. Intention is an emotional reaction ("actu de natural apetit") that causes the will and understanding to search for the natural perfection owed to an object or idea.[12]

Clarifying for his son, Ramon Llull differentiates two types of intention related to material things based on personal preference; for instance, when you ask a clerk to pen a book, your first intention is the writing of the book and the second paying the clerk to do it because you love the book more than the money. For his part, the clerk prefers the money; otherwise, he would not give you the book

---

[11] Augustine's passage reads, "'Caritatem' voco motum animi ad fruendum Deo propter ipsum et se atque proximo propter Deum" (*De doctrina christiana* III, x, 16).

[12] Entenció es obra de enteniment e de volentat quis mou a donar compliment a la cosa desijada e entesa; e intenció es actu de natural apetit qui requer la perfecció que li cové naturalment (Llull 5). All the translations into English, unless indicated otherwise, are mine.

in exchange for it. In relation to intellectual things, however, the only intention is charity. Elaborating upon the example of the book, Ramon Llull notes that the act of writing is the secondary intention, while transmitting the content ("la sciencia") is primary; in turn, the content is secondary to the act of understanding it; the acquired wisdom is secondary to its worth; wisdom's value is secondary to the glory it begets; the glory of Paradise —if you enter ("si y entres")— is secondary to the ultimate knowledge of God and His love ("la conexença que auràs de Deu e la amor," 7).

Ramon Llull is describing the *rationes* that, according to Augustine, make thinking possible by moving memories into various relationships with one another (Carruthers, *The Craft of Thought* 32–35). In the case of sinners, Ramon Llull warns, an accident affects their will, which alters the *ratio*, or the order of intentions, so that they love a beautiful book for its beauty, not its content.[13] From the paternal affection naturally owed to a lovable child or the purchase of a desirable book to the beatific vision of God, Ramon Llull articulates for his son the *rational* progression of charity's intention from the sensitive to the spiritual, what Leclerq memorably described as the love of learning and the desire for God.[14]

Around the same time that Ramon Llull composed *Llibre d'intenció*, the Valencian physician Arnau de Vilanova wrote *Tractatus de amore qui dicitur heroicus*. He was responding to a letter from a former Montpellier classmate, a physician practicing in Sardinia, who asked about the cause of the irrational movement that manifests itself as lovesickness.[15] Medical, literary, and philosophical discourses converged in addressing the nature of this disease, and the letter sheds light on Ramon Llull's concern with the *accidental* disordering of intentions among sinners.

---

[13] "Accidentalment, fill, amen los homens peccadors ab les dues intencions desordonades en lurs amor; car amar son beyll libre per ço quor es bell, e no amarlo per ço quel entena, es desordonament de entenció; e en aytal manera amor lo libre bell es per la primera intenció, e amarlo entendre es per la segona; car hom desordonat fa major força de volentat en fer bell libre que entendrelo" (7).

[14] The same logic informs Dante's *Comedy*. In the ninth canto of *Paradiso*, Bishop Folco compares his youthful passion to that of Dido but, as Heinrichs remarks, "The difference between him and the lovers he names, all of whom may be presumed to repose in the inferno, is that he ended using his passionate nature as an instrument of transcendence" (*The Myths of Love* 69–70).

[15] For a review of Arnau's medical views in the letter, see Serés's *La transformación*, especially 69–72; Jacquart and Thomasset; and McVaugh's introduction to the treatise (Arnau de Vilanova 5–45).

Arnau de Vilanova studied medicine in Montpellier in the 1260s and taught there at least from the end of 1291 until 1301. As at other centers of medical learning, like Paris and Bologna, Constantine the African's *Viaticum*, an adaptation of a tenth-century Arabic medical handbook, was a major textbook. Medieval commentaries on the chapter on lovesickness often cited Ovid's *Remedia amoris*, drawing serious medical conclusions from a burlesque poem, and transforming the Roman poet into a *doctor amoris*, a tradition that extended to sixteenth-century Spain when Lope de Vega still referred to him as "galeno de los amantes" (Giles 4–6). In contrast, Arnau's *Tractatus*, composed around the 1270s, is a monograph reviewing contemporary medical views of obsessive thinking. Arnau does not consider love an illness, which must involve an organic defect ("mala dispositio membri"), but an accident, damage or corruption of the energy that acts in the organ, triggered by an opposite inclination.[16] He defines lovesickness as a potent recurring thought ("cogitatio") about the desired object that is sustained by the hope of instant gratification.[17] Arnau speculates that, since a mere figment of the imagination could not possibly activate such irrepressible longing, it must be triggered by a kind of perturbation that causes the natural instinct, or *virtus aestimativa*, to make erroneous judgments. In response to his colleague's query, he proposes that for desire to become activated and activate the nagging *cogitatio*, an inclination ("intentio") must make the *aestimativa* judge the promised pleasure within immediate reach. Arnau concedes that physiology plays a role in such malfunctioning: perception of the desirable object raises the intense heat of the heart.[18]

Because *amor heroicus* is one of the "occupational hazards" of the aristocracy and its courtship rituals, as Minnis puts it, and because the *Tractatus* shares its ideas on love with the Italian surgeon

---

[16] "[N]ociva seu mala actio virtutis operantis in organo que causatur ex eiusdem dispositione contraria, dicetur proprie accidens et non morbus" (Arnau de Vilanova 56–58). Giralt, who edits and translates into Catalan the *Treatise*, renders *virtus as facultat* and "ex dispositione contraria" as "la malaltia d'aquest organ," which distorts Arnau's definition.

[17] "[A]mor talis (videlicet dicit hereos) est vehemens and assidua cogitatio supra rem desideratam cum confidentia obtinendi delectabile apprehensum ex ea" (Arnau de Vilanova 60).

[18] "Cum enim anime gratum seu delectabile presentatur, ex gaudio deletabilis apprehensi spititus in corde multiplicati subito calefiund, et calefacti subito –prout in de motibus animalium inquisitum est ea parte qua de motu cordis agitur– delegantur ad membra corporis universa" (Arnau de Vilanova 68).

Dino del Garbo's commentary on Cavalcanti's "Canzone d'Amore," the offending object is easily associated with a woman. However, nothing in Arnau's definition implies that exclusive connection; in fact, he considers the passion born between a man and a woman only a particular case of *amor heroicus*, a mental illness more appropriately translated as a type of obsessive-compulsive disorder. As Jacquart proves, for Arnau the expression *amor heroicus* is equivalent to *amor dominalis*, not only because it mostly affects lords, but because it lords over the human spirit and heart (150).

In the homosocial world of medieval schoolrooms, the object students most likely encountered first was their Latin textbook with its lurid rape scenes and gendered grammatical metaphors.[19] Its effect on young minds would have been similar to the effect of *Lancelot* on Paolo and Francesca: it condemned them to the Dantean hell.

Some critics (William R. Cook, Ronald B. Herzman, and John Freccero) consider their story a parody of "the all-important role of the 'book' as initially manifested in the topic of the conversion in Augustine's *Confessions*" (Cocozzella, "Ausiàs March Text" 25). This interpretation of one of the most famous episodes in Western literature partly supports my theory that sentimental fictions distort moral reading; in fact, Deyermond proposed it as an indirect catalyst of the Iberian genre. Still, as Heinrichs remarks, Dante's position is "doctrinally correct, the lovers have not been acted upon by an uncontrollable passion, but have freely willed to follow the promptings of their irrational nature" (*The Myths of Love* 69). Dante was merely illustrating the dangers of exposing the young to carnal reading. Their sin is a consequence of the accidental disordering of their intentions; a lethal combination of suggestive reading material and close proximity of physical beauty caused a surge in their already torrid body temperature. The image of Lancelot and Guinevere kissing conquers Paolo's will. He impulsively kisses Francesca, and she enthusiastically responds. Young and foolish, their emotional reaction causes their *aestimativa* to judge only immediate satisfaction; lacking *ratio*, they fail to arrange in their minds the beautiful images in the book and *en face*, derailing the proper progression of their intentions toward true natural perfection, or loving God.

The mental risk posed by improper use of material likenesses was well known. Bernard of Clairvaux censured the use of physi-

---

[19] See, for instance, Ziolkowski's *Alan of Lille's Grammar of Sex*. For the Hispanic world, Francomano's *Wisdom and Her Lovers*.

cal images and other people's fiction as aids to meditation because they encouraged distraction and mental laxness, yet what Stock calls "reading as thinking" was the schools' only method of rational analysis and composition. Books, even Ovidian literature, were morally good because "as Augustine said, a picture's value lies not in the image itself but in the cognitive and ethical use someone makes of it" (Carruthers, *The Craft of Thought* 210).

The problems this ambivalent approach raised for schoolmen are shown in the prose introduction to manuscript S of Juan Ruiz's *Libro de buen amor*, the erotic pseudo-autobiography of a foolish Archpriest (De Looze, *Pseudo-Autobiography*; Rico, "Sobre el origen;" Lida de Malkiel, "Nuevas notas"). Manuscript S, the lengthiest witness which may have been copied around 1415–1417 either by Alfonso de Paradinas or at his request, was housed at the Colegio de San Bartolomé in the University of Salamanca after 1440.[20] The academic origin of the *Libro* as a whole is evident in its Castilian adaptation of Ovid's *Ars amatoria* in the advice that Don Amor administers to the Archpriest; and its version of the medieval *Pamphilus* in the episode of Doña Endrina's seduction by Don Melón, a passionate lover into whom the Archpriest character inexplicably morphs at some point.[21] The Archpriest's adventures are modeled on the Ovidian tradition of first-person storytelling from personal experience.

The prose prologue considers interpretation as a logical extension of Augustinian hermeneutics and memorial practices (Brownlee, *The Status of the Reading Subject*), or as Curtis more recently argues when analyzing its punning on the mind as *çela*, is fundamentally concerned with interpretive and cognitive processes. The critical debate on its challenges has been quite lively.[22] Following Rico ("Sobre el origen") and Lawrance ("The Audience"), I place it within the Latin exegetical tradition of Ovid's *corpus eroticum*, even if Juan Ruiz also incorporated images and references from Iberia's

---

[20] The name of Alffonsus Paratinensis —or Alfonso de Paradinas— appears in the colophon. The identification of Paradinas with a famous churchman of the same name by Menéndez Pidal "has been called into question, and the appearance of Paradinas's name in a rubricated colophon without the normal scribal identification, such as *scripsit* ("wrote"), may suggest that Alfonso de Paradinas is the name of the manuscript's owner, patron, or commissioner, not its scribe" (Dagenais, *The Ethics of Reading* 121). For the textual issues raised by the *Libro*'s manuscripts and editions, see Dagenais's *The Ethics of Reading* and Blecua.

[21] On Ovidian influence, see Schevill (28–55). On the influence of Ovid and *Pamphilus*, see Rico ("Sobre el origen") and Seidenspinner-Núñez (38–57).

[22] See a review in Haywood and Toro's *Juan Ruiz, Arcipreste de Hita.*

Semitic cultures throught his *Libro*.[23] My interpretation also follows Gerli's seminal article basing its didactic structure on Augustinian rhetoric and moral voluntarism as presented in the theory of teaching outlined in *De magistro* (1981–1982). Finally, I rely on Brownlee's application of Augustinian doctrines to the status of the *Libro*'s reading subject (*The Status of the Reading Subject*).[24]

The prologue is structured as a prose sermon and begins with a meditation on Psalm 31:10 ("Intellectum tibi dabo et instruam te in via hac, qua gradieris, firmabo super te oculos meos"), interpreted as pertaining to what "algunos doctores philósophos" say are the three faculties of the soul: understanding, memory, and will.[25] When these faculties are good, the sermon expounds, they "bring comfort to the soul and prolong the life of the body and bring to it honor and profit and good reputation. For through true understanding man understands the good and from this, knows the bad" (23).[26] In a well-trained mental inventory ("a recollection of works is always in the true memory")[27] an act of the will displaces memories that prevent the true love of God in order to attain salvation.[28] The dangers of an untrained *memoria* ("the poverty of memory, which is not instructed by true understanding")[29] are not so much forgetfulness and ignorance ("it cannot love good or call it to mind")[30] as the lack of focus caused by sensual distractions that bend the soul toward material

---

[23] The literary influence of Arabic *maqamat* was posed by Américo Castro in 1948 and enthusiastically followed by Lida de Malkiel ("Nuevas notas"). For Pérez López the *Libro* is part of the Western tradition but is Mudejar because the old kingdom of Toledo and its archdiocesis, where the book was born, were Mudejar (284–85). The most recent iterations of the *Libro's mudejarismo* in Barletta and Hamilton.

[24] Accorsi's critique of Augustinian influence is based on direct comparison. According to this scholar, most interpretations depend on a partial, deformed reading of Augustinian works ("una lectura parcial y algo deformada"). But that is exactly what medieval authors do; they perform on a tradition of moral conversion based on the generic models of Augustine and Boethius.

[25] I cite from Zahareas's 1978 bilingual edition (Juan Ruiz 22–28). The sermon's meditative quality was first pointed out by Ullman, who categorically rejected its interpretation as a *sermon joyeux*, as later developed by Burke.

[26] "Las cuales, digo, si buenas son, que traen al alma conssolaçión, e aluengan la vida al cuerpo, e dan la onra con pro e buena fama. Ca, por el buen entendimiento, entiende onbre el bien e sabe dello el mal."

[27] "[O]bras siempre están en la buena memoria."

[28] "Que con buen entendimiento e buena voluntad escoje el alma e ama el amor de Dios por se salvar por ellas;" "which, in order to be saved by them, the soul chooses with true understanding and true good will, loving the love of God."

[29] "[L]a pobredad de la memoria, que non está instructa del buen entendimiento."

[30] "[N]on puede amar el bien nin acordarse de ello para lo obrar"

needs ("human nature is more ready for and inclined toward evil than good").[31] To educate memory's innate sensual disposition and progress toward the *summum bonum*, one must study "books of law and justice, and admonitions and customs and of other knowledge ..."[32] After it proclaims the *Libro*'s *intentio* to be moral, the sermon concedes, "inasmuch as it is human to sin, if anyone should wish (which I do not advise) to have a taste of this worldly love, here they will find some models for doing so."[33]

Leaving aside the debate over whether the sermon is tongue-in-cheek or serious, the prologue offers a conventional explanation of the Augustinian understanding of sin as caused by a perversion of the will's priorities. *Amor*, which in Augustine is synonymous with will, is misdirected to become *inordinatus*. This idea was widely disseminated in late medieval confessionals (Gerli, "'Recta voluntas'" 505); we saw it in Arnau de Vilanova's *Tractatus de amore heroico* and Ramon Llull's educational treatise to help his son fulfill his potential. Proper arrangement of the memorial inventory through a willed displacement of those secondary *intentiones* that chain the soul to the body will dig out Truth. Brownlee calls it a "conversion mechanism" that Augustine presents "simultaneously as a record of [his] own conversion and as a paradigm for his universal (Everyman) reader" (*The Status of the Reading* 29).

Brownlee believes that the prologue illustrates "not only the narrator's exegetical mastery —but at the same time— his profound skepticism regarding the didactic efficacy of exemplary literature per se" (*The Status of the Reading* 31). Such ambivalence is not original to the *Libro*'s prologue; instead, as Rico indicated, it is a direct reflection of the tensions originating in the medieval understanding of Ovid ("Sobre el origen").[34] "Systematic mora-

---

[31] "[L]a natura humana, que más aparejada e inclinada es al mal que al mal que a bien, e a pecado que a bien."

[32] "[L]os libros de la ley e del derecho e de castigos e costunbres e de otras çiençias."

[33] "Porque es umanal cosa el pecar, si algunos, lo que non los consejo, quisieren usar del loco amor, aquí fallarán algunas maneras para ello." In a fascinating study, Hamilton relates the analogy that Ruiz develops soon after (stanza 70) to Jewish biblical hermeneutics. Ruiz compares the *Libro* with a stringed instrument whose tune depends on the performer's skill. Hamilton identifies two Hebrew poems that deploy the same analogy to demonstrate that along with Latin and Romance, Juan Ruiz had recourse to the Semitic tradition.

[34] Medieval glosses on the Ovidian corpus were well known in Castile and are another source of Juan Ruiz's prologue (Dagenais, "A Further Source").

lization together with an ultimate harmonizing of discords" relied on Ovid's "eventual repentance, as recorded in the *Remedia*, and indeed (for those who were prepared to take the pseudo-Ovidian *De vetula* on trust) to his conversion to Christianity" (Minnis, *Magister amoris* 69–70). As a consequence, by the fourteenth century, Ovid had been transformed into a lovesick poet-physician, much like Juan Ruiz himself, and the therapy proposed in Ruiz's *Libro* "can be understood in both Augustinian and Ovidian terms, allowing the Archpriest to pursue the spiritual restoration of *Christus medicus* while at the same time taking on the narrative voice of pseudo-Ovid, the *doctor amoris* turned lovesick patient of medieval lore" (Giles 10).

The fourteenth century was the golden age of Ovidian aprocrypha all over Europe (Rico, "Sobre el origen" 307). In the Iberian peninsula, along with Juan Ruiz, we must remember Alfonso X's translation of the *Heroides* in the *General estoria* and the interest in the Roman poet that Violante de Bar at the Aragonese court manifested in her request for the "letres d'Ovidi en pla" and a copy of the "Ovidi mathamorphoseos moralisat" from her French relatives in the last decades of the 1300s. Bernat Metge, an illustrious member of the court, translated *De vetula* under the title *Com se comportà Ovidi essent enamorat* [How Ovid Behaved When in Love]. At some point before his early death in 1424, the Valencian poet Jordi de Sant Jordi (c. 1399), royal chamberlain at the court of King Alfons V of Aragon and I of Naples, the Magnanimous, composed the allegorical poem *Passio amoris secundum Ovidium* [Passion of Love According to Ovid] and Schevill demonstrated "the subtler influence of Ovid, 'the great lover,'... in the spirit of some of the [*cancionero*] poets themselves as well as in the peculiar phraseology that characterizes their amatory lyrics" (57–58).[35]

Ovid's cure sought to heal the hearts of adolescents experiencing the same amorous afflictions he had; his later spurious conversion to Christianity, a forerunner of Don Juan waiting for old age to atone for earlier excesses, was likely inspired by Augustine. Recanting youthful amatory verse at life's end became commonplace among late medieval Castilian poets (Green 123) and drew from yet another schoolroom classic, Boethius's *Consolation of Philosophy*.[36]

---

[35] See also Cristóbal.

[36] Weiss points out the influence of Boethius's *Consolation* in Mena's *Coplas de los siete pecados* but claims that "the notions that underlie Boethius's retraction had already been transformed into aphorisms" ("La *Afección Poetal*" 179).

A case in point is Diego de San Pedro's poem "Desprecio de
Fortuna" [Contempt of Fortune], composed around 1498 for his
patron, Count Juan Téllez-Girón, who had lost his twin brother and
most of his wealth. A restrained San Pedro describes himself "lleno
de canas" [gray haired] and at an age when he can admit the errors
of his youth ("donde conozco mis yerros"). He recants his earlier
amorous compositions, particularly his best-seller *Cárcel de Amor*,
branding them trifling ("obras livianas") and seasoned with a zest
for sin ("salsa para pecar").[37] The poem's sober stanzas, as Keith
Whinnom observed, render Boethius's theme of worldly misery and
the agonies of aging without resorting to Petrarch or Boccaccio (San
Pedro, *Prison of Love* 77), a proof that Italian influence was second
to that of the medieval schoolroom *auctores*.

Other Boethian echoes chime in Juan de Padilla's *Retablo de la
vida de Cristo* (1528), when he recoils from the damaging Muses of his
youth to celebrate sacred topics, a clear allusion to *The Consolation*'s
opening scene.[38] Green mentions the earlier testimonies of Pedro de
Portugal, who dismisses the sweet venom spilled by the Sirens of his
young age in his *Coplas del menosprecio e contempto de las cosas fermosas del mundo* [Stanzas on the Contempt for Worldly Beauties],
and the initial invocation of Jorge Manrique's celebrated *Coplas a la
muerte de su padre* [Stanzas for the Death of His Father], in which
he repudiates the writings of classical poets and orators as flavorful
meals laced with poison ("traen yeruas secretas sus sabores"). These
rebuffs, Green points out, "make clear that the turning away from
the delights of secular poetry is analogous to the turning away from
the delights of courtly love" (116) or, more emphatically, from the
utter delight of reading for entertainment.

BOETHIAN DREAM VISIONS AND LITERARY CREATION

If Ovid eased the hearts of the young, Boethius sought to cure the
sufferings of those tired of engaging in worldly pleasures or forceful-

---

[37] "Aquella Cárcel de Amor / que assí me plugo ordenar, / ¡qué propia para amador,
/ qué dulce para sabor, / qué salsa para pecar!" (San Pedro, *Obras completas* III 276).

[38] Huyan, por ende, las musas dañadas / a las Estigias do reina Plutón, / en
nuestro divino muy alto sermón / las tienen los santos por muy reprobadas. / Aquí
celebramos las cosas sagradas. ... Dexa, por ende, las falsas ficciones / sus fábulas
falsas y sus opiniones / pintamos en tiempo de la juuentud, / agora mirando la suma
virtud / conozco que matan a los corazones (Green 116).

ly removed from them. Later medieval schools glossed over *The Consolation*'s neoplatonism and the more revolutionary ideas contained in its fourth book, focusing instead on Stoic therapy to heal the ravages of Fortune. By way of medicine, Lady Philosophy demonstrated the way the afflicted prisoner could detach peacefully from worldly cares, encouraging complete severance from the sensual bonds that anchor the soul and prevent its spiritual flight from the body.

The Consolation opens on Boethius, crying silently in his prison bed, reflecting on the poem he is composing —meter 1. Suddenly, Lady Philosophy appears and drives out the poetic Muses standing over the bed, speaking to the prisoner. Carruthers calls the scene "a familiar moment of pure creative vision" that spells out the initial steps of memory work and composition. Boethius is lying down to think, one of the positions said to encourage invention, while experiencing the preliminary mental distress and anxiety that initiate a vision that may lead to spiritual knowledge (*The Book of Memory* 173–75).[39] A similar scene in which "reading, inventive memory work, and vision 'take place'" is Augustine's conversion in the garden of Milan (Carruthers, *The Book of Memory* 175). Boethius's prisoner and Augustine's reader are two grief-stricken protagonists who modeled the process of morally converting classical authors and their own sinful pasts for generations of students. More important, Boethius's introductory narrative offers a memory image with enormous inventive power that gave way to an enduring consolatory tradition of religious treatises and amusing parodies.[40]

Medieval literary composition entailed a rhetorical performance based on classical sources (Copeland) —what Albesano calls "unfaithful" translation— adapting the original work to a specific audience. A fascinating case is a treatise on carnal love (*Tractatus amoris carnalis*) entitled *Rota Veneris* [Venus's wheel]. This burlesque

---

[39] In the opening scene of Ramon Llull's *Libre d'intenció*, Llull is prostrate in bed ("jaent en mon lit"), searching his memory ("fuy membrant"), profoundly uneasy about the world his son is about to enter ("con lo mon es en torbat estament per privació de vera intenció, absentada al humà enteniment per defalliment de voler ordonat en membrar e entendre" 3).

[40] For the Boethian tradition in general, Courcelle's study is indispensable. See also *The Medieval Boethius*, edited by Minnis. *The Consolation* in late medieval Europe has received ample critical attention recently; Albesano; Cancel; Kaylor and Philips; and Elliott all attest the popularity of Boethian readings and vernacularizations. For the religious and parodic traditions based on Boethius's opening vision, see Astell (*Job, Boethius*; "Visualizing Boethius's *Consolation*") and Heinrichs ("'Lovers' Consolations of Philosophy'").

of Ovid's *Ars amatoria* and Boethius's *Consolation* was composed by Boncompagno da Signa (c. 1165–1240), who taught rhetorical composition, or *ars dictaminis*, at the University of Bologna.[41] In proposing methods for writing love letters that might help in seducing women, it must have encouraged distracted adolescents to focus on their writing techniques and enlivened an otherwise dull writing course. Boncompagno as both narrator and protagonist becomes *auctoritas* as a second *magister amoris*.[42]

The *Rota Veneris* begins with fictional Boncompagno falling asleep in a garden. He has a vision in which Venus appears surrounded by a choir of women —a catalog of all the possible types available for seduction— and recriminates him for having neglected lovers in his treatises. Cortijo Ocaña places the opening scene within the Provençal tradition of the love vision in a *locus amoenus* (Boncompagno, *El Tratado de amor carnal* 16), but the fact that the protagonist is not yet asleep but instead mulling over intimate thoughts ("infra mentis archana plurima resolverem") makes this scene a spoof of the inventive vision that initiates a memorial composition. The chirping birds and blooming trees by the river caricature Augustine's Milanese garden and the monastic paradises on which Gonzalo de Berceo (1190–1264), an author just a generation younger than Boncompagno, models his allegorical dream introducing a translation into Castilian of Marian miracles.[43] Venus herself, a congenial maiden of perfect beauty wearing a golden dress, a crown, and holding a scepter, is a mocking reverse of Lady Philosophy, who manifests herself to Boethius as a daunting figure of extremely old age, dressed in clothes darkened by the passage of time, and holding books in one

---

[41] Cortijo Ocaña analyzes *Rota Veneris* as a parody of the biblical *Song of Songs* based on Boncompagno's parting words, but its compositional techniques ("mecanismos de ficcionalización") are those of the two major textbooks: initial vision, pseudo-autobiography, and epistolary exchange or debate (*El Tratado de amor carnal* 9–10; *La rueda del amor* 41). In his 2005 edition, Cortijo Ocaña admits that there may be other classical and medieval models, including Ovid (Boncompagno, *La rueda del amor* 42–43).

[42] See Jonathan Newman, who studies the influence of the *Rota's* Ovidianism that inform Chaucer's *Troilus and Criseyde*. The Rota "mixes language and human relationships to conflate lovers' desirous language with their desiring and desired bodies." Newman understands the *ars dictaminis* as clerical performance of masculinity that "assimilates acts of love to dictaminal textuality" (114).

[43] The verdant meadows, sweet-smelling flowers, fruit-bearing trees refresh the pilgrim. The narrator subsequently glosses them as the paradise and Mary's miracles while the birds that regale him with their songs become Augustine, Gregory, and Old Testament profets.

hand and a scepter in the other. Venus's *rota*, probably a pun on rote memory, is a facetious reminder of another powerful image in *The Consolation*, Fortune's wheel. Unlike Lady Philosophy, Venus does not chase away the Muses but encourages Boncompagno to compose passionate letters, and he immediately obliges. After she leaves, he confesses that perhaps she remains *potencialiter presens*, a donnish pun most likely having to do with male sexual arousal. While he is ashamed of the lascivious things he wrote and thinks of destroying them, he agrees to surrender his *Rota Veneris* at his friends' request, so they can learn *urbanitas*.[44]

The treatise ends with a request to place it under the ethical mantle. The fictional Boncompagno compares his writing to Solomon's *Song of Songs*; its verses, if taken literally, could arouse the flesh instead of Christian morals.[45] But Solomon was joined with Wisdom, God's helper, and wise men interpret their bond as representing the union of the Church and Jesus Christ. The audience must have guffawed at the *double entendre* of this passage: Solomon copulated with Wisdom ("meruit assistrici Dei, is est eius sapience copulari") and, by implication, at God's bidding since the Bible is the divine word communicated to men with Wisdom's assistance.[46] The naughty conclusion is that moral intention is an equally apt justification for Boncompagno's union with Venus to compose the treatise's lewd episodes at his friends' request ("Credere autem debetis quod Boncompagnus non dixit hec alicuius lascivie causa, sed sociorum precibus amicabiliter condescendit;" *El Tratado de amor carnal* 9–10). The presence of the *Rota Veneris* in a fourteenth-century manuscript in the Colegio de San Bartolomé's library at the University of Salamanca and the existence of a *Boncompagnus* in Barcelona in 1489 indicate that the treatise enjoyed wide currency in Iberian schools (Boncompagno, *La rueda del amor* 45). In fact, Cortijo Ocaña posits its amorous epistolary content as an indirect influence on sentimental fiction.

---

[44] Cortijo Ocaña translates *urbanitas* as "cortesía y buenos modales amorosos" (Boncompagno, *El Tratado de amor carnal* 148) or "refinada cortesía" (Boncompagno, *La rueda del amor* 101) but in both cases, he is clear to distinguish *urbanitas* from *curialitas*. *Urbanitas* likely implies donnish wit in this context, certainly not courtliness.

[45] "[S]ecundum lit[t]eram magis possent ad carnis voluptatem quam ad moralitatem spiritus trahi" (*El Tratado de amor carnal* 106).

[46] Copulare means to join, to unite, as Cortijo Ocaña translates it, but the sexual misuse of grammatical terms is amply documented; see Adams (39–40) and Ziolkowski's Alan of Lille's *Grammar of Sex*. It fits with the treatise's burlesque intent.

It is not a mere coincidence that manuscript S of the *Libro de buen amor* was also housed at the Colegio de San Bartolomé. Different from the other two witnesses, manuscript S is not a private copy; it is signed, which means that was destined to be read at the library and its epigraphs facilitate its reading (Pérez López 32). Furthermore, the presence of a dream vision in the Archpriest's autobiographical account places his *Libro* in the same humorous tradition as Boncompagno's *Rota*. In the *Libro*'s dream vision the Archpriest's debates successively with Don Amor and Doña Venus before the episode of Doña Endrina's seduction by Don Melón. Deyermond, who maintains, correctly, that the Endrina episode is part of the dream-vision sequence, takes pain in justifying it as a type of consolation for a clumsy lover that can be found "only in a dream" ("Was It a Vision" 121). But it is precisely the rhetorical energy liberated by the internal debate with Ovid's arguments —Don Amor's reasons are a paraphrasis of Ovid's *Ars amatoria*— that gives way to the Endrina's narrative sequence as a re-enactment of, or performance on, the plot of twelfth-century elegiac comedy *Pamphilus de amore*.

Heusch considers the *Libro* a work in progress that follows the Archpriest's injunction to his readers to improve it in *copla* 1629 ("Los 'tiempos çiertos'").[47] Lyric interpolations and emendations to the original narrative, Heusch hypothesizes, could have been added in the context of the first Trastamaran courts when poets began to compose *cancionero* poetry in Castilian, transforming the *Libro* into a manual for writing love poetry. The prose prologue added to manuscript S, as that of Baena's *cancionero*, is addressed to those interested in the science (*çiençia*) of poetry. If Heusch is correct, and Gerli's analysis of its impact as a "key subtext of early fifteenth-century Castilian poetic discourse" supports this assumption ("Fernán Pérez de Guzmán" 368; "On the Edge" 2), the *Libro*'s later readers approached it as a manual of rhetorical composition, similar to Boncompagno's *Rota* and displaying the same fictional mechanisms. Dagenais accepts as much when he states that the rubrics, textual divisions, marginal notations, and included works in manuscripts G and S treat the *Libro* as a collection of exempla bound together by the story of the Archpriest's love adventures (*The Ethics of Reading* 124). In S, furthermore, rubrics stress the autobiographical compo-

---

[47] "Qualquier omne que lo oya, si bien trobar sopiere, / puede más aí añadir e emendar si quisiere." [Whoever hears it, if he knows the art of poetry, / May add more to it, change, improve, if he wishes to].

nent; the Archpriest is a voice of authority and in the final rubric by Paradinas his imprisonment "becomes the circumstances of the book's creation" (*The Ethics of Reading* 127). Following on Dagenais's footsteps, Folger claims that the paratexts and prose prologue understand the *Libro* as a parody of Boethian narrative ("Alfonso de Paradinas").[48] More likely, the prologue and paratexts approach the *Libro* as a characteristic Ovidian-like compendium of moral exempla and attempt to apply its teachings to human behavior with the expected ethical intervention: Ovid morphes to Boethius.

A later and tamer example of a dictaminal literary performance of a classical source initiated by an inventive vision is Jordi de Sant Jordi's *Passio amoris secundum Ovidium*. In this case, the poet is not a school don but a Valencian knight at the court of King Alfons, the Magnanimous. In the poem, the allegorical description of the castle where love dwells is the fictional mechanism that binds together fifteen fragments borrowed from Occitan troubadours.[49] It is also the memorial image that sparks Sant Jordi to retrieve sections of other amorous poems from his memory bank. Critics suggest that this image must be borrowed from the *Roman de la Rose,* and it probably was, but buildings served as inventive images at least as far back as Cicero's tale in *De oratore,* where Simonides discovers the principles of mnemonic techniques by organizing his memories within an edifice.

Sant Jordi practices the rhetorical craft of literary creation by arranging recollected readings and personal experiences according to the compositional techniques of dream vision and fictional autobiography.[50] Poetic treatises of the Provençal troubadour tradition —*Las Leys d'Amors* by Guilhem Molinier (1330–1350)— and their translation to Catalan practice in Lluís d'Averçó's *Torcimany* (c. 1400); letters from the poetic Consistories in Barcelona; and references in Metge's *Lo somni* all con-

---

[48] As Pérez López notes, the *Libro* is the work of a young man whose school years were still fresh in his mind (40) and it parodies liturgical texts, institutions, customs, and feast days (249–317).

[49] See Isabel de Riquer (342). Martín de Riquer identifies poems by Guillem de Berguedà, Arnaut de Maruelh, two by Bernart de Ventadorn, Rigaut de Berbezilh, Folquet de Marsella, Clara d'Anduza, Ponç d'Ortafà, and Raimbaut de Vaqueiras (*Història de la literatura catalana*, vol. 3, 699)

[50] Christine de Pizan's *Livre de la Mutacion de Fortune* (completed in 1403) is a universal history preceded by an allegorical autobiography. It borrows from William of Conches to divide *memoria* into two faculties: the *Retentive*, memories of one's own perceptions and thoughts —and *Memoire*, which records what one hears or reads (Cancel 259).

nect vernacular poetry to rhetoric and ethics.[51] Pujol presents three examples: Bartolomeu Sirvent, who translates *inveniendi scientia* in 1393 as
"ciència de trobar;" Metge, who asserts that vernacular poetry —"la gaia
ciència"— is "saviament e ornada dictar ... fundada en rectorica" and
"mesclada ab saviesa" [learned and ornamented composition ... based
on rhetoric and mixed with wisdom]; and the scholar Felip de Malla
(c. 1372–1431), who equates *gaia ciència* and "alegre and plasent studi"
[joyful and pleasant study] and applies the adjective "studiosos" to those
"trobadors" who practice it ("Els 'trobadors estudiosos'" 83, 87). In all
cases, *trobar* and *trobador* refer to those who *invent*; that is, who find
knowledge (*compilatio*) and organize it according to rhetorical *ordinatio*.

Understood within this rhetorical tradition, the term *tractatus* proposed by critics years ago to indicate a didactic intent in sentimental
fictions does not define a genre but a dictaminal exercise (Krause, "El
'tractado' novelístico"). Dagenais limits its use to academic grammatical explanation of canonical authors. However, the fact that, as he
himself proves, the term is rarely mentioned in Latin *accessus ad auctores* except in discussions of *forma tractatus*, or rhetorical structure,
is proof that we are dealing not with the genre of individual works but
with a compositional process ("Juan Rodríguez del Padrón's Translation" 136n18). Indeed, Rodríguez del Padrón's translation of Ovid's
Heroides confirms that the Castilian *tractado* translates both the act
of composing (*tractandum est*) and its outcomes (*opus, liber, scripta*),
regardless of form: prose, verse, or prosimetric. Dagenais notes that
the term is used "to alert the reader that the author is taking some
position vis-à-vis the tradition of academic (and generally moralizing)
commentary in the work" ("Juan Rodríguez" 136). Sant Jordi's compositional mode does not denote a moralizing stance but youthful exhibition of his considerable reading and poetic skills, much like those
of other aristocrats, including Íñigo López de Mendoza, Marqués de
Santillana, and James I of Scotland, to whom we shall return.

The Late Iberian Boethius

The Consolation appeared in over four hundred manuscripts and
countless translations from the ninth century on. It inspired com-

---

[51] See Weiss ("La *Affección Poetal*" 68–73); Pujol ("Els 'trobadors estudiosos';"
"'Gaya vel gaudiosa'").

mentaries and other works, both in Latin and vernacular languages, and passing references attest to its lasting influence on generations of readers who found solace in Lady Philosophy's advice to the despairing prisoner. Besides its use as a Latin grammar textbook and mythological encyclopedia, it raised philosophical questions that became part of the intellectual equipment of educated men and a few women. Arguments on free will made their way into Jean de Meun's *Roman de la Rose* and Chaucer's *Troylus and Criseyde*; several passages of the *Vita nuova* and Beatrice's remarkable similarity to Lady Philosophy in the *Comedy* show Dante's debt, just to cite a few examples proposed by Howard R. Patch in his pioneering study on Boethian presence in medieval culture. By the fifteenth century, *The Consolation* was "absorbed into aristocratic lay culture to the extent that quotations from it may pretend to be expressions of natural intellect" (Léglu and Milner 5). Weiss points to the epistolary exchange between the author and an unindentified "discreta señora" (a wise lady) in Fernando de la Torre's *Libro de las veynte cartas e quistiones* (*The Book of Twenty Letters and Questions*). Her firm understanding of Boethian moral philosophy suggests a familiarity with one of the Iberian translations of *The Consolation* circulating at that time ("What Every Noblewoman" 1134).

While markedly sparse and slightly delayed compared with fourteenth-century French, English, and Italian *volgarizzamenti* and adaptations of *The Consolation*, translations into Catalan and Castilian increased at the end of that century and fully bloomed in the fifteenth. They expanded to Castile from the kingdom of Aragon (Briesemeister); the paucity of evidence in fourteenth-century Castilian may reflect the difference in their legal systems, as legal archives were established in Aragon much earlier (Faulhaber, "Rhetoric in Medieval Catalonia" 122).

The inventories of Menéndez Pelayo (*Bibliografía*) and Schiff (*La Bibliothèque*) document *The Consolation*'s presence in the Iberian peninsula, but it did not receive full critical attention until the last quarter of the twentieth century, beginning with Riera i Sans's groundbreaking study "Sobre la difusió hispànica de la *Consolació de Boeci*" and Keightley's checklist of early translations ("Boethius in Spain"). Riera i Sans asserts that Boethius's Iberian impact was similar to that of Seneca and much deeper than that of Dante and Boccaccio (297).

Pere Saplana, a Dominican friar without any known academic title or relevance to Aragonese cultural circles, composed the first romance version of *The Consolation* in Catalan prose. It is addressed to the *"Infant* en Jacme," son of the King of Majorca, who was in solitary confinement at the Castell Nou in Barcelona between 1358 and 1362. Saplana presented his version of a moral tract, composed by another famous prisoner, to relieve the prince's sufferings. This translation is now lost, but a few fragments survive in a manuscript copied by Jaime Villanueva in the nineteenth century; an anonymous adaptation in the manuscript Ripoll 113, also very incomplete; and Pedro de Valladolid's 1436 Castilian translation riddled with Aragonisms for the king of Navarre, the future Joan II of Aragon, which is now housed at the Biblioteca Nacional de España with signature 10193 (Riera i Sans 302–3).[52]

An adaptation of Saplana's version by Pere Borró around 1360–1370 for King Pedro *el ceremoniós* is mentioned in the 1417 inventory of Alfons the Magnanimous's personal library. It is said to have presented Boethian meters both in the original Latin and "en lenga limosina" and translated the prose passages into "lenga catalana" (Riera i Sans 305–6; Briesemeister 64). A third version by another Dominican, Antoni Ginebreda, reviewed and completed Saplana's anonymous adaptation in 1390 at the request of a young nobleman, the *doncel* Bernat Joan of Valencia (Riera i Sans 308; Briesemeister 65; González Rolán y Saquero Suárez-Somonte 335). Ginebreda's adaptation was translated into Castilian in the 1497 and 1499 print editions of Sevilla and the 1511 print edition of Toledo (Doñas, "Introducción").

Riera i Sans's meticulous archival research found ample evidence of the circulation of these Catalan translations at Aragonese courts during the fourteenth century, and readership expanded to the urban upper ranks in the fifteenth. Royal and aristocratic libraries contained copies both in Latin and the vernaculars, but so did the smaller collections of royal and town clerks, physicians, and merchants.[53] An often cited proof of Boethius's popularity is a payment made to the "honrat maestre Guillem Venecià, poeta," hired by the Casa del Consell in Valencia to teach Virgil's *Aeneid* and Boethius's *Consolation* in the city schools ("legir públicamente") during academic year

---

[52] According to Cátedra, Pedro de Valladolid's version is a literal translation of Saplana's original, including the glosses attributed to Saint Thomas (Villena, *Los doce trabajos de Hércules*, vol. 2, 149n10).

[53] For the complex transmission of *The Consolation* in the Iberian peninsula and a description of its manuscript witnesses and print editions, see also Briesemeister; Doñas; González Rolán and Saquero Suárez-Somonte; and Ziino.

1424–1425 (qtd. in Riera i Sans 326).[54] Another remarkable testimony is the anonymous adaptation of Saplana's version among the twelve volumes on medical subjects owned by Joan Vicenç, a barber-surgeon in Barcelona.[55]

By the later Middle Ages, Latin copies of *The Consolation* appeared as commentaries. Teachers wishing to instruct their students in grammar, history, and basic moral concepts wove exegetical glosses into the original Boethian text. As a consequence, they abounded in mythological and narrative detail but, as Courcelle laments, failed to exert their earlier philosophical power (336–37). Since all the Iberian versions translate these hybrid medieval commentaries, reading them was interminable, frustrating, and impenetrable for laymen, if we are to believe Ruy López Dávalos, Constable of Castile (1357–1428). He asked an anonymous translator to produce a version of *The Consolation* free of glosses because, he admitted in exasperation, after attempting to plough through the massive commentary by Nicholas Trevet, they became a hindrance that rendered the text incomprehensible.[56] In his dedication to *Infant* Jaume, Saplana discloses that he did not translate Boethius's original text but some writings by Saint Thomas on it ("l'escrit lo qual féu lo beneventurat sent Thomàs … sobre lo libre de Boeci de Consolació") that he found in his monastery's library. Encouraged by a few eminent individuals in Catalonia ("algunes notables persones de Cathalunya") who were outraged by the prince's incarceration and wished to offer him moral support, the Dominican's basic, unadorned translation aims to convey Boethius's obscure philosophical subtleties ("ho treledat en pla per ço que·l entenau mills … car lo libre és molt escur e molt subtil de entendre").

---

[54] Delgado Criado (378) cites this testimony and provides further information on Valencia's religious and urban schools (374–82).

[55] The translation is listed in the inventory of assets executed by his son and universal heir, Miquel Climent Vicenç, in 1464. Item 46 records "un altre libre scrit en paper, a corondells, de forma comuna, ab posts de fust cubertes de cuyro vermell, ab dos gaffets, apellat *Boeci, De consolació*. E comença en lo negra: 'A major e pus perfeta declaració' et cetera. E fenex: 'al qual sie donada honor, laor, e glòria e benedicció per tostemps, in secula seculorum. Amen'." (Cifuentes, "La promoció intelectual" 467).

[56] "Non es de mí entendido ansy como quería: et creo que sea este por falta de mi ingenio é aun pienso faserme algun estorbo estar mezclado el testo con glosas, lo qual me trae una grant escuridad" (qtd. in José Amador de los Ríos, vol. 5, 112). Lawrance also mentions the case as evidence of the spread of lay literacy in Castile ("The Spread of Lay Literacy" 82–83). The anonymous translator has been erroneously identified as Pero López de Ayala (Saquero Suárez-Somonte and González Rolán).

Saplana translated the Latin commentary by William of Aragon, which he mistakenly ascribed to Thomas Aquinas.[57] Little is known about William; from the scant evidence available, Olmedilla Herrero presumes that he was the physician of Jaume II, King of Majorca, and *magister* of medicine at the University of Montpellier, as indicated in the colophon of some manuscripts. He may have been Arnau de Vilanova's disciple or, at the very least, familiar with his work. His commentary was necessarily composed before 1305, when Jean de Meun incorporated its prologue into his own translation of Boethius's *Consolation*. It is the first known Aristotelian commentary and clearly precedes that of Nicholas Trevet (c. 1305).[58] William's text is much more original than Trevet's and enjoyed a wider readership in the Iberian peninsula through Saplana's Catalan translation, revised by Ginebreda, and their later translations into Castilian (González Rolán and Saquero Suárez-Somonte, "Boecio en el medievo" 321).[59] In fact, the anonymous Castilian translation of Trevet's commentary —BNE 10220, erroneously attributed to Pero López de Ayala— contains numerous passages borrowed verbatim from William (González Rolán and Saquero Suárez-Somonte, "Boecio en el medievo").

The Saplana-Ginebreda translation adapts William's commentary for lay readers by eliminating all philosophical or linguistic sections

---

[57] See González Rolán and Saquero Suárez-Somonte ("Boecio en el medievo hispánico"). Ziino surmises that Saplana's *amplificationes* of William's text are interlinear or marginal glosses, which were commonly added to Latin manuscripts of *The Consolation*; she cites Ms. Cambridge Gonville and Caius College 309 (707), where William's commentary is preceded by a *Consolation* with a marginal gloss based on Remi de Auxerre's commentary ("Some Vernacular" 50–54).

[58] Olmedilla Herrero addresses the problems in dating William's commentary and his presence at Montpellier (*Edición crítica* vi–xi, xliii). She discusses the limited biographical information and describes the manuscripts and the edition of the commentary. My sincere gratitude for her generosity in providing me with a copy.

[59] William's commentary survives in four manuscripts. Ziino mentions the book inventory of Ramon Vinader, "doctor en lleis i ciutadà de Barcelona," as evidence of its presence in Catalonia ("Some Vernacular" 44). Manuscript witnesses of the Catalan and Castilian translations can be divided into two groups: those derived from Saplana's original version and those that translate Ginebreda's version (Doñas, "Versiones hispánicas"). For the sake of convenience, I offer my English translation and in footnotes, quote from the Castilian version of Saplana's original made by Pedro de Valladolid (N) and the anonymous Castilian translation that appears in the Sevilla print edition of 18 February 1497 (Se1). Se1 belongs to second group, and Doñas, its editor, speculates that it may be based on a Catalan version of the same branch that preceded all extant Catalan witness. I also provide, when available, the fragments conserved in Ms. Ripoll 113 at the Archivo de la Corona de Aragón, edited by Bofarull y Mascaró (R). For the sake of brevity, I refer to them by their signature.

to focus on the more narrative parts (González Rolán and Saquero Suárez-Somonte, "Boecio en el medievo" 328; Ziino, "Some Vernacular" 46–7). Following the trend pointed out by Courcelle for the later Middle Ages, the translation dispenses with Boethius's platonic vision of the cosmic wheel whose immutable center, God, cannot be fully contemplated from the chaos of its rim, the realm of fate, disorder, and decadence. The interest lies in the most medieval of allegories —Fortune's ever-turning wheel; Saplana-Ginebreda elaborates on Lady Philosophy's defense of virtue as a remedy for the wounds inflicted by Fortune, with passing references to divine providence, but ignoring Boethius's striking image of Providence's role as mediator between the eternal and the transient. The embattled prisoner is a synecdoche of Every Man on the path toward spiritual enlightenment.[60] In book 3, meter 11, Lady Philosophy says, "Every man who wishes to understand and attain pure truth must alter the priorities of his will, disentangling his reason's light and his understanding; with their power, he must subjugate carnal delights to reason's straight moral judgment, instilling it in his heart and dispelling the dark clouds of error."[61] The echoes of Augustine's *De libero arbitrio* indicate the old monastic practice of using *The Consolation* to evoke its views on morality and free will (Carlos 26). In the end, Saplana-Ginebreda reduces Boethian philosophical subtleties to an explanation of the metaphor of man's bondage to *cupiditas*, which blocks the intellect's light ("empacha la lumbre del entendimiento") and prevents the proper functioning of the imagination.[62] Fortune is not the fickle overseer of human fate but is simply equated with erotic desire.[63]

---

[60] Ginebreda's prologue, taken from Trevet, explains Boethius's seven names; the first is "never defeated by wickedness" ["siete nombres del dicho Boecio, por los quales son entendidas las sus perogativas. E primeramente es llamado *Avici*, que quiere dezir "sin vicio" o "non vencido," como jamás ningund vicio no lo pudo vencer" (Se1)]. The prose *vulgarizzamenti* analyzed by Albesano exhibits the tendency to universalize Boethius's individual experience.

[61] "Todo omne que ha deseo de saber e quiere buscar aquella cosa que es pura verdat trastorne bien e desenbuelua la lumbre de la su razon e del su buen entendimiento e faga su poder en someter e sojuzgar los deleites carnales e umanales al derecho juyzio de razon dotrinando claramente el su coraçon aluñando todos nublos e escuredades de error" (N 52r–53v). "Todo hombre que dessea saber e quiere buscar la cosa que es pura verdad rija bien e aclare la lumbre de la su razón e del su entendimiento e faga fuerça en someter los desseos terrenales e humanales y enseñe claramente el su coraçón alongando todos nublos de escuridad de error" (Se1).

[62] Aristotle derived *phantasia* (imagination) from *phos* (light) because it channels *sensibilia* (images) to the intellect (Serés, *La transformación* 59).

[63] William's commentary merely indicates the rejection of *temporalia*: "In hoc expresse innuit Philosophia quod intus per operaciones intellectus debemus inquirere

The Saplana-Ginebreda version moralizes Orpheus's tale at the
end of the third book in this light. The opening lines of the meter
—"Felix qui potuit gravis / terre solvere vincla"— are rendered in
a long-winded interlinear gloss as "blessed is the man who can see,
understand, and break the bonds of the ponderous earth; that is,
those disordered desires incited by the senses which obstruct understanding with their fetters and alter its rightful course, pulling it
back to worldly cravings."[64] It follows William's moral *expositio* on
Eurydice's flight from Aristeus and Orpheus's descent to the underworld after she dies from a snake bite. William's commentary clearly
differs from Trevet's, departing from William of Conches in favor of
Fulgentius. Following the mythographer, it interprets Eurydice as
rational judgment but introduces the serpent, which it identifies with
low passions biting the heart.[65] The Saplana-Ginebreda explanation
["la espusiçión de la dicha fabla ... segund que dize Fulgencio en el
libro de natura de los dioses" (N 55r)] reads:

> Orpheus signifies a wise man, fine-looking and eloquent; Eurydice
> is rational judgment and good deed, and she is Orpheus's wife be-
> cause every fine-looking, eloquent man is expected to make accu-
> rate judgments and benefit others by educating them with his elo-
> quence. [Orpheus] signifies a virtuous man and must be powerful
> enough to take what belongs to him. His search for Eurydice sig-
> nals that he must work to attain rational judgment and good deeds,
> implying that worldly delights prevented him from reaching her.[66]

---

uerum et bonum propium eciam uel summum, non in exterioribus et caducis" (208).
Circumscribing evanescent things to carnal desire and equating them with Fortune
are typical features of both penitential and sentimental fictions, also found in *The
Kingis Quair*: "At a most basic level, then, *The Kingis Quair* is about James' suffering
and feelings of impotence in the face of fortune (or the goddess Fortuna) in both his
life and his love" (Mooney and Arn).

    [64] "bien aventurado es aquel que puede veer e entender e alongar de si las ata-
duras de la tierra pesada, conviene saber los deseos dessordenados mouidos por los
sesos corporales los quales ligan e empachan el entendimiento e lo desuian tirando
contra las cosas mundanales" (N 54v). "Bienaventurado es aquél que puede alon-
gar de sý los gigantes del pensamiento pesado, esto es los desseos deshordenados e
movidos por los fechos corporales, los quales ligan y empachan el entendimiento e lo
desvían" adding, "Otrosý entiende de los desseos e deleytes de las cosas mundanales
e terrenales, los quales atan y empachan al ombre fuertemente. E desaventurado es
aquél que se dexa vencer a las cosas de suso dichas segund que paresce en la fabla de
Orfeo" (Se1).

    [65] Most likely following the "Vulgate Commentary" on the *Metamorphoses*, al-
though here the serpent symbolizes the deceits of this life (Coulson 133).

    [66] "Orfeo quiere dezir omne sabio e fermoso e fablante; Erudiçen quiere de-
zir buen juyzio e buena obra e es dicha muger de Orfeo ca a todo fermoso e bien

Orpheus, the hero whose sweet voice and captivating songs allow him to return from the underworld, is moralized as any classical myth; it teaches wisdom and eloquence.

However, Saplana-Ginebreda expands its telling details into a cautionary tale "against vices and sins hidden in our thoughts. And these are the underworld because they are concealed."[67] Orpheus becomes a young man mulling over his *archana*, the promiscuous thinking that Boncompagno playfully revealed to his peers and students. Although Saplana-Ginebreda does not elaborate on Fulgentius's allegorical explanation, the mythographer's interpretation of Orpheus as a young *dictator* informs the Catalan moralization. In Fulgentius's exposition:

> ... Orpheus stands for *oreafone,* that is, matchless sound, and Eurydice is deep judgment. In all the arts there is a first and a second stage: for boys learning their letters there is first the alphabet, second learning to write; at the grammar level, first reading, second clear speech; at the rhetorical level, first rhetoric, second dialectic ... It is one thing for teachers to recognize different aspects of their subject, another to put them into effect; it is one thing for instructors in rhetoric to have *profuse, unbridled,* and *unrestrained* fluency, another to impose a *rigorous and scrupulous control* over the investigation of truth. (96–97, my emphasis)

The "rigorous and scrupulous control" over one's eloquence in the mythographer's *enarratio* parallels the moral control of one's passions with the assistance of good judgment in the Saplana-Ginebreda

---

fablador se pretende que deue bien juzgar e bien obrar a los otros con el su buen fablar adotrinar. Eurich quiere dezir ombre virtuoso. Aqueste deue alcançar e fazer su poderio de tomar. Erudiçen quiere dezir que deue trabajar que pueda alcançar buenos juizios e buenas obras mas por tal como los buscaua por los prados, quiere dezir por los plaçeres e deleites mundanales no la pudo alcançar" (N 55r–55v). There is an obvious scribal error in N; I have tranlated "Eurich quiere dezir ombre virtuo-so" as "Orpheus." "Orfeo quere [sic] tanto dezir como fermoso hablador; Euréditen quiere dezir buen juyzio e buena obra, y es dicha muger de Orfeo ca fermoso e buen fablador se requiere de buen juzgar e bien obrar y en aquellas mesmas cosas. Eurusch quiere tanto dezir como hombre virtuoso, e sigue a Uréditen ca a persona virtuosa pertenesce seguir buenas obras e buenos juyzios e trabajar por alcançar aquéllas" (Se1).

[67] "el sabio e buen fablador [que] castiga los viçios e los pecados escondidos en nuestros pensamientos. E aquestos son entendidos por los infiernos que son escondidos" (N 55v–56r). "La persona sabia e buena e bien fablante, [que] haze corregir contra los vicios que avemos dentro en nuestros pensamientos, los quales son entendidos por los infiernos, que son ascondidos" (Se1).

translation. Fulgentius circumscribes that process to the educated man: "Eurydice was desired by the best; that is, by Aristaeus —for *ariston* is the Greek for best— as art itself avoids the common level of men." The snake bite that kills her is likened to lack of rhetorical skill, while Saplana-Ginebreda identifies it with another human error: the sting of lust that accidentally disrupts learning.

The Saplana-Ginebreda translation presents Orpheus's disciplined eloquence and moral restraint as the reverse of the behavior of the "scenicas meretriculas," the Muses of poetry. At the beginning of *The Consolation*, they stand over the tearful prisoner, and an incensed Lady Philosophy asks, "Who allowed these filthy harlots to harass this sufferer?"[68] Pedro de Valladolid's Castilian version renders Lady Philosophy's tongue-lashing in indirect speech and expands on the Muses' threat:

> When [Lady Philosophy] saw the causes of his aching, which were making [the sufferer] sicker and hindering his return to rational judgment, she said of those who were allowed to stand by his side: these filthy harlots have given this patient poison for medicine, which worsens his agony because he cannot be cured and increases his anguish.[69]

The offending Muses are further equated with those secret cogitations that bring moral disorder:

> The wise man must not dwell on them but stop thinking about them because following your wishes instead of reason turns man into a defiled beast; that's why Lady Philosophy called them filthy harlots because they incite man to do dirty things like harlots, who drive men crazy and make them take pleasure in filthy things.[70]

---

[68] A fragment of Saplana's original texts says, "Qui a lexades acostar a aquest malaut aquestes putanyones soylades?" (R).

[69] "E quando ouo vistas las razones del su dolor las quales le agrauiauan e non le dexauan tornar al derecho juyzio de la razon dixo de aquellas que ha dexadas açercar asi aqueste enfermo: aquestas putañonas ensuziadas las quales por manera de medezina le dan venino el qual faze crescer los sus dolores porque no puede guaresçer antes se angustia quanto mas va mas" (N 10r). "Quando ovo vistas las razones del su dolor, las quales lo agraviavan e non le dexavan tornar al juyzio derecho de razón, un poco somovida, ca persona sabia non se deve fuertemente ensañar, dixo de las dichas razones que turbavan a Boecio que ha dexadas a cercar aqueste enfermo: Estas putanas ensuziadas, las quales por manera de melezinas le davan vino con qual los sus dolores más se agravavan que non guarescían" (Se1).

[70] "la persona sabia no deue retener[los] consigo, mas deuelos arrestar de si mesmo. E es por esto ca seguir mas la voluntad que la razon faze ha ome seer casi bestial e suzio e por aquesta razon la filosofia dixo de las cogitaçiones seguientes a la

The identification of fiction (the "scenicas meretriculas") with erotic temptation is certainly the Dantean reading of the Paolo and Francesca's episode. Similarly, Castilian authors renounced poetry's sweet poisons, the secret herbs that flavored their salad days, in the palinodes of their advanced years.

Saplana-Ginebreda fails to assign blame to fiction itself —a good moralization and ethical classification would take care of that— and points the finger at those unrestrained lascivious thoughts that drive men insane. By no accident are promiscuous ruminations and pleasant words aligned with women in Lady Philosophy's harsh remarks: "go away and good riddance because you are like the sirens who sing pleasingly and kill people. The fables say that those sirens, *who have a womanly form*, sing very pleasingly and attract ships, lulling sailors to sleep with the sweetness of their songs so that they can kill them" (my emphasis).[71] More important, such hidden thoughts are caused by an emotional perturbation whose symptoms are those of obsession: "and the more enjoyable those cogitations, the more they increase the pain to the point that they drive man to despair if they last long."[72]

---

voluntad que eran putañonas suzias ca tales cogitaçiones mueuen al omne ha cosas suzias afalagando con cosas plazientes ansi como fazen las putas que sacan los omnes de la razon e fazenlos deleytar en suziedades. (N 10r)."Persona sabia non deve en sý retener[los], mas alongarlos de sý; e porque seguir más la voluntad que la razón, la qual haze al ombre quasi bestial e suzio, por esta razón la Philosofía dixo de las cogitaciones que eran putanas y ensuziadas, ca tales cogitaciones mueven al hombre a cosas suzias, assí como las putas falagan los ombres e los tiran de razón" (Se1). "On devets notar que persona savia no deu retenir ab si los pensaments que torben la raho mas deulos lunyar de si matexa. E per ço car seguir mes la volentat que la raho fa hom esser quaix bestial e sutze e per aquest raho la Philosophia dix de les cogitacions seguens la volentat que eren putanyones soylades car aytals cogitacions meven hom a coses sutzes afalagant ab coses plasents axi com fan les putas giten los homens de raho els fan delitar en sutzures" (R).

[71] "ydvos a la mala ventura ca soys ansi commo las serenas del mar que cantan dulcemente e matan las gentes. E dizese en las fablas que las dichas serenas son en forma de fenbras, las quales cantan muy dulcemente e tiran las naos contra si faziendo adormir los marineros por el dulçor del su cantar e desi mantanlos" (N 10v). "Ydvos dende e no estedes aý que soys asý como las serenas que cantan dulcemente e matan los ombres. Las serenas son en el mar, e dízese que son en forma de mugeres las quales cantan dulcemente, tiran las naves e fazen adormir los marineros por dulçor del su canto, e quando duermen mátanlos todos e fuyen" (Se1). "Anatsvosen en mala ventura car sotz axi com les serenes de la mar que cantant dolçament maten les gents. –Diuse en les faldes que les dites serenes son en forma de fembres les qualls canten molt dolçament e tiren les naus faent faent [sic] adormir los homens per la dolçor de lur cant e puis aucienlos" (R).

[72] "E ansi a tales cogitaçiones parescen plazientes mas fazen crescer el dolor en tanto que fazen al omne venir en desesperaçion si mucho las atura consigo" (N 10v). "E assý tales cogitaciones parescen plazientes e después crescen el dolor y el tristor en tanto que traen a la persona a desesperación si mucho le dura" (Se1).

As Ziino noticed, the remark about the sirens is not in William's commentary ("Some Vernacular" 53), which addressed a clerical readership; Saplana-Ginebreda presupposed a reader, if not younger, at least more distracted by frivolous poetry and worldly cares and less experienced in disciplining them —a courtier needing instruction from a patient preacher. Some of the Saplana-Ginebreda explanations have a penitential tone more appropriate to the confessional than the schoolroom. After the Muses exit, the commentary describes an ashamed Boethius, who "looked down in expectation of what the lady would do," while Lady Philosophy, a stern preacher, wags her reprimanding finger: "notice that a man subject to sensuality by his evil thoughts, before he can straighten himself with the light of reason, must wage a war between sensuality and understanding in order to forcefully sever sensual bonds so that he can recognize himself."[73]

The Saplana-Ginebreda version restricts Boethius's journey toward true understanding under the guidance of Lady Philosophy to a psychomachy between Will and Reason provoked by an accidental disturbance that threatens possible onset of *amor hereos*. As in academic tradition, it problematizes the role of Fortune in the workings of an imagination, albeit exclusively carnal, that mediates between tangible realities and intellectual perception. Fortune takes the form of voluptuous sirens who spin man's thinking and volition. Hence, it is deeply concerned with what Archer called "the problem of Woman." Feminist critics faulted the phrase for failing to recognize the variety of women's experiences, yet in the binary gender system that pervaded medieval schoolrooms, "Woman" was, first, a problem for adolescents working on their Ovid and, later, for young men at court; she was a constant concern for the teachers and confessors

---

[73] "boluio los sus ojos fasta la tierra e la vista esperando firmemente que faria la dicha dueña ... notad que el ome que es sometido a la sensualidat por malos pensamientos antes que se pueda del todo leuantar por la lumbre de la razon ha primeramente batalla en si mismo entre la sensualidat e el entendimiento e con gran fuerza quebranta onbre las ligaduras de la sensualidat reconosciendo a si mismo" (N 11r). "tornó los ojos e la su vista fuertemente contra la tierra esperando qué faría, ca el ombre sometido a las passiones e a la sensualidad antes que del todo se pueda levantar por la lumbre de la razón, primeramente abatalla en sí mesmo e con gran fuerça quebranta los ligamentos de la sensualidad" (Se1). "E gira los seus huyls e la viste fortment envers la terra e espera que faria la dita dona. Notats quel hom qui es sotsmes a la sensualitat per avols pensaments ans ques puza de tot leval per la lum de la raho ha primerament batayla dins en si entre la sensualitat e lenteniment fort trenca hom los ligams de la sensualitat regonexent si mateix" (R).

in charge of reining in the boys' natural tendencies on their path toward wisdom. When the moral path failed to focus their scattered thoughts and curb their overheated hearts, young men could take by force the real women whom their elementary textbooks presented as pawns in games of seduction or inimical harlots and sirens.

Pedro de Valladolid's Castilian translation of the Saplana-Ginebreda commentary adds in a revealing aside that Orpheus represents a man "powerful enough to take what belongs to him" ("deue alcançar e fazer su poderio de tomar" N 55r). Furthermore, while other versions correctly translate Orpheus's etymology "oris phonos" as "fermoso hablador" (Se1) —literally, "beautiful speaker" in the sense of silver-tongued orator— Pedro de Valladolid amplifies it as "omne sabio e fermoso e fablante," turning Orpheus into a poet endowed with the classical virtues of eloquence and wisdom, but also handsome, a courtly nobleman, perhaps not unlike the King of Navarre, the future Joan II of Aragon, for whom he composed his translation.

HEALING THE MIND

Interest in the symptoms and therapies of the *aegritudo amoris* and the abundant production of *materia de amore* by members of the *enamorada generació* in late medieval Iberia are hardly surprising. The body of medical knowledge derived from the doctrines discussed by the faculties at Montpellier, Bologna, Paris, and Salamanca was informed by the same Aristotelian natural philosophy that informed the work of Albertus Magnus and Dante.

At the University of Salamanca, discussions of passionate love gave way to doctrinal treatises, such as Alonso Fenández de Madrigal's *Libro de amor y amicicia* [*Book on Love and Friendship*], composed in Latin around 1440 and translated into Castilian by its author for the profit of many at the request of King Juan II of Castile.[74] Its popularity was not limited to university circles; this personal version of Aristotelian thought gained currency at the royal court, where it was disseminated among lay circles and influenced courtly love lyrics.[75]

---

[74] "[E]l dicho latino comento en romançe castellano mando jnterpretar, porque si en la dicha obra algund fructo oujesse, a todos fuesse maniffestado" (fol. 1r).
[75] A study of Aristotelian naturalist tradition on love passion is found in Serés's *La transformación* (53–86).

Alonso Fernández de Madrigal, *el Tostado*, was a professor of moral philosophy and Rector of the university's Colegio Mayor de San Bartolomé between 1437 and 1449 before becoming Bishop of Ávila.[76] His *Libro* contains the expected compilation of scholastic tradition on love as a natural passion, the most impetuous, but also the most excellent. He defends its inherent goodness by demonstrating that love for God is passionate, and evil but misplaced love. One chapter devoted to carnal desire encapsulates contemporary medical ideas that coincide with those we saw in Saplana-Ginebreda. The *Libro* comments on the inevitability of love as it appears in Aristotle's *De anima* and the idea, common to jurists, doctors, professors of natural philosophy, and poets since Andreas Capellanus and Guido Cavalcanti, that love is a natural inclination to engender something similar to us. Initiated by, not reason, but an active principle, "el grande aguijón de delectación," this prickling of pleasure, which Fernández de Madrigal compares to a bee sting, is driven both by instinct and the vision of beauty. Love is stronger in men than in beasts because the intellect participates, activating memory, which allows the pleasurable reproduction of the loved thing in the mind and calms the inner fire. However, relentless reproduction of images, even if they are calming and delightful, may cause memory malfunction or corruption, leading to the loss of reason known as *amor hereos* or *aegritudo amoris*.

Following the prevalent medical opinion, Fernández de Madrigal considers the nobility significantly at risk because only those moved by imagination, not just physical pleasure, can properly be called lovers and, contrary to the opinion of Montpellier Professor of Medicine Bernard de Gordon (fl. 1270–1330) as stated in his *Lilium medicinae*, finds the physiological root of the illness in, not the sexual organs, but fantasy. He concludes that erotic melancholy affects neither intellect nor will. Animal fantasy is corporeal and can be treated medically.

By the later Middle Ages, cures for a condition so closely associated with the imagination proposed offering opposing images, based on Galen's principle of humoral balance. Folger calls this treatment an *ars oblivationalis*, an art of forgetting, and points to Ovid's *Re-*

---

[76] The information on the chapter on passional love from the *Libro de amor* is extracted from Cátedra (*Amor y pedagogía* 22–56). On the whole treatise see Heusch's unpublished dissertation *La philosophie de l'amour dans l'Espagne du XVe siècle. La corónica* devoted a critical cluster to Fernández de Madrigal edited by Recio and Cortijo Ocaña in 2004. More recently, Henry Berlin analyzes the concept of civil friendship and its political implications.

media amoris, which teaches that love can be unlearned through the arts of memory; here, by altering the image of a woman one wishes to forget (*Images in Mind* 52).[77]

However, as Arnau de Vilanova explained in his *Tractatus de amore heroico,* compulsive ruminations are not exclusively about a woman. The Saplana-Ginebreda commentary seems more concerned with the enticing power of fiction; similarly, Diego de San Pedro recanted his youthful works' taste for sin. The therapy of forgetting does not differ substantially from the techniques used to convert one's sins or moralize an *auctoritas* by coloring it with the opposite emotion and reversing its orientation. As in the meditative tradition Carruthers analyzes, forgetting is "a matter largely of *willed* 're-placement' and displacement," resisting the natural inclination toward crowded thoughts and wandering licentious ruminations in favor of intellectual clarity (*The Craft of Thought* 97–99). The role of the liberal arts in the struggle against sensual impulses that prevent intellectual concentration and moral uprightness is explained in a little-known rhetorical performance on *The Consolation,* entitled *De consolatione Rationis.*

THE MONTPELLIER CONNECTION

De consolatione Rationis is a prosimetrum, first mentioned by Patch in 1935, authored by a Petrus Compostellanus. It is addressed to Berengarius de Landora, a French nobleman and archbishop of Santiago de Compostela from 1317–1330. Briesemeister dates the work around 1330 and considers it "the only example of a major Hispano-Latin composition of the fourteenth century" (67). However, González-Haba's archival and manuscript research identified the author as Petrus de Stagno, a *magister,* most likely a Benedictine, of the University of Montpellier, who was an admirer of Archbishop Berengarius; she delays the date of composition to 1340–1360, when Petrus de Stagno taught in the law faculty.[78]

The treatise opens with a distressed Compostellanus tempted by Mundus (World) and Caro (Flesh), personified as beautiful young

---

[77] Folger's *Images in Mind* is an essential review of lovesickness according to premodern physiology and psychology and its impact on sentimental fiction.

[78] Santos Paz (2006) confirms González-Haba's conclusions after tracing most of the classical and medieval sources of this *compilatio.*

women. As he hesitates, Caro expatiates on Mundus's delightful garments, fashioned from the four elements, animals, and plants.[79] When she falls silent, Ratio appears as a discreet, blushing maiden surrounded by light —"inmensa claritate corusca, vultu submisio ac viginalis pudicicie rubore perfusa"— and fumes at the other women: "What are these harlots doing here, away from their brothel, these forgers of flattery, crafters of lies, who tempt the inexperienced heart and under the pretense of friendship act like hostile sirens, singing their melody and driving men to perdition?"[80] She then excoriates Compostellanus and to help him forget the strumpets' alluring words, adduces the arts of the *trivium* —grammar, logic, and rhetoric— which, Compostellanus admits, soothed his afflictions in the past ("quibus olim meas moderatur mesticias" 61).[81] She goes on to present the arts of the *quadrivium* —arithmetic, astronomy, geometry, and music— and the seven virtues. Now Caro decides to fight her with the armies of sins, her daughters, in a psychomachia that follows the template set by Prudentius. Ratio routs Caro's forces with the help of the seven virtues and the liberal arts and declares victory. Finally remembering his school training, Compostellanus listens to Caro's conversion (*conversio carnis*), advising him to avoid women's touch and embrace ("tactus vel manuum vel complexus mulierum" 95, v. 11) along with heavily seasoned foods that may arouse lust ("vires veneri piperata cibaria prestant" 95, v. 17).

---

[79] For the origin of Nature's garments in medieval cosmology, see Rico ("Las letras latinas"). An obvious source is Alain de Lille's *Anticlaudianus*. In his edition of Alanus de Insulis's *Anticlaudianus*, James Sheridan analyzes its connection to this popular school text, so closely indebted to Boethius's *Consolation*, although he thinks *De consolatione Rationis* preceded it. See also Fleming (*Reason and the Lover* 10).

[80] "Quid hic iste astant, cenule meretrices, adulacionis artides, artifices figuli falsitatis, cordis aucupes imperitii, que sub hostili amicicia tanquam sirenes melodiam proferentes usque ad mortis perducunt excidium?" (Blanco Soto 60). *Artides* is an obvious error for *artifices* that is repeated later in the manuscript. The correct reading would be "adulationes artifices, figuli falsitatis." The suffix *–ule* is a diminutive added to cena; the literal translation would be "harlots of a little supper," but I have translated it as "harlots away from their brothel" because at a brothel, prostitutes might entertain their clients with refreshments. Rico reads *scenule*, which would translate the Muses' theatrical nature. Rico ("Las letras latinas") and González-Haba point out the defective nature of the only witness of *De consolatione Rationis* in the library of San Lorenzo del Escorial; it was obviously penned by a scribe who did not know Latin.

[81] In the second book of Alain de Lille's *Anticlaudianus*, the *puelle septem* come to rescue Phronesis.

Petrus Compostellanus is presented as a young student "cordis imperitii," with an inexperienced heart, the common metaphor for a poorly trained memory. Tormented by Caro's siren song, his emotional state at the opening of *De consolatione Rationis* reflects mental clutter and wantonness. With the help of the liberal arts that Ratio places within his memorial reach, his will is able to divert him.

Beyond Ratio's initial rebuff of World and Flesh, *De consolatione Rationis* has little in common with Boethius's *Consolation*. Substituting a personification of reason for Lady Philosophy, as Briesemeister notes, imparts a scholastic mood that feels incongruous with *The Consolation*'s original philosophical orientation (67). Indeed, superficial similarities obscure closer affinities with Alain de Lille's moral allegory *Anticlaudianus*, William of Aragon's commentary, also composed at Montpellier, and the Saplana-Ginebreda Catalan translations, written at around the same time that Petrus de Stagno was teaching there. They all share a taste for stories and exempla of Fortune's vagaries; that is, the novelistic tendencies that Brieseimeister identifies in the French translations of Boethius's *Consolation* and the "Boethian fictions" studied by Dwyer.[82] More significantly, they all emphasize free will.

In *De consolatione Rationis*'s second book, Ratio instructs Compostellanus on theology, paying close attention to the Augustinian doctrine of human freedom as an explanation of volition's turn to material things:

> Unless the movement of the will by which we direct our emotional *intentio* here or there is made voluntarily and under our power, man must not be praised when he turns toward superior things nor blamed when he turns toward inferior things; similarly, the will, which is one of our prized possessions, must not be considered corrupt. Evil is a distancing from the *summum bonum*. However, because this distancing is not coerced but done voluntarily, it carries equal shame.[83]

---

[82] The examples adduced to illustrate Fortune's whims are generally coetaneous events, like Saint James's miraculous appearance when the community rose in revolt against Archbishop Berengarius; some of the events are fully fictional or mixed with miraculous tales (González-Haba 30).

[83] "Motus enim voluntatis quo huc atque illuc convertimur, nisi esse voluntarius et in nostra positus potestate, nec laudandus cum ad superiora, nec vituperandus homo esset cum ad inferiora retorquet, nec etiam ipsa voluntas que in quibusdam cencetur bonis mala dicendam est, sed malum fit eius a sumo bono aversio; que tamen aversio quia non cogitur, sed voluntaria est, digne eam miserie pena subsequitur" (Blanco Soto 82).

The Saplana-Ginebreda commentary commends virtue —under-stood as the restraint of sensual impulses and performance of good deeds— as a shield against Fortune using edifying *exempla* and the righteous tone of a confessor. *De consolatione Rationis* is more inter-ested in explaining the *conversio Carnis* as a moral transformation brought about by liberal education. Ratio instructs young Com-postellanus in prudence and wisdom to escape guilt or *confusio*, the torments of Hell whose description closes the treatise. In the original Boethian treatise, self-knowledge is acquired through personal expe-rience of Fortune's turns; here, it results from the *memoria* of school texts, the experience of scholarly training. Both the commentaries and *De consolatione Rationis* transform Lady Philosophy's intellectu-al clarity into the rigid hierarchy of *Ratio* that disciplines wandering thoughts, prioritizes *intentiones*, and, in *De consolatione Rationis*, classifies knowledge into the seven liberal arts whose *memoria* in-structs and consoles Compostellanus.

De consolatione Rationis is an imitative work of little literary mer-it that had no influence on later authors.[84] It received some critical attention as one of the few examples of Hispano-Latin composition (Briesemeister; Rico, "Las letras latinas"), but González-Haba's proof of a later date and identification of its author in Montpellier contradict that proposition. The fact that Petrus de Stagno was a law professor there, probably a Benedictine, places his prosimetrum within the French tradition of penitential literature and in the cultur-al orbit of the Crown of Aragon.

When Jaume I (1208–1276) received the city of Montpel-lier as part of his maternal inheritance and endowed the original Benedictine school with the legal status of *studium generale* in 1272, the Crown of Aragon became one of the first European kingdoms to host a university (Delgado Criado 561). Even after the territory passed on to French dominion in 1347, and despite the founding of *studia* in Lerida (1297), Perpignan (1350), and Huesca (1354), Montpellier maintained an international reputa-tion for the quality of its teachings, particularly in the fields of law and medicine, deemed second only to the medical school of

---

[84] Briesemeister relates it to Alfonso de la Torre's Castilian *Visión deleytable* (c. 1430), a dream vision composed for Carlos de Viana, heir to the throne of Navarre, that allegorically depicts the instruction of a young man. González-Haba could not find any reference to either work or author and rightly claims that an allegorical Rea-son is insufficient evidence to merit the comparison (51, 51n12).

Salerno.[85] Arnau de Vilanova was one of its famous physicians; his colleague Bernard of Gordon's *Lilium medicinae* was first translated into the vernacular from a lost Catalan *Pràctica del Gordó* or simply *Lo Gordó* (Cifuentes, "L'Université de Médecine" 280).[86] Abundant documentation on the Spanish college at the University of Bologna, established by Gil Álvarez de Albornoz in 1358, has allowed historians and cultural critics to study its juridical status and educational operation in detail, positing a strong Bolognese influence on peninsular universities, but Amasuno Sárraga contends that Montpellier enjoyed the same, if not greater, cultural weight (141). In fact, Di Camillo states that the number of students going to Italy did not increase until the first decades of the fifteenth century, with the return of the popes to Rome: "Until this time most university students who chose to complete their education abroad had gone to Paris for theological studies or to Toulouse or Montpellier for civil and canon law" ("Humanism in Spain" 64). Medical knowledge propounded at those two universities was central to late medieval science (15). Furthermore, the medical faculty at Montpellier was strongly connected to the Avignon papacy; for much of the fourteenth century, it had direct papal support (Singer 63) and provided another opportunity for early Iberian interaction with Italian humanism.

Instruction, even for medical students, was closely connected to the liberal arts. Rational thinking, as Stock explains, was complemented since late antiquity by a program of spiritual exercises that involved the body and those "combined mental and corporeal practices became associated with one type of activity —reading" ("Reading, Ethics" 6–7). In medieval cathedral schools the Ciceronian formulation *studium bene vivendi* was taken over to indicate the double aim of their academic program, the *cultus virtutum*, that identified the "stuy of living well" and "the study of speaking well" in accordance with the principles of philosophy and rhetoric.[87] Schoolboys progressed from the *trivium* and *quadrivium* to more specialized subjects, and their familiarity with other disciplines completed their

---

[85] For Aragonese universities, see Delgado Criado 318–45. An in-depth study of Montpellier's faculty of medicine and medical practices in Dumas.

[86] For the vernacular dissemination of medical works in the Crown of Aragon, see Cifuentes ("Vernacularization").

[87] For the *cultus virtutum* see Jaeger's *The Envy of Angels* (76–117).

worldview (Amasuno Sárraga 138). At the colleges of late-medieval universities, educational training in virtuous living, meant to prepare them for public life, stressed continence, sacrifice, and charity. Delgado Criado terms it *pietas litterata*, the amalgamation of virtue and letters (602).

Weiss traces the admixture of eloquence and virtue in the Catalan poetic tradition to the ideal orator of classical antiquity, the "vir bonus peritus dicendi." He comments, "If the science of poetry was discovered in order to enable men to 'miels dir sa voluntat,' this 'voluntat,' or will, must first be given a spiritual, courtly, and ethical education" ("La *Affección Poetal*" 73). The strong penitential component in the Saplana-Ginebreda commentary and *De consolatione Rationis* fits squarely into the *modus vivendi* of lettered religiosity for young dictators.

Gerli ("*Siervo libre*"; "The Old French Source"), Cátedra (*Amor y pedagogía*), and Conde ("De las fuentes") demonstrated the profound impact of penitential literature on Rodríguez del Padrón's *Siervo libre de amor*, traditionally considered the forerunner of the sentimental genre. Gerli finds that it mimics the lexicon and rhetorical conventions of the allegories in Guillaume de Deguileville's *Pèlerinage de la vie humaine*, which portrays the voluntary renunciation of sin in "a tripartite structure that moves from a recognition of *amor concupiscentiae* to the free, voluntary *electio* of *amor benevolentiae* followed by the triumph of reason and the regret of having willfully consented" ("*Siervo libre*" 95). Without fully rejecting Siervo's connection to Deguileville's allegories, Conde mentions the emergence of a wider penitential tradition in thirteenth-century French confessional treatises, whose compositional mechanisms expanded into other, more literary works. By the fourteenth century, a type of penitential literature that connects individual salvation with strenuous journey, articulated in allegorical terms, was consolidated.[88]

Petrus de Stagno's *De consolatione Rationis* is consonant with this tradition. Its dull reiteration of commonplaces and uninspired deployment of penitential compositional techniques make it a prime example of a scholarly exercise in *docta pietas*: dream vision, allegorical debate among the soul's faculties, descent into hell or ascent into heaven coalesce in an autobiographical, or pseudo-autobiographical, narrative. Along with a taste for stories and *exempla*, these dic-

---

[88] See the examples mentioned in Conde ("De las fuentes").

taminal mechanisms were employed in rhetorical performances on the topos of *contemptus mundi,* whose most important school text was Boethius's *Consolation.* Late medieval voluntarism, emphasizing freedom of the will to alter worldly inclinations toward love for God, not only determines a penitent's confession of sin and contrition. It is a rhetorical practice that arranges emotional reactions and authorial purposes according to their proper *ratio,* which, for *rational* schoolmen, must be charity. As Karras points out, schoolmen did not reject sex, just the disordered mind infatuation provokes; only rationality differentiated them from women and wild beasts. Similarly, they did not object to Ovid's lascivious tales if they could be colored with an ethical purpose and placed under the aegis of Lady Philosophy.

Rhetorical performances like that outlined in *De consolatione Rationis* must have been conventional among students. A pertinent example is the *Memorial del pecador remut* by the Catalan scholar Felip de Malla (c. 1372–1431), Master of Arts at the University of Paris, where he also studied theology. Malla was close to the intellectual circles of the Avignon papacy and corresponded with French humanists; in Barcelona, he engaged in intense political and bureaucratic activity as a member of the Diputació del General de Catalunya (city governance) and died just two days after Queen Violante de Bar. He preached his last sermon at her funeral.[89]

Composed between 1419 and 1428–1429, his *Memorial* meditates on the passion of Christ to stimulate theological knowledge and love for God. Its dictaminal nature is evoked by the title, its reliance on dream visions to articulate doctrinal points, and a debate on achieving redemption among the three arms of humankind —gentiles, Jews, and Christians— presided over by God the Father. In the proem, Malla presents his work as an "ordenat compendi" of the passion's mysteries (87) and formulates the journey to salvation as a pilgrimage on the ship of understanding, commanded by conscience, with the heart as watchman.[90]

We can safely hypothesize that Catalan clerks and clerics attending Montpellier or the other Aragonese universities modeled on it

---

[89] On Malla, see Izquierdo ("El segon llibre") and Badia (ed. *Història,* vol. 3, 370–90) from where I summarize the biographical notes.

[90] "Car protest denant lo jutge de ma consciència e scrutador de mon cor, Déu factor meu, al qual no vull ni puch mentir, que sola veritat he e vull haver, tots los dies de la mia peregrinació sobre la terra, per regina e directiva e gloriosa timonera de la naveta de la mia intelligència" (88).

were familiar with similar exercises.[91] Some of them owned a copy of William of Aragon's commentary on Boethius's *Consolation*, either in Latin or the Saplana-Ginebreda versions, and the penitential fictions they composed —discussed in chapter 2— arose at the intersection of the medical, literary, and confessional discourses that structured university life.[92]

LAY READERS AND *CABALLEROS SÇIENTES*

In the conclusion to her doctoral thesis on the resurgence of Boethius's *Consolation* in fourteenth-century France, Cancel identifies the reliance of lay French writers on its translations and commentaries to define their status as poet-philosophers. They clarified the essential concepts of *memoria*, the debate between the active and contemplative life, and the notion of poetry as allegory (384–85). By the end of the century, we find a similar pattern in the emergence of vernacular humanism in the Iberian peninsula. As Weiss noted, the spread of lay literacy opened new domains between clerisy and courtliness for literate but not learned authors ("What Every Noblewoman"). Critics have studied this phenomenon under the rubric "arms vs letters" (*sapientia* vs *fortitudo*), which pitted aspiring authors like the well-read Count of Haro and Enrique de Villena against professional men of letters, who, like the Bishop of Cartagena, disparaged them.[93] Of particular interest for my argument are the debates over Fortune, organized around sexual and intellectual desire, that created a field of lay learning (Weiss, "What Every Noblewoman" 1142).

A figure stands out as representative of these newly literate aristocrats —Enrique de Aragón, better known as Enrique de Villena (c.

---

[91] A comparable Italian case analyzed by Albesano is the "unfaithful" translation by Arrigo da Settimello, *De diversitate Fortunae et Philosophiae consolatione*, which became very popular and was used with Boethius's *Consolatio* to teach Latin in schools. The author-protagonist complains about Fortune, and Phronesis (practical wisdom) instructs him on morality.

[92] The 1356 book inventory of jurist Ramon Vinader notes a Latin copy of *The Consolation*. For the dissemination of Boethius's Catalan translations among clerks, pharmacists, merchants, and noblemen, see Riera i Sans; Cifuentes ("Vernacularization;" "La promoció;" "Traduccions").

[93] Lawrance ("On Fifteenth-Century") qualifies Round's ("Renaissance Culture") and Russell's ("Las armas contra las letras") argument that aristocrats were prejudiced against learning, citing Cartagena's objections to lay learning.

1382/1384–December 1434). Related by birth to the kings of Castile
and Aragon, he spent his formative years at his grandfather's Valencian court in Gandia. Here, he encountered such important intellectuals as the March family, which included the famous poet Ausiàs
March, and the Franciscan friar Francesc Eiximenis, author of the
treatise *Dotzé del crestià* [Twelfth Book of the Christian, 1384] on
the education of the ruling class, and the Dominican Antoni Canals,
author of *Scipió e Anibal*, both dedicated these works to his grandfather. In 1387, Queen Violante de Bar invited the child Villena to
visit her royal court, where he came into contact with the Catalan
literary world. While not derived from the official academic culture,
Villena's abundant literary production mediates scholarly learning
and vernacular lay culture. He translated into Castilian Dante's *Comedy*, the pseudo-Ciceronian *Rhetorica ad Herennium*, fragments of
Titus Livius, and the twelve books of Virgil's *Aeneid,* adding a mon-
umental gloss on the first three before death interrupted. He composed tracts on topics as varied as leprosy; evil eye; the arts of poetry;
carving at the table; and a translation of, and commentary on, a Petrarchan sonnet.[94]

His treatise on mythological exegesis, *Doce trabajos de Hércules*
[Twelve Labors of Hercules], outlines the features of the *caballero
sçiente* [learned nobleman]. It is a prime example of the *pietas litterata* fostered by school training. He composed it in Catalan as *Dotze
treballs de Hèrcules* on 3 April 1417 at the request of the Valencian
knight Pere Pardo and translated it into Castilian on 28 September
at the request of one of his retainers, Juan Fernández de Valera.[95] In
translating his own work, Villena demonstrates his pivotal role in the
intellectual exchange among vernacular humanists in the kingdoms
of Aragon and Castile; *Doce trabajos* is a testament to their tastes and
interests.[96] Its style, a notoriously difficult Latinate euphuism, led an
exasperated Carr, the first contemporary critic to become interested
in Villena's work at large, to dub him "awful Henry."

In an introductory letter addressed to *Mosén* Pere Pardo, Villena
boasts about his memorial inventory of "istoriales que d'esto han

---

[94] For Villena's biography, see Cátedra and Carr ("Datos para la biografía"; *Epistolario*); Cátedra's introduction in Villena (*Obras completas*, vol.1, xi–xxvii).

[95] The Catalan version, now lost, survives in a 1514 edition (Cátedra "Algunas
obras perdidas" 55).

[96] For Villena's self-translation, see Cátedra ("Un aspecto de la difusión"). On
the *Doce trabajos*, see Cátedra and Cherchi's introductory studies (Villena, *Los doce
trabajos*).

tractado e poetas que con ello guarnesçieron sus ficçiones" ("Los
doce trabajos" 5), a commonplace combination of poetic myths and
their commentaries, and asks him to disseminate his work among the
nobility as a useful moral mirror. He defines its subject matter as "satire, even if tragic poets presented it."[97] In interpreting this remark,
critics have suggested that Villena collected some of his materials
from Seneca. However, Villena is simply opposing his work to fictional narrative. Medieval theorists classified both satire and tragedy
as types of historical narrative whose characters served an exemplary
function.[98] Satire exposed the naked truth, in stark contrast to tragedy's poetic veil, or *integumentum* (Minnis, *Magister amoris* 18–20).
Accordingly, Villena places his *Doce trabajos* as, not a poetic piece
demanding interpretation of concealed truths, but a straightforward
exposition of the ethical teachings contained in Hercules's labors.[99]
His vocabulary implicitly connects his own hermeneutical labor of
penetrating the dense *integumentum*, the veil covering myth, with
the moral labor of disentangling reason and understanding from
the weft of vices by restraining beastly inclinations ("desfaziendo *la
texedura* de los viçios e domando la feroçidat de los monstruosos
actos"; my emphasis). The whole interpretive act is modeled on penitential literature as a school exercise defending the myth of Hercules
as a consolatory balm.

   Cherchi indisputably demonstrated that Villena borrowed both
the number and sequence of his fourfold *expositio* from Guido da
Pisa's *Fiorita d'Italia*. The explanation for each labor follows a very
similar structure, beginning with a summary of the events (*historia*),
followed by the allegory (*alegoría*) or its moral utility, and the truth
(*verdad*) or euhemerist interpretation. However, as Cherchi admits,
Villena adds a fourth category of his own creation, the myth's benefit (*aplicación*) for each social station, making his text four times
longer than Guido da Pisa's. Furthermore, Villena appears to rely
on Fulgentius, a source unmentioned in the *Fiorita* (124). The Sa-

---

   [97] "[E] la comuniquedes en lugar que faga fructo e de que tomen enxemplo, a
cresçimiento de virtudes e purgamiento de viçios. Así será espejo actual a los glorio-
sos cavalleros en armada cavallería" ... "[L]a materia presente más es satírica que
trágica, ya sea trágicos la ayan deduzida" (6).
   [98] Nicholas Trevet defines tragedy as "carmen de magnis criminibus uel iniqui-
tatibus" [a poetic composition about great crimes and injustices] (qtd. in Torró, "El
mite de Caldesa").
   [99] As Weiss indicates, sátira, "does not indicate the content, stylistic, or narrative
structure of the work, but simply denotes that it possesses a moral function" (Juan
de Mena's *Coronación* 123).

plana-Ginebreda commentary and Stagno's *De consolatione Rationis* are also significant references. Villena's acquaintance with the former has been demonstrated (Saquero Suárez-Somonte and González Rolán, "Las glosas"); as for *De consolatione Rationis*, even without direct knowledge, the very triteness of Stagno's dream vision makes it an apt example of the exercises on *pietas litterata* that students of the *ars dictaminis* regularly performed and religious orders disseminated in their sermons and confessional treatises.[100]

The model that Villena propounds for the *caballero sçiente* conflates Hercules and Orpheus: a strong warrior endowed with intellectual curiosity and eloquence. Saplana-Ginebreda moralized Orpheus as a wise, eloquent man who admonishes against concealed vices and sins, while Hercules possessed "the virtue of strength and must endure many different labors and risk many dangers to maintain his virtue."[101] The Saplana-Ginebreda expositions of the fourth and ninth labors connect these two myths with the educational path Villena proposes for the nobility.

In the fourth, Hercules must find golden apples in the garden of the Hesperides. Saplana-Ginebreda understands the apples as "the many parts of science."[102] The Hesperides, the commentary expounds, citing Fulgentius, "are intellectual learning, remembering, and eloquence; this means what the wise must gather from the garden or orchard, that is, from the writings that must be reoriented to the *intentio* of loving God."[103]

Villena summarizes this moralization, which does not substantially differ from Guido da Pisa's simpler equation of the orchard produc-

[100] Three of Malla's sermons take the form of a dream vision with allegorical personifications (Badia ed. *Història*, vol. 3, 374).

[101] "el sabio e virtuoso e que ha virtud de fortaleza el qual deue ser aparejado de sofrir muchos e diuersos trabajos e de ser puesto en muchos peligros por conseruacion de virtud" (N 70v). "el ombre sabio que ha virtud de fortaleza en sý, el qual deve ser aparejado a sofrir muchos trabajos e deve ser puesto en muchos peligros por conservación de virtud" (Se1).

[102] "mançanas de oro ... es entendida sçiençia la qual ha muchas partes las quales son en el vergel de las esperides" (N 70v).

[103] "Aquestas donzellas ... segun los latinos quiere dezir estudio entender, remembrar, bien fablar. Quiere dezir que la persona sabia deue sacar del huerto o del vergel muy rico e deleitoso conviene a saber de las escripturas que son ordenadas a dios" (N 70v–71r). I am translating "ordenadas a Dios" in N as "must be reoriented to the *intentio* of loving God" to summarize the process of arranging those writings' intention in the proper *ratio* of charity. "[L]as dichas donzellas, segund Fulgencio fueron nombradas assí. E que la medusa Fetusa, que quiere dezir según los latinos estudio y entender e bien membrar e bien fablar del huerto d'estos, pues deve traer los pomos de oro la persona sabia, que es sciencia"(Se1).

ing golden apples with the sciences that produce delight for the wise ("prefigura la delettazione, che l'uomo savio piglia delle sette scienzie" Muzzi 197). However, Villena emphasizes scholastic learning by personifying the Hesperides as, not the intellectual powers of memory, understanding, and will, but the stages of *enarratio* —memorial recollection, understanding, and interpretation.[104] Eloquence is equated with oratorial *inventio* which, according to Copeland, is equivalent to the *modus interpretandi* in rhetorical treatises and *artes poetriae* (7). For Villena, the fourth labor's aptness for moral allegory classifies it as poetical fiction ("este fablar, segúnd la alegoría ha declarado, fue fabuloso e ficçión pohética"), and as satire demands, he proceeds to uncover the truth about the knight Hercules "who was rich in virtues and did not lack the will or the intellectual aptitude to know."[105] Hercules's trip to Libya is equated with the aristocratic desire to find and to use scientific knowledge here and now. When Hercules offers the apple of knowledge to King Eurystheus, "he enlightened a region that was in the darkness of ignorance and enriched the minds of its inhabitants, who were lacking in knowledge."[106] Therefore, Villena's display of the myth's true *intentio* both justifies his role as cultural mediator and defends learning as critical to the education of the aristocracy:

> This story was written by historians in Hercules's lasting memory so that noblemen would not feel contempt for devoting their time to learning and the sciences, as he devoted his, because learning will not dampen their fighting skills, contrary to the opinion of many contemporaries who insist that a basic knowledge of reading and writing is more than enough for a knight.[107]

Villena's defense of a noble education in his satire of Hercules's fourth labor is complemented by the moral allegory of the ninth. Here, Hercules must defeat the giant Antaeus; in Saplana-Gine-

---

[104] "[E]s a saber sigue los estudios e apazigua las dichas donzellas, dándose al entender, membrar e demostrar lo aprendido" ("Los doce trabajos" 32).

[105] "[Q]ue habundaba en virtudes e non fallesçié en él desseo de sçiençia nin la dispusición para ella" ("Los doce trabajos" 32).

[106] "E así alumbró aquella región que de antes por ignorançia era obscura e enriquesçió los entendimientos de los moradores d'ella, que de antes eran pobres de saber" ("Los doce trabajos" 34).

[107] "Esto fue escripto a perpetual memoria del dicho Ércules por los istoriales, a fin de que los cavalleros non menospreçiasen darse a aprender a las e las sçiençias, segúnt aquéste fizo, ca por eso non perderán el uso de las armas, contra la opinión de muchos bivientes en aqueste tiempo o modernos, que afirman abaste al cavallero saber leer e escribir" ("Los doce trabajos" 34).

breda's commentary, "it is understood that you must hold in contempt all worldly desires because *giant* means *earth* according to the
Greeks."[108] The *Fiorita* moralizes the episode as a simple struggle of
flesh and spirit. Villena follows this reading in principle but clarifies
that Antaeus is "a great giant in the world because of the natural pro-
pensities that magnify the body."[109] He inserts a revealing comment:
Antaeus lived in Libya, "which is also a very hot land, to show that
the sin of the flesh thrives in hot lands, and there it gains strength
and control."[110] This moral *expositio* recalls *The Consolation*'s fourth
meter in the second book where Boethius praises "the prudent man
intending to build a house to last, stable, not to be tumbled down by
the southeast wind with its noisy blast, nor crumbled by the sea with
its threatening waves," and urges avoiding "the mountain top and
the thirsty desert sand."[111] Saplana-Ginebreda's version follows William of Aragon's interpretation of the poem as a warning against the
dangers that the wise avoid and the ignorant seek, allegorizing dry
sands as worldly desires that dry up the brain.[112] The tortuous translation struggles to render Boethius's pristine language and its gloss:

> Who could have such certainty as to place his perpetual accom-
> modation in happiness and not suffer your [Fortune's] assaults,

---

[108] "[E]s entendido que deues menospreçiar e matar todo deseo terrenal ca gigante segun los griegos quiere dezir tierra" (N 71r). "[E]s entendido que deve meno-
spreciar e matar en sý todo desseo terrenal, ca gigante segund los griegos quiere
dezir tierra" (Se1). William of Aragon's commentary says: "Dicitur eciam sapiens
prostrasse Antheum gygantem eo quod eius menti est omne terrenum prostratum.
Gygas enim dicitur a Ge, quod est terra" (Olmedilla Herrero, *Edición crítica* 300).
[109] "[E]ntendiendo por Anteo la carne, que es grant gigante en el mundo por las
naturales inclinaçiones que magnifican el cuerpo" ("Los doce trabajos" 68).
[110] "[F]ue en Libia, que es tierra muy caliente además, a mostrar que el viçio de la
carne en las tierras calientes más se demuestra e allí tiene su fuerça e señoría" ("Los
doce trabajos" 68).
[111] "Quisquis volet perennem / Cautus poenere sedem / Stabilisque nec sonori /
Sterni flatibus Euri / et fluctibus minantem / Curat spernere pontum, / Montis cacumen alti, / Bibulas vitet harenas." Boethius's quote and its English translation from
Loeb's bilingual edition (Boethius, *The Consolation* 198–99).
[112] William expounds, "Docet Philosophia qualiter agendo securus erit homo ab
omnium fortuitorum tumultu, et hoc facit methaphorice tangendo similia in rebus
nature, dicens: Quisquis uolet perhennem cautus ponere sedem, id est perpetuam
sibi procurare felicitatem, que, id est et, ipse, dico, stabilis nec, id est non uolet sterni, id est agitari, atibus Euri sonori, id est inatiuis uanitatibus bonorum fortune que
ualde sonore sunt in hac uita, et curat spernere pontum minantem uctibus, id est
fortunam cum suis aduersitatibus, *uitet bibulas arenas, id est opum cupiditates que
ita siciunt ut arena*, uitet eciam cacumen montis alti, id est dignitates magni honoris"
(Olmedilla Herrero, *Edición crítica*, vol. 2, 99; my emphasis).

which often play to the ears, which are worldly futilities? They engorge men with a pleasant song, but they are thin like the strings made out of animal guts that sound in musical instruments. And he who scorns death with its stormy waves, which are worldly sorrows, should indeed stay away from *dry sands, which are worldly desires and greed.* (My emphasis)[113]

Saplana-Ginebreda glosses over the physical effects of dryness and insists on a penitential mistrust of pleasant music, with an implicit rejection of trifling poetry and womanly temptation; they seem to cause the same physical swelling in men, and the translation adds the disturbing image of deflated intestines strung out in tension.

Villena's reading, on the other hand, emphasizes the body of medical knowledge on obsessive compulsion summarized in Arnau de Vilanova's *Tractatus de amore heroico.* During unremitting passion, Arnau explained, the mind is dry as though exposed to burning heat.[114] A yellowish complexion is a clear sign of the withered mind of the most famous of emaciated characters, Alonso Quijano's alter ego Don Quixote de la Mancha. Folger has shown that, according to the medical theories presented by Huarte de San Juan in his classification of psychological types, *Examen de ingenios para las ciencias* (first published in 1575), the *ingenioso hidalgo's* malfunctioning

---

[113] ¿Quién podríe aver tal certidumbre que pusiese la su cáthedra perpetual en bienandança e non fuesse movido d'ella por los vuestros hechos que a menudo suena[n] a las orejas, que son las vanidades mundanales? Fincha[n] al ombre con plazentero son, empero son flacos assí como las cuerdas de las tripas que suenan en los estormentes. E aquél que menosprecia la muerte con las sus ondas tempestosas que son las amarguras d'este mundo, por cierto este tal devría esquivar *las arenas secas que son las cobdicias d'este mundo e de las riquezas mundanales.* (Se1). Pedro de Valladolid misunderstands the text and muddles the end of prose four and the beginning of meter four: Siguese que la nuestra bien auenturança deuemos poner en ella coujene saber el anima por la qual según que sabemos muy bien muchas personas buenas & sabias an sofrido non tan solamente mverte mas muchos & diuersos dolores & crueles tormentos por tanto que despues de la vida corporal & despues de la muerte pudiesen alcançar el fruto de la verdadera bien auenturança perpetual & que non [N fol. 38r] fuese removido de aquella por los quales vientos que suenan a las orejas conujene saber por las uanidades mundanales que finchaba omne con plaçiente son enpero son muy febles ansi commo las cuerdas de los istrumentos que suenan. E aquel que menospreçia la mar con las ondas tempestuosas conosçe bien lo que façe ca esquiua *las arenas sedientes dela cobdiçia de las rriqueças mundanales* (N 38v). My emphasis.

[114] "[N]on videtur frigiditas sed caliditas verius male disposuisse partem organicam, quamvis eidem ex continua furia videatur aliqua siccitas coadiungi" (Arnau de Vilanova 66).

aestimativa is a consequence of the pneumatic heat produced by his fevered readings. Quijano also feigns passionate love as a necessary attribute of a true knight-errant, a freely made choice that differentiates him from sentimental heroes who appear unaware of their misjudgments (*Images in Mind* 234, 240–43). Villena's vernacularization of mythological exegesis in the *Doce trabajos* constructs the *caballero sçiente* as Don Quijote's opposite. It conflates medical and penitential discourses with scholarly traditions of learning in which choice is a rhetorical, stylistic, and moral act. The impact of this model on sentimental production, whose protagonists, contrary to what Folger proposes, are as aware of, and committed to, their choice as Alonso Quijano, will be developed in the following chapters.

Villena's moralization of Antaeus also draws on Saplana-Ginebreda's etymology of *giant* as derived from *ge*, earth. He adds, "by this sin [of the flesh], studies are hindered and undermined wherever it holds sway, and all laws and practices of reason are undone. Because of it, men behave like beasts and sometimes are even transformed into beasts, as Ovid tells in his *Metamorphoses* and Boethius in his *Consolation*."[115] The allusion to the animalizing effect of sin both supports the *Metamorphoses*' utility —revealing the transcendent through the transient— and recalls the myth of Circe, one of the three *The Consolation* mentions. Saplana-Ginebreda moralized her transmutation of Ulysses's shipmates into swine as the loss of *ratio* that turns men into wild animals and adds lions and wolves as representatives of capital sins.

Villena's own explanation of the ninth labor relates it to social stations, aligning Hercules with teachers who wrestle with their disciples, on the one hand, and, on the other, with physicians advising their lords about the dangers of binging. Villena quotes Boethius "where he states that he who wants to sow truths and virtues in the field of knowledge must first clear out and completely eliminate natural inclinations and sins."[116] Taken at face value, the passage is an alarming document of the trials and tribulations *magistri* must have endured when educating unruly young aristocrats:

---

[115] "[P]or este viçio los estudios se destorvan en Libia e se desfazen donde quiera que reina, e todas leyes e usos de razón se quebrantan por éste. Por él son fechos los omes bestiales e muchas vegadas transformados en bestias, segúnt Ovidio en el su *Metamorfóseos* e Boeçio en el suyo *De consolaçión*" ("Los doce trabajos" 69).

[116] "Boeçio en suyo *De consolaçión* libro [que] declara que quien quiere en el campo del entendimiento verdades e virtudes sembrar, antes debe las afiççiones dichas e viçios purgar e arredrar dende" ("Los doce trabajos" 73).

[I]f a teacher is armed with virtue, he must not hesitate to rebuke a student in his school and in his class, no matter how powerful by wealth or lineage, when he sees him growing like a giant in vices and carnal sins, even if that means crossing a sea of threats and going to Libya, which is the place where those sins are carried out, fighting earnestly and dispassionately, following Hercules's example.[117]

Again, physical swelling is emphasized; Villena depicts arrogant aristocrats who literally puff up to intimidate their teachers. Is he recalling his own educational experience at his grandfather's seigneurial court? Did teachers pursue and rescue their charges from places of sin? Saplana-Ginebreda's insistence on comparing the Boethian Muses to "filthy harlots who drive men crazy and make them take pleasure in filthy things" suggests widespread extracurricular activity. In that light, Villena remarks that a teacher's Herculean struggle must include enough virtuous scholarly exercises ("trabajos virtuosos e actos scholasticos") to engage the young and to keep them in eyeshot. After so killing the carnal giant, the teacher "shall restore freedom and righteous order to the schools, delivering them from such a tyrannical and depraved bondage that robs body and soul, mind and reason, from its subjects."[118]

Villena's model of the pious lettered gentleman stems from medieval commentaries on the three myths mentioned in *The Consolation*, and may ultimately derive from the Augustinian Christian orator who, like Christ, teaches through words and deeds. As word-made-flesh, Orpheus is the author. He enters the hidden abyss of the underworld to regain his good judgment and discovers a new subject matter, deploying his eloquence to disseminate its wisdom. Hercules represents the wise man's strength, moral *fortitudo*, in fighting vice. Ulysses embodies the prudence of those who resist siren songs and do not become beasts. The intertwining of eloquence and exegesis, of *auctor* and interpreter, defines dictaminal literary creation as rhetorical performance: after defeating his passions, an author's elo-

---

[117] "El maestro dubdar no debe, si de virtud es guarnido, por grand omne que sea de riquezas o de linage en su escuela e so su dispçiplina, que si lo vee gigantizar en viçios e carnalidades de reprehenderlo, aunque sepa passar la mar de menazas e ir en Libia, que es lugar mesmo do tales viçios se obran, combatiéndose esforçadamente sin enojo, siguiendo a Hércules por exemplo" ("Los doce trabajos"73).

[118] "E cuando esto fiziere, el buen maestro fará recobrar e restituirá a las escuelas libertad e derecha orden, librándolas de tan tiránica e viçiosa servidumbre, que roba a los súbditos suyos el cuerpo e el ánima, el seso e la razón" ("Los doce trabajos" 73–74).

quence uncovers and conveys the human sin and consolation figured in classical myths. This model also articulates the liberal arts as a shield against the dangers and symptoms that Aristotelian naturalism attributed to erotic desire and Saplana-Ginebreda, Petrus de Stagno, and Villena locate in human nature and carnal reading.

LAY AUTHORS

Villena struggled all his life to present himself as the epitome of the *caballero sçiente* he so deftly articulated in his works. Alas, he utterly failed to show aristocratic *fortitudo;* his contemporary Fernán Pérez de Guzmán portrayed him as learned but lacking the military prowess and political savvy his lineage and position demanded. The Marqués de Santillana, an accomplished poet to whom Villena dedicated his treatise on the art of writing poetry (*Arte de trovar*) and for whom he translated Dante's *Comedy*, composed a heartfelt *planctus* after his death (*Defunsión de don Enrique de Villena*). He praised him as a *poeta,* by which he meant a vernacular author endowed with eloquence and wisdom gathered from the *auctores.* In the third stanza, he compares the sweetness of Villena's style to Orpheus's lyre ("O cíthara dulçe más que la de Orpheo"), his encyclopedic knowledge to a library of moral interpretations ("O biblioteca de moral cantar"), and awards him authorial status as a fountain of sweet-as-honey eloquence from which Santillana strives to sip.[119] In stanza 20, Santillana mourns similar losses, a quite revealing mix of classical authors (Titus Livius, Virgil, Valerius Maximus, Salust, Lucan, Seneca, Cicero, Boethius, Terentius, Juvenal, Statius, Quintilian); their medieval commentaries (Macrobius, Alain de Lille, Fulgentius); penitential literature on free will (John Cassian); and the *moderni* —Dante, paradigm of the poet-philosopher, and Petrarch, often cited in association with Thomas Aquinas as an authority on memory, whose poetic style Santillana helped to introduce in Castile.[120]

---

[119] "Mas yo a ti sola me plaze llamar, / O cíthara dulçe más que la de Orpheo, / que sola tu ayuda non dubdo, mas creo / mi rústica mano podrá ministrar. / O biblioteca de moral cantar, / O fuente meliflua, do mana eloquençia, / infunde tu graçia e sacra prudençia / en mí, porque pueda tu planto expresar" (156–57). For an analysis of Villena's construction of his own authorial status, see Miguel-Prendes's *El espejo,* in particular 19–105.

[120] "Perdimos a Libio e al Mantuano, Macrobio, Valerio, Salustio e Magneo; / pues non olvidemos al moral Eneo, / de quien se laudava el pueblo romano. / Per-

Like Villena, Santillana passionately defended literary training to help noblemen fulfill their role in governance.[121] As the first of his time to conjoin science and chivalry, the breastplate and the toga, in the words of a nephew, he embodied the *caballero sçiente* represented in fiction as Curial [lit. *courtly*], epitome of the valiant knight and genteel lover. Deyermond placed his allegorical trilogy on Fortune's workings —the narrative poems *Triunphete de Amor* [Love's Triumph], *El infierno de los enamorados* [Lovers' Hell], and *El sueño* [The Dream]— on the frontier of the sentimental genre.[122]

El sueño (c. 1428?) is considered the most mature of the three. Santillana sings of love servitude as physical imprisonment, a topos that, especially since the protagonist is reading a book, immediately brings to mind dictaminal practice and its moralizing strictures. Critics have puzzled over the perversion of the *locus amoenus* into a barren landscape to symbolize falling in love and, indirectly, the theme of Fortune (Beard). Further, Lapesa attributes the lack of formal coherence of its heterogeneous elements, connected only by a purpose that gives them meaning ("una sucesión de heterogéneos elementos ligados por una finalidad que les da sentido"), to the lack of single model, in contrast with the other two poems in the trilogy modeled after Petrarch's *Trionfo d'Amore* and Dante's *Inferno* respectively (123). However, these questions are resolved when we see *El sueño* as a clear example of the dictaminal *modus tractandi* on the penitential topic of erotic passion and the poet's search for deliverance by reading the *auctores*.[123]

It opens with a complaint against Fortune, who has sent Venus and her armies to disrupt the carefree life of the poet's *persona*. One

---

dimos a Tulio e a Cassilano, / Alano, Boeçio, Petrarca e Fulgençio; perdimos a Dante, Gufredo, Terençio, Juvenal, Estacio e Quintiliano" (62). Only the reference to Gaufredo is unclear in this list.

[121] See Lawrance for the ritual defense of learning by Santillana and other fifteenth-century noblemen ("On Fifteenth-Century"). To refute Bishop Cartagena, Santillana picks up Villena's argument that "la sciencia non embota el fierro de la lança, nin faze floxa el espada en la mano del cavallero" in the *prohemium* to his *Proverbios* (218–19).

[122] See Gómez Moreno's introduction to Santillana's works (xlv–xlvii); Deyermond ("Santillana's Love-Allegories"); Beard. Fifteenth-century manuscripts also associate the three poems; see Kerkhof ("Sobre la transmisión textual").

[123] In relation to Dante, Foster notes that "particularly when Santillana deals with Passion," his interest "was the rhetorical device of a setting similar to the Italian's, rather than any preoccupation with the ultimate vision of the *Divina commedia*" ("The Misunderstanding of Dante" 363).

night, in bed reading Lucan's *Pharsalia*, he falls asleep.[124] In the ensuing dream vision, he is blissfully accompanying the nightingales on his harp in a fragrant garden when, suddenly, dark clouds obfuscate his high thoughts. The shady trees become gnarled trunks; the melodious songs, screams; the birds, venomous snakes; and his harp, an asp that strikes at his heart. When he wakes up in the morning, his Heart and his Intellect debate the meaning of the terrifying dream. The contest ends undecided.

The poet searches for consolation. On the eighth night, he runs into a Homeric character, the blind priest Tiresias, who tells him that the only defense against Fortune is Free Will ("libre alvedrío") and advises him to search for Diana, goddess of chastity.[125] The poet journeys through the literary sources he has read, indicated by the frequent use of verbs like *vi, leí, he leído, leo, recordéme* [I saw, I read, I remembered]. The memorial inventory from which he draws the materials for his "trágico tractado" is composed of what Gómez Moreno characterizes as an unusual array of sources ranging from Boccaccio's *Fiammetta* to Petrarch, Egidius de Columpnis, and Bernat Metge (Santillana xlvi–xlvii). These authors all helped to define the emergence of the sentimental genre.

Diana and Venus's armies fight. A charge by Perfect Beauty throws the poet's cavalry unit into disarray; Skill and Nobility wound his understanding and chase it off; Grace and Youth take his standard. In spite of Diana's efforts, he has sustained a mortal blow and lies imprisoned in love's unyielding fetters.

El sueño, the poet repeats, is a *tractado*, a gathering of the inner meaning of texts read and mentally recreated (st. XLVII, v. 369; st. LII, v. 415). Love passion is presented as Fortune's work and framed as a snake bite. The invasion of desire in the garden of knowledge —that is, reading an *auctoritas*— creates disorder and confusion in the poet's mind. The dream may or may not have been borrowed from Boccaccio's *Fiammetta*; dream vision was a widespread method of rhetorical *inventing* —that is, recollecting and reassembling— an author's *memoria*.

---

[124] "En mi lecho yazía / una noche, a la sazón / que Bruto al sabio Catón / demadó commo faría / en las guerras que bolvía / el suegro contra Ponpeo, / según lo canta el Anneo / en su gentil poesía" (Santillana 117).

[125] "Pero, maguer que seamos / governados por Fortuna, / quédanos tan solo una / razón en que proveamos, / de la cual, si bien usamos, / anula su poderío: / éste es libre alvedrío / por donde nos governamos. / Assí, buscad la deessa / Diana de castidad" (Santillana 124–25).

The dictaminal practice of literary composition as a rhetorical performance was encouraged as routine exercise for those who had fallen from Fortune's wheel and grace. Saplana advised the *Infant* Jaume to occupy his time versifying the copy of *The Consolation* he presented to him: "E serie'm semblant, senyor, que vós, que sabeu l'art de trobar, vos ocupàseu en lo dit libre de fel-lo en rims per ço que fos plasent de legir a vós mateix e als altres, e que mils ne passeu lo vostre temps" (qtd. in Riera i Sans 299). Jordi de Sant Jordi's deeply sad poem "Presoner" [The Prisoner] also reflects the rhetorical practice of meditating on, and composing after, the Boethian model under similar conditions. Captured in Naples by the forces of Francesco Sforza in 1423, he pleaded for his freedom to King Alfons the Magnanimous feeling abandoned by all ("deserts d'amics, de béns e de senyor") and unable to think ("ma voluntat e pensa caitivada").

Alberto della Piagentina's *Della filosofica consolazione* (1322–1332) and *The Kingis Quair* (c. 1423–1427), a dream vision attributed to James I, King of Scotland (1394–1437), show the pervasiveness of this practice and its varied forms.[126] Della Piagentina, a Florentine notary public, spent the last ten years of his life in a Venice prison. His translation of Boethius's *Consolation*, one of the Italian *volgarizzamenti* studied by Albesano, stays close to the original, rejecting the explanatory amplifications typical of medieval commentaries. He endeavored to render *The Consolation*'s post-classical Latin into his Florentine notarial language and replaces its metrical variety with *terza rima*. The direct, graceful result is closer to the spirit of later humanists, while *The Kingis Quair* is more in tune with late medieval dictaminal practices.

James I's *Quair* is ignited, as in Santillana's *El sueño*, by desire while reading an *auctoritas*. Composed immediately after James I's long captivity in England, it is attributed to him based on his widely documented penchant for literary composition, and the second scribe's colophon in the only extant manuscript (Summers 66). As a performance on several authors, the *Quair* demonstrates James's mastery of different topoi and styles recalled from his memorial inventory by the rhetorical power of two inventive images, Fortune's wheel and feminine beauty. The author's powerful emotional drive structures the poem around the theme of the love prisoner.

---

[126] Other examples may be found in Summers.

On a sleepless February night, the protagonist reaches for *The Consolation*. Inspired by the illumination of Fortune at her wheel, he writes a poem about his capture and how he fell in love at first sight with a beautiful lady walking in the garden under his prison window. Tormented by passion, he falls asleep and begins to dream. As in *El sueño*, the poet-*persona* visits mythological dreamscapes. In Venus's realm, he sees all manner of lovers, and Venus offers him the guidance of Good Hope, who leads him to the palace of Minerva, personification of reason. Patience admits him to her presence, and she teaches him how to win the lady's love. He continues on to the realm of Fortune for further advice. She explains how her wheel moves, and James wakes up. A turtledove appears, bearing a poem that announces heaven's decree: he shall fulfill his desire. He narrates his courtship, expresses gratitude to all who played a part in his discovering love, and ends with an envoy recognizing God's omnipotence and a prayer for his predecessors, not in prison, but in art —Chaucer and Gower.

The version of *The Consolation* that James I read was almost certainly Chaucer's translation, based, like Jean de Meun's, on the Latin commentary of Nicholas Trevet around 1305 (Minnis, ed. *The Medieval*; Gleason, "Clearing the Fields"). Critics have identified Chaucer's influence on the narrative frame; reading a book to get to sleep recalls *The Book of the Duchess,* and the topos of love-at-first-sight may be taken from *Troilus and Criseyde* (Mooney and Arn). I am not denying Chaucer's direct impact nor suggesting that James's *Quair* was one of Santillana's "unusual array of sources." It is highly unlikely he would have had access to it. However, Santillana could have known the Castilian translation of Gower's *Confessio amantis, Confysión del amante*, which was composed before 1454 in the literary circles associated with the Portuguese court of Avis, the Castilian court of Juan II, and his own seigneurial court (Cortijo Ocaña, *La evolución genérica* 63). It is another consolatory dream vision based on Boethius's *Consolation*, but, as noted, this fictional mechanism was part of clerical training, as further attested by its deployment of Ovid's *Metamorphoses*. In a salient difference, it is a recantation written in the poet's old age, while the *Quair* and *El sueño*'s protagonists are still suffering the agonies of lovesickness.

What interests me is that both *El sueño* and *The Kingis Quair* are a web of the dictaminal conventions used by young noblemen in love, particularly the introductory vision fired by a memory image and first-person narration of personal experience. In their transfer to the lay world of aristocratic poets, these conventions are deployed to articulate a discourse on erotic passion that draws equally from medical doctrines, penitential treatises, and school hermeneutics.

The resort to first-person narration was profitably engaged by Latin and vernacular authors alike. It appears in the burlesques of Boncompagno da Signa and Juan Ruiz's erotic pseudo-autobiography but also structured more sober, late-medieval works like Dante's *Vita nuova*, Guillaume de Machaut's *Voir-dit*, or Froissart's *Prison amoureuse*.[127] They all describe a surge of passion upon the sight of a beautiful maiden. Physicians like Dino del Garbo cited Arnau de Vilanova's medical doctrine to explain its role in Cavalcanti's poetry. At Salamanca, professors like Alonso Fernández de Madrigal used it to distinguish true love from lust. However, as in the tale of Paolo and Francesca in the Dantean Hell, *El sueño* and *Quair* are precipitated by parallel acts of falling in love and reading: they narrate a precise reversal of moralization in which the poet *persona* is abruptly distracted by lust.

---

[127] All of these texts, with the exception of Ruiz's *Libro de buen amor*, have been singled out as inspiring the sentimental genre (Deyermond's "Las relaciones genéricas" and "El punto de vista," most notably; Cortijo Ocaña's "La ficción sentimental;" *La evolución genérica*; "'De amicitia'").

CHAPTER 2

RECANTING LOVE

ALLEGORICAL literature in late-medieval Iberia bloomed with the bureaucratization of state affairs, which profoundly changed governance.[1] A new form of subjectivity shifted away from aristocratic ideals and reflected the culture wars over access to knowledge and the written word waged by the clerical and aristocratic castes in *cancionero* poetry and sentimental narrative.[2] The debate about Woman, reified as fickle Fortune, was intertwined with the exegetical, penitential, and medical discourses of Christian ethics; "the fact that Woman was put into question so frequently and with such virulence at this time is also an index of conflicts and changes that were taking place in the very structure and definition of the nobility ... and its long transformation from a warrior to a courtier caste" (Weiss, "¿Qué demandamos?" 240).

The two warring parties were particularly attracted to the humanistic trends coming from Italy, but university-trained *letrados* "had a deeper understanding of the cultural renovation [and] were able to assimilate the lessons of antiquity and utilize them in matters relating to their educational, social, and religious concerns" (Di Camillo, "Humanism in Spain" 80). Those working for the Crown of Aragon were exposed to Italian humanism earlier than those in Castile

---

[1] See Folger (*Escape*); also Martín, for whom this "modern and economic subjectivity ... prompts, in return, new courtly aristocratic and intellectual features" ("Allegory and the Spaces" 134).
[2] See Weiss "La *Affección Poetal*;" "¿Qué demandamos?;" "What Every Noblewoman."

for several reasons. First, the installation of Pere the Great's dynasty
in Sicily in 1282 increased circulation between the two peninsulas.
The Catalan language then acted as a cultural bridge with Castile as
demonstrated by the numerous translations of Catalan versions of
Italian and French texts into Castilian and the decisive influence of
the Catalan poetic tradition on the debate about Woman that raged
in fifteenth-century Castile (Cifuentes, "Traduccions i traductors"
127).[3] Second, the turn of the thirteenth century saw increased dissemination of such scientific works as the *Regiment de sanitat per al
rei d'Aragó*, a Catalan translation of Arnau de Vilanova's *Regimen
sanitatis ad regem Aragonum* commissioned by Queen Blanca d'Anjou (Naples 1285–Barcelona 1310), to "profit those who do not understand Latin and must resort to books in romance" ("pusca tenir
o fer profit a aquels qui no entenen latí" and must "ajudar amb los
libres qui *són* en romanç"; qtd. in Cifuentes, "Traduccions i traductors" 127). The Saplana-Ginebreda version of Boethius's *Consolation*
is a case in point; we might not consider it scientific, but the private
libraries of physicians and lowlier barbers held a copy. Third, the
Crown was historically and intellectually connected with the University of Montpellier and the papal see at Avignon, where Petrarch's
Latin output circulated after the 1370s.

The *letrados*'s scholastic training had a significant effect on
the style of the Aragonese royal bureaucracy, while the chancery's
written production since the early fourteenth century had a clear
influence on Catalan's expressive model. Its clerks —among them,
the distinguished Bernat Metge— produced a rhetorically ornate
prose sometimes known as *valenciana prosa*, not for any geographical reason but merely denoting medieval Catalan artistic prose.[4]
This elegant language controlled access to courtly and city offices
and enjoyed international standing: King Robert of Naples corresponded in his own hand in Catalan with Jaume II, and Catalan
ambassadors spoke in their own language with Popes Clement V
and John XXII.[5]

---

[3] For the debate's Catalan background, see Cantavella (13–41).

[4] Martín de Riquer indicates that the phrase "designava el català retòric i am-
pul·lós ... Un estil poètic i aritificiós (*Història*, vol. 3, 319). For Badia, it means "prosa d'art catalana medieval" ("'En les baixes antenes'" 155n19). A useful overview of
the royal chancery's impact on Catalan is in Badia (ed. *Història*, vol. 2, 115–19). See
also Wittlin (157–61).

[5] All the information on the Catalan royal chancery and its clerks' linguistic and
cultural influence is taken from Badia (ed. *Història*, vol. 2).

Catalano-Aragonese clerks were not usually affiliated with the church. The royal chancery was their training center from the entry-level position of *escrivan de registre*, or copyist, to notary, and ultimately to secretary and *protonotari* keeper of the privy seal that authenticated royal documents in charge of personally correcting their style. Although little is known about the curriculum bureaucrats studied before entering office, it is safe to assume they were trained in the *ars dictaminis,* a rhetorical preparation similar to that at the Universities of Montpellier, Bologna, or Salamanca. Regularly circulating among European chanceries, dynamic centers of cultural production and dissemination, they would have developed common instruments of composition and organizational systems. A similar situation may be posed for Castilian professional men of letters although with a stronger presence of the clergy; learning became an opportunity for social mobility in the service of the royal court and city governments.

In both crowns, the connection between education and government progressively increased during the fifteenth century. Well-trained bureaucrats were favored over those of noble birth for administrative jobs, particularly by the end of the fifteenth century at the court of the Catholic Monarchs. Closely related to changes in the model of government is the transformation of the nobility into a courtier caste as they migrated to the court and urban residences. This process, which Gómez-Bravo terms *letrado* culture, fostered close contact between the "working low and middle nobles" and other bureaucrats, many of whom were of *converso* origin. In the struggle for power and influence, "textual productivity and mastery over stylized language would prove to be a key element in the processes involved in ... identity and its modes of self-constitution" (*Textual Agencies* 31).[6] Members of the Trastamaran courts of Juan II of Castile and Alfons V, the Magnanimous, of Aragon in Naples composed with equal ease in Catalan, Castilian, and Latin, and interest was sufficient for Alonso Fernández de Madrigal to translate some of his university lectures into Castilian (Cátedra, *Amor y pedagogía*). Noblemen and bureaucrats, high and low, were also part of what the Catalan *Lançalot* termed *enamorada generació.* Speaking of the new artistic prose, Cátedra notes that the translations generated to meet the craze for contact with Italy were less significant than the

---

6　See also Cátedra's analysis of bureaucratic literature [*literatura funcionarial*] at the court of the Catholic Monarchs ("La literatura funcionarial").

interaction of the Aragonese and Castilian crowns, particularly the border-crossing efforts of Enrique de Villena ("Presentación" 13).[7]

Two of the penitential fictions analyzed in this chapter were composed by courtly clerks, Bernat Metge (1348/1350–1413), a royal secretary of the Barcelona royal chancery, and Juan Rodríguez del Padrón (1390–1450), who served Cardinal Cervantes. Two other authors treated here, Romeu Llull (c. 1439–1496) and Francesc Moner, were educated at multilingual royal courts. We know little about the early years of the Valencian knight Francesc Carrós Pardo de la Casta (second half of the fifteenth century), but his participation, like Moner's, in the joint Catalan-Castilian military campaigns against Granada places him in a similar cultural environment.

Metge and Rodríguez del Padrón, whom I consider the genre's creators or at least its earliest practitioners, composed in Catalan and Castilian, respectively, although their ornate style betrays a clerical mastery of Latin —and almost certainly Italian and French. Carrós, Romeu Llull, and Moner are equally comfortable in Catalan and Castilian, reflecting the bilingual nature of Trastamaran courts.

All of them had close ties to Franciscan spirituality. Rodríguez del Padrón and Moner entered the Franciscan order at the end of their lives. Metge, Carrós, and Romeu Llull lived in Valencia and Barcelona, where Franciscans had tremendous cultural clout as royal confessors and political advisers. The Franciscan Observance had held unsurpassed prestige since 1402, when Queen Maria de Luna inaugurated it in the Iberian peninsula with the foundation of the Valencian Convent of Sancti Spiritus.[8] Carrós belonged to the same Valencian literary circles as Roís de Corella, whose personal and literary ties to Franciscanism are well documented.[9] In Romeu Llull's case, the connection is more tenuous. Turró [Torró] traces *Lo despropiament*'s advocacy of conjugal love to the humanist reassessment of the family as a pillar of the city; this discourse was common among Italian friar minors, and Romeu Llull might have picked it up from one of Bernardino de Siena's sermons (Llull, Romeu, *Obra completa* 44–45).

---

[7] An excellent summary of that interaction, with a focus on the court of the Catholic Monarchs, in Silleras-Fernández (*Chariots of Ladies* 162–74).

[8] See Silleras-Fernandez's study of Maria de Luna's piety and devotion (*Power, Piety* 115–37). For the Franciscan Order in the Crown of Aragon and its cultural impact, see Webster (*Els Menorets*).

[9] See a biographical summary and useful bibliography by Josep Lluís Martos Sánchez (Badia, ed. *Història*, vol. 3, 211–15). For an exhaustive biographical study, Chiner Gimeno.

The penitential fictions I consider are the last two books of Metge's *Lo somni*; Rodríguez del Padrón's *Siervo libre de amor*; Carrós Pardo de la Casta's *Regoneixença o moral consideració*; Romeu Llull's *Lo despropriament d'amor*; and Pedro Moner's *L'Ànima d'Oliver* and *La noche*. They all purport to tell an autobiographical story, but their plots are minimal, even irrelevant, focusing instead on elaborate dream visions of the moral conversion implied in *pietas litterata*. The exception is Rodríguez del Padrón, who inserts the *novella* "Estoria de dos amadores" in the middle of his *Siervo*.

These works, with the obvious exception of *Siervo*, are well known among Catalan scholars but fail to appear in most discussions of the sentimental genre. The canon privileges Castilian production —more specifically, action-packed works by Diego de San Pedro and Juan de Flores— while acknowledging the relevance of allegory in the initial stage represented by *Siervo*.[10] Catalan allegorical narratives are still relegated to the tower of regional peculiarity even when Rodríguez Risquete ("La regoneixença"), for example, recognizes the clear echoes of Rodríguez del Padrón's *Siervo* in Carrós's *Regoneixença*. As a consequence, Catalan critics have identified the visionary setting as the marker of a Catalan genre that Martín de Riquer labeled "proses sentimentals i allegoriques" (*Història*); Pacheco, "novelletes sentimentals" (ed. *Novel·letes*); Torró "prosa sentimental" ("El mite de Caldesa"); and Pellisa Prades "ficció sentimental catalana" (*La ficció sentimental*). I believe that separating Catalan and Castilian works clouds our understanding of the period.[11] The works analyzed in this chapter comprise a single genre, penitential fiction, the moral consolation of a wretched lover, which narrates the sometimes-problematic victory of reason over desire.

Critics like Rohland de Langbehn have closely analyzed the narrative features of *Siervo*'s *novella* but dismissed the effect of its visionary setting on the final configuration of the sentimental genre. Haywood made the first attempt to systematize the role of allegory in the sentimental corpus, but her otherwise insightful analysis is limited to earlier works (*Siervo*; *Sátira*; and *Triste deleytaçión*) ("La

---

[10] See Rohland de Langhben on the three stages of the genre (*La unidad genérica*).

[11] As Torró suggested and Pellisa Prades after him (*La ficció sentimental* 30), a study of the literary relations of Catalan and Castilian-speaking areas and their sentimental fiction in the context of *cancionero/cançoner* production is needed.

escura selva'"). Martín followed her approach ("Allegory", "Love's Subjects"), trying "to trace the shift from the sentimental allegorical mode to a narrative one," but like Brownlee (*The Severed Word*), he thinks allegory fails in these experimental early works, that "the didactic limitations imposed upon allegorical conceptualization" inhibit narrative ("Allegory" 134). From a different perspective, I called attention to allegory's productive role in both crafting individual narrative ("Tratar de amores") and driving the genre toward the novel ("La retórica", "Otra frontera").

Building on my earlier arguments, this chapter focuses on the rhetorical environment and distinctive features of the penitential genre. Based on Boethian consolation, penitential fictions are *tractatus* —both compilation or translation *and* rhetorical performance. They construct a rational subject by offering the therapy of moral conversion against the accidental disorder brought on by infatuation for a woman and poetry. I bring Roís de Corella's *Parlament* into the discussion to illustrate the violence that allegory demands and the emergence of narrative desire, which will generate the sentimental contrafacta studied in chapter 3. The examination of the authorial positions occupied by Íñigo López de Mendoza, Marqués of Santillana, clarifies the genre's purpose and focus: penitential fictions are the communicative form chosen by aging authors —or at least their fictional persona— to engage in the debate on Fortune's mutability, under the guise of either the "Woman Question" or castigating the dangers of poetry.

THE CONSOLATION OF ORPHEUS: BERNAT METGE'S *LO SOMNI*

Bernat Metge (1348/1350–1413) illustrates the formative role of the Catalano-Aragonese royal chancery and the transference of a polished administrative style to literary practice; Cabré compares this literary and social situation to early humanism in northern Italy.[12] Metge learned his trade in the service of Queen Elionor of Sicily, third wife of Pere III the Ceremonious, whose moniker is the consequence of the extensive bureaucratic reforms carried out at his

---

[12] Metge's biographical information is abridged from Martín de Riquer (ed. *Obras*), which remains the most complete and best documented work on the subject; Barnett's introduction (Metge, *Book of Fortune*); Cortijo Ocaña's introduction (Metge, '*The Dream*'); and Cabré, Lluís ("Bernat Metge").

decree.[13] Metge's stepfather, Ferrer Saiol, a well-known translator of Latin, became the protonotary in charge of the queen's correspondence in 1365, so Metge, as he recalls in *Lo somni* [The Dream, 1399], was raised and "nourished" in Elionor's court.[14] He was trained as an administrator and entered the queen's chancery in 1371 as registry assistant [*ajudant de registre*]. When Elionor died, Metge continued as the scribe of her son Joan, Duc of Girone, who ascended to the throne in 1387. In 1390, Metge became his secretary and visited the papal court at Avignon in 1395 as royal ambassador. However, Joan's suspicious death in a hunting accident precipitated an immediate succession crisis. Metge and all the king's counselors landed in criminal court.[15] Whether Metge was imprisoned, as he claims in *Lo somni*, is unclear, but he managed to secure a post as the new king's secretary in 1405 and served until Martí I died in 1410. Metge died in Barcelona as a private citizen in 1413.

Pere III's *Ordenacions* required royal clerks to compose letters and documents in the chancery's three official languages, Latin, Catalan, and Aragonese. These linguistic skills allowed Metge to translate into Catalan the pseudo-Ovidian *De vetula* (*Com se comporta Ovidi enamorat*) and Boccaccio's *Griseldis* (*Història de Valter e Griselda*).[16] He also composed three verse works whose dates remain under debate. Two of them are clearly satirical: *Sermó* (c. 1381) parodies contemporary sermons, and *Medecina apropriada a tot mal* [Medicine Suitable for All Ills] is a mock prescription that imitates the poets' electuaries for curing love sickness and pokes fun at pharmaceutical jargon. The third and longest is *El libre de Fortuna e Prudència* [The Book of Fortune and Prudence, 1381], a work that some critics consider a serious reflection on Boethius's *Consolation* based on a scholastic reading of Arrigo de Settimello's *Elegia*, but that Marco, one of its most recent editors, places with *Sermó* and *Medicina* as a burlesque (qtd. in Metge, '*The Dream*' 7).[17]

---

[13] As Barnett indicates, thanks to Pere's reforms, the Archive of the Crown of Aragon is today one of the richest medieval record repositories in the world (Metge, *Book of Fortune* 9).

[14] Among Saiol's translations is Palladio's *Opus agriculturae* as *Tractat d'agricultura* between 1380 and 1385.

[15] For the conflict's details, see Torró ("*Il Secretum* di Petrarca" 57–58) and Badia (ed. *Història*, vol. 2, 199–203).

[16] This title appears in the manuscript and may not be Metge's. See Butiñá's "De Metge a Petrarca".

[17] See Fleming (*Reason and the Lover*) and Barnett's introduction to his edition and translation of Metge's *Book of Fortune and Prudence*.

Metge's most famous work is unquestionably *Lo somni*, a prose dream vision in four books. The author persona is visited by the spirit of the recently deceased Joan I, who initiates a dialogue on the soul's immortality. Critics have focused on *Lo somni*'s historical context and literary models, especially its relation to Italian humanism.[18] Since Metge is unlikely to have composed it in prison, a more plausible date would be sometime after 1398, when he had been absolved of the accusations. The fact that Metge presents himself as *Lo somni*'s protagonist "en la presó," however, associates him with Boethius, as someone unfairly condemned by his enemies' envy or perhaps God's secret judgment ("estant en la presó, no per demèrits que nos perseguidors e envejossos sabessen contra mi ... mas per sola iniquitat que m'havien o, per ventura, per algun secret juý de Deu" 31).[19] The obvious allusion places *Lo somni* within the Boethian consolatory praxis we saw operating in the poems of Jordi de Sant Jordi, James I of Scotland, and Alberto della Piagentina and as the pastime Saplana recommended to the *Infant* Jaume to distract himself while in solitary confinement.

Critics have traced the source for *Lo somni*'s title, dialogic structure, and moral intention to the *Somnium Scipionis*, Petrarch's *Secretum*, and Augustine's *Confessions,* respectively. Metge's ultimate intention, most concur, would have been political: to counteract accusations of moral turpitude and to show his unfailing loyalty to the new king.[20] His original manipulation of source materials and mature, elegant prose make *Lo somni* the first humanist book ever written in the Iberian peninsula, but as Cortijo Ocaña also acknowledges, it exhibits "the mixture of Classical and Christian elements that defined early Humanism. In fact, Metge's main literary sources include a combination of Italian fourteenth-century works, classical titles, Christian authors, and the Bible" (Metge, '*The Dream*' 5).[21]

---

[18] See a useful review in Cortijo Ocaña's introduction (Metge, '*The Dream*' 4–5).

[19] I cite from Cortijo Ocaña's bilingual edition.

[20] Cortijo Ocaña points out that those *demèrits* of which enemies accuse Metge mean "offenses implying moral turpitude" (Metge, '*The Dream*' 30n8). See also Torró ("*Il Secretum* di Petrarca").

[21] Metge's mental library as reconstructed from his citations contains Ovid "mestre d'amor" and *Ovidius maior*, Virgil, Cicero, Lucan, Macrobius, Boethius's *Consolation* —most likely filtered through the Latin manuals of Alain de Lille's *Anticlaudianus* and Arrigo de Settimello's *Elegia*— along with penitential works (Saint Gregory, Ramon Llull, Aquinas) and the moderns Dante, Petrarch, and Boccaccio (Cabré, Lluís, "Bernat Metge" 192–93). For specific sources in *Lo somni*, see Cingolani's "Bernat Metge e gli *auctores*."

Lo somni is a clear instance of *pietas litterata* curriculum and compositional techniques, based on the Boethian and Augustinian model of the suffering author-penitent. To the grieving Metge persona, the visionary dream offers the balm of meditative reflection and moral conversion. The first two books debate the troubling question of the soul's immortality, but the focus changes radically when God sends an old man, the blind seer Tiresias, and his young companion, musician Orpheus, to remind Joan I of his sinful love of astrology and music. Their introduction tempts Pellisa Prades to include *Lo somni* in her catalog of Catalan sentimental fictions, but she ultimately finds its treatment of the sentimental theme "marginal" (*La ficció sentimental* 51, 69).

Lo somni's last two books address the dangers of confusing memory with imagination; their permeable boundaries must be disciplined into the strict logic of *ratio*. Contemporary Catalan scholars have mined Petrarch for the many references Metge elegantly incorporates; the *Secretum*'s spirited dialogue probably inspired *Lo somni*'s. Closer inspection reveals another model: the *Consolation*'s initial scene. In *Lo somni*, Orpheus stands for the offending Muses; fictional Metge is the suffering prisoner; and Tiresias plays the therapeutic role that Boethius assigned to Lady Philosophy. Friedlein makes this association but attempts to adduce philosophical similarities throughout *Lo somni*'s four books. My interpretation focuses on Metge's reworking of *The Consolation*'s initial triangle in *Lo somni*'s last two books and its impact on penitential narrative.

Metge's mythography derives from the scholarly *Ovidius maior,* and his Orpheus takes many traits from Boccaccio's *Genealogia deorum gentilium* (Alemany Ferrer 2–3). However, the more unique features spring from the rhetorical and penitential tradition, best exemplified by the Saplana-Ginebreda commentaries and *De consolatione Rationis*, which we saw at work in the vernacular reconfiguration of Villena's *Doce trabajos de Hércules* and Santillana's *El sueño.*

The moralization of the Orpheus myth pervades *Lo somni*'s last two books. Orpheus may seem the humanist orator, the *vir bonus peritus dicendi*, but fits more comfortably in the category of silver-tongued *dictator* in the Fulgentian sense of "oris phonos." The narrator sees an Orpheus blessed "with a benevolent countenance and pleasant semblance," who speaks "very graciously" ("fort graciosament ab bon gest e alegra cara, començà dir"). Orpheus calls attention to his own tender age and gentle manners: "Among those who advocate the use of courtliness," he concedes to Tiresias, "it is customary for the young to speak first, and for the elders to correct their errors and to con-clude" ("Entre·ls volents usar de curialitat és costum que los jóvens parlen primerament e los antichs, suplint los defalliments d'aquells, concloen" 104–5). He embodies what Pedro de Valladolid amplifies as "omne sabio e fermoso e fablante" in translating Saplana-Ginebre-da into Castilian and Villena extols as *caballero sçiente.*

In his journey to the underworld, Orpheus moves Cerberus to open the doors by "playing the *rota* that Mercury had given" him ("sonant la rota, la qual a mi havia donada Mercuri" 104–5). Alemany identifies the *rota* Metge substitutes for Orpheus's lyre as the harp of medieval minstrels and troubadours (3). Martín de Riquer translates it as *lira* (ed. *Obras* 259), most likely steered by the mention of a *rota* among the instruments that come out to receive Sir Love after Lent in Juan Ruiz's *Libro de buen amor.*[22] However, as a gift from Mercu-ry, *rota* suggests *memoria,* both rote repetition and the recollection of, and musical performance on, the *auctores,* a process allegorized in the marriage of Mercury (eloquence) and Philology (learning) and lampooned by Boncompagno's *Rota Veneris* as the copulation of Solomon and Wisdom.[23] Ruiz's metaphorical association of his ambiguous *Libro* —a metonymy for poetry— with a musical instru-ment in the critically debated stanza 70 supports this interpretation, and it accords with Ovidian *enarratio.* Orpheus is the silver-tongued *dictator* who plays his memorial instrument to invent and compose.

In *Lo somni,* Orpheus is the vernacular poet. He explains that after losing his adored wife twice, he withdrew from the company of women to sing virelais, ballads, and chansons in praise of solitude ("sonant la rota, canté alguns virolays, bal·lades e cançons, loant vida lunyada de companya de dones" 107). Solitary retreat is a common feature of the martyr's life, a genre in monastic meditation in which the saint's journey toward holiness is interspersed with constructive visions. Madness as penitential process, Saunders notes, is also part of a wider literary tradition exemplified in the Middle English nar-rative poem *Sir Orfeo,* composed around the turn of the fourteenth century (77). There, Orpheus is an English king who, after losing his queen, abandons the court to live as a wild man in the woods.

---

[22] "El rabé gritador, con la su alta nota / cab él el orabín taniendo la su rota;" "The noisy, shrill rebec, with note so high it seems a squawk, / was join in the tunes the Moor was twanging on his harp" (st. 1229ab). Cortijo Ocaña does not commit and leaves it as *rota* without further explanation.

[23] See chapter 1 pages: 55–57.

Scholars trace it to an Old French lay mentioned in such romances as *Floire and Blancefor* and the vulgate *Prose Lancelot*, which, we saw, appealed so much to the *enamorada generació* in its Catalan adaptation, *Tragèdia de Lançalot*.[24]

In the English poem, Sir Orfeo happily returns to court and his throne. In contrast, *Lo somni* closely follows Ovid's account in *Metamorphoses* XI. Orpheus complains that he was tracked and stoned by a mob of angry women, but when the rocks, moved by his sweet lamentations, fail to harm him, the raging viragos work to silence him with an "uproar of horns, cymbals, basins and bowls." The maenads end up decapitating him and throwing his head and his *rota* into a river (108). A similar version appears in Alfonso X's *General estoria*, and Juan de Mena summarizes it in the learned commentary to his poem *Coronación*.[25] Unlike the Castilian renditions, *Lo somni* translates the reason for the maenads' violent attack, amplifying Ovid's line ("'en,' ait, 'en, hic est nostri contemptor!'" XI, 7), when Orpheus appears to accept blame for his demise:

> Seeing and hearing this a great multitude of women, whose wrath and hatred I had incurred, one of them began to speak and said: "Whoever wants to avenge so great an injury done to all women, follow me!" (108)

> Veyent e oynt açò gran multitud de dones, la ira e oy de las quals encorreguí, una d'aquelles començà a parlar, e dix:
> —Qui tant gran injúria feta a la universitat de les dones volrà venjar, seguesque-mi. (109)

Metge's rendition provides the script for the gruesome end of the eloquent women-hater Torroella in Juan de Flores's *Grisel y Mirabella* (c. 1475). The fictional character was based on real-life poet Pere

---

[24] For *Sir Orfeo's* sources, see Bliss's introduction to his edition (xxxi–xxxii). In *Lo somni*, Tiresias mentions Lancelot's popularity among the ladies at court; she castigates them for "reciting the stories of Lancelot, Tristan, King Arthur and of all the lovers that lived in their time" ("reçitar les istòries de Lançelot, de Tristany, del rey Artús e de quants amorosos són stats a lur temps" '*The Dream*' 142–43).

[25] "Cogieron se unas duennas a que llamavan cicones por que eran de tierra de Ciconia, dont era natural Orpheo … fizieron pieças e esparziéronlo por muchos logares, e tomaron la cabeça e ell arpa e dieron con ello en un río que corríe e acerca que llamavan Ebro" (II, 324b). Mena abridges it as "fasta que la dueñas çicones lo mataron e fezieron mill pedaços e echaron su cabeça e su vihuela en el río de Ebro" (152, 152n14).

Torroella (c. 1420–c. 1492), who claimed that women's cruelty has no limits —"the man in love who courts / a woman, destroys himself" ("Quien bien amando persigue / dona, a sí mesmo destruye")— in his famous *Maldezir de mugeres* [Slander against Women], a provocative *cancionero* poem composed around 1440.[26] In *Grisel y Mirabella*, Torroella is murdered by courtly ladies bent on avenging the great injury done to them all after he defeated Braçayda's arguments in defense of women.[27]

Orpheus is a mirror image of the lovesick Metge persona, which shows Metge's profound understanding of Boethius's *Consolation*. As Astell has shown, the triangle formed by the prisoner, the Muses, and Philosophy represents Boethius's *Consolation* as a whole and is mirrored "midway through the *Consolation*," in the third book, when "the weeping Boethius sees himself reflected in the person of the grief-stricken Orpheus, whose backward glance at Eurydice inspires his upward glance at Lady Philosophy" (*Job, Boethius* 128). Unlike Boethius, *Lo somni*'s fictional Metge is not weeping but enjoying Orpheus's tale when he is suddenly interrupted by Tiresias. "I beseech you not to deprive me of what gives me pleasure" ("Precht-te que no·m me tolgues mon plaer" 108–9), the irritated Metge complains, and Tiresias replies by reenacting Lady Philosophy's arguments. He reads Metge's reflection in Saplana-Ginebreda's moralizing light, which aligns Eurydice with rational judgment, Orpheus with the prudent man who lost her, and his exit from hell as a relief after being sickened by lewd thoughts.

Tiresias, as Lady Philosophy, claims to be acting as a good doctor ("bon metge") whose job is to counteract the myth's toxic effect on the passion that already perturbs Metge's mind ("car lo meu ofici no és dir pasenteries ne lagots, sinó desenganar. Tot lo delit que trobes en les paraules d'Orfeu és com ha parlat d'amor, e són verí a la passió del teu coratge, torbat per aquella" 109). He reprimands Metge's lack of judgment and decorum for falling in love despite his old age and vast learning:

---

[26] For a useful summary of the cultural and literary questions, see Francomano's introduction to her bilingual edition of *The Spanish* Querelle *Texts*, which includes Torroella's *Slander* and Juan de Flores's *Grisel y Mirabella*. The quote and translation are taken from that edition (Flores, "Grisel y Mirabella" 54–55).

[27] The similarity of Orpheus's death to the fictional Torroella's was pointed out by Cocozzella, although he does not relate it directly to Metge's Orpheus (*Fra Francesc* 59). For an analysis of *Grisel y Mirabella* see chapter 3: 278–81.

Oh, what a fool you are, he replied, and how easily you believe! You do not know what women are as well as I do. Are these the words of a man with a sound mind? Are these the words befitting your age? Are these the words of someone who loves learning and has read as much as you have? Leave such things to iddle, vain and ignorant men, for your mind is not to be wasted in love, as it is suited for higher things. (108)

O com est foll –respòs ell– e de leugera creença! No saps què són dones tant bé com jo. Són açò paraules de home ab sana pensa? Són açò paraules convenients a la tua edat? Són açò paraules de home qui am sciència e hage legit tant com tu? Lexa semblants coses a hòmens ociosos, van e il·literats, car lo teu enginy no·s deu distribuir en amor; pus altes coses li són legudes. (109)

The treatment selected by Tiresias, a longwinded invective against women in general and Metge's lady in particular, is borrowed from Boccaccio's *Corbaccio* and inspired by Juvenal's *Satire VI*.[28] It takes up most of the third chapter and rehearses the conventional misogynistic arguments on female physical decay and depravity foretold by Orpheus's ghastly murder.

Despite the medicinal diatribe, the protagonist remains melancholy and disconsolate ("Trist jo ladonchs e desconortat" 151) at the beginning of the fourth book. He whines about Fortune, but Tiresias places the blame on the lover's *bestialitat* and asserts the power of free will:

Do you know who has forced you? Nothing but your folly which, having left reason aside, has followed disorderly desires. Fortune gives wealth, power, dignity, and the like, and she takes them away when she pleases; but the choice to love or to hate, to do right or wrong belongs to free will and is within the reach of everyone to use it as they please. (150)

Saps què te n'ha forçat? No àls sinó la tua bestialitat que, lexada la rahó, ha seguit lo desordonat voler. Riqueses, potències, dignitats e semblants cosas dóna fortuna, e tol·les com li plau; mas elecció d'amar o avorrir, obrar bé o mal, voler o no voler, en franch arbitre està, e en la mà de cascú és que n'ús a son pler. (151)

---

[28] Specific borrowings from Boccaccio are pointed out by Martín de Riquer in notes to his edition and translation (ed. *Obras* 286–319). See also Moll ("El 'Corbatxo' de Giovanni Boccaccio") and Cingolani ("Bernat Metge e gli *auctores*").

Cortijo translates *bestialitat* as folly, and Martín de Riquer as "stupidity" ("tu propia tonteria" ed. *Obras* 321), but the term has a more specific meaning in moral discourse, referring to the minds of beasts and women, which lack the *ratio* afforded by scholastic training. This meaning is suggested in chapter 248 of *Tirant lo Blanc* (1460–1464), borrowed almost verbatim from *Lo somni*, as Martín de Riquer noticed (ed. *Obras* 320n1). Joanot Martorell remembered *bestialitat* as "lack of knowledge" ("lo vostre poc saber"), no doubt motivated by the inventive, biblically inspired trope that initiates *Lo somni*'s last book, "the ploughman who wants to cut the wheat and finds the ears empty" (Metge, '*The Dream*' 150).

Fictional Metge replies to Tiresias's slander with praise of famous women of classical antiquity, recast from Petrarch's epistle 8 of *Familiarum rerum* XXI (Riquer, Martín de, ed. *Obras* 326–37), followed by a list of contemporary ladies. The oration in defense of women and its counterpart, the discourse *in mulieres*, Heinrichs reminds us, was a common dictaminal exercise often incorporated into sermons on Fortune's fickleness; Augustine deployed it as such in Petrarch's *Secretum* (*The Myths of Love* 81). *Lo somni* introduces two novelties: the denunciation of men's faults and a clever game of references, which, while seeming to counter Tiresias's arguments, actually endeavors to correct Boccaccio and Petrarch (Cantavella 31).

Tiresias relishes the challenge and, with the bright smile of a proud teacher, admits to great pleasure when Metge answered all charges against women "with eloquence and in a brilliant manner." He still asserts that such a skilled, articulate tirade sharply contrasts with the endless chatter and gossip he deems characteristic of women ("lur parlar e rallar" 139). The technical terms Tiresias uses to praise Metge's speech —"disertament et acolorada" (187)— allude to the Fulgentian *oris phonos*: the ornamental use of rhetorical colors and the "rigorous and scrupulous control" of a disciplined mind. Nonetheless, Tiresias warns Metge that all his oratorial might has not altered the truth about the evils brought about by womankind; his final recommendation urges him to turn his erotic energy into love of learning and desire for God ("Converteix, donchs, la tua amor d'aquí avant en servey de Déu e continuat studi" 189).

Metge resorts to a scholastic convention, using classical myths to characterize foolish lovers, while a wise counselor, who acts as the voice of reason, moralizes the stories to remind reckless lovers that they have forgotten their *integumenta*.[29] The identification of irrational love and classical myths, with or without moralization, appears in all of the texts that critics have mentioned over the years as direct or indirect stimuli of sentimental fiction: *Fiammetta*, *Roman de la Rose*, *Voir Dit*, or even Dante's association of his imperfect desire for Beatrice with that of Pyramus for Thisbe in *Purgatorio*. In *Lo somni*, Orpheus mirrors the infatuated Metge persona and is endowed with all the traits of a vernacular poet. His story, a patent synecdoche for poetry, is a source of amusement and delight, the joy and happiness ("gaug" and "alegrier") that the Barcelona poetic consistories attributed to classical myths.[30]

Tiresias warns about fiction's toxic effect on reasoning. As a consolation, he invites moral conversion, both exegetical and personal, of the irrationality that ethical discourse locates in adolescent vulnerability to sex and unrestrained imagination. The model he proposes coincides with the "trobador estudioso," which Dominican preacher Felip de Malla recommended to the *vulgares eloquentes*, the Catalan troubadours at the royal court: a new King David who combines eloquence and divinely inspired wisdom, *dolç parlar* and *gratiosa doctrina*.[31]

The fact that *Lo somni* characterizes Metge as an old man in love alludes to the ridiculous episodes that school tradition blamed on Ovid's and Virgil's senility and speaks to the lethal, enduring power that preachers attributed to women's wiles. Later Castilian *cancionero* poems and school tracts, such as *De cómo al hombre le es necesario amar* [How Man Must Necessarily Love], wrongly attributed to Salamanca professor Alonso Fernández de Madrigal, will exploit the humorous implications of the weaknesses that affect aged clerks, but the psychological stages of love's unfolding and purification are also referenced. As Astell remarks about the use of Orpheus in *The Consolation*, poetic myth in *Lo somni* "mysteriously embodies the abstract double potentiality of temptress and guide in a diachronic fashion that displaces the synchronic opposition of the Sirens and Philosophy into a developmental continuum of 'before' and 'after'"

---

[29] I am summarizing Heinrichs's argument (*The Myths of Love* 258–60).

[30] See Pujol for Catalan theorization of vernacular poetry during Metge's time ("'Gaya vel gaudiosa'").

[31] According to Pujol, this model is based on late fourteenth-century French tradition that looks back to the Fathers of the Church and twelfth-century Christian humanism ("Els 'trobadors estudiosos'" 205–06), which is consonant with my analysis of *pietas litterata*.

(*Job, Boethius* 128). Orpheus and Tiresias represent the consecutive stages of sinful temptation and moral conversion.

Cortijo Ocaña (Metge, *'The Dream'*) and Friedlein point out that *Lo somni* is a consolation that ends paradoxically with a disconsolate protagonist. For Cortijo Ocaña, Tiresias's attack on women "serves as a gloomy final reflection on human nature" (188n201), while Friedlein considers *Lo somni* a transgression of the model offered by Boethius's *Consolation*. Both interpretations underline unequivocal traits, yet they fail to account for the distinctive behavior of the three characters who so diligently enact the roles of the *Consolation*'s initial triangle. Compare *Lo somni*'s perplexing ending to Juan Ruiz's *Libro*, another exercise on *enarratio ad auctores* that pokes fun at its dissonances. I am not suggesting any direct or even indirect influence other than the shared exegetical, medical, and penitential discourses of *pietas litterata*. Both Juan Ruiz and Metge assign responsibility to their readers' free will to choose either a poet's youthful passion or the harsh strictures of an aged moralist. No wonder *Lo somni*'s protagonist wakes up sore and melancholic from a dream as exacting as a gloss on Boethius's *Consolation*.

Both Cingolani ("Bernat Metge") and Friedlein puzzle over Metge's deployment of his extensive knowledge of classical and penitential literature to produce a text that does not correspond to the norms of the classical consolatory genre. Their narrow understanding of the genre misses the many disguises that Boethius's *Consolation* adopts here and throughout the Middle Ages. Metge manipulates Boethian dream vision and arguments about Fortune's workings to describe and to justify his own authorial status, garnishing it with a bookish display of classical and modern *auctores* carefully selected from his well-appointed *memoria* in order to safeguard his position at court. He exhibits his proficiency at what Weiss calls the courtier's rhetoric of display and dissimulation ("¿Qué demandamos?") by both pretending love and advancing its respite, being simultaneously patient and cure, becoming, de facto, a Catalan *doctor amoris*.

The learned parade was obviously successful since Metge remained close to the king until Martí I's death. More important for my purposes, *Lo somni* exhibits the most distinctive traits of the scholastic exercise on *pietas litterata* that I term penitential fiction. It is the first instance of a genre that spreads throughout the Catalan and Castilian courts and clerical parlors over the fifteenth century. *Lo somni*'s admixture of rhetorical mastery and an elegance fashioned from the most up-to-date and brilliant Italian *auctores* could not but dazzle courtly dilettantes like Santillana, who solicitously copied it. The future marquis became acquainted with Catalan letters in 1413 during his early post as cupbearer (*copero mayor*) to Alfons the Magnanimous, then heir to the throne, and his profound admiration is documented in the poetic treatise *Proemio e carta al Condestable de Portugal* [Proem and Letter to the Constable of Portugal].[32] A comparison of *El sueño*'s motifs with those of Metge's *Lo somni* will elucidate the types of rhetorical environment that give form and meaning to clerical and aristocratic sentimental productions.[33]

THE TWO AGES OF THE POET: SANTILLANA'S *EL SUEÑO* AND *PROEMIO E CARTA*

Santillana's familiarity with *Lo somni*'s moral reading of Orpheus in particular and classical myth in general is evinced in his magnificent library among whose volumes was an anonymous Castilian translation of the *Morales de Ouidio*. Schevill notes that in a 1445 letter to his son, then a student at the University of Salamanca, Santillana urged him "to cultivate the classics, and to translate them into Castilian, he himself having instigated at a previous date various translations, among them *Las Transformaciones de Ouidio*" (69). The advice to engage in the dictaminal practice of *translatio* as rhetorical performance accords with that of Saplana's to the *Infant* Jaume. But while paraphrasing Boethius was meant to offer consolation on fortune's downturns, translating, and moralizing, Ovid was an exercise better suited to the young man's age.

Two members of Santillana's inner circle, Juan de Mena and Enrique de Villena, added moral glosses to their works. Mena added a lengthy commentary to his own poem *La coronación del Marqués*

---

[32] Santillana visited the great urban centers of the Aragonese crown —Zaragoza, Valencia, Perpignan, Gerona, and Barcelona— in the company of the heir; when the prince succeeded his father as Alfons V, the Magnanimous, Santillana remained at the court until his majority (Pérez Bustamante 40–42).

[33] A different connection between Metge's *Lo somni* and Santillana's crafting of his own authorial status that merits further exploration is Santillana's interest in the soul's immortality, the subject of *Lo somni*'s first two books. Pero Díaz de Toledo translated Plato's *Phaedo* for Santillana. Metge's ideas, although he cites Plato's dialogue, are taken mostly from Cicero's *Tusculanae* with a brief reference to *Laelius sive de amicitia*, as Martín de Riquer demonstrates (ed. *Obras*). On Díaz de Toledo's cultural background and his translation's impact on Castile, see Round (*Libro llamado Fedron*).

de Santillana [The Coronation of the Marquis de Santillana], composed in 1438 to celebrate the nobleman's victory at Huelma. Each stanza is followed by a prose commentary that clearly separates a myth's literal story ("estoria e verdad") from its ethical application ("moralidad e aplicación"), in an exegetical labor as rigorous as Villena's interpretation of the *Doce trabajos de Hércules*. In the gloss on the Orphic myth, Tiresias stands for any righteous person who teaches moral living and God's service ("qualquiera persona buena que amonesta a omne a bien bevir e que sirva a Dios" 124); Orpheus represents "a rational man's judgment" ("el seso e el juizio e entendimiento del onbre cuerdo" 152), and Eurydice, "our flesh over which our judgment must rule like a husband over a wife" ("devemos entender la nuestra carne, la qual el seso e entendimiento de cada uno de nos deve señorear como a muger" 153). According to this moral logic, the snake that bites Eurydice unavoidably signifies "mortal sin whose bite poisons our flesh" ("el pecado mortal que muerde e enponçoña la nuestra carne" 154).

For his part, Villena began the massive commentary to his translation of Virgil's *Aeneid* in 1427 for the King of Navarre but ultimately dedicated it to Santillana. Its learned prologues and extensive marginal glosses elucidate the rhetorical operation at work in interpretive and ethical conversion. Both the rhetorical motif of *exercitatio* and rivalry with Servius's commentary on the *Aeneid* drive his performance, extracting from Virgil's *intentio* a practical knowledge that he deems indispensable for the "lector romancista" [vernacular reader]. As the work progresses, the marginal glosses cease to be merely referential and relate a *caballero sciente*'s penitential journey in search of atonement. Villena invents his own moral *Aeneid*, focused on the motif of conversion.[34]

Santillana's narrative poem *El sueño* was composed some ten years before Mena's *Coronación* and around the same time as Villena's commentary. In choosing his title and mythical characters from Metge's most famous work, he signals its dependence —today we would call it a tribute— but beyond pointing to *Lo somni* as a source, to my knowledge, no critic has yet analyzed the impact of *El sueño*'s intertextuality.

---

[34] See Miguel-Prendes (*El espejo y el piélago*). For the "atracción novelesca de la glosa," what Lida de Malkiel called "el novelar desinteresado," among Castilian authors in the first half of the fifteenth century, see Weiss ("Las 'fermosas e peregrinas'").

El sueño is a quest for consolation against the instability of Fortune, represented, unsurprisingly, as erotic passion, which threatens
the poet's rational thinking and freedom. Critics have puzzled over
the initial motif of the blasted garden in which the poet's harp turns
into a desert asp and lacerates his left side.[35] As Haywood points out,
quoting Deyermond, the corrupted *locus amoenus* is typically "an image of a disastrous love affair" ("'La escura selva'" 423). In *El sueño*,
the garden morphs into the landscape moralized by Boethian commentaries as a desert drained of intellectual juices by worldly desires,[36]
while the author persona is both Orpheus and Eurydice, inspired
poet and victim of the bite of erotic fire that overcomes his senses ("la
flama es estensa e çircunda los sentidos" vv. 13–14). The intellectual
confusion brought about by Fortune's sudden turn is structured as
a debate between Mind and Heart ("Seso" and "Coraçon"), which
Coraçón appears to win before Seso abruptly changes:

> Difinida la porfía
> de los dos que litigaron,
> mis sentidos reposaron
> commo nave quando çía;
> e fallé que me conplía
> en tal caso bien pensar
> e morir o deffensar
> libertad que posséya. (St. XXIII)

At first, the comparison of a boat rowing backwards ("nave quando çia") and the poet's senses at rest seems incongruous. However,
consider it as the beginning of a creative vision in which the poet as
young Orpheus will be instructed on the importance of free will by
the aged Tiresias ("en hedat ser declinante, a la senectud bolante"
vv. 203–4). The Theban priest advises the poet to search for Diana,
goddess of chastity, as a way of *reversing* ("ca ella sola *revessa*" v. 269)
love's darts. It is a reformulation of Tiresias's final advice to Metge
in *Lo somni* to convert —that is, to change the direction of— his
human love to charity.

El sueño's quest begins when the poet enters his memorial storeroom of classical references —whether from the Italians or the Cata-

---

[35] "E la farpa sonorosa, / que recuento que tañía, / en sepes se convertía de la
grand sirte arenosa, / e con ravia viperosa / mordió mi siniestro lado" (st. XIII).
[36] The mention of dryness recalls Villena's moralization of dry sands ("sirtes") in
Doce trabajos.

lans, their source is irrelevant to my argument— and his bookish mind's eye conceives a vision ("vi," "he leído," "recordeme"). He gathers them in a "trágico tractado" without further commentary ("non methaphoro ni gloso" vv. 414–15) as examples of virtuous men who may help him to recover his liberty. As in *Lo somni*, despite the *exempla* recalled from memory, suggesting a penitential craft organized around moral reading and literary performance as a medicine for erotic fire, *El sueño*'s lovesick protagonist remains melancholy. The fact that Santillana presents himself as a victim of amorous passion and not simultaneously as its learned cure, as Metge did, may be a consequence of his youth or his aristocratic credentials; being in love attests to his nobility. At the same time, he is mounting an impressive display of poetic prowess to compete with, if not to emulate, the most learned productions of fashionable Catalan clerks.

Santillana waged his personal battle in the culture wars against Castilian professional men of letters. Their attacks on aristocratic learning must be framed by the larger debate over the mutability of culture that Weiss identified, cloaked in debates about Woman and Fortune. Booklearning was thought to weaken the nobleman's command of the sword, but vigorous opposition was based on clerical misgivings about lay access to classical myths. Without proper moral conversion, they alleged, delightful words and magnificent meters incite profligacy.[37] Weiss cites Cartagena's stern lesson to the Count of Haro on the kind of literature appropriate for the *militari vires* who wished to combine the active and contemplative life (*The Poet's Art*). This eloquent summary of the arguments wielded by *letrados* deserves quotation in full:[38]

> You must abstain from those books that appear to induce immorality such as amorous or bucolic tales and other poetic fabrications, which in spite of being composed in eloquent style and with clever inventions, and although they exhibit an immense talent in concocting sweet flavors through an admixture of excellent metrical composition and exquisite words, still their subject matter is obscene and encourages licentiousness. In the same manner that there are some foods that provoke lust ... words that deviate from rectitude often harm the spirit.[39]

---

[37] See Kohut; Lawrance ("La autoridad"); Gascón Vera.
[38] I cite the complete Latin passage from Lawrence's *Un tratado de Alonso de Cartagena*.
[39] "A libris itaque illis abstinendum erit, qui ad inhonestatem videntur allicere, uti sunt amatoria, bucolica, aliaque poetarum figmenta, que, licet eloquenti stillo et

The passage appears in the letter that Cartagena enclosed with
a gift of two of the Latin books of the *Cathoniana confectio* intended for children's grammatical training.[40] This moral candy, in his
learned opinion, was more appropriate to the count's social station
than the pagan literary sweets most aristocrats enjoyed. The gift's implied insult speaks of the bishop's aversion to aristocratic amateurs
encroaching on the turf traditionally reserved for professional scholars. *Letrados* commonly proposed that noblemen had better things
to do than read or, worse, produce extravagant tales that harm moral
health like overly rich food harms the body. The spread of lay literacy
made a variety of forms previously restricted to the clerical domain
available to a wide public.[41] Cartagena engages in a lengthy comparison of viands and readings whose consumption must be strictly
regulated by wholesome ethical principles.[42]

If *El sueño* is a youthful display of literary erudition, the *Proemio e carta*, composed when Santillana was approaching fifty (c.
1445–1449), can be read as a carefully planned response to each of
the charges wielded by *scholastici vires* like Cartagena. In defending
poetry as the highest form of eloquence, he vindicates his own *intellectual* nobility and clarifies an aspect of poetic decorum critical
to my argument on the generic status of penitential and sentimental
works. As Weiss cautions, the concepts that Santillana proposes in
his definition of poetry may seem directly borrowed from Italian
humanism, but they "belong to a common heritage of literary theory, employed in one form or another from the time of the early
Christian Church until well beyond the fifteenth century" (*The Poet's Art* 199); that is, the dictaminal toolbag of *pietas litterata* used
by Metge. In response to Cartagena's disparaging comparison of
poetry to spicy foods that incite lust, a common clerical charge that
we saw articulated in the "Conversio Carnis" of the trite *De consolatione Rationis*, the nobleman extols poetry as "insaçiable çibo del

---

acuta inventione composita sint, magnamque ingenii elevationem ostendent, cum
mirabili compositione metrorum exquisitisque verbis coagulata dulcem saporem
conficiant, in nonnullis tamen eorem materia obscena et provocativa libidinum est.
At sicut cibi aliqui sunt qui pre ceteris libidinem provocant ... sic et verba que ab
honestate declinant plerumque animo nocent" (Lawrance, *Un tratado de Alonso de
Cartagena* 50). Lawrance notes that the objection to classical poetry is taken from
a passage by Saint Basil, the same that Italian humanists deployed to elaborate its
praise (*Un tratado de Alonso de Cartagena* 50n49).

[40] See chapter 1: 42.

[41] See Weiss ("Medieval Vernacular").

[42] See chapters 6 and 9 in the *epistula* (Lawrance, *Un tratado de Alonso de Cartagena* 42–46).

ánimo," a definition drawing on the web of memorial associations that equate meditative reading with the most basic food for daily nourishment; Peter of Celle called such activity "a steaming oven full of breads of the best wheat flours" (qtd. in Carruthers's *The Craft of Thought* 109). This metaphor clarifies Metge's trope of creative distress in finding the ears of wheat empty: *Lo somni's* protagonist is starving for poetic bread but receives instead a bitter dose of castigation.

Santillana also praises poetry as "un zelo çeleste, una affecçión divina" (439). Weiss traces this definition to biblical scholarship and understands its meanings as ranging from the "violent fervour which consumed so many Old Testament priests and prophets" to the "irrational impulse ... often used to highlight the conflict between man's reason and his emotion" in penitential texts. From late fourteenth century on, the meaning of *affecçión*, a learned equivalent of the Latin *affectio*, could range from *love* or *desire* to *irrationality* (*The Poet's Art* 182–83). I want to call attention to three occurrences of the term that Weiss mentions in his discussion of Santillana's poetics. He warns that, although none can be pinpointed or completely ruled out as the direct source of Santillana's phrase, they were certainly part of the network of texts that helped him to articulate ideas deeply familiar to him and his contemporaries (*The Poet's Art* 200). More to the point for my argument, they help to clarify the rhetoric of conversion and the social meaning of form that support my taxonomy of penitential and sentimental fictions.

The first instance appears in Cartagena's Castilian translation of Cicero's *De inventione,* which Weiss relegates to a footnote. Cartagena renders the rhetorical term *affectio* in the accurate Ciceronian sense as "a mutation that happens in the heart or in the body at some point caused by joy, greed, fear, sadness, illness, weakness or similar things" ("aquella mudación que acaece en el coraçon o en el cuerpo en algunt tiempo por alguna cabsa, como alegría, cobdicia, miedo, tristeza, dolencia, flaqueza o otras cosas semejantes" *The Poet's Art* 183n27).[43] Cartagena's faithful translation bears an uncanny resemblance to Arnau de Vilanova's definition of medical *accident* as a type of physical perturbation of the *virtus aestimativa's* inclination, or *intentio*, affecting its judgments. It also brings to mind

---

[43] "Adfectio est animi aut corporis ex tempore aliqua de cause commutatio ut, laetitia, cupiditas, metus, molestia, morbus, debilitas, et alia, quae in eodem genere reperiuntur" (*De inventione* 1, 25, 36).

Saplana-Ginebreda and Villena's insistence that a sudden upsurge of desire or fierce anger causes physical swelling and affects the emotional coloring of the heart's (i.e., memory's) contents. Both suggest the conflation of rhetorical and medical discourses characteristic of *pietas litterata*.

Villena uses a narrower sense of *affecçión* in his Castilian translation of, and commentary on, a Petrarch sonnet, copied at the end of the manuscript containing his translation of Dante's *Comedy* for Santillana.[44] He makes no effort to understand Petrarch's poem and its cultural context, but his misinterpretations encapsulate the poetic theories of his and Santillana's literary circle (Weiss, "La *Affección Poetal*" 72). Villena reads the sonnet as an example of "affecçión poetal uirtuosa" [virtuous poetic *affectio*]. Weiss claims, correctly, that it corresponds to *studium* in classical rhetoric ("La *Affección Poetal*" 76), but taken with Cartagena's rendering of *affectio*, Villena's phrase brings out the ethical range of the term; it encompasses the strong emotion that inclines memory to allow imaginative work. In contemplative reading, a rhetorical operation based on memorial manipulation converts a sensual impression —of an image, a poetic myth, an upsurge of lust— to the intention of Christian charity; Augustine called it *amor* and identified it with human will. *Lo somni*'s Tiresias intends this meaning when he advises Metge to convert his *love* to the service of God and *continuous study* ("Converteix, donchs, la tua amor d'aquí avant en servey de Déu e *continuat studi*" 189; my emphasis).

The third instance appears in a Castilian translation of Leonardo Bruni's *Vite di Dante e del Petrarca,* contained in fols. 25–62 of Ms. 10171 in the Biblioteca Nacional de España, which belonged to Santillana's extensive library.[45] The anonymous Castilian translator, Weiss acknowledges, renders Bruni's terms quite literally. It qualifies *affecçion* as "inward" and defines it as a movement that awakens the mind ("interior affecçión e mouimiento e despertamiento de mente" 43r). It distinguishes two kinds of poets. The first, like Saint Francis, are stirred by some inner force or mental frenzy ("furor e ocupaçion de mente"). Saint Francis may have lacked scholastic

---

[44] See Weiss *The Poet's Art* and "La *Affección Poetal*". He still presents the translation and commentary as anonymous although Carr's meticulous analysis of scribal hand and vocabulary unquestionably attributes it to Villena.

[45] The classic study on Santillana's library is Mario Schiff's; an updated summary and study appears in Gómez Moreno's introduction to Santillana's *Obras completas* (xxi–xxxiii).

training, Bruni admits, but he knew God better than theologians.[46] This form of poetry is the highest, and Bruni also mentions Orpheus and Hesiod as poets who have been called divine, *vates*, or seers because of their poetic fever.[47] The second, like Dante, are poets who attain wisdom through study ("los estudios"), or the strenuous effort of gathering many books and converting them to Christian ethics ("tractar e boluer muchos e uarios libros velando e sudando") with the help of rhetorical skill and good judgment ("por arte e por prudencia").[48] It may be objected that the term *boluer* just means turning the page, but its later use in *Siervo libre de amor* supports my interpretation of it as the change of direction —the reordering of *intentio*— implied in moral conversion. It is synonymous with Tiresias's advice to Metge about converting love and Santillana's backward-rowing boat in *El sueño*.[49] After the taxing exercise of *los estudios*, the poet's task consists in adorning, arranging, and explaining the found wisdom ("ornar, conponer e esplicar con los sus uersos") in his verses. In studious authors like Dante, *affectio* implies a form of *translatio* in which love's earthly elements are left in the past and its purest element becomes *caritas* (Minnis, "Authors in Love" 185–86).

Villena, in his characteristic convoluted style, appears to echo Bruni's distinction in a gloss on the phrase "generosos entendimientos," which he applies to vernacular poets like himself in the "Prohemio" to his massive translation of, and commentary on, Virgil's *Aene-*

---

[46] "Digo que los poetas son e se fazen en dos maneras, el un modo es por ingenio propio despartado (sic) e comouido de algun uigor interior e oculto o ascondido, el qual se llama furor e ocupaçion de mente ... Çierto es que san françisco non por çiençia nin por disçiplina escolastica mas por ocupacion e comouimiento de mente aplacaua su animo asi fuerte a Dios tanto que se trasfiguraua casi allende del seso humano e conoçia de Dios mas que nin por estudio nin por letras conoçen los theologos, asi es en la poesia que alguno por interior e intrinseco mouimiento e aplacaçion de mente se faze poeta" (42r–42v).

[47] "E aquesta es la mas alta e mas perfecta especie de poesia, e commo quier que dize que los poetas son diuinos e los llaman sauios e commo quier que los llaman uates o adeuinos la su apellaçion o nonbre es tomado de aqueste furor o intrinsico mouimiento que yo digo. E cerca desto auemos exenplos de orfeo e de essiodo" (42v).

[48] The whole passage reads, "La otra espeçie es por çiençia por estudio e por diçiplina por arte e por prudençia e de aquesta segunda espeçie fue dante, ca por estudio de filosofia e de teologia e astrologia e de arismetica e de geometria e por lecçion de estorias e por tractar e boluer muchos e uarios libros velando e sudando en los estudios alcanço e la çiençia, la qual deuia ornar, conponer e esplicar con los sus uersos" (43r–43v).

[49] For its use in Siervo *libre de amor* see chapter 2: 127.

id. Contrary to lowly chroniclers, poets' minds must first be trained ("habituados a la soliçitud e cura de las otras sçienças antiguadas e aprovadas") to receive poetry's nourishment ("E tales entendimientos como éstos ansí dispuestos nudre e cría la poesía;" Villena, *Obras*, vol. 2, 48). He struggles to translate the mnemonic technical term *sollicitudo* as "soliçitud e cura," which indicates the "good *curiositas* or carefulness and attentive mindfulness" (Carruthers, *The Craft of Thought* 99) implied in *los estudios* that dispose the mind (*dispuesta*) to be fed but, more important, free it from nagging distractions and focus it.

By Santillana's time, the association of inspired madness with Orpheus in love had become "a literary motif, so familiar as the emblem of great love that it may be adopted as self-conscious pose" (Saunders 78). We saw it in Metge's *Lo somni* and Santillana's reworking in *El sueño*, opposed to the learned *prudentia* embodied by Tiresias. The *Proemio e carta* also contrasts youthful inspiration and reflective maturity. In the exordium, Santillana apologizes to his young friend Pedro de Portugal for his reluctance to send him some of his "dezires e cançiones," as requested; their subject matter and uncontrived rhetorical composition, he regrets, make them undeserving of written record ("no son de tales materias, ni asý bien formadas e artizadas, que de memorable registro dignas parescan" 438). Santillana's clichéd rehearsal of the humility topos hides a more important distinction. If he finally sent his poems to Pedro, it would be because such joyful pastimes are the pursuit of courtly young men ("estas tales cosas alegres e jocosas andan e concurren con el tiempo de la nueva hedat de juventud, es a saber, con el vestir, el justar, con el dançar e con otros tales cortesanos exerçiçios") in which he once engaged ("Cum essem paruulus cogitabam ut paruulus, loquebar ut paruulus"). However, such activities that now so much delight his young correspondent cannot, or should not, bring pleasure to someone of Santillana's age ("muchas cosas plazen agora a vos que ya no plazen o no deven plazer a mí" 438). His allusion to decorum is framed by a display of wisdom that suits his age: he quotes St Paul's first letter to the Corinthians and Dante's *Comedy*.[50]

---

[50] Commenting on Santillana's decorum, Gómez Moreno quotes a marginal note, possibly by Santillana's hand, in his Italian manuscript with Villena's translation, saying "nota cómmo todo onbre en la madura edat deue cesar el malbeuir." Villena's translation reads, "Quando me bi junto aquella parte / de mi hedat donde cada vno deuía / baxar las belas e recoger la xarçia / lo que primero me plazía entonçe me desplogo" (Gómez Moreno, *El Prohemio* 86n2).

Thus, age places an author in two distinct rhetorical environments: either he is Orpheus, an infatuated, bewildered poet who identifies with myths, forgetting their *integumentum* —the Boethius who despairs about Fortune while composing his meter— or he is Tiresias, a wise teacher, a Lady Philosophy, who dispenses moral therapy. In the *Proemio e carta*, Santillana performs the role of the mature poet whose years of learning and detachment from the passions that disturbed him in youth taught him how to break poetry's sweet crust to feed on its wholesome contents. Weiss is mystified that Santillana's definition of poetry here —"fingimiento de cosas útyles, cubiertas o veladas con muy fermosa cobertura"— places a very medieval emphasis linking poetic craft to allegory, whose striking veil conceals useful knowledge (*The Poet's Art* 191).[51] Such definitions simply correlate the treatise with his present circumstances: he is claiming his authorial status as another Dante by explaining his love poems as a juvenile version of his love of wisdom, both human and divine. His formidable ego and aristocratic credentials allowed him to play the prudent Tiresias, but aging clerks and knights of lower social status were more circumscribed to penitential discourse. First, they humbly recanted their poetic compositions and amorous infatuation; then they wrestled with the recklessness of their ways before offering the soothing balm of moralization to cure the debilitating madness brought about by erotic desire and poetic imagination.

THE VIOLENCE OF CONVERSION: *SIERVO LIBRE DE AMOR*

Few sentimental works have generated as much critical controversy as Rodríguez del Padrón's *Siervo libre de amor* (c. 1440). Long considered the first sentimental monument, most scholars initially traced its themes and structure to Italian models,[52] until Gerli ("*Siervo libre*") and Cátedra (*Amor y pedagogía*) placed it squarely within

---

[51] The association of poetry and allegory is developed in Mena's commentary to *La coronación* where he justifies his own deployment of fiction "so that the listener's imagination may see and understand more plainly some of the moral reasons covered by fiction's rhetorical color" ["porque más palpablemente la maginativa conprenda del oyente las fiçiones que yo sobre aquesto he pensado traher so la color de las quales presumo, veamos algunas filosóficas siquier morales razones"], a convoluted way of describing a dream vision.

[52] For the Italian influence, see Weissberger's "'Habla el *auctor*';" Andrachuk's "A Further Look;" Brownlee's "The Generic Status;" Castro Lingl's "Back to the Text."

the penitential tradition.[53] Gerli's eventual identification of its source in Deguilevile's *Pèlerinage de la vie humaine* ("The Old French Source") or the wider French penitential tradition, as Conde ("De las fuentes") proposes, clearly excludes *Siervo* from the sentimental canon, as Gwara and Gerli suggested, to position it among clerical penitential fictions that recant shameful passion and poetry.

Siervo's ambiguous title can be translated as either *Love's Willing Slave* or *The Slave Free of Love* (Impey's "Los enigmas" 110; Deyermond's "On the Frontier" 101). It already hints at the loss of personal freedom fictionalized in Metge and Santillana's dreams and the process of conversion that may bring deliverance.[54] The first page presents the author at the service of Cardinal Cervantes, Archbishop of Seville ("criado del Señor don Pedro de Çervantes, Cardenal de Sant Pedro, Arçobispo de Sevilla" 10), to whom he may have been related and in whose company he traveled to Italy.[55] Rodríguez del Padrón was a member of the emerging class of Castilian bureaucrats and, like most *letrados*, including Gonzalo de Medina, the Mondoñedo judge to whom *Slave* is addressed, he attended the *studium generale* in Salamanca (Cátedra, *Amor y pedagogía* 156). *Siervo* was composed sometime between 1339 and 1441, when Rodríguez del Padrón took Franciscan orders in the Convent of Jerusalem and entered the Friar Minors.[56]

Siervo is prefaced by an academic prologue, and the term *tratado* that describes the work points, as in Santillana's *El sueño*, to a dictaminal mode of composition.[57] Allegory is the chosen poetic method, or *forma tractandi*, and the tripartite structure, the *forma tractatus*, consecrates each of three allegorical paths and their associated trees to a deity and one of the three faculties of the soul.[58]

---

[53] Impey ("Los enigmas") also pointed out linguistic French borrowings.

[54] Dolz interprets the title within a Franciscan context as referring to the Friar Minors, who, after rejecting worldly desire, serve the love of God ("El simbolismo" 114–21).

[55] I cite from Dolz's 2004 edition of *Siervo libre de amor* (Rodríguez del Padrón); for the translation I take advantage of Dolz's substantial notes and useful glossary. For Rodríguez del Padrón's biography, see Lida de Malkiel ("Juan Rodríguez del Padrón").

[56] See Dolz ("El vocabulario" 87–88).

[57] Cátedra compares it with the method deployed in his *Bursario*, the translation of Ovid's *Heroides* (*Amor y pedagogía* 154).

[58] *Siervo*'s allegory attracted numerous studies. See, in particular, Herrero; Brownlee ("The Generic Status," "The Counterfeit," and *The Severed Word*); Cátedra (*Amor y pedagogía*); Haywood ("'La escura selva'"); Dolz ("El simbolismo"); and Martín ("Allegory" and "Love's Subjects").

On the first path, we find the one who loved and was loved, whose tree is the green myrtle consecrated to Venus and the heart or memory. On the second path of unrequited love, the tree of paradise, or the white poplar, is consecrated to Hercules and free will. The final path of the one who did not love and was not loved is a narrow track presided over by the green olive consecrated to Minerva and knowledge.

This passage led critics to propose a missing third part to the work.[59] The fact that the only manuscript witness is located in a truncated codex whose first 124 pages are lost gives credence as does Gerli's comparison with Deguilevile's *Pèlerinage de la vie humaine*, a work that clearly develops three specific stages in a penitent's pathway to conversion. Martín sees "a mimetic reflection" among sections, trees, chronological steps, and a three-part allegorical construction, but the difficulty of identifying those correspondences in the existing *Siervo* leads him to conclude that neither the allegory nor the narration are linear but develop "by means of psychological inversion and reversion ... to objectify emotional desperation" (Allegory" 133–34). However, Folger (*Images in Mind*) and Conde ("De las fuentes") warn that neither the proemial division nor *Siervo*'s penitential source guarantee that some final section would relate the narrator's adventures in not loving or being loved. More emphatically, Conde demonstrates that Deguilevile's *Pèlerinage* could not have been *Siervo*'s only penitential source. Since Rodríguez del Padrón was well acquainted with the topos, the confessional triple paths mentioned in the preface merely indicate the choices available in mapping the protagonist's process of confession and contrition.[60]

Folger analyzes the following section, "Síguese la primera, de bien amar y ser amado," as a second prologue that introduces a different reading (*Images in Mind* 110), but it may be more aptly understood as the beginning of the *tractatus* itself. It is conceived as a prosimetrum letter from the author to Gonçalo de Medina, the Mondoñedo judge, who, *Siervo* asserts, demanded to know the "case" in writing. Martín Baños notes that *dictatores* like Guido Fava, Boncompagno da Signa, and Conrado d'Hirsau considered epistles a mean to keep secrets between friends (136, 136n17). In this type of clerical correspondence, composed, *Siervo*'s narrator claims, "en señal de amistad" (as

---

[59] See Andrachuk ("On the Missing Third"); Fernández Jiménez ("La estructura" and "*Siervo libre*"); Herrero; and Gerli ("The Old French").

[60] See a different interpretation related to friendship in chapter 2: 135–39.

a sign of friendship), writers parade their knowledge of classical *auctores* as a conscious act of self-presentation; these complex literary productions have little connection with historical events. Missives penned by Godfrey of Reims (c. 1015–1040 / c. 1094) to his friend Baudri of Bourgueil are early instances; note that in Godfrey's *Epistola de Odone*, Orpheus appears as personification of poetry, and Lady Philosophy, contrary to *The Consolation*, playfully defends it (Carlos). We have seen how Boncompagno's *Rota Veneris* lampoons such scholarly consolations.[61] In this tradition, *Siervo*'s "spiritual autobiography," as Lakarra labels it (*"Siervo libre"*), may not be autobiographical at all; rather, it reinforces *Siervo*'s placement within a dictaminal tradition where Ovidian and Boethian recantations and spoofs are an excuse to display the author's rhetorical skill.[62]

The author persona who narrates the "case" presents himself as a fearful lover ("temeroso amador"), filled with anxiety and shame ("pavor y vergüença"). Critics believe he is expressing remorse for a past love affair. Dolz relates his feelings to the triple *via* of Saint Bonaventure's mysticism ("El vocabulario" 97–99). Similarly, Gerli restricts them to "the narrator's voluntary repudiation of a concupiscent love" (*"Siervo libre"* 97), although in a subsequent and very influential article, he acknowledges metafictional structures and conceits in *Siervo*: "the representation of a writer writing within the text" ("Metafiction" 57). I propose to build on these later insights to interpret the narrator's strong emotions as the engine that fires his intellectual activity and leads him to compose the fictional "Estoria de dos amadores," a long narrative parenthesis, labeled *novella* in the manuscript's margin, inserted without explanation in the middle of the dream vision.[63]

Siervo's initial section, then, details the mental state that fosters his project: relating a penitential journey in the dictaminal tradition of visionary first-person narration. To measure up to the judge's rhetorical skills, comparable to the eloquence of Virgil and Cicero ("Más

---

[61] For the impact of Boncompagno's ideas on letter writing and friendship, see Cortijo Ocaña ("'De amicitia'") and his introduction (Boncompagno, *La rueda del amor*).

[62] See Gerli: "the narrator's story is, in sum, little more than fiction transparently disguised as autobiography" ("Metafiction in Spanish" 57). Cortijo Ocaña compares *Siervo*'s frame letter with the anonymous *Tratado de cómo al hombre le es necesario amar* as examples of self-exculpatory epistles ("Notas" 70–71).

[63] Cátedra states that Deyermond conceived a related interpretation, seeing *Siervo*'s supposedly missing third part as the act of writing it (*Amor y pedagogía* 150n333), but I have not been able to locate it in any of Deyermond's published work.

como tú seas otro Virgilio e segundo Tulio Çíçero, príncipes de la
eloqüençia"), the narrator feels he must imitate the style of "los antiguos Omero, Publio Maro, Perseo, Séneca, Ovidio, Platón, Luca-
rio, Salustrio, Estaçio, Terençio, Juvenal, Oraçio, Dante, Marcotulio
Çiçerio, Valerio, Luçio, Eneo, Ricardo, Plinio, Quintiliano" (11), the
traditional admixture of grammatical authors and moral commentaries, if we agree with Dolz that "Ricardo" is Richard of Saint Victor
(Rodríguez del Padrón 11n14), author of a mystical treatise on the
four degrees of violent love that begins, "I have been wounded by
love" (275).[64] The narrator will compose a tale in the style of classical
myths ("trayendo fiçiones segund los gentiles nobles de dioses dañados e de deesas") but with a moral intention ("the poético fin"): to
herald their errors by exposing the allegorical meaning inside their
crude literal cover. When interpreted with sound judgment, his tale
provides weapons against love.[65]

Nowadays, scholars tackling a hermeneutic job initiate their research in a library and peruse their notes. Medieval intellectuals like
Aquinas or Anselm, Carruthers shows, either cry or burn with love,
as a reaction to the familiar anxiety of facing a blank page (*The Book
of Memory* 202).[66] Like the weeping Boethius at the beginning of
The Consolation, *Siervo*'s protagonist is facing a crisis while reporting
on past events he identifies with turns of Fortune's wheel ("yo aver
sido bien affortunado, aunque agore me vees en contrallo" 12). Notice that his older friend has demanded more than simple facts ("los
passados tristes y alegres actos"); he wants to know the protagonist's
solitary contemplations and intimate thoughts ("esquivas contem-
plaçiones e innotos e varios pensamientos" 11).

After this brief enigmatic account and three poems that oscillate
between a *reprobatio* of love and a missive to his lady, the narrator
accepts her hostility. The memory of their affair, which may have
involved one of his friends,[67] forces him to solitary contemplation:[68]

---

[64] From Kraebel's edition of Richard of St Victor's "On the Four Degrees of
Violent Love;" see also his introduction.

[65] The whole passage reads, "Ficçiones, digo al poético fin de aprovechar y venir
en ti en plazer con las fablas que quieren seguir lo que naturaleza no puede sufrir;
aprovechar con el seso alegórico que trahe consigo la ruda letra, auqnue pareçe del todo
fallir; la cual, si requieres de sano entender, armas te dizen contra el amor" (11–12).

[66] See also Minnis's remarks on authors in love ("Authors in Love;" "The Author's").

[67] For Cortijo Ocaña, *Siervo* contrasts the chaos brought about by carnal love to
peaceful friendship yet is also an indictment of deceitful friends ("'De amicitia'").

[68] Parrilla quotes Impey's observation that the smooth linking of prose and verse
in this section represents the full temporal course of the narrator's love affair ("Can-

My fear and great shame, mixed with my loyalty, made me retreat
into the temple of great solitude, in company of its high priestess,
sad bitterness. There, at the time when the old fathers in the isolation of the desert habitually devote themselves to devout prayer
in solitary delight, I, accompanied by tears, sighs, and moans, remembering the past every day, devoted myself to the following
contemplation.

Cuyo temor e grand vergüença mesclada con lealtad me hizieron
retraher al templo de la grand soledat en compañía de la triste am-
argura, saçerdotissa de aquélla, donde a la acostumbrada hora que
los padres antigos en la esquividat del desierto se dan a la devota
oración, de plazer solitario e acompañado de lágrimas, gemidos
e suspiros, todos días remembrándome lo pasado, me dava a la
siguiente contemplaçión. (18)[69]

The passage likens creative effort to monastic prayer, a delightful
solitary occupation paradoxically initiated by a state of grief and fear,
the *compunctio cordis*, or remembrance of sins in this case, an intense
prickling caused by the slave's devotion to the lady, which moves him
to shame and contrition.[70]

The creative process is figured in a dream vision in which the
narrator wanders through the dark forest of his thoughts until he
arrives at the crossing of the three paths. His cogitation combines silent composition with sobbing recollection of memorial images. The
passage's convoluted syntax and obscure references make interpretation a challenge, but we can still discern the expected conversion of
the *locus amoenus* into a horrid antechamber of chaos and panic that
opens into a memorial storeroom of subject materials. When the narrator arrives under the shade of Venus's lovely myrtle, the tree loses
its leaves ("fue despojado de su vestidura"), and the nightingale's
song suddenly transmutes into screams. Minerva's green olive, the
signpost of contemplative life, remains in bloom. *Libre alvedrío* [Free

tar y contar" 223). I refer to Parrilla's study for an insightful analysis of the metric
compositions in *Siervo*.

[69] Dolz adds a comma after "oración" so that "de plazer solitario" modifies
acompañado" (in the company of solitary joy and tears). The monastic tradition considers contemplation a blissful activity so I translate "de plazer solitario" as a mod-
ifier of "la devota oración" (devout prayer in solitary delight or a delightful solitary
occupation).

[70] For the long tradition of the beloved's image imprinted in the lover's memory,
see Serés's *La transformación*.

Will] faces a choice, symbolized by the odd fact that his literary boat has two "*lemes*," or helms, to orient its direction. In his misery, Free Will selects Hercules's path, marked by the white poplar, and leading to the Lethe, river of oblivion.[71] *Entendimiento* [Understanding] discourages his choice and reminds him of a number of wretched lovers who succumbed to a deplorable death as a consequence of women's wiles.

The Elysian fields that Entendimiento recalls are not configured like the Dantean hell, as critics initially assumed, but taken from the *Aeneid*'s sixth book, the *Heroides,* and the *Metamorphoses*.[72] Hell functions as a mnemonic diagram from which to extract mythical *exempla* as Pero Díaz de Toledo explains in a gloss to Plato's *Phaedo*; he presented his Castilian translation, *Libro llamado Fedron*, to Santillana around 1447: "En el infierno fazían logares distintos apartados donde se penavan los malos e los peccadores, e donde eran remunerados e galardonados los buenos e los virtuosos, segund pone Séneca en la primera trajedia, e Virgilio en el sexto libro de los Enoydos" (Round, *Libro llamado* 232). [In hell, there were separate places to punish wicked sinners and reward the virtuous, as Seneca says in his first tragedy and Virgil in the Aeneid's sixth book]. An easy metaphorical transfer links the dark underworld and its hidden entrance to the secret cell where the mind stores its memories: texts read (most by dead authors), images seen, private cogitations, the secret poisons of classical poets and orators that so tormented aging poets. Hell's geography places them in convenient order ("aquestas cosas assí dispuestas e ordenadas" 323). In *Siervo,* hell opens the narrator's way to compose the "Estoria de dos amadores," the tale of the ill-fated lovers Ardanlier and Liessa, which is also heavily influenced by Arthurian romance.

Once the "Estoria" concludes, the narrator wakes from his deep dream. He now follows Entendimiento's advice down Minerva's bitter path ("la muy agra senda donde era la verde oliva consagrada a Minerva qu'el entendimiento nos enseñava quando partió airado de mí" 35) but remains intellectually restless. Parrilla notes that critics

---

[71] The choice of Hercules's path alludes to Villena and Cartagena's moralization of Hercules as the prudent man. In the latter's translation of Cicero's works (*Los libros de Tulio*), Hercules chooses virtue over delight after the excesses of youth (Beceiro Pita, "De las peregrinaciones" 119). In Siervo, however, the emphasis is on the hero's tragic end.

[72] Dolz lists the similarities with Villena's translation of the *Aeneid* in his edition of *Siervo* (Rodríguez del Padrón 21n90).

construed this passage as the beginning of the last stage of the narrator's penitential journey but ignored the implications of the section's metric compositions, which go far beyond the prose. Continuing Impey's argument, she stresses that the poems disagree with the ideology of courtly love and present a particular concept of servitude ("Cantar y contar" 230–31).

As the narrator crosses the hills of his thoughts once again, descending to the valleys of his first inclination ("desçendiendo a los sombrosos valles de mis primeros motus" 35), he recites two long poems. The first, "Aunque me vedes así, / cativo, libre nací" [Even if you see me captive now, I was born free], highlights the ambiguity of the work's title. It also establishes a fine modal distinction —"no soy siervo, mas sirviente"— between the permanence of *siervo*, which the poetic voice rejects, and the temporary nature of the present participle *sirviente*, implying the possibility of reversal, and supported by the narrator's pressing command to *libre alvedrío* to change directions ("buelta, buelta mi esquivo pensar") immediately after he wakes up. As in the Castilian translation of Bruni's *Vite del Dante e del Petrarca*, *bolver* implies moral conversion. Indeed, in the second poem, the landscape turns into a pleasant meadow with birds singing a "discor," a type of amorous composition equivalent to a Provençal *descort* in which the stanzas disagree (Rodríguez del Padrón 38n212). *Siervo*'s "discor" encourages mad lovers like the protagonist who sing of love to *bolver* their passion to the Lord's service.[73]

Out of the valleys of his dark desires, the narrator continues wandering through the thickets of his thoughts, climbing their high trees. Finally, he discerns a large ship carrying a black-clad old dame, her seven daughters, and a large retinue. There is no agreement on the image's precise allegorical meaning, which most likely was meant to prompt a wide range of memorial connections. My own interpretation clarifies Gerli's understanding of it as the ship of the Church ("The Old French Source" 10). The old dame's location "with pomp on a high platform" ("la antigua dueña cubierta de duelo era a la pompa en muy alto estrado" 40) suggests a professorial chair or priestly pulpit;[74] perhaps scholastic Ratio and its cortege of the seven liberal arts and the seven virtues that we saw in *De consolatione*

---

[73] "[S]ervid al Señor, / pobres de andança. / Y yo, por locura, / canté por amores, / pobre de favores, / mas no de tristura" (39).

[74] As Dolz indicates, the manuscript clearly says *pompa* not *popa* (stern) which suggests authority (Rodríguez del Padrón 40n216).

Rationis. In this light, the large ship would correspond to Christian exegesis navigating the sea of texts —and its mortal dangers— with human reason as the pilot.

Critics commonly associate the ship's mistress with Sindéresis, but *Siervo* clearly indicates that she is just one of Ratio's attendants.[75] Ratio organizes the ship's company and commands Sindéresis to approach the narrator:

> The old dame, covered in black, [arriving] with pomp on a high platform the color of her clothes, arranged her daughters in this formation: one each on the ship's left and right sides, two guarding the upper deck, other two the quarterdeck, and one on the main topsail, the highest point. She instructed the rest of the ship's company to remain hidden under the deck, with the exception of prudent Sindéresis, whom she commanded to get in the skiff and approach the land in search of relief, refreshments, and subject matter as a plan of action against the enemies. She [Sindéresis], rowing vigorously, came to the shore in front of me. And then, after a greeting, she demanded to know my adventures, and so I told her.

> La antigua dueña cubierta de duelo era a la pompa, en alto estrado del triste color de sus vestiduras, ordenando a sus hijas en esta reguarda: dos a las bindas diestra y siniestra e dos que guardavan el castil davante e las otras dos el alcáçar de proa e una a la gabia, a la mayor altesa, comendando a las otras compañas, por no hacer muestra, que todas fuesen so sota cubierta, salvo la muy avisada Sindéresis que entrase en el esquilfe a çercar tierra firme por algunos reparos, refrescos, afferes, en ardit y deffensa de sus enemigos. La qual muy rexio bogando deçendió a la ribera enverso de mí. E luego, después de la salva, vino en demanda de mis aventuras y yo esso mesmo en recuenta de aquéllas. (40)

Cátedra interprets Sindéresis as the knowledge that emerges from the ship of the Church and the sea of tears; it is a habit of the

---

[75] Cátedra does not make up his mind; while initially he places Sindéresis in the old lady's retinue ("la imagen de esa *urca* ... comandada por una anciana vestida de negro, que tiene a su servicio siete doncellas vestidas del mismo paño, y otras compañías ... entre las que se destaca Sindéresis" *Amor y pedagogía* 148), on the next page, he identifies Sindéresis as the ship's captain ("son presididas en el gran barco que viene de alta mar por la dama Sindéresis" 149) and later with human will ("la gran dama que preside la *urca* sería la mismísima voluntad, vestida de negro por la esclavitud y postración" 150).

will that inclines man toward moral goodness, a spark that awakens conscience.[76] Building on that insight and expanding on *Siervo*'s Franciscan context, Dolz understands Sindéresis as closely related to free will ("El simbolismo" 111); she is the experiential knowledge brought about by divine grace that delivers the individual from the bondage of sin (Dolz, "*Siervo libre*" 256).[77]

While I have no objection to these interpretations, I am drawn, first, to the similarity of Sindéresis vigorously rowing and Santillana rowing backwards in *El sueño*. Second, as Folger points out, Sindéresis comes "not to rescue the author-persona, but in search of 'material' that can help her fight her enemies ... establishing a circular narrative closure" (*Images in Mind* 131). What "material" does Sindéresis demand? Folger believes *Siervo libre de amor* is the *historia* she wants (*Images in Mind* 131). Certainly, it begins with the judge's request to see the author's "case" in writing, but —and critics gloss over this important fact— he also demands an account of his correspondent's contemplations and intimate thoughts. The narrator spends very little time remembering; most of the work is dedicated to poems and the narrative parenthesis. He expresses his emotional state by means of an allegorical vision in which, as Folger perceptively noted, "no hermeneutic effort is required from the narrator or the reader" because the secondary meaning of its elements is conventional and clearly explicated in the text: there is no veiled sense.[78] Like Augustine and Boethius, the protagonist cries when he remembers his past and composes poetry, but the same tears allow him to enter his memorial cell and *invent*. The dream vision, then, needs no interpretation; it is a rhetorical device —a metafictive conceit in Gerli's terms— for thinking and composing the poems and "Estoria."

Most critics have difficulty interpreting *Siervo* because they read it exclusively as an allegorical account of individual conversion in which "Estoria" acts as a negative example. For instance, even admitting the importance of imagination and memory in sentimental works, Hay-

---

[76] "Un hábito que inclina al hombre al bien moral ... chispa despabiladora de la conciencia" (*Amor y pedagogía* 146–49). A useful review of Thomist and Franciscan theological concepts of synderesis can be found in Folger (*Images in Mind* 127–32). Folger further relates it to memory but still identifies it as the ship's commander.

[77] Sindéresis's Franciscan context is further developed by Dolz ("El simbolismo").

[78] As Quilligan explains, allegorical narratives "do not need allegoresis because the commentary ... is already indicated in the text" (*The Language* 29).

wood limits *Siervo*'s allegory to the exploration of "the psychodynam-
ics of sexual love through the articulation of the lovers' consciousness" ("'La escura'" 423), overlooking the dream vision's rhetorically
productive power. Martín even denies it, affirming that "while ...
allegory is central to developing the plot, this centrality is qualified
by the possibility of opening new narratives and spaces." For him,
the allegory fails because "Estoria" performs its dissuasive function
("Allegory" 136). However, Grieve warns against reading "Estoria"
solely as a negative *exemplum*. Rather than a complete condemnation
of earthly love, it conceives a hierarchy in which this fine sentiment is
a stepping-stone to the finest kind, the love of God (24). Cocozzella
agrees, asserting that "rather than rejecting the values of courtly love,
Juan Rodríguez del Padrón, by his insight into the role of Ardanlier,
makes considerable strides toward transposing those values from a
profane to a religious mode" ("The Thematic" 195). In similar terms,
Dolz finds that *Siervo*'s story acquires meaning only as an account of
the transformation of its author's value system from worldly to divine
love ("El simbolismo" 92). Such interpretations are certainly more
in accord with the ethical progression of *intentiones* toward wisdom
explicitly described by Ramon Llull to his son and the exercises of
pietas litterata. "Estoria de dos amadores" performs a role similar to
that of the Orphic myth in *The Consolation* and Metge's *Lo somni*: it
reflects the protagonist's desire and is an incitement to change, em-
bodying fiction's potential as both poison and cure. The battleship of
moralization, under Ratio's command, brings a whole army to reorient the story's "poético fin" with Sindéresis's help: it may be adapted to Christian ethics by those of sane mind ("sano entender") and
provide weapons against love ("armas te dizen contra el amor" 12).

Critics' assessment of *Siervo* also muddles allegory and allegoresis. The narrator's encounter with the mysterious ship and Sindéresis
is not, as Folger believes, the only scene that calls "for hermeneutic
operation" (*Images in Mind* 103–6). We may need an explanation
of the ship's image, but its currency in biblical exegesis, expanded
to vernacular creation, makes it a well-attested *topos* that the Mondoñedo judge would readily understand. The metaphor's scholastic pedigree goes back to the Roman poets who compare the act of
composing to seafaring —Ovid repeats it in his *Ars amandi,* and
Propertius equates poetic imagination and a *cymba ingenii*.[79] Medie-

---

[79] See Curtius (*Literatura europea y edad media latina*, vol. 1, 189–93).

val monks adapted it to biblical exegesis by comparing the sea to the sacred scriptures, which human reason navigates as the pilot of rightful interpretation (Jeauneau, "Le symbolisme de la mer" 389). Sailing into more perilous textual waters, school manuals, such as the Vatican Mitographer III, the *Ovide moralisé* and later prose versions, and Petrus Berchorius's *Ovidius moralizatus*, read risky seafaring as erotic passion, as in the story of Leander's night swim across the ocean to reach his beloved Hero.[80] As Blumenberg points out, "odysseys are an expression of the powers that denied Odysseus a homecoming, senselessly driving him about and finally leading him into shipwreck" (8), an apt image for the perplexing downturns of love and fortune. We have seen it as a metaphor for penitential conversion in Malla's *Memorial del pecador remut*, where the journey to salvation is presented as a pilgrimage on the ship of understanding governed by conscience, with the heart as watchman (see chapter 1). It is implied in Tiresias's command when the fictional Metge hesitates to follow his advice, "Do not turn back as Orpheus did; and since you have lived in the stormy seas, do your best to die in a calm and secure port" ("no·t girs detràs, axí com féu Orfeu. E pus en la tempestuosa mar has viscut, fé ton poder que muyres en segur e transquil·la port" 189). Cortijo Ocaña traces Metge's nautical metaphor to Petrarch's *Secretum* iii (Metge, 'The Dream'), but the passage also reads as a loose version of Boethius's fourth meter in the second book, praising the prudent man ("quisquis volet perennem / cautus poenere sedem"). The same moral tradition interpreting stormy waves as worldly sorrows informs William of Aragon's commentary on *The Consolation*; Saplana-Ginebreda rendered it into Catalan as "las sus ondas tempestosas que son las amarguras d'este mundo" (Se1). A related interpretation is found in Mena's commentary to his *Coronación del Marqués de Santillana,* where a "barca sin remos" indicates the body exposed to seven marine dangers, or the seven

---

[80] See a summary and analysis of the sea as symbol in Roís de Corella's *La istòria de Leànder y Hero* in Martos Sánchez's *Les proses mitològiques* (vol. 1, 366–406). The source is obviously Martianus Capella's *De nuptiis*, where Psyche is an allegory of the human soul's desire for Love (Cupid) and sustained suffering before ultimate union (vol. 1, 84). This is the reference that Boccaccio has in mind when he asks young men distracted by love to pay attention in the introduction to *Il Filocolo*: "Adunque, o giovani, I quali avete la vela della barca della vaga mente dirizzata a' venti che muovano dalle dorate penne ventilanti del giovane figliuolo di Ceterea, negli amorosi pelaghi dimoranti disiosi di pervenire a porto di salute con istudioso passo, io per la sua inestimabile potenza vi priego che divotamente prestiate alquanto alla presente opera lo 'ntelletto ..." (6).

deadly sins (155–56, 159).[81] Petrarch deploys the boat in *Canzoniere* to signify both life's pilgrimage and reading's mental journey, which Cortijo Ocaña (*"El Siervo libre"*) aptly compares to *Siervo*'s psychological introspection, while authors like James I, Santillana, Villena, the poet Ausiàs March, and Dante (his "picoletta barca" in *Paradiso* II, 1–8) use it to refer to their vernacular works.[82] Nautical images and vocabulary pervade the medical explanation of *amor heroicus*. In Arnau de Vilanova's treatise on the illness, its cause —the intense *impetus* exerted by *cogitatio* that keeps the lover sleepless— and movements are compared to a tempest and fluidity, while its symptoms belong to the semantic domain of burning aridity (Jacquart and Thomasset 155).

We may assume the learned Mondoñedo judge grasped this wide-ranging network of associations, so the material in need of "hermeneutic operation" —what Sindéresis demands for moral conversion— is neither the dream vision nor the closing image of the battleship. Instead, the narrator's dark thoughts and ruminations expressed in his poems and "Estoria" are deemed incoherent with *caritas*. The conversion may be effected by free will choosing —the surprising two *lemes* of the boat— to translate the fantasies "invented" in the narrator's dream vision into Christian faith —prudence's purview— by a rhetorical move: reorienting their *intentio* as a penitential consolation. The spark of clarity brought by the ship of Christian education offers this option at the end.

Moral conversion as a therapy for the disruptive power of uncontrolled imaginings informs *Siervo*. The narrator's erotic itch alludes to both intentionally fostering strong emotions as a starting point for meditation and the dangerous influence of fiction's sweetness and eloquence on the untrained mind. As in *Lo somni*, the narrator's passion —feigned or felt— moves him to compose, like Orpheus, and to offer, like Tiresias, its cure. Rodríguez del Padrón, like Juan Ruiz and Metge, does not commit: his *Siervo* tells a story in the style of classical

---

[81] Mena's scholarly gloss is clearly indicated by the pairing, in couplet xxxviii of the *Metamorphoses*, of the very useful *dictator* and consolatory Boethius with its meters and prose ("dictador muy oportuno / del gran Metamorfoseos" and "el consolable Boeçio / con los sus metros e prosa").

[82] For the image of a maritime adventure in search of riches inspired by Virgil, Horace, and Seneca, and its fortune in Early Modern Spain, see Gómez Moreno ("Revaluación"), especially 392–94. He provides a remarkable woodcut illustrating "De nauigantium temeritate" from Josse Bade's 1505 *Navis stultifere collectanea*. Further consideration of the image's philosophical underpinnings can be found in Blumenberg.

myths for the enjoyment of any mad reader, but only those of sound judgment, like his learned correspondent, will find its true intention and convert its unpolished letters —"ruda letra"— into a shining weapon against carnal love —"armas te dicen contra el amor."

Siervo's early critics were not off track when they compared it to Dante's *Comedy*. In a chapter whose title —"Infernal Inversion and Christian Conversion: *Inferno* XXXIV"— supports my understanding of devotional rhetoric, Freccero traces the Platonic and Christian roots of the Pilgrim's spiritual change, represented by the inversion of the *crux diaboli*. Disseminated through the *Legenda aurea*, among other channels, the passage of Plato's *Timaeus* that describes the newborn soul and the *mutatio* effected by *paideia* materializes in Dante's *Comedy* in the inversion of the cross (Freccero 184). What I wish to stress, beyond the motif's intellectual origin, is the shared template of *pietas litterata*: intellectual and spiritual disorder is figured in the *Comedy* by the Pilgrim's disorientation, and education's role consists in straightening the upside-down world, represented by the physical inversion of the Pilgrim and his guide at the center of the universe. Physical inversion and the reorientation of intention accomplished by meditation coincide; as Freccero states, "it marks the transition from sin to penance, through a first 'conversion'" (185). Nevertheless, Teskey explains in his analysis of the *Comedy*'s allegory, this transition is an act of violence in which Dante, moved by "the crushing exigencies of the poem's intellectual design," is able to depreciate the complexities of life and feeling by means of "allegory's primary work, which is to force meaning on beings who are reduced for that purpose to substance" (25–26).

In *Siervo,* the narrator's agitation is transmuted into meaning by, first, the personification of his physical senses and intellectual faculties and, second, topification —the translation of such abstractions as thoughts, choices, and intellectual progress into the dream vision's geography.[83] The rift, in Teskey's words, between the self and the world, the literal and the allegorical, is concealed by imagining the hierarchy of meanings that Ramon Llull explained to his son as moving upward in the rational progression from material desire to loving God. Such movement —inward, then upward— is the *interior affección* that later awakens the mind. It corresponds to the intellectual journey modeled by Boethius. As Astell remarks, "By the

---

[83] Haywood divides allegorical narrative into topification and personification ("'La escura'").

end of Book III the prisoner is able to read the story of his own life allegorically, as a heroic descent to the underworld comparable to that of Orpheus" (*Job, Boethius* 42). In the Saplana-Ginebreda commentary, the allegorical aim is noted in the initial scene, after Lady Philosophy chastises the Muses. Filled with shame, the prisoner lowers his eyes to earth ("boluio los sus ojos fasta la tierra"), and a battle between sensuality and understanding takes place before he can get up, with the help of reason's spark ("antes que se pueda del todo leuantar por la lumbre de la razon" N 11r).[84] The same movement is echoed in Orpheus's entrance into, and exit from, the underworld. Boethius sees himself reflected in it, but *The Consolation* alludes to a philosophical quest that proceeds from external to internal causes, as "Boethius learns to probe into the deeper meaning of things" (Astell, *Job, Boethius* 42). Saplana-Ginebreda aligns the Orphic hero's journey with a dictator who must enter the dark recesses of his thoughts and keep them under control before becoming "el sabio e buen fablador," the Fulgentian *oris phonos*.

Siervo's tearful narrator travels a similar road. His intellectual progress is indicated by the move from Discreçión to Sindéresis.[85] Discreçión, who addresses him in his initial crisis, is equivalent in contemporary Castilian texts to the moral virtue of prudence but has a wider range of meaning in literary creation (Rodríguez del Padrón 13n30). As Miriam Cabré explains in her analysis of the troubadour poetic tradition, in the process of acquiring knowledge, *prudentia* deals with transient things and is essential for rhetorical effectiveness and decorum. It is opposed to *sapientia*, which, aided by reason, is concerned with the immutable (*Cerverí de Girona* 86–90). In *Siervo,* the dictaminal skill that the narrator exhibits in composing the poems and the "Estoria" progresses to fulfill the moral intention demanded by Sindéresis, and Rodríguez del Padrón gains the literary authority of former patient and current healer.

---

[84] "[T]ornó los ojos e la su vista fuertemente contra la tierra esperando qué faría, ca el ombre sometido a las passiones e a la sensualidad antes que del todo se pueda levantar por la lumbre de la razón, primeramente abatalla en sí mesmo e con gran fuerça quebranta los ligamentos de la sensualidad" (Se1). "E gira los seus huyls e la viste fortment envers la terra e espera que faria la dita dona. Notats quel hom qui es sotsmes a la sensualitat per avols pensaments ans ques puza de tot leval per la lum de la raho ha primerament batayla dins en si entre la sensualidat e lenteniment fort trenca hom los ligams de la sensualitat regonexent si mateix" (R).

[85] Cortijo Ocaña accepts that Discreçión and Sindéresis are different but both perform the same role helping to recover rationality after a period of irrationality ("'De amicitia'").

Siervo's dream vision is a cognitive image that powers literary creation, while moralization controls intellectual disorder and excessive imagination. Moral allegory is a consolatory therapy for human subjection to earth-bound erotic desire and the threat posed by the disorderly fantasies that fiction may elicit; it arranges them in their proper *ratio* —"ordenando la lectura a Dios," as Saplana-Ginebreda indicates. It operates by offering the possibility of channeling desire through the academic discourses of *integumentum* and satire to transform "Estoria de dos amadores" into a *reprobatio amoris* and reorient its *intentio* toward an ethical *utilitas*. Erotic burning, intellectual restlessness, and the carnality of literal reading are soothed by their conversion into symbol. The upward progression to the calm unity of a soul liturgically reintegrated into the community of the faithful leaves behind a web of intemperate emotional needs and desires for symbolic stillness. In doing so, *Siervo* exposes the violence with which meaning is imposed on both the body and allegory's Other, narrative temporality: Ratio is not the blushing maiden surrounded by light who visits Compostellanus in his *De consolatione Rationis,* but the captain of a menacing army intent on capturing carnal desire and joining it to *caritas* by force as different aspects of a single transcendental truth.

AMONG FRIENDS

The "unfeigned confidence and mutual love of true and good friends," Augustine asserted in *Civitas Dei* XIX, 8, is the "one solace in human society." It should come as no surprise that friendship was a popular topic in the homosocial atmosphere of dictaminal schools. One professor, Boncompagno da Signa, presented it as the only source of stability and happiness, opposed to the madness of blind servitude to lust, in the treatise *De amicitia*, his take on the Ciceronian dialogue *Laelius sive de amicitia*.[86]

The interest in friendship peaks in fifteenth-century Aragon and Castile. Heusch studied two representative instances, the *Theologia naturalis seu liber creaturarum*, a tract on the science of love (*amantia*) in all its human and divine aspects, composed between 1430 and 1436 by Raymond Sebond, a Catalan living in Toulouse (*La philoso-*

---

[86] See Cortijo Ocaña's introduction to Boncompagno's *El Tratado de amor carnal.*

phie).[87] In the Crown of Castile, another professor, Alonso Fernández de Madrigal, summarized some of his lectures in *Libro de amor y amicicia* (c. 1440) at the request of King Juan II. Along with the brief section on passionate love that we discussed in chapter 1, the larger work develops a sustained argument on friendship based on books VIII and IX of Aristotle's *Nichomachean Ethics*, the main text in the new field of ethics at the University of Salamanca.[88] While these two treatises respond to very different conceptions of naturalism —Sebond inspired by the Lullist ontological ascent to perfection, Fernández de Madrigal by Aristotelian pragmatism— both accentuate human freedom. For Sebond, love is a mode of action that guides the human will, and Franciscan voluntarism is the ideological support for his theological exposition on the transformation of human into divine love (Heusch, *La philosophie* 38). For Fernández de Madrigal, love is a passion, unconnected to moral acts, and the will directs human behavior:

> Virtues are under our will's command because no one becomes virtuous except by willing and acting. And it is impossible to take virtues away from anyone against his will, no matter how adverse his fortune and how frequent the hardships. Because virtues are the product of our will and by our will are lost.[89]

Fernández de Madrigal stresses moral autonomy to develop his discourse on friendship as a shield against the disorder and chaos wrought by amorous infatuation. Friendship, unlike love, is a rational act, the assiduous fellowship of those who share their deepest secrets (Heusch, *La philosophie* 267).

Fernández de Madrigal's definition brings into sharper focus Gonçalo de Medina's demand at the beginning of *Siervo* for a written account of his younger friend's recondite thoughts ("innotos

---

[87] All the information on Sebond and Fernández de Madrigal is from Heusch's unpublished dissertation (*La philosophie*).

[88] Cátedra maintains that the chapter on passionate love is formally different and may have been a youthful exercise that Fernández de Madrigal incorporated when he composed the *Libro* for a courtly audience (*Del Tostado* x–xi).

[89] "Las virtudes estan so el poderio de nuestra uoluntad ca non se faze alguno uirtuoso sinon queriendo et obrando et non pueden a alguno contra su voluntad por muy dura que le sea la aduersidad de la fortuna et abastança de sobreuenjentes males las virtudes seer tiradas ca las virtudes ansi como por nuestra uoluntad sola se vsan ansi por nuestra uoluntad sola se pierden" (fol. 21v). I cite from the semi-paleographic transcription by Sánchez, Herrera, and Zabía (Fernández de Madrigal, "Libro de amor y amicicia") but eliminate textual abbreviations and marks.

e varios pensamientos"). Cátedra considers *Siervo* an expurgatory letter in which Rodríguez del Padrón atones for a supposed moral blunder (*Poesía de Pasión* 302), while Cortijo Ocaña contends that its main theme is actually friendship, not love, and finds many similarities with Boncompagno's *De amicitia* ("'De amicitia'"). In fact, along with those connections, *Siervo*'s much debated three parts outlined in the *accessus* illustrate, not the consecutive stages of love or penance, but the three types of emotional relationships studied in Fernández de Madrigal's *Libro*. The time to love and be loved ("el tiempo que bien amó y fue amado") is associated with friendship, in Fernández de Madrigal's sense of the *habitus* or disposition that demands reciprocity of affection and action, freely binding two souls. The time to love and not being loved ("el tiempo que bien amó y fue desamado") corresponds to what Fernández de Madrigal defines as erotic passion:

> Loving is more appropriate to the nature of friendship than being loved because, although a friend loves and is loved, one is not called a friend because one is loved by another but because he loves. In the same manner as the *habitus* corresponds to the action, friendship, which is the consequence of the practice of virtues, corresponds to an action. Therefore, *seer amado* is not action but passion, and loving is the action of friends.[90]

"Seer amado" may just indicate passively receiving love, but Fernández de Madrigal defines it as a movement against reason that matches the state of infatuation[91] and demonstrates its toxic consequences in a series of old stories ("Estorias antiguas prouantes como el amor muchas vezes fizo dapno"), the classical myths that schoolmen deploy to characterize foolish lovers. Similarly, Rodríguez del Padrón composes *Estoria de dos amadores* in the style of those classical fables ("trayendo fiçiones segund los gentiles nobles de dioses dañados e de deesas").

---

[90] "[M]as conjuncto es a la naturaleza de los amjgos amar que seer amado ca avnque el que es amjgo ame et sea amado enpero non se dize alguno amjgo de otro porque es amado de el mas porque lo ama. Otrosi ansi como a los habitos corresponden los actos ansi a la amjçiçia la qual consigue a los habitos de las uirtudes correspondera algund acto enpero seer amado non es acto mas passion pues amar sera el acto de los amjgos" (fol. 33v).

[91] "[L]as cosas que son causadas por passion non se fazen por juyzio de razon mas contra razon peruertiente la malicia a la razon" (fol. 2r).

Siervo's third part, the time when he did not love nor was he loved ("el tiempo que no amó ni fue amado"), refers to a moment of solitary introspection.

> This happens when man, leaving aside all the annoyances, considers only himself and his actions, and how much each day he progresses or relapses; this is called being man with himself because in the same manner that we said one is or lives with his friend only if he considers what pertains to his friend, we say that one is with oneself when, leaving aside everything else, one considers only oneself.[92]

This type of inner dialogue, Fernández de Madrigal insists, characterizes the virtuous man ("el varon uirtuoso") engaged in intellectual speculation:

> When all his things are in order and the impetus of his struggling passions calmed down, the virtuous in his solitude is the lord of himself and has power over himself, and he draws from it not an insignificant delectation because he considers his past actions, and when he draws all these things one by one from the secret places of his heart where they lie hidden as in a heap, notices the many good things he did and delights in them.[93]

Fernández de Madrigal is describing the enjoyable process of creative *inventio*, gathering up ("en vn monton ascondidas") and drawing in ("sacare vna a vna") the contents of one's *memoria*.[94] *Siervo*'s protagonist takes this steep narrow path ("agra y angosta senda") in the company of Discreçión after freeing himself ("por donde siguió

---

[92] "Esto acontesçe en el onbre quando apartadas todas las occupaçiones de las cosas fazientes moujmjento & estoruo a si mjsmo solamente considera el onbre & solamente acata sus obras cognosçiendo quanto cada dia cresçe o quanto mengua & esto llaman estar el onbre con si mjsmo ca ansi como dizimos que alguno esta o viue con su amjgo si solamente considera lo que pertenesçe a su amjgo ansi diremos que esta con si mjsmo quando apartadas todas las otras cosas a si solo considera" (fol. 44v).

[93] "[O]rdenadas todas sus cosas & los jmpetus de las peleantes passiones amansados el uirtuoso estando solo es sennor de si mjsmo & sobre si tiene poderio leuantase de otra parte sin esto al varon virtuoso non pequenno logar de delectaçion ca el considera sus fechos passsados & quando todas estas cosas de los logares secretos de su coraçon ansi como en vn monton ascondidas sacare vna a vna acata muchos bienes que el fijo de los quales non puede passar alguno sin delectaçion & cada vno de ellos sta speçialmente acatando & de cada vno resçibe gozos non vulgares" (fol. 46r).

[94] Remember that the slave describes contemplation as a "plazer solitario" (18).

después de libre, en compañía de la discreçión" 10) and immediately before he catches sight of Ratio and her attendants arriving in the moral warship. The path is symbolized by the olive tree consecrated to Minerva, and the slave identifies it as the contemplative life of not loving ("la vida contemplativa de no amar" 19). It is not, Rodríguez del Padrón comments in the *accessus*, as popular as friendship or love ("no es tan seguida como la espaçiosa de amar bien y ser amado ni como la deçiente de bien amar sin amado") because it is the easiest to deviate from and the hardest to follow ("por ser la más ligera de fallir y más grave de seguir" 10). The verb *fallir*, Dolz notes in the glossary appended to his edition of *Siervo*, indicates *to err* in its double meaning of deviating from the true course and going astray morally (Rodríguez del Padrón 71 *sv*). It stresses the dangers that lurk in the pleasures of solitary contemplation, which conversion endeavors to channel to its proper ethical end.

The fact that penitential fictions appear enclosed in letters points to a type of consolatory practice articulated around male friendship and self-reflection. Metge may omit the letter frame in *Lo somni*, but the plot of its first two books is a dialogue between himself and Joan I, who appears in his dream to discuss the soul's immortality. In addition, the direct quotes from Cicero's *Laelius* in support of the protagonist's grief at the king's death place *Lo somni* in the context of the dictaminal curriculum.[95] That one of Fernández de Madrigal's *repetitiones* addresses the soul's beatitude after death (*De statu animarum post hanc vitam*, 1436) and that Santillana had Plato's *Phaedo* translated by Pero Díaz de Toledo in 1447 are not irrelevancies. Metge's *Lo somni* encapsulates the questions that were debated at schools and most appealed to a courtly audience of *caballeros sçientes*. This context may clarify Juan II's request that Fernández de Madrigal summarize and translate his lectures for the profit of many. Heusch notes that in the *Libro,* a work by Aristotle resonated with the interests and tastes of a nonprofessional class for the first time (*La philosophie* 248). Fernández de Madrigal's translated lecture certainly helped to disseminate Aristotelian naturalism among courtly dilettanti and deeply influenced their poetry, as Cátedra points out (*Amor y pedagogía*), but the intertwined topics of friendship and the soul's immortality belonged to the dictaminal curriculum of *pietas litterata* that Metge's *Lo somni* popularized at the court of Martí I.

---

[95] Cicero's quotations are noted by Martín de Riquer (ed. *Obras* 203n28, 203n29). See also chapter 2: 135n210 on Santillana's interest in the soul's immortality.

SAILING IN GOOD COMPANY: ROÍS DE CORELLA'S *PARLAMENT*

The force of the rhetorical operation Ratio demands at the end of *Siervo libre de amor* may be brought into sharper focus by comparing Rodríguez del Padrón's *forma tractandi* with two Catalan works, Roís de Corella's *Parlament* (1471) and Metge's *Lo somni*. Keeping in mind the social and temporal span separating them, we can still discern several instances of the common dictaminal practice of *los estudios* involved in *pietas litterata* in which vernacular readers —Villena's *lectores romançistas*— invent their own literary *auctoritas* as *caballeros sçientes* by unveiling and artfully displaying poetic fiction's ethical *intentio*.

Parlament is a record of a literary gathering that took place at the home of Berenguer Mercader. The host and five friends —Joan Escrivà, Guillem Ramon de Vilarrasa, Lluís de Castellví, Joan de Pròxita, and Roís de Corella— enjoy a light supper and afterward amuse themselves with the tragic stories of mythical lovers. The meeting may be a narrative device, as in more famous Italian *convivia*, with Roís de Corella as chronicler. Fictitious or not, *Parlament* echoes a cultural phenomenon in Valencia at the time, when dilettantes of the urban oligarchy and merchant ranks dabbled in the latest literary fashions.[96]

Parlament's full title, *Parlament o col·lació que aprés de sopar sdevench en cassa de Berenguer Mercader entre alguns hòmens de stat,* describes the friends as members of Valencia's upper social ranks. From the host, who served Alfons the Magnanimous as royal chamberlain and ambassador to Castile, to Pròxita, baron of Palma i Adlor, and Roís de Corella, a member of the lower nobility who later became master of theology, they were an admixture of high-ranking *bureaucrats* and noble *lletraferits* not dissimilar to those of the royal chancery at the time of Bernat Metge.[97] As Torró explains, the lack of

---

[96] See Martín de Riquer (*Història*, vol. 3, 313–15); Rico ("Imágenes"); Badia ("'En les baixes'" and ed. *Història*, vol. 3, 228–31); Martos Sánchez (176–83); Torró ("Una cort"); Pérez Bosch (*Los valencianos* 48–54).

[97] The meaning of *homèns de stat* is clearly indicated in a document addressed to the king by the Majorcan *síndicos forenses* (officers in charge of collecting and managing taxes) assessing the detriment to the economy brought about by the increasing number of noblemen: "dins la ciutat per lo menys stan e viuen con á nobles personas sus de mil mil personas las quals tenen stat de barons e nobles, ço que en temps antich no era, car fort poch hi havia homens de stat, sino grans mercaders ab grossos stats ab grans credits que per tot lo mon tenían, e así aumentavan dit vostre regne" (Quadrado 325–26).

a permanent royal court in Valencia and Catalonia meant noblemen and courtly officers were educated in the multilingual atmosphere of Alfons the Magnanimous's Neapolitan court or his brothers' itinerant courts in Navarre, Zaragoza, and Castile ("Una cort"). Bilingual Catalan and Castilian literary production took place in urban social circles; gatherings in Valencia have been documented, but Torró surmises their existence in Barcelona and other capital cities of the Aragonese Crown as well.[98]

The nature of the gathering is indicated by term *col·lació* in the title as a synonym for *parlament*. It alludes to prose eloquence in the sense used by Petrarch in his *Collatio laureationis* and connects it to the monastic ritual of public reading and interpreting spiritual texts after a light evening meal, here contextualized as a pleasant conversation among friends.[99] Like Petrarch's *Collatio*, *Parlament*'s topic is poetry, but its understanding is closer to that of Santillana's *Proemio e carta* —a beautiful veil of beneficial wisdom. Each participant summarizes a story from Ovid's *Metamorphoses,* introduced by a moral explanation.[100]

Parlament opens with a programmatic declaration:

> Descending from the sublime apex of sacred theology, master of all the sciences, to the blooming green fields of easier poetry by way of delightful study, I have raised the anchor of idleness, leaving the ports of bountiful silence, and set the white sail of enjoyable exercise on the low mast of vernacular prose. After redirecting the prow toward Venus's stormy sea, I shall describe the shipwrecks of those who, foolishly navigating its waters, find a harrowing end.

> De la transcendent celsitut de la senyora de totes les sciències, sacra theologia, devallant ab delitós studi en los florits e verts camps de afable poesia, he llevat les ànchores de pereós oci, dexant los ports de reposat silenci, per stendre les càndides veles ab plaent

---

[98] A very detailed overview of the political and cultural atmosphere in the Crown of Aragon with special emphasis on the Neapolitan and Navarran courts can be found in Rodríguez Risquete's introduction to his edition of Pere Torroella's works (Torroella, vol. 1, 115). See also Badia for further bibliographic information on literary gatherings and feminine salons (ed. *Història*, vol. 3, 306–9).

[99] "The collation was originally a monastic tradition, recapitulating during the evening the main theme of that day's biblical reading. The mendicants adopted the collation as part of their religious life, and at times, developed it into lengthy conferences" (Roest 89n18).

[100] As Rico pointed out, Roís de Corella filters Ovid through dictaminal theory and practice ("Imágenes" 18).

exercici en les baxes entenes de vulgar prosa. A la tempestuosa mar de Venus la proha de ma scriptura endreçant, descriuré naufraigs de aquells qui en ella follament navegant, dolorosa e miserable fi pervenen (2: 829–30).[101]

Roís de Corella observes the expected separation between theology, which provides a superior kind of knowledge, and poetry, further differentiated as Ovidian myths in Latin and vernacular prose interpretations.[102] Martos Sánchez points out the divergent reading of the two manuscript witnesses in which *Parlament* survives: while the Cambridge codex reads "vulgar prosa," the option Martos selects for his edition, the *Cançoner de Maians*, uses "vulgar poesia" (vol. 2, 829n166). In any case, this discrepancy just reinforces the rhetorical understanding of vernacular *inventio* as the unveiling of classical myth in either prose or verse. Unlike lofty theology, poetry allows easier access to its delightful meadows of blooming flowers —I am reading *afable* as a Latinism indicating both *enjoyable* and *approachable*— not an unlikely remark by someone who would later become master of theology. What interests me in Roís de Corella's proemial words is the dictaminal context in which reading the classics and vernacular creation occur.

The definition mentions two key terms, *delitós studi* and *reposat silenci*. For Badia, *reposat silenci* implies interruption of the silence that precedes literary creation as a way of avoiding idleness, the traditional role assigned to poetry ("'En les baixes'" 154). However, in the monastic vocabulary alluded to in *Parlament*'s title, *silentium* has a more technical meaning: the disciplined cognitive activity involved in rhetorical composition.[103] In that light, the binary *delitós studi* and *reposat silenci* corresponds to Metge's "continuat studi," Villena's "affecçión poetal uirtuosa," and "los estudios" in the anonymous Castilian translation of Bruni's *Vita di Dante*: the strenuous yet enjoyable process of extracting from the classics a wisdom to be later conveyed with the rhetorical skill and decorum ("por arte e por prudencia") of the great Italian masters.[104] It is the delightful solitary occupation that *Siervo* attributed to the desert fathers, and while *Parlament* does not begin with the narrator's tears —he

---

[101] I cite from Martos Sánchez's edition in his *Les proses mitològiques* unpublished dissertation.

[102] See Badia ("'En les baixes'" 153–54) and Cingolani (*Joan Roís* 45).

[103] See Carruthers's explanation of *competens silentium* (*The Craft* 3).

[104] Also compare Felip de Malla's definition of the *gaya ciència* (cap. 1: 64).

is merely recording the event— the attending friends cry their eyes out, moan, and lament while considering the stories' moral repercussions: "Grief, commiseration, and reasonable condolence brought a fountain of compassionate tears to my weeping eyes while considering the story's wretched ending," exclaims Berenguer Mercader halfway through his narration.[105] His companions join in when he falls silent: "Our eyes, along with Berenguer Mercader's, were not lacking in sympathetic tears when the sad story reached its painful end."[106]

The product of such a pleasurable, not to mention cathartic, exercise is described with an extended nautical metaphor that, as Martos Sánchez remarks, recasts a passage in Dante's *Convivium* (vol. 1, 172).[107] Like Dante, but also like Malla, Metge, and so many other vernacular authors, Roís de Corella associates his white-sailed boat with vernacular creation, which reason or desire steer through the stormy sea of Ovidian stories.

Parlament follows traditional moralizations of the Ovidian myths. For Martos Sánchez, who meticulously traces Roís de Corella's classic and medieval sources, the stories articulate a moral program in two sections: in the first, the tragic cases of two happily married couples (Cephalus and Procris, Orpheus and Eurydice) serve as an excuse to deliberate on human destiny and the need for Christian faith. In the second, the tales of Scylla and Pasiphae illustrate the consequences of women's immoderate lust, and Tereus's rape of Philomela, his wife's sister, condemns the same vice in men. In that sense, *Parlament*'s final section reproduces the debate on women in the last two books of *Lo somni* and is one more instance of Roís de Corella's philogyny (vol. 1, 183–86, 241).

Although Joan de Pròxida, *Parlament*'s last speaker, does claim that Tereus's story of sexual abuse, mutilation, and deceit proves that "dishonest love" leads men to commit the same excesses as women, I have trouble accepting his narration as a defense of women. Philomela and her sister Progne are presented first as innocent victims of

---

[105] "Dolor, pietat e rahonable conplany font de piadoses làgremes als meus plorosos ulls descobren, pensant la miserable fi de la ystoria que recite" (vol. 2, 842).

[106] "Los nostres ulls, ensemps ab los de Berenguer Mercader, staven no exuts de piedoses làgremes, quant acabava la dolorosa fi de tan trista ystòria" (vol. 2, 846).

[107] "Poi che proemialmente ragionando, me ministro, è lo mio pane ne lo precendent trattato con sufficienza preparato, lo tempo chiama e domanda la mia nave uscir di porto; per che, dirizzato l'artimone de la ragione a l'òra del mio desiderio, entro in pelago con isperanza di dolce camminno e di salutevole porto e laudabile ne la fine de la mia cena" (qtd. in Martos Sánchez vol. 2, 172).

male brutality but quickly turn into exemplars of female wrath and cruelty motivated by extreme grief and slow understanding, a trait that brings them closer to fearsome beasts ("fora de seny ... la strema dolor canvià en oy de terrible ira, seguint lo costum de la femenil conditió, que, si ja crueldat l'ímpetu d'elles sguarda, perquè llurs obres molt tart lo enteniment refrena, a les feres implacables bèsties avancen" vol. 2, 881). As in the Ovidian myth so closely summarized, Progne murders her own son with the help of her abused sister Philomela and serves him for dinner to her rapist husband as vengeance. Any similarities with *Lo somni* may be found in the penchant for episodes that emphasize female spitefulness, like that of the enraged harridans who chop off Orpheus's head because he spurns women to sing in peaceful solitude.

More in tune with the discourse of *pietas litterata*, Roís de Corella understands Ovidian myths as repositories of the truth in human behavior ("la veritat dels humans actes ab exemples millor se mira"), which consists in attachment to an inferior material desire that obfuscates rational thinking and prevents individuals from reaching their highest potential.[108] The first two myths are about happily married men, Cephalus and Orpheus, much like the five companions whose speeches Roís de Corella records; however, their content attachment to their faithful wives is their hubris. The sea of stories is roiled by the frenzied depths of worldly sorrows into which men are drawn by treacherous Fortune's siren song, as Johan Scrivà comments when moralizing Orpheus's story:

> Orpheus's sad story shows that, in the bitter sea of this world, very rarely —or never— may anyone navigate with a propitious wind and, reaching a secure port, keep at bay adverse fortune. And if ever the calm waters of a lucky chance invite us to accommodate the white sails to the breeze, it is so that we may suffer a cruel shipwreck more rapidly and with a greater personal loss. Similar to the mortal siren's sweet song, deceitful fortune never dotes on us unless it is to achieve a greater triumph by hurling us from a higher point.

---

[108] "[L]o major goig de nostra mísera vida se causa en la falça stima del que amam, torcent lo camí de nostre ésser. Primer en strem volem que no conegam si tant devem amar e, aprés que amor té nostres penses entenebrades ab ofuscat entendre, falç stimam tant com nostra benevolençans empeny. Perjudicant l'altitud de nostra condició humana, dexam la infinida fi del subran bé, elegint en les criatures, egualment o més que nosaltres miserables, útima benaentura fent contra regla no solament de la sancta fe cristiana, mas de natural rahó, quens mostra la fi de les altres causes més noble sia, de més vàlua que les coses que a ella s'endrecen" (vol. 2, 831).

[D]e Orpheu la dolorosa faula, per mostrar que, en la amarga mar de nostre habitable terra, molt tart —o nunqua— ab tan pròsper vent algú navega, que, venint a segur port, de la adversa fortuna defendre's puga. E, si alguna vegada les tranquilles aygües de la sort pròspera nos conviden que les blanques veles acomanem a l'ayre, és perquè més prest e ab dolor de major pèrdua, sens repar trabucant, encorregam cruel naufraig de nostres béns e persona. Quasi semblant al dolç cant de la mortal serena, la enganosa fortuna jamés no·ns afalagua, sinó perquè, ab més gran cayguda, en triünpho de major victòria de nosaltres triünphe. (vol. 2, 848)

Women ("la femenil condició") are identified with the lowest, most bestial inclinations. Immediately after Orpheus's story, Pasiphae's *contra natura* desire for a bull is described, and in the final one, Progne's fearsome wrath is compared to that of a lion. Tereus's story shows that men are not free from similar debasing urges, but —now Pròxida comes to the point— they remain rational creatures ("criatures rationals") endowed with free will ("libera voluntat de arbitre"). They can choose a virtuous life and become god-like angels or surrender to disordered desire and lose their intellectual capacity becoming animals or irrational women.[109]

Despite their moralizing claims and proud advertizement of mythical heroes' sin and excess in a few lines at the beginning of each tale, each speaker spends an inordinate amount of time describing the chosen characters' afflictions, doubts, and feelings, reproducing their words in rhetorically elaborate letters and emotional digressions. The five mature, happily married companions carefully explain how free will orients the prow of their literary boats and colors their lives with virtue, but, if anything, their accounts illustrate the dangers of a well-crafted tale: uncontrolled imagination collapses fiction into lived experience. In a telling moment, the chronicler comments:

> Johan Scrivà had captivated our sad thoughts with his well-reasoned fable so that it seemed each of us had lost Eurydice. And

---

[109] "Mas, encara nosaltres, hòmens, si amor desonesta nostre voler asalta, cometem viltat de tals actes, que, de ésser hoyts, fere porten. D'on clarament se mostra les criatures rationals líbera voluntat de arbitre tenen, que·ls animals de rahó exemps no jamés en lurs obres passen los llímits que lur stint natural condició·ls comporta. ... Però nosaltres, si virtuós viure nos acompaya, fet quasi déus, lo ésser nostre al dels àngels se transporta. ... E, per ço, si·l desorde de nostre voler, quant a vils coses se endreça, no refrenam, incorrent crims de ineffable malícia, perdem de hòmens la intellectual figura" (vol. 2, 871–72).

the power of the mindful imagination forced all of us to imitate Orpheus's motion, looking over our shoulders to see if Eurydice was following. But Guillem Ramon de Vilarasa quickly put an end to our false imagination with his tale as I repeat here faithfully.

Axí havia transportat Johan Scrivà en la ben rahonada faula nostres entrestides penses, que a cascú de nosaltres semblava Eurídices havia perduda. E lo poder de la attenta ymaginativa pensa forçà a tots per aquell gest que de Orpheu se rahonava, girant-nos a les spatles per veure si Eurídices venia. Però no tardà Guillem Ramon de Vilarasa a nostra falça ymaginació donar terme en stil tal, com ací felment recite. (vol. 2, 858)

Like weeping Boethius and fictional Metge, the enthralled companions forget their *integumenta* and instead see themselves reflected in Orpheus's fear of losing a beloved wife. Scrivà must tear them away from the tale's mesmerizing power and direct them back to moralizing discourse, which, not surprisingly, consists in a misogynous tirade not unlike Tiresias's chastisement of the infatuated Metge. In *Parlament*, the horrid tales of Scylla and Pasiphae slander women as ugly and dishonest ("los leigs desonests actes en la femenil condició" vol. 2, 858), and Joan de Pròxida's final tale, the longest, warns against adultery because it releases murderous female anger. "Heaven has no rage like love to hatred turned/ Nor hell a fury like a woman scorned" (William Congreve, *The Mourning Bride*, 1697) —a theme that continues to mesmerize Hollywood. In Pròxida's retelling of the Ovidian myth, the final metamorphosis of a chaste wife and an innocent maiden into murderous monsters merely confirms women's mutability as an index of life's uncertainty.

Parlament's narrative tendency and its Latinate, highly emotional style lead Pellisa Prades to include it in her census of Catalan sentimental fictions (*La ficció sentimental*). *Parlament*'s ornate expression and lachrymose subject fit comfortably within the sentimental tastes of the *enamorada generació,* but it is certainly not a penitential fiction since the first-person narration merely chronicles, like the *Auctor* who narrates *Cárcel de Amor,* although he is less engaged in events. No metafictional dream vision signals the beginning and end of the compositional journey: the companions have already engaged in *delitós studi, reposat silenci*, and what Roís de Corella reports is not the creative process but its outcome. *Parlament* stands on the border between the penitential genre and the narrative contrafacta that will be the subject of chapter 3.

Roís de Corella's fluctuation between the delight of telling tales and the need to moralize them elucidates the choice presented to *caballeros sçientes* when reading fiction: Orpheus's youthful infatuation and desire for narrative detail or the wise maturity of Tiresias's moral allegory. *Parlament*'s identification of uncontrolled desires with female irrationality and Fortune's unfathomable turns reflects the tension between the material/literal and spiritual that moralization aims to soothe. Its project of allegorical capture is comparable to the fighting vessel intent on seizing the narrator's story in *Siervo*. In *Parlament,* Tereus not only rapes Philomela but cuts off her tongue. Pròxida's disingenious attempt to exculpate women does not prevent the relegation of Progne and Philomela to memory —the dark reign of Pluto ("als oscurs regnes de Plutó")— as personifications of female viciousness and Fortune's sudden turns. Still, his emotive account of their earlier happiness and misfortunes —Progne's sisterly affection and chaste love for Tereus, Philomela's suffering, eloquently expressed before Tereus silences her forever— keeps reorienting the literary boat away from allegory into the treacherous waters of story telling. It resists moral conversion. Other contemporaneous works succeeded in imposing the full force of allegorical meaning upon imagination; here, its fearsome power holds a moment's sway.

"LET THE SOUL HER SLUMBERS BREAK:" CARRÓS PARDO DE LA CASTA'S *REGONEIXENÇA*

The Valencian knight Francesc Carrós Pardo de la Casta composed his *Regoneixença e moral consideració contra les persuasions e forces de amor* [Soul-searching and Moralistic Treatise, Countering the Temptations, Vices, and Powers of Love] in the last stages of his life, around 1478.[110] The treatise bears a close resemblance to his Castilian poem, "Consuelo de amor" [Love's Consolation], compiled in Hernando del Castillo's 1511 *Cancionero general*; in fact, it can be read as an extended commentary on it. *Regoneixença*'s apparent success —it merited a 1490 print edition— belies Carrós's initial re-

---

[110] For Carrós's biography, see Reyes-Tudela's introduction to his edition of the complete works (15–34) from which I also cite *Regoneixença*. The English translation of *Regoneixença*'s title is by Cocozzella (*Fra Francesc* 51). See as well Rubió i Balaguer (178–81) and Rodríguez Risquete ("La regoneixença"). Carrós's adaptation of Italian sources is treated in Recio ("El humanismo" and "Intertextuality").

luctance to share it with the unnamed friend who requested it. A letter, addressed to either *Vostra Senyoria* or *Vostra Mercé*, discloses that Carrós hid it for two years under the scholarly pretext that his little boat lacked oars and prudence's helm.[111] Only the friend's resolve to see it and his own desire to reveal the errors of his blindness persuade him to consent to the petition. Reyes-Tudela sees no reason to doubt Carrós's words (58), but his humility *topos* is suspiciously similar to the commonplace qualms that Boncompagno da Signa —always the professor— parodies in his *Rota Veneris*: my friends made me do it. If anything, the opening letter reveals the rhetorical environment that structures courtly moralization. Carrós resorts to the clerical practice of learned correspondence between two friends that we saw in *Siervo libre de amor*, where, following Dante's model, the author justifies his literary authority by displaying the ability to interpret his own past and poetry. As in dictaminal performances on the *contemptus mundi*, Carrós adopts the double position of student and teacher, Boethius and Philosophy, and demands that his readers assume the contemplative stance that befits aging *caballeros sçientes*.

Carrós's moral authority acquires full force in his appeal to both readers and, surprisingly, *Regoneixença* itself at the work's end. He urges the former to follow his model: to stay awake ("no durmau, que temps és de vellar. ¡Vellau, vellau!" 149), to enlist reason's forces to clear the blinding clouds, and to acknowledge life's inconstancy.[112] In addressing his own work, Carrós compares the passions and labors he endured —in life and writing— to yappy little dogs that never cease to annoy ("los cans mordedors, y més, los chiquets, que per gran iniquitat nunqua cessen de ladrar e de mordre" 152); he cleverly encourages *Regoneixença* to endure any yapper's criticism with the Virgin's guidance. *Regoneixença*'s main themes and motifs

---

[111] "E si lo príncipi de aquella, la difficultat de la sua fi me for a presentada, ab la mia poqueta barca, guiada sens rems o govern de la discreció, no tentara yo navegar en la mar e fondura de tant saber quant per a tal empresa fora necessari" (118).

[112] "Múden-se los temps, cámbien-se los stats, les coses baixes de aquells son exalçades, les altes són atterades. ¿Quina novidat? Costuma és les coses no fermes no ésser segures: la segura e ferma, fermetat guarda; la movible, moviment. Cada qualsegons lo seu ésser té la condició: lo mal, del mals no·s turmenta: lo bé que és la sola e perfeta rahó, descansa, remeya, e consola" (150).

[Times change, so do states, the low are exalted, the high brought back to earth. What's new? It is habit of changeable things not being steady: the certain and steady stay stable; the fickle stay in movement. Each is according to its own condition: evil torments us, goodness, which is the only perfect reason, offers repose, remedy, and consolation].

—the soul's awakening, life's joys as maddening dogs, the rejection of pagan literature in favor of Christian truth, the journey toward wisdom as a shield against Fortune's vagaries— bear a remarkable resemblance to Jorge Manrique's *Coplas* (c. before 1479) and may indicate direct knowledge, although the scarcity of facts on Carrós's life does not allow such a claim. More likely, the similarities point to the shared discourse of *pietas litterata. Regoneixença* is a fully convencional performance of moral conversion but also provides the backdrop for the consolatory procedures that coalesce in Manrique's moving poetic elaboration.

Regoneixença's repository of Ovid's stories conceives them as memorial signposts of human errors. They mirror the protagonist's sinful past as the first step in the moral metamorphosis charted in Boethius's *Consolation*. Bartolomeu Muntaner and Angel Aguiló, *Regoneixença*'s first modern editors, pointed out its debt to *The Consolation* and added it, quite tellingly, to their 1873 edition of *Libre de consolación de Philosophia ... en romanç catalanesch*, the Saplana-Ginebreda commentary contained in Biblioteca de Catalunya Ms. 68. They justified its inclusion as an appendix to the Catalan *Consolation* because of the treatise's rarity ("la raresa del present tractat fet per lo poeta valenciá"), but they also perceived the notable similarities. More recently, Cocozzella noted the Boethian mood that pervades *Regoneixença* from the role attributed to reason to its plaintive stance (*Fra Francesc* 51–56). Numerous echoes confirm the resemblance: the supplication for divine inspiration rehearses a Boethian rejection of the Muses and Roman eloquence, and, as Reyes-Tudela believes, it may recast the ninth poem in the third book, where Philosophy requests divine intercession to demonstrate that God is the supreme good (140n614). *Regoneixença* acquires its full meaning in the context of a Boethian *contemptus mundi* and the protagonist's realization that human truth is affected by Philosophy's arguments with the help of "la poca centilla." As Rodríguez Risquete claims, this tiny spark illuminates *Regoneixença*'s strong penitential component; it is no other than synderesis —the innate *scintilla conscientiae* or *scintilla rationalis* to which Franciscans and Dominicans attributed the capacity to distinguish good from evil and to repent. It appears at the end of *Siervo* to demand conversion ("La regoneixença" 1387).[113]

---

[113] For Franciscan and Dominican doctrinal stands on synderesis, see Rodríguez Risquete's argument; he admits that their positions tend to converge ("La regoneixença" 1386–87). See also Dolz ("El vocabulario del alma" 105–14).

Carrós's choice of autobiographical dream vision as the appropriate rhetorical genre to chart his exegetical and ethical progress is not unexpected. An old man, *el Actor*, suddenly inspired by reason, contemplates his wretched life:

> I had already gone through the time of vain and dangerous youth; and finding myself closer to the end than to the beginning of life, my age tormented by the experience of so many errors, terrified by considering the examples of our miserable being, moved by a certain spirit, although I believe that I was touched by a reasonable inspiration, I comprehended the great abyss of wretchedness in which I lived and still live.

> Lo temps de la vana e perillosa joventut era ja de mi trespassat; e trobant-me yo prop de la fi més que del principi de la vida, la edat per speriencia de tantes errós turmentada, aterrada la pensa en los exemples de nostre miserable ésser; no sé de quin sperit mogut, mas stime que de rahonable inspiració tocat, yo regoneguí lo gran abís de misèria en lo qual vivia e viu. (119)

The veil of passion ("lo vel de cega passió") produces a blind stupor that makes his will lose heart and exclaim in pain: "go away, leave me, darkness of mine, go away deceiving hope that forces me to despair" ("Fogiu, fogiu de mi, tenebres mies, fogiu, enganosa esperança, per qui desesper" 119). He begins crying uncontrollably and withdraws at night to his secret cogitations until the morning light finds him free of his captivity ("libert de la captivitat" 120). He then realizes the deceitfulness of the senses and meditates on how to attain the supreme good and human solace.

First, Actor rejects fame, beauty, strength, and Midas's riches. He denies the liberal arts the capacity to deliver men from material bondage by rehearsing Seneca's arguments in his *Epistula ad Lucilium*, which Carrós may have known in either a Catalan or Castilian translation.[114] He passes the day in these considerations, but restlessness overcomes him again at night, when a tempting voice (*la Veu*),

---

[114] Rodríguez Risquete points out the debt to Seneca's *Epistula* ("La regoneixença" 1384). The number of translations circulating in fifteenth-century Castile and Aragon attests to its popularity. Valero Moreno lists a Catalan version from a French translation in the first decades, a Catalan translation from Latin in the second half, a mid-century Castilian version from a Tuscan translation commissioned by Fernán Pérez de Guzmán (c. 1376–c. 1460), and Alonso de Cartagena's version (1434), known as *De las artes liberales*, which survives in thirty-one manuscripts (148–54).

evocative of Caro in *De consolatione Rationis*, announces that she is Love's messenger, come to claim his former servant. She presents the argument of Aristotelian naturalism —love as an inescapable inclination— which we saw articulated in Alonso Fernández de Madrigal's *Libro de amor y amicicia*. Like the Salamanca professor, Veu resorts to the customary examples of classical lovers, among them Orpheus and Hercules, followed by modern classics like Paolo and Francesca ("Paulo e Francisca, segons Dant recita" 129) and Petrarch's *Canzoniere*. Love is an ennobling passion —claims Veu after Virgil— and when praising its beneficial effects on the soul, she compares the pleasure of composing and reading a love letter with the sirens' song:

> Which sweet melody by the harmonious sirens ... can equal the discreet notes and hearing the delightful news that the diligent hand, moved by a passionate desire, writes with the pen's black water on the white paper, where the pure intention and hope of future reward are represented?

> ¿Ni qual melodia suau de les acordants serenes ... és egual ab los discrets reports, ab lo sentir aquelles agradables noves, que la diligent mà dapassionat voler moguda, prenent la ploma ab les negres aygues en lo blanch paper descriu, on la pura intenció, e la sperança del sdevenidor bé stan figurades? (130)

The nautical metaphor extends from the material support of a lover's discourse —paper as white sail— to a manipulation of Boethius's fourth meter in the second book, praising the prudent man:

> Fully opening your eyes, opening your ears, and continuing to navigate with the compass of loving hope as guide toward firm north means arriving at the secure port of propitious fortune.

> Obrir bé los ulls, obris les orelles, e seguint navegan ab brúixola d'enamorada sperança la dreta guia de la sus ferma tramuntana, és arribar al repós e port segur de pròspera fortuna. (130)

In the sea of love, Veu continues, the song's melody makes the deaf hear, the blind see, and the moribund revive.[115] The metamor-

---

[115] The argument is fully conventional but Carrós's Veu seems to enunciate the same reasons presented by Pere Torroella in a letter to the Aragonese knight Hugo de Urriés. See Rodríguez Risquete's edition (Torroella, vol. 2, 207–09).

phosis effected by love will secure happiness, Veu insists, before calling on Justice to settle the case. Once she falls silent, the disturbed
Actor considers her words and the clouds of his sadness turn to bitter
downpour ("dels núvols de la mia tristor aygues amargues e ploro-
ses abundaren" 132). He acknowledges the power of her imaginings
and, aided by a glint of his former clarity, remembers his true nature
as a rational man. He calls on Reason (*la Rahó*) to help him to control the yearnings aroused by Veu's cunning words, which, he warns,
blind understanding, shackle free will all over again, and delight the
eyes ("l'enteniment ceguen, e la liberta voluntad dislliberten, la vista
deliten" 133).

Rahó's appearance initiates the recantation of past errors by revealing the fraudulence of Veu's arguments. Human folly is figured
as Cupid; his *puerilitat* signals adolescence's error and *ignorància*; his
nakedness, its lack of virtue and shame; his wings, youthful vanity,
and their variegation colors the thoughts of sad lovers ("de innu-
merables colores pintades, descobren que colora la pensa dels trists
amadors"). His darts wound the soul (137–39). Rahó invokes a mysterious poet ("O poeta, pintor bienaventurat") whom Reyes-Tudela,
after Farinelli, identifies as Dante (139, footnote to lines 598–604).
Described as a landmark ("fuyst monjoya") for discovering the paths
of errors and signaling the right course toward the true haven, he
could indeed be Dante. However, other remarks point in a different
direction: "qualsevol que tu foses" [whoever you were], "si bé fos
considerat" [if rightfully understood], "gran és lo deute, gran la ob-
ligació que dels mortals ab tot que mal conegut, tes deguda" [great is
the debt, great the obligation owed to you by mortals even if you are
not well known; 139–40]. By the second half of the fifteenth century,
the *Comedy*'s allegory would hardly be misinterpreted nor its cre-
ator unrecognized. More suitably, Rubió i Balaguer believes that the
unidenfied poet is the one who fashioned the mythological image of
Cupid that Rahó interprets (179). Carrós does not seem to recognize
the *Triumphus Cupidinis*, where the god dons "due grand'ali di color mille," perhaps Petrarch's inventive rendering of the glimmering
brilliance that Apuleius attributes to the white feathers of Cupid's
wings.[116] The image was commonplace among Catalan authors like
Ausiàs March or Alegre, who cites Petrarch's work verbatim (Pellisa

---

[116] "[P]er umeros volatilis dei pinnae roscidae micanti flore candicant" [on the
winged god's shoulders white feathers sparkled like petals in the morning dew] (*Psyche et Cupido* 4.22).

Prades, *La ficció* 141). Carrós may have learned it from them, which would explain his glossing over the author's name. More remarkable, however, is his acquaintance with the exegetical, medical, and penitential discourses in both Cupid's moralization and the association of his multihued wings with the rhetorical colors that cause the will to alter memories' *intentio*. Akbari's study of the optical theories that underpin medieval allegories shows that by the 1400s, vision was questioned as a metaphor for certain kinds of knowledge, and the spectrum was taken to represent decay and chaos (236). Cupid's iridescent wings signal the unsettling agitation of *curiositas* —in monastic vocabulary, "mental fornication"— and Rahó must adjust memories' color and bring them back from error, chaos, and confusion to the true course toward moral stillness and focus.

The motif of conversion is at play in the story of Orpheus that Veu offers as a mirror to the confused protagonist. She presents the conventional image of the inspired poet. Intoning his tearful song, he does not fear the sight of infernal punishments, hoping to take back his life and reclaim his lost Eurydice ("lo qual entonant la trista veu del seu plorós cant ab les delitoses acordances de amor, no teme amant la presencia de infernals penes mirar, per sols reveure la perduda vida, e la vista de la sua infernada Euridiçe" 128). Critics point to Metge's *Lo somni* and Roís de Corella's *Parlament* as Carrós's obvious sources (Reyes-Tudela 19; Rodríguez Risquete "La regoneixença"), but Orpheus is first and foremost the myth that articulates *The Consolation*'s journey. We saw its specular reflection in Rodríguez del Padrón's configuration of love's slave. In *Regoneixença*, Rahó comes in lieu of Philosophy to straighten the myth's mental image, and Orpheus's lyre becomes King David's zither, imploring divine intercession to compose a *reprobatio amoris*:

> Celestial harmony, for whom the voice of David's zither was so pleasant, you can see that I do not claim to reach the Muses's register or the Caucasus's heights ... nor do I call on the great eloquence of Titus Livius and Cicero, but my only hope is being inspired by you as the light of divine wisdom; assist my feeble mind, *straighten my memory*, and may you direct my hand so that with my tongue as instrument and the pen writing against Love's vices and forces, truth may attain its victory.

> Mas tu, celestial armunia, per qui la veu de la Cíthara de David fon axí agradable, puix veus que yo, no les scientífiques Muses,

ni de Caucasso les altures reclame ... ni de Tito Livio, ni de Cicero la gran eloqüència cride, mas sols de tu sola com a llum de la divina sapiència ésser inspirada spere; socorre la dèbil pensa, *endreça la memòria*, e la mà sia per tu regida, perque l'instrument de la mia lengua preferint, e la ploma scrivint contra los vicis e forces de amor, lo ver atenga la sua victòria. (140; my emphasis)

Rahó's rejection of classical eloquence entails the moralization of a number of Ovidian myths, most of which, Reyes-Tudela points out, coincide with those elaborated by Roís de Corella (17).

After Rahó's long speech, Actor achieves understanding. Next, not unexpectedly, Justice rejects Veu's sophistry ("sofistichs arguments") and declares Rahó the debate's winner, which frees Actor from bondage. Wisdom is achieved in a beatific vision of human nature and divine essence. Reyes-Tudela noted that this scene is the first —and only— descriptive scene in *Regoneixença* and relates it to an altarpiece dedicated to Saint Ursula without providing further explanation (68–69).

The iconography of Saint Ursula and the eleven thousand virgins appears frequently in late-medieval Iberian altarpieces, as Ferreiro Alemparte documents in studying the legend's peninsular cycles. The earlier date and greater number of altarpieces dedicated to the saint in the Crown of Aragon suggest that her cult spread from there. A fine example is a well-preserved *retablo* now housed at the Museu Nacional d'Art de Catalunya; the Catalan master Joan Reixach, who set up his workshop in Valencia in 1437, created it for the monastery of Santa Maria de Poblet (Tarragona) in 1468. As in Carrós's description, the saint is recognizable by the arrow of her martyrdom, but even considering that meditational ecphrases are not supposed to be mimetic, Actor's words make clear that Saint Ursula is not his vision's center. His contemplative journey establishes a hierarchy that matches the configuration of a typical fifteenth-century *retablo*: a central post with the image to which the altarpiece is dedicated; above it, a painting of Christ; and flanking them, additional panels depicting other saints or episodes from their lives.[117] The altarpiece as a meditational center triggers a sequential pattern of thought, a perambulation that mimics Actor's conversion from the material to the spiritual.

---

[117] See Sobré.

The name that Carrós assigns to *Regoneixença*'s protagonist is not casual either. Books of hours —portable meditational artifacts— often refer to the individual engaged in prayer as *actor*. Actor paints Saint Ursula's scene in the vivid, sensuous terms of *enargeia*: along with the arrow she ("una victoriosa penonera") carries as a standard a cross ornamentted with drops of blood and leads the army of the eleven thousand virgins. White lilies and golden crowns symbolize their virginity ("tenien en les mans flors de blanchs e agradables liris ... portaven en lo cap corones d'or e d'esmalts diversos"); their garments' bright colors ("de fin atzur, ab cerca de color vermella") and the phylactery's inscription ("laor e glòria sia per tostemps de tanta caridat, al fruyt que ha produit la florida verga de la real de Jesse" 146–47) are minutely detailed. Still, Saint Ursula and her court are placed to one side, symmetrical with a depiction of Saint Agnes surrounded by red roses and the symbols of her martyrdom ("el tiran Quíncia" with "les torçudes e arrancades mamelles" 147) in the company of Saint Susan. Actor sees the Man of Sorrows high above:

> I discovered, in the elevation of my spirit, that from those victorious wounds that he had in his feet and hands, in his head and side, a light and rays emanated, glorifying the faith, merits and martyrdom of the saints' assembly.

> Yo descobrí, en elevació de sperit, que d'aquelles victorioses naffres que en los peus e mans, en lo cap e costat la sacratíssima humanitat de Déu tenia, naixia una lum e raigs de tanta claredat, que la fe, los mèrits e martiris de tota la multitud glorificaven. (147)

Underneath, as the other focal point for Actor's devotional experience, the Virgin Mary appears, accompanied by the cardinal virtues:

> And in her I saw Justice, Wisdom, Truth, Temperance, Fortitude, and Prudence ... And at the feet of such great majesty, humble and obedient, burning in love, there was a holy Virgin ... and from two brimming fountains that she had in her sacred breasts ... I saw the manna of divine love endlessly flowing over the plants and soil of our mortality.

> Y en ella mateixa viu star Justícia, Sapiència, Veritat, Temprança, Fortitut e Prudència ... El als peus de tanta magestat humil e prostrada, tota de caritat encessa, residia una sanctíssima verge, ... y,

de dos abundoses fonts que·n los pits sagrats tenia, ... yo viu abun-
dar e brollar sens fi sobre les plantes e terra de nostra mortalitat la
manna de la caritat divina (146).

Devotion to the *Virgo lactans* was widespread after the thirteenth
century. Numerous panels and sculptures in Castile and Aragon represent Mary, sitting on a throne or standing, offering her breast to the
infant.[118] A similar representation is the mystical scene known as the
lactation of Saint Bernard (*lactatio Bernardi*). For example, a panel
painted by Pere Lembrí, active at the beginning of the fifteenth century in Castellón, represents Mary, sitting on a Gothic throne with
the child on her knees, both adorned with golden haloes as signs of
spiritual radiance, but the milk flowing from her breast falls, not into
the child, who appears to be helping by squeezing the unnaturally
positioned breast, but on the lips of Saint Bernard, kneeling at her
feet (see fig. 1). A line indicates the milk's trajectory. The image is
traditionally interpreted as divine wisdom flowing through Mary's
intercession, and this particular depiction highlights it by placing
open books in the hands of Bernard and his companion, Saint Benedict of Nursia.[119] Trens documents an analogous representation of
Mary's milk feeding devout souls, nourishing human mortality with
divine love. The central panel of an altarpiece in Valencia by Pere
Nicolau (d. 1421) depicts Mary breastfeeding the child, but her milk
also falls into the plates, pots, and vases extended by individuals of
all social ranks. Such devotion appears to be related to the Joys of
Mary as documented by a stanza of *Gozos a Nuestra Señora de la
Leche* venerated in the cloister of the Real Convento de Predicadores
in Valencia (Trens 476–77).

Actor's final advice to his own work to rely on the Virgin Mary as
its guide may seem a devotional cliché, but it acquires fuller meaning when we compare the image of the Mary *lactans* to allegories of
grammatica and philosophy. Clerical personifications of *grammatica*
as a lovely woman with uncovered nipples alluded to the delights
that their sweet milk offered in preparation for more wholesome,
yet hard-to-chew doctrinal lessons. Even Sapience appears in some
cases nursing "David and Solomon at her breasts, her milk being

---

[118] For the Spanish iconography of the *Virgo lactans*, see Trens (457–80).
[119] The Museo del Prado holds the panel and indicates that it must have been part
of a larger *retablo* in a monastery, most likely the Cistercian monastery of Benifasar in
Castellón.

Figure 1. *La Virgen de la Leche with the Child between Saint Bernard of Claraval and Saint Benedict*, Pere Lembrí, 1410–1415. Guilded, tempera on panel.
© Museo Nacional del Prado.

the souce of the psalms and the books of wisdom" (Teskey 45).[120]
Saplana-Ginebreda personifies Philosophy in *The Consolation* as a
breasfeeding mother:

> This woman was Philosophy, and she is a woman because just like
> a woman's role is giving birth and nourishing man, and this is
> mandated by natural law, in the same manner, philosophy makes
> man perfect and complete by nourishing and forming him.[121]

A subsequent gloss comments on ancient representations of Philosophy:

> Others painted her in courthouses in the likeness of a queen on a
> professorial chair; at her feet were the men of antiquity, who had
> one knee on the ground, and each of them was suckling from her
> breasts, and she extended her arms over all of them. The meaning
> of it is that the milk of philosophy makes, forms, and nourishes
> justice's truth and goodness.[122]

Carrós's depiction of Mary highlights a comparable intellectual
connection, particularly in the context of the *Verge dels consellers*,
a panel from a lost altarpiece commissioned by the Barcelona *Consell de Cent* in 1445 to the Valencian master Lluís Dalmau and now
housed at the Museu Nacional d'Art de Catalunya. Noting a Catalan
tendency to associate the cardinal virtues with the Virgin Mary, Molina i Figueras interprets the *Verge dels consellers* as a political allegory
in which Mary offers wisdom and the virtues necessary for a ruler
(*Arte, devoción*; "La Virgen"). He acknowledges that the virtues are
not represented in Dalmau's *retablo* but surmises that Mary's depiction as throne of Solomon implies the privileged inspiration that she

---

[120] For a clever analysis of the eroticized bodies of female personifications and
their parodies in medieval and early modern Hispanic literature, see Francomano
(*Wisdom and Her Lovers*).
[121] "Aquesta muger era Philosophía, y es dicha muger porque assí como a la
muger pertenece segund la su condición de parir al ombre e de nodrirle, y esto es or-
denado naturalmente, assí la filosofía faze al ombre perfecto e acabado nodriéndolo
y enformándolo" (Se1).
[122] "Otros la pintavan en los lugares de las justicias assí como reyna estando en
cáthedra, e a los sus pies estavan los ombres antiguos, los quales tenían la una rodilla
fincada en tierra e mamavan cada uno d'ellos las sus tetas, cada uno la suya, y ella es-
tendía los sus braços sobre ellos. Por la qual cosa es entendido que verdad e bondad
de toda justicia es hecha e formada e nodrida con leche de philosofía, e por ella es
fructificada e acabada" (Se1).

infuses in the *consellers* (*Arte, devoción* 217; "La Virgen" 125). In *Regoneixença*, Mary is not seated on a physical throne, but Actor's mind sees her on the throne of eternity ("en lo tro de la immensa eternidat," 146). His plea for Mary's guidance supports a similar interpretation of her loving mediation in the transmission of heavenly virtues.

The whole ecphrasis exudes the pictorial quality, attention to detail, and emotivity that Franciscan spirituality adopted to contemplate silently on the life of Christ as an illuminating and purgative act for the devout. Franciscans had a prominent role in Valencian literary circles at Carrós's time. Roís de Corella translated Ludolph of Saxony's (1295–1377) *Vita Christi* as *Lo Cartoixà*; printed in four volumes between 1495 and 1496, it became a best-seller. He and his family were benefactors of the Poor Clare convent where Abbess Isabel de Villena (1430–1490) composed her unfinished *Vita Christi*, printed in 1497. In it, Sor Isabel presents Mary to her nuns as the means to acquire wisdom through divine inspiration, the only path open to women, who were barred from scholarly training (Twomey 220). By birth and family ties, Carrós was part of this intellectual milieu. Reyes-Tudela surmises that Carrós's familiarity with the members and texts of the literary circle that Roís de Corella fictionalizes in *Parlament* stemmed from his relationship to Lluís de Castellví, one of *Parlament*'s members —Carrós's older brother married Castellví's daughter (17–19).

Marian devotion was encouraged by the mendicant orders, but Dominicans propagated the cult of Our Lady of the Milk and passionately opposed the notion of her Immaculate Conception, which Franciscans defended with equal passion. Metge discusses the question in the second book of *Lo somni,* and it was the subject of many poetic competitions in the fifteenth century —at least ten of the fourteen celebrated in Valencia. Works recounting her life in Catalan and Castilian prose and verse proliferated (Arronis Llopis and Baños Vallejo 73–74). Carrós's *Virgo lactans* dispenses with the physicality the Dominicans attributed to her —the narrator does not see her breasts, but fountains of wisdom— and underscores her purity. The whole ensemble of Mary in the exclusive company of virgins counters the promiscuous examples adduced by Veu; Mary's charity is the reverse of erotic desire.

Regoneixença involves a set of oppositions and transitions from Ovidian metamorphosis toward Boethian conversion: sensual perception leads to the soul's awakening; David is Orpheus's divinely

inspired reverse, the harmony of his song a respite from the distract-
ing colors and rhythms of poetic fiction. In the final analysis, *Regoneixença* incorporates the debate on Woman and materiality that
underpins penitential literature. To the youthful display of courtly
love and its defense of women as a stimulus for poetry, it opposes
the mature contemplative stance of a private reader converting material cravings into affective energy in preparation for the spiritual
inspiration of Christian charity that, flowing through Mary, guides
the author's hand. Mary supplants Francesca and Lady Philosophy.

ORPHEUS GETS MARRIED: ROMEU LLULL'S *LO DESPROPIAMENT D'AMOR*

Lo despropiament was composed around 1480, when Romeu
Llull (c. 1439–1496) finally married in Barcelona at the age of 40.
The title references the legal term for a regular cleric's testament, issued before death or leaving the order, to narrate the author's departure from youthful follies and delayed entrance into maturity (Llull,
Romeu 210). According to Torró, it stands at the crossroads of the
Italian petrarquism in vogue at the Neapolitan court of King Alfons
the Magnanimous; Castilian *cancionero* poetry; and the Catalan poetic tradition with which Romeu Llull may have come in contact
through Pere Torroella, a poet related to both the Neapolitan and
Castilian courts.

Lo despropiament is enlivened by abundant motifs, echoes, and
direct quotations from Dante, Boccaccio, Ausiàs March, and above
all Petrarch, which Torró conscientiously details in the footnotes to
his edition. This humanistic attire should not distract us from identifying the compositional devices and penitential motifs it shares with
Siervo and *Regoneixença*: first-person remembrance of past errors
and translation of sinful love into virtue within the framework of
allegorical vision.[123] Against this backdrop, it fits squarely in the category of Iberian penitential fictions: the protagonist's recantation and
moral conversion are offered as a therapy that soothes the pernicious
intellectual effects of his earlier uncontrolled passion.

In his extensively documented biography, Torró surmises that
Romeu was educated at Alfons the Magnanimous's Neapolitan chan-

---

[123] For critics who place *Lo despropiament* in the sentimental fiction category, see
Torró (Llull, Romeu, *Obra completa*); Pellisa Prades (*La ficció*); Badia (ed. *Història*,
vol. 3).

cery before moving to Barcelona in 1479.[124] As the youngest of six brothers and three sisters, upon the untimely death of his parents in 1447, he was left under the tutelage of Joan, the oldest sibling and a member of the king's close circle, who served as governor of Sorrento and Capri. Unlike his brothers —one was a prebendary, another a Benedictine monk, a third a doctor of the law— Romeu did not follow a military or clerical career. In 1483, he was a prosperous member of the Barcelona *Consell de Cent* [municipal government] after a series of fortuitous events made him the only heir to the family fortune and an extensive library that contained, not surprisingly, "algun Boeci" among the sacro-military mix characteristic of vernacular humanists and the professional tomes of his clerical brothers.

Lo despropiament begins by accepting the inevitability of erotic desire:

> It is a common opinion of medical and theological doctors that all rational human creatures are inclined from birth to a certain natural inclination, which more than any other dominates them, and they are forced to follow it and obey it willingly.

> Comuna opinió és, no solament dels naturals encara dels teòlechs doctors, que tota racional e humana creatura en la creació sua és inclinada a certa natural inclinació, la qual més que tota altre en ella domina, e a sseguir e obehir és voluntàriamente forçada. (211)

As in *Regoneixença*, the proem articulates the painful truth in terms of Aristotelian naturalism: love is an innate tendency that rules all others —Arnau de Vilanova called it *amor dominalis*— and bends rational creatures' will ("tota racional e human creatura en la creació sua és inclinada a certa natural inclinació, la qual més que tota altre en ella domina, e a sseguir e obehir és voluntàriamente forçada" 211).[125] Youthful desire is figured in the deceiving beauties of Cupid's court, rendered through allusions to Petrarch's *Canzionere* and *Triumphus Cupidinis*. The author also alludes to his own past, when he composed one his most interesting poems, "Lo consistori de Amor," which is addressed to the families of the Barcelona oli-

---

[124] For Romeu Llull's biography, see Torró's introduction to his edition of Llull's works (12–24).

[125] Torró refers to the astrological naturalism studied by Cátedra (*Amor y pedagogía*) in relation to Juan Ruiz (Llull, Romeu, *Obra completa* 218 n1–19), but I find no evidence in *Lo despropiament* to justify this assertion.

garchy, the honorable citizens (*ciutadans honrats*) whose close ties
with the monarchy led them to imitate the royal custom of organizing "love courts" (Llull, Romeu, *Obra completa* 37). The entirety of
Romeu Llull's poetic work, including *Lo despropiament,* survives in
a single manuscript —the *Jardinet d'orats*. It contains five other brief
narrations set in Cupid's court, where amorous passion is put on trial
(Pacheco, "L'anàlisi" 35).

In *Lo despropiament,* the sixteen-year-old protagonist, dressed
with Love's first emblems but inexperienced in its service, follows his
will ("per la voluntat guiat") to the beautiful Temple of Love, located in the sweet-smelling, flowery green meadow of cliché. There he
finds Hope [Speransa], a red-haired lady dressed in green, who leads
him to another building, oddly small, narrow, and low, where Cupid holds his tribunal. Upon Speransa's request, Cupid takes Romeu
Llull as his faithful servant. Love's ministers —Fear and Jealousy,
Toil and Illness— remove Romeu Llull's clothes and dress him in the
order's symbolic habit and a stole bearing their own initials T.G.T.Ff.
—"ço és, Temor, Gelosia, Treball e Ffermedat"— the four passions
on which the religion of Love is built. Hope for a reward is their
only ruler ("a significança que lo àbit de la religió de Amor és fundat
sobre aquestes quatre pacions, de les quals Speransa de galardó és lo
sol govern de aquelles" 214).

The passage implicitly associates sensual beauty and courtly
games with the veil of ignorance that the protagonist willingly accepts
in servitude to his base desires. Love's ministers dress his nude body,
literally, with a device that turns him into a walking metonymy of one
of *cancionero* poetry's most characteristic categories, the enigmatic
invención that invites quick-witted dialogue.[126] Wearing his master's
colors and wounded by one of his arrows, Romeu Llull addresses
a lovely lady, who, with serene and joyful countenance ("ab serena
cara e molt alegra"), tells him her name, Serena, and teases him before disappearing. He searches for her through the jagged geography
of his dark desires, falling and getting up, suffering fatigue and endless dangers, until he finally recognizes her, but now her infuriated
stare and repellent, horrific smile blind him.[127] Topification figures

---

[126] For *cancionero* poetic categories, see Chas Aguión (*Amor y corte; Categorías
poéticas*). For a detailed analysis of the *invenciones y letras,* see MacPherson (*The
invenciones*).

[127] Torró traces the association of the lover's sufferings with a dangerous journey
to Petrarch's "errar per locs deserts e tenebrosos" (Llull, Romeu, *Obra completa*
211), but we should not forget the comparison's penitential pedigree.

his struggles as a frightful landscape leading only to disappointment. The realization comes in a moment of penitential fire and brimstone, when, without warning, Serena —her name recalling at once composure and the treachery of the sirens— turns into a Medusa. This image suggests the grinning skull under rosy cheeks or Roís de Corella's innocent heroines metamorphosed into execrable monsters: woman as token of human deceit, rottenness, and mortality.

Inspired by divine will ("de la divina voluntat inspirat" 217) and remembering that he is a Christian, the protagonist becomes aware of his *integumentum* and reads through Serena's beautiful veil, her deceiving *claror*, undressing her truth. What follows is his own undressing, slipping off the uniform he wore for twenty-four years, seven months, and nine days; as for most addicts, the date forever commemorates past pleasurable excesses. The process is articulated in the legal language of Barcelona's merchants and jurists:

> I took as counselor Understanding, which I saw obfuscated by depravity; as defenders Memory, which had forgotten all virtue, and ailing Reason, and Conscience as judge; after turning each of them back into his original virtuous state, at their instruction, I composed a petition to Cupid to dispossess me of all the benefits of vain love to bring repose to my life.

> [L]'entaniment que per lo mal e viciós viura offuscat tenia per procuredor pres, la memòria de tota virtut oblidada e la rehó malalta per advocats, e la consiència per jutge, tornat cascú en lo primer e virtuós stat, aconsellat per ells e ordenada una suplicació la tenor de la qual fou que de tots los béns de vana amor, per dar repòs a ma vida, me despropiàs. (217)

Having received a favorable sentence, Desdeny [Disdain], as notary, inventories the benefits to be repossessed: fluctuating cogitation, vain hopes, foolish thoughts, sinful desires, unrewarding services ... and in conclusion, lost time and a ruined life (218). Stripped of the bright colors of his former life, Romeu Llull dons the honest, albeit drab habit of virtuous love for the rest of his life; he enters the sacred religion of honest matrimony and offers his experience as a deterrent to those who wish to escape foolish love (218). No woman is harmed in the process of allegorical capture, but Romeu Llull's naked body, treated as a text, is covered and uncovered with the rhetorical ornaments that point to either *amor hereos* or conjugal virtue.

Does Romeu Llull's subsequent production support the conversion narrated in *Lo despropiament*? In 1488, we find him in Valencia, participating in a poetic competition to honor Our Lady with his "Responsiva com Nostra Dona en los vint trihumphos trihumpha."[128] Other Marian composions and repentance poems, such as "Obra contrita fugint a foll i deshonest amor" [Contrite Work Escaping from a Foolish and Dishonest Love], indicate that he left behind courtly praise of female beauty's passing joys in favor of spiritual belief. However, the impossibility of precisely dating his production leads Torró to warn about the trap of establishing two poetic cycles articulated around *Lo despropiament*. Nothing would prevent Romeu Llull from addressing love poems to his wife, as Jorge Manrique did, or proposing conjugal love as a prison filled with freedom that does not blind or deny virtue, as in his poem "celebrant un amor virtuós i feliç" (Llull, Romeu, *Obra completa* 39).

Romeu Llull may be addressing a mixed public, closer, as Torró proudly remarks, to that of Italian humanism, even if their assumptions differed greatly. They were the men and women, *ciutadans honrats,* and wealthy merchants of Barcelona, who imitated courtly games and rituals (Llull, Romeu, *Obra completa* 45). But *Lo dispropiament*'s arguments on love's pernicious influence that frame the vision reveals that this audience was similar in its tastes to those of the all-male Valencian tertullias. Like Roís de Corella's happily married friends, Romeu Llull valued marriage as a pillar of society while maintaining a healthy distrust of comforting uxorial affection.

TIRESIAS IN LOVE: FRANCESC MONER'S *L'ÀNIMA D'OLIVER* AND *LA NOCHE*

The last instances of penitential fictions in this chapter are the work of Francesc Moner (1463–1492), a member of the Catalan lower nobility. Of his fifty-six poetic and eighteen prose compositions, sixteen are in Catalan and fifty-eight in Castilian (Cocozzella, *Fra Francesc* 24).[129] Like Carrós, Moner participated in one of

---

[128] It is copied in fols. 37r–41r of *Jardinet d'Orats*, (Arronis Llopis and Baños Vallejo "Las vidas" 77). See also Torró's edition and commentary (Llull, Romeu, *Obra completa* 83–93).

[129] All the information on Moner's biography comes from Cocozzella's dissertation, where he surmises that Moner wrote most of his works in the last five years of his life (*The Two Major* 31); his introduction to *Obres catalanes* (Moner, Francesc 7–97); and further remarks in his introduction to the study on Moner's poetics (*Fra*

the military campaigns against Granada (c. 1481) before joining the household of the Duke of Cardona, where he is supposed to have produced most of his poems and treatises from the mid-1480s to 1492. At the end of his life, like Rodríguez del Padrón, he entered the Franciscan order and changed his given name, Pere or Pedro, to that of the order's founder.

Pellisa Prades (*La ficció*), and Badia (ed. *Història*, vol. 3, 205–09) after her, place his two major narrative works, *L'Ánima d'Oliver* [Oliver's Soul] and *La noche* [The Night], in the mixed bag of sentimental fiction because of their formal structure and content: they are first-person accounts of allegorical visions with abundant personifications who debate the moral consequences of passionate love and stress women's destructiveness. Cocozzella, the critical authority on Moner, groups them with Carrós's *Regoneixença* as examples of the dramatic genre *auto de amores*. His highly pertinent insights on Ausiàs March's spatial poetics in exploring the lover's subjectivity, which Moner faithfully followed, can be fruitfully applied with equal ease to the allegorical topification characteristic of penitential fiction, but fail to convince in the matter of the major prose works' theatricality. Other critics have insisted on the theatrical or choral component of texts dealing with the *materia de amore* (Blay Manzanera, "Espectáculos cortesanos;" Severin, "Audience and Interpretation;" Cortijo Ocaña, *La evolución genérica*), but as penitential fictions, *L'Ánima* and *La noche* construct a private, contemplative reading position. Cocozzella accepts as much when he proposes that *La noche* transforms ceremonial theatricality into the *locus* of absolute solitude, the privacy of the psychic space, and a soulful place ("Fra Francesc Moner y el auto" 74–75).[130] His claim that *La noche*, *L'Ánima*, and Carrós's *Regoneixença* belong to the subgenre of "the *consolatio* of the naive and ill lover —ill physically, psychologically, and morally"— points in the same direction (*Bilingual Poetics* 56).

L'Ánima and *La noche* exhibit the rhetorical features of the consolations analyzed in this chapter. An author persona presents a dream vision as a love *case,* but it is really a disquisition about for-

---

Francesc). I cite *L'Ánima* from the *Obres catalanes* edition and the English translation from Cocozzella's 1966 dissertation (*The Two Major Prose Works of Francisco Moner*). Quotes from *La noche* and its English translation are from the 1966 dissertation as well. On *La noche's* interpretation, see also Ruiz-Gálvez Priego, although she adds no significant insights to Cocozzella's.

[130] See further considerations in Cocozzella (*Bilingual Poetics*; "Psychic Space").

tune, providence, and free will, after Boethius's *contemptus mundi.*
Ignorance is the consequence of the bodily passions' obsfuscating
veil, synecdochically represented by *amor hereos,* the obsessive-compulsive mental and physical disorder that medical treatises viewed as
ruling the human spirit and heart.[131] As a defense against Fortune's
incomprehensible turns —nature's overpowering urges and the always unfathomable female mystery— a teacher appears to tell the afflicted protagonist how to straighten out his fixated imagination with
the help of free will. Any penitent's moral conversion repeats this
journey, but *La noche* emphasizes the association among rhetorical
colors, confusing emotions, and poetic craft. In *L'Ánima,* the protagonist is a lover who retreats into solitude to ruminate on his chaotic
delusions and despair; *La noche*'s lover is more narrowly identified
as a poet. In both, a supernatural figure reminds the protagonist of
the falsity of his fictions, but *La noche* delves deeper into the human
truth that poetry hides under its multicolored veil. Here, "we witness
a momentous shift from the Boethian mode of comforting ratiocination to a phenomenology of love, in which the presence of reason
is or would be in itself problematic" (Cocozzella, *Bilingual Poetics*
12). The final products of both are learned display and penitential
cure, offered to the correspondent as a sign of friendship. However,
L'Ánima is dedicated to a man; *La noche,* to an unnamed "Illustrious Lady" (Egregia Señora), which opens to question its purportedly
moral intention and places it in a no-man's land between the penitential genre and its sentimental contrafacta.

   Dating Moner's two major prose works is difficult, although *La
noche*'s dream vision displays a more scholarly description of the passions that affect a lover and problematizes their cure. Information on
his life is gathered exclusively from a letter addressed to Ferran Folk,
Duke of Cardona, by Moner's cousin, Miguel Barutell de Barutell,
in the 1528 *editio princeps.* According to Barutell, Pedro Moner
served as a page in Joan II's royal court, then in the military, and was
then admitted to the service of Joan Ramon Folk, Ferran's father and
predecessor in the dukedom. He suffered a psychological crisis as a
consequence of an unfortunate love affair that prompted his entry
in the Franciscan Observance, dying a year later in Barcelona on the

---

[131] Cocozzella traces Moner's assignment of love's primacy over the other passions
to Thomas Aquinas (*Bilingual Poetics* 94). Moner may have indeed drawn from the
Summa, but love's precedence is the traditional medical explanation for its designa-
tion as *amor dominalis.*

day he took his final vows. The *princeps*'s title indicates merely that his works were composed at different times with different and noble purposes ("compuestas en diuersos tiempos y por diuersos y nobles motiuos").[132]

Badia warns that Barutell's biography, addressed to a Castilian readership, is but a literary construct to lend Moner's works unity and project his authorial figure as the Catalan counterpart of Rodríguez del Padrón (ed. *Història*, vol. 3, 206). The woodcut that illustrates *La noche*'s opening page may support Barutell's editorial strategy by connecting Moner to two Castilian best-sellers. It represents a massive fortress that Cocozzella relates to the elaborate *castells* and *roques* of courtly and religious spectacles and his thesis about *La noche*'s dramatic nature ("Fra Francesc Moner y el auto" 74–75).[133] If Badia is right, however, Barutell or even the printer may have selected the woodcut to attach the popularity of *Cárcel de Amor*, Diego de San Pedro's hit. *Cárcel*'s title page in the 1493 Catalan translation by Bernardí Vallmanya and the 1496 Castilian edition consists of a woodcut representing a man entering the prison of love. Deyermond surmises that the same woodcut illustrated *Cárcel's* first edition as demonstrated by the 1493 Saragossa edition studied by Pallarés ("The Woodcuts" 523). *La noche*'s illustration might have also reminded readers of the *Fortalitium fidei* (1458), a treatise by the friar minor Alfonso de Espina defending the fortress of Christian faith from its enemies. Its widespread success gave way to luxurious manuscripts with fine miniatures and enjoyed wide dissemination in printed form, although the print editions lack illustrations.[134] Yarza Luaces found a manuscript, housed in the Biblioteca y Archivo Capitular of El Burgo de Osma cathedral, that Bishop Pedro de Montoya (1412–1491) commissioned for his private use. A member of the Franciscan Observance, rector at the University of Salamanca, and confessor of Enrique IV of Castile, the bishop commissioned his personal artist to illustrate the manuscript with a splendid miniature of the fortress and its defenders ("La imagen del rey" 278–80). *Fortalitium*'s miniature of a stronghold with several towers surrounding

---

[132] I cite the title from the *Obras nueuamente imprimidas* facsimil edition (1951), which has no pagination.

[133] Those ideas were further developed in "Ausiàs March Text" and inform his analysis in *Fra Francesc Moner's Bilingual Poetics* and "Fra Francesc Moner's Psychic Space".

[134] This information comes from the Biblioteca Nacional de España's webpage on "Biblias de Sefarad" exhibit: www.bne.es/es/Micrositios/Exposiciones/Biblias/.

the keep is closer to *La noche*'s woodcut than *Cárcel*'s edifice represented as a single turret.[135] Barutell's choice or the printer's was probably meant to trigger a meditational network of metaphorical associations, including the rocks and *castells* of courtly spectacles mentioned by Cocozzella, to appeal to the widest possible readership, courtly and spiritual. As examples of *arquitecturas efímeras* [ephemeral architectures], *roques* and *castells* point to the transcience of human life that can only be buttressed by Christian faith.[136]

La noche and *L'Ánima* begin with the protagonist's strong desire for solitary retreat at sunset, and both dream visions take place over the course of one night. Their endings are clearly marked by the arrival of dawn: in *L'Anima,* the bells are ringing for matins as the protagonist returns home through the Gate of the Angel ("Entrava per lo Portal de·l Angel quant tocavena matines" 344), and in *La noche,* he wanders until sunrise ("hasta tanto que se hizo de día" 203). The moment of crisis is translated into the barren geography of confusion, chaos, and fear, the shattered *locus amoenus* that initiates cogitation. *La noche*'s landscape morphs into a rocky climb of thorny bushes as night sets in. In *L'Ánima,* the night's absolute darkness leaves the protagonist completely blind. Tears, wailing, and despair accompany his writer's block; he moans, "Big tears and frequent sighing came forth from me because there were no words for my ills because they were so strange" (354).[137] In *La noche,* two thousand bats strike his eyes with their wings, filling him with dread.

These painful, inexplicable emotions signal the creative instant. In *L'Ánima,* a mysterious voice identifies itself as the soul of Oliver, the hapless lover who killed himself when spurned by the Countess of Luna (355–56).[138] Cocozzella notes Moner's "multifarious textuality" (*Bilingual Poetics* 16), the thick weft of allusions that here points

---

[135] The fortress miniature is available on the "Biblias de Sefarad" webpage www.bne.es/es/Micrositios/Exposiciones/Biblias/Exposicion/seccion5/Obra5.html?origen=galeria. The woodcut of the 1493 Saragossa edition is available at visigodo.faculty.ku.edu/CARCELDEAMOR/CARCEL1493/FOLIO1_93.html

[136] Another association might have been related to fortune if we consider a much later English dream vision, a 136-line poem by one T. S. P. in which "the poet-narrator finds himself viewing a huge mountain … and countless scores of people straining to mount to the summit" representing "foolish people laboring to scale Fortune's mountain" (Davidoff 70).

[137] "Soccorrien grosses làgrimes y redoblats sospirs perquè mos mals, d'estrengés, faltaven de vocables" (140).

[138] Bassegoda identifies her as Violant-Lluïsa de Mur. The mythic Oliver committed suicide in the 1450s (256).

to Metge's *Lo somni* and Carrós's *Regoneixença*. Oliver's soul will interpret the protagonist's strange ills and remedy them with the advice to substitute charity for "that cruel love that blinds you" (355).[139] In *La noche*, the protagonist arrives at the gate of a wondrous fortress and a longwinded moralization on human life that entails a rehash of *cancionero* conceits; Thomist theories on the passions of the soul (Cocozzella, *Bilingual Poetics* 83–128); and Boethian *consolatio* (*Bilingual Poetics* 40–81).

La noche's most original aspect is in articulating a lover's passions within a system of colors and mottoes taken from *cancionero* poetry to a personified Razón [Reason] for further interpretation. Upon his arrival at the fortress, the narrator is met by a young beautiful lady with bared breasts, who invites him in. She wears a green velvet gown embroidered with verses: "when the sun of doctrine / Does not shine upon rulers and the common folk, / I am considered the law" (211).[140] Cocozzella interprets this personification, who identifies herself as Custom, as "the embodiment of bad habits or vices, and perhaps, the perversion of all virtues" (*The Two Major* 89), but read in the context of Romeu Llull's *Lo despropiament*, she takes on the more restrictive Aristotelian meaning of the innate inclination to procreate that rules the world. The protagonist's reaction confirms this view. Enticed by not only Costumbre's exposed breasts but her "gentle voice" and "pleasing gesture," he remembers his past and exclaims:

> Oh womanly beauty! How can you be so deceiving yet so powerful? O foe of those who most desire you! He who does not know you well pursues you. Avoid those who gaze upon you longingly, for wherever you are, there rule Pride, Cruelty, Ingratitude. Salted as you are with whims and fickleness, people pursue you without reason. (212)[141]

The discourse *in mulieres* as the ultimate sign of instability implicitly frames the discussion on the ten passions derived from Amor

---

[139] "[L]'amor cruel que t'enbena" (140).

[140] "Trahía vestido un brial de terciopelo verde, broslado al rededor d'unas luzérnigas muy naturales y de letras que dezían: Quando el sol de la doctrina / falta en los grandes y grey / yo soy tenida por ley" (89–90).

[141] "O mugeril hermosura, ¿por qué, siendo tan engañosa, puedes tanto? ¡O enemiga de quien más te quiere! Quien no te conosse te sigue. Húyete de quien detrás te mira, porque donde tú eres mandan Soberbia, Crueldad, y Desconosimiento. Salada d'antojos y mudanssas, a tu te siguen sin causa" (92–93).

[Love]. They are, in this order, Odio [Hate], Desseo [Desire], Aborrescimiento [Abhorrence], Deleyte [Delight], Tristeza [Sadness],
Sperança [Hope], Desesperaçión [Despair], Temor [Fear], Denue-
do [Daring], and Yra [Anger]. They correspond to a lover's paradoxical responses to a capricious lady's fancies. Each allegorical
figure wears colorful attire embroidered with an emblem. Amor
is a handsome youth ("la edad jusgué de viente años" 94) "with a
cheerful countenance and a courteous bearing." He wears a crown
of flowers, "a long surcoat of mauve satin lined with taffeta of various colors," and a white breastplate in which the protagonist sees
his own reflection under the light of a torch found at the fortress's
entrance. The motto on Amor's shield reads: "The purpose of this
armour is to prevent / Anyone from paying homage / To Reason, my
enemy" (213).[142] Cocozzella asserts that Moner "disregards the traditional representation of the winged Cupid" to portray "Love as a
young knight or courtier;" his variegated surcoat recalls the clashing
colors of Cupid's wings that Carrós attributes to the evils inherent in
courtly love (*The Two Major* 94–96). Moner places wings, now black,
not on Amor's shoulders, but on his son Desseo's surcoat made of
"very finely woven crimson damask and a satin doublet appliquéd all
around with some wings and letters which read: Let those who wish
to fly / Arm themselves with their hearts / For this is where the wings
are" (223–24).[143]

Love's insidious nature is revealed not only in the mismatched
hues of Amor's attire, as Cocozzella proposes, but more emphatically in the dizzying antithesis of brightness and darkness that defines
his offspring and attendants: the rich velvets and satins in bright
blue, yellow, green, and white that Deleyte and Sperança boast offer
a stunning contrast to the surcoat of Aborrescimiento, "dyed two
shades of black" (226). Tristeza and Desesperaçión are dressed in
black as well, while Odio and Desseo combine intense black and
varied shades of vivid red —crimson, poppy— and Yra is bizarrely

---

[142] "Un hombre con gesto galán, hermoso, y alegre. La edad jusgué de viente
años. ... Traýa una ropa rosegante de carmesí morado raso en taffetán de colores.
... En la cabeça una corona de muchas y diversas flores. Y ensima de todo, un peto
d'arnés blanco. ... y unas letras que dezían: Todas estas armas son / porque no se den
las paryas / a mi enemiga, Razón" (93–99).
[143] "La edad era de page, el rostro mugeril ... Vestía una ropa d'estado de damas-
co carmesí de muy sotiles obras, un jubón de raso, chapado de unas alas y letras al
derredor que dezían: Los que quisieren bolar / ármense del coraçón / que las alas
aquí son" (115–17). "Negras alas son las tuyas, hijo del cruel padre" (118).

characterized as "a bearded old lady with a headdress like that of Navarrese women" wearing "a red gown of unusual design, and, on top, a short mantle of black cloth fastened all the way down" (241).

The whole description of the mental turmoil induced by erotic desire smacks of clerical mnemonic tricks. Each personification occupies its place after the protagonist opens a door in his arduous ascent of a stairway he can barely see in the dim light of his torch. It fits within the wider penitential tradition that Conde sees as the base of *Siervo*'s allegorical structure ("De las fuentes"). Confessional manuals, such as the influential *Summa de vitiis* (ca.1248) by Dominican preacher Guillaume Peyraut (Guilielmus Paraldus), mentioned in passing by Conde, offered a model for personifying each sin, and the penitent is figured as a knight who fights them, carrying a shield with inscriptions referring to the Trinity.[144] At the same time, if *La noche*'s allegory and its protagonist's moralistic protests against each passion are typical of clerical penitential strictures —his invective against Amor's deceits recalls Juan Ruiz's attack on Sir Love— each passion's colorful ecphrasis also recalls the splendor of courtly pageantry and poetic pastimes.

Poetic conceits in penitential fictions are attested in *Siervo*. Rodríguez del Padrón, like Moner, was an accomplished poet before entering the Franciscans. Dolz has studied the symbolic function that color performs in *Siervo,* following Le Gentil's analysis of the synaesthetic devices *cancionero* poets deploy to express a lover's agony and sadness, which he also traces in contemporary French compositions ("El simbolismo" 125). René of Anjou's prosimetrum *Livre du coeur d'Amour épris*, completed in 1477, is perhaps the best example.[145] It is impossible to ascertain whether Moner knew

---

[144] *The Summa de vitiis* survives in more than 500 manuscripts, many originating in Dominican and Franciscan environments, and a few dozen early printed editions. See www.narcis.nl/research/RecordID/OND1294348. A critical edition and translation of Peraldus's *Summa de vitiis* is under way by a team of researchers. See www. public.asu.edu/~rnewhaus/peraldus/. A remarkable example of compilations that a preacher may have consulted can be found in a manuscript housed at the British Library (Harley MS 3244). It contains extracts from Peraldus's *Summa de vitiis* along with Alain de Lille's *Liber penitentialis* and *De confessione* or pseudo-Bernard's *Tractatus sive meditatio Bernardi de interiori homine* among others. The digitized version is available at www.bl.uk/manuscripts/FullDisplay.aspx?ref=harley_ms_3244. A miniature of the knight fighting the vices is at www.bl.uk/manuscripts/Viewer. aspx?ref=harley_ms_3244_f027r. See also the allegorical journeys to the heavenly city listed by Cornelius (69–72).

[145] René (1409–1480), who claimed rule over Sicily and Naples, lost them to Alfons the Magnanimous. He was involved in French-Catalan territorial disputes, and

of this work or to define exact correspondences between *La noche* and *Livre au coeur*'s minutely detailed allegories, but some attributes and devices of the personifications along with their elaborate color schemes speak to a similar tradition of courtly games and witty displays that Moner reworks for his own consolatory purposes.[146]

Livre du coeur narrates the complex allegorical journey of René's Heart, torn from his body by Love. Desire arms Heart as a knight with the halberd of pleasure and shield of hope and accompanies him on his quest, leading Heart into personifications of a lover's conflicting emotions before they arrive at Love's Castle. A bare-breasted woman meets them as they enter the castle of Despair; the moment is captured in an image in a richly illuminated manuscript, although the woman embodies, not Costumbre, but Sloth, dirty and disheveled.[147] *Livre du coeur*'s miniatures paint Desire, not Amor, dressed in white, but, like Amor, Desire's contrasting black boots express paradox, and he rides a cinnamon-colored horse. Heart wears completely black armor and a helmet embellished with golden wings, while *La noche* assigns black wings to Desseo. Hope, not Costumbre, is a red-haired damsel in a bright blue gown.[148]

Moner rehashes René's admirable display of luxurious fabrics and gems, elaborate poetic conceits, and clever conversations not without his own wittiness, resorting to the *invenciones y letras* so characteristic of *cancioneros*. In contrast, *La noche* opposes the protagonist's distrust and painful memories. He argues with Amor, covers his ears to ignore Desseo, begs Yra not to remind him of past outrages and sufferings —"For God's sake, Madam, no more! I beseech you, let not my memory recall things I cannot endure" (242)— before he drops his torch. *La noche*'s moralistic bent, absent in René's

---

when Aragon revolted against Alfons's brother, Joan, in 1466, Louis XI of France supported René's claim to Aragon and Naples, and René declared himself king of Aragon and count of Barcelona that year without ever actually reigning (René I x–xxx).

[146] For the role of colors in *Livre du coeur*, see Scheidegger; Early. In *La noche*, Deleyte is dressed in the French fashion ("todos sus aparejos françeses" 123), bolstering the stereotype.

[147] A few of the mansucripts are richly illuminated. Several miniatures of Cod. Vid.2597 at the Austrian National Library are available in wikimedia commons. See Sloth welcoming Heart and Desire at Wikimedia commons (File:Livre du cœur d'amour épris - vindobo2597 - f25v.jpg). All the miniatures are reproduced in Viereck Gibbs and Karczewska's edition (René I).

[148] See Wikimedia commons (File:Livre du cœur d'amour épris - vindobo2597 - f21v.jpg).

Livre du coeur, is further developed by the appearance of Razón, who will explain the true meaning of the allegory the protagonist just encountered and, like Boethian Philosophy, enlighten him about the workings of fortune, free will, and providence.

The close association of colors and emotional states that structures the protagonist's initial journey in *La noche* is similar to the metamorphoses from bright to dark to bright that unify *Siervo*'s apparently unconnected sections, as Dolz noted ("El simbolismo de los colores"). *Siervo*'s first transformation takes place during the narrator's "dolorosa contemplaçión" before he enters hell. In the process, a *locus amoenus* is corrupted in a series of impossible mutations: the grass is burnt; perennial trees lose their leaves; and his "alazán" turns black. Dolz clarifies that *alazán* refers to a horse of a red, blonde, or cinnamon color ("El simbolismo de los colores" 120–21), and it may be a significant detail in this complex language of color. The lively miniatures that embellish *Livre du coeur* in Cod. Vid.2597 paint Heart's mount a rich reddish brown. *La noche*'s protagonist takes his quest on foot and wears no symbolic colors, but a comparable fluctuation of brilliance and obscurity defines the characters that personify love's contradictory moods. He examines them until his altercation with Yra, when he collapses, accidentally shattering his torch and almost quenching its flame. To this point, he has not directly considered his past; he was completely absorbed in the rhetorical colors and poetic conceits that reminded him of his sufferings. "I beseech you" —he implores Yra— "let not my memory recall things I cannot endure." Seeing his reflection in Amor's dazzling bright breasplate, he is another sad Boethius, scrutinizing himself in Orpheus's sad story. Critics of the *Roman de la Rose* note the narcissistic paradigm of falling in love with the image of a rosebud reflected on a fountain near the home of the God of Love. The fountain and mirror, Early explains, "typically evoke a visual process by which a male lover becomes enamored with the reflection" and "has a direct correlation to the acts of both writing and authorial doubling" (19). In Moner's narrative works, reflection betokens the lover's self-absorption —the protagonist sees *himself* on Amor's breastplate— and poetry's fictitious but strikingly beautiful *cobertura*.

Moner's concern with what he deems the lover's sin of idolatry is explicitly stated in *L'Ánima*. Its first-person account begins when the narrator feels on the verge of death, and a friend fails to assuage his pain. He leaves for the "nearby valley of St. Jerome of Hebron to hear that sound called an echo" (353) and spends a long time crying and moaning —and listening to its reverberation— in the middle of the night. Then he hears Oliver's voice, exhorting him to forsake his blinding love for the love of Jesus Christ, "for without charity virtuous deeds are dead."[149] The narrator explains the cause of his pain —unrequited love, death wish, consuming fire. Oliver feels sorry "for those few lovers who are like you because, as you yourself confess, they are idolaters" (360).[150] To lighten the burden of such miseries, Oliver encourages him to get "rid of the delight that sustains them, avoiding their causes —looks, thoughts, speech concerning the worth of your beloved, whether you are with her or not;" that is, he admonishes against love poetry. Those who fight such amorous battles, Oliver continues, "are demoralized and covered with shame and lead a miserable life; an exile, full of strange judgments of deranged minds; and, at the end, Hell is, without doubt, their everlasting reward" (363).[151] Oliver compares this state to a "shipwreck of freedom" and advises the protagonist "before the tempest to seek refuge in the secure port of the love of God, for we may enter that harbor whenever we wish, in any winds" (365).[152]

In *La noche*, the nautical reference comes from Desesperación, an old woman who, in lieu of a device, carries a piece of paper that she hands to the protagonist. In it, he sees a realistic painting of a boat in a tempest, its sails torn, about to "crash violently against a very high crag," enveloped by raging flames that "started on the stern from where the wind was blowing" (234).[153] The textual nature of the boat is emphasized by its material support and painterly image, but

---

[149] "Ab furia dresí los passos a la vall vesina de Sant Yerònim de Ebron per hoyr aquel son nomenat èchon, de qui ere cert que, sin·m me respongués, diguera lo que yo, y, sens fer-me contrari, ensempt ab mi se dolguera" (138–39) ... "Mes, pus creus bé en Jesuchrist, Déu y senyor nostra, ama'l per matex, que sens caritat les obres virtuoses són mortas" (142).

[150] "Mas dels pochs que són tals com tu, és de dolre, perquè tots son ydòlatres, com tu confesses" (147).

[151] "Axí que si vols destroir-los, lo delit que·ls sosté destruu, fugint a la causa sua, que és mirar, pensar, parlar, present y absent, en lo valer de la que amas. ... en aquesta guerra los que van avant són envergonyits y aminvats, y en vida miserable, bandeig de consell strany y destruccions de seny, y en fi, en infern paga eterna y certa" (149).

[152] "Axí que mira lo naufraig de la libertat ... Gran discreció és, donchs, ans de la fortuna, salvar-se en lo segur port de la amor de Déu, pus a tots vents y podem entrar, si volem, perquè sa Magestat inmensa tostemps nos acull, sy ajudam, ajundant-nos" (151–52).

[153] "Stava de dentro pintado: una nave en el mar con muy gran tormenta, el mastel y velas rompidas, y ella con furia para dar en una peña cortada, muy alta sin reparo; y por más desventura, muy gran fuego metido en la popa, por donde el viento venía" (133–35).

it comes into full focus when Desesperaçión illuminates, literally, the text of the protagonist's life by offering him the miniature for interpretation as a moral mirror. The narrator sees in it the foolish lover whose disordered desire steers him into Venus's stormy waters; he attempts to reject the reflection ("quise excusarme de lo que me culpaba") but finally admits that his will offers the same advice ("pero lo que me consejava era lo mismo que tenía en la voluntad" 137).

The transition from intellectual confusion to understanding is marked by the appearance of a wondrous woman ("una mujer de milagrosa manera" 149). Left in the dark with his broken torch, the protagonist manages to save the smallest piece, and its faint light guides him up another staiway where he stumbles into a familiar figure:

> Her eyes were so bright, like two big stars. She was much bigger than any woman, the proportions of her body so ideal that they conformed to the standards of beauty in every detail. On top of her long blond hair, she wore a gold crown, studded with many precious stones, shining so brightly that it was impossible to look at them. I saw no clothes on her, but she was enveloped in a very white cloud. (243–44)[154]

La noche's Razón is not Boethian Philosophy but scholastic Reason. Cocozzella comments that, like "the good Thomist that she is," she carries the protagonist from darkness to light (*Bilingual Poetics* 122). She takes command of the helm by reminding him of his *integumentum* and revealing the wisdom hidden "under a veil, by means of signs" (261). The fortress and its inhabitants cease to be chaotic figments of the imagination; Razón's exegesis refocuses them as the rhetorical colors that signal a different mood and direction, pointing the protagonist toward the ethical journey. He does not dismiss memories from his mind —"let what you have recalled up until now be enough," he tells Yra; "This I do not forget" (242)— but refashions their *intentio*. Against the deceits of the world symbolized by Amor —"the first and most important passion … a chain which

---

[154] "Y tenía los ojos tan claros como dos grandes estrellas. Era muy major que ninguna mujer, sus faysiones de proporción tan igual que no desmentían en nada de la mesura de beldad. Ensima sus cabellos, largos y ruvios, traýa una corona de oro, sembrada de muchas piedras presiosas que reluzían a no podellas mirar. No le vi otros vestidos sino que venia cubierta de una nuve muy blanca" (149–50).

binds all your operations" (249)—[155] Razón offers the shield of free will and a true "dyfinycion" of fortune.

Remarkably, she prefaces it with yet another lesson in textual interpretation:

> I come here to warn you about the deceptive nature of woman you see on this scaffold. Her name is Fortune. They say that her work is changing things. Men of the world complain a great deal about her, but they do not know her well. Many have written about her. Most attribute to her what she does not possess. If I told you the many saying of poets and philosophers concerning her I would be prolix. But I want to give you a brief and true definition, and if you bear it in mind, you will never feel toward her fear or affection, which would be harmful to you. (265)[156]

The definition itself is a crude summary of Boethian arguments on fate, fortune, and providence, developed in book IV, prose VI of *The Consolation*. Fortune, Razón instructs,

> when considered in itself, has no being. But if you ask what this word "fortune" means, I will reply that it is the secret of God's great and deep judgments of which we perceive only the effects. And since human nature, covered by the veil of ignorance, is inept at understanding them, it slips into the mistakes I have told you about, complaining of fortune, as if it had a will and a freedom of choice with which it could give to some and take away from others. And the truth is that they are complaining about God because there is no other cause for necessary and immutable effects —the best possible effect— except the will of God. (265–66)[157]

---

[155] "La primera passión y más principal ... una cadena que ata todas vuestras operaciones" (159–60).

[156] "Aquí te vengo avisar del engaño d'esta que vehes en el cadalso. Su nombre es Fortuna. Sus obras dizen que son mudanças. Los hombres del mundo lamentan mucho, y conosçenla poco. D'ella han muchos escrito. Los más le atribuyen lo que no es suyo. Ca si yo te dixiesse la diversidad de las sentencias de los poetas y philósophos sobre ella, sería prolixa. Mas quiérote dezir una dyfinyción breve y verdadera, la qual si presupones, jamás le havrás miedo ni amor que te dañe" (183).

[157] "Mas fortuna no tiene ningún ser si por sí la consideramos. Pero si buscas qué es lo que se significa debaxo d'este nombre 'fortuna," dígote que el secreto de los juyzios de Dios grandes y profundos, de los quales no alcançamos sino los effectos. Y porque la humana naturaleza con el velo de ygnoracia no abasta a compredelles desvara en los errores que te he dicho, quexándose de la fortuna, como si tuviesse voluntad y eleción con que diesse a los unos y quitasse a los otros. Y es cierto que de

Razón's words constitute the *contemptus mundi* that strives to display the truth behind appearances. In *L'Ánima*, that role is performed by Oliver's soul, which reminds the lover of his free will and rants against women. In *La noche*, after they visit the Hall of Fortune, Razón leads the protagonist to the Hall of Fame, introducing her as the other side of Fortune and "none the less unreliable" (267; "toda vez no es cyerta" 187). "Wisdom teaches," continues Razón, "that those who desire fame miss their aim through it itself because virtuous deeds take on their perfection from Charity, and they they will not have this virtue unless they direct their acts of intense and fervent love to God" (268–69).[158] Razón does not ask him to discard ardent love; she merely castigates its intent to stray from the rightful path ("desvían del hito"), a misdirection she attempts to *adreçar*, or reorient, by appealing to his free will.

Barutell's preface to the *editio princeps* of Moner's *obras* also assigns a significant role to volition. In his twin role as critic and biographer, his comments must not be underestimated, Cocozzella warns, as they point toward Moner's cultural and literary underpinnings (*Bilingual Poetics* 3). He relates Barutell's mention of Moner's "derecho juizio" to Baena's proemial definition of the outstanding poet as one endowed with wholesome and rightful judgment ("muy sano e derecho juyzio") but detects a substantial difference: while for Baena, the poet must be a lover who takes pride in pretending to be in love ("se preçie e se finja de ser enamorado"), Barutell stresses that Moner loved his lady so truly that we must excuse the frivolities that often accompany love affairs ("con tanta verdad, que basta para descargo de la liviendades que suelen traher los amores"). Cocozzella finds in Moner's disparagement of pretense in favor of truth, as Barutell's comment implies, the influence of Ausiàs March; specifically, his aesthetic principle of "*veritat* without *escalf*" [truth without excessive heat]. The new meaning assigned to the poet's "derecho juizio" is indebted to his contact with the Castilian *cancionero* poet Alfonso de Cartagena, whom he met during military service for Fernando the Catholic (*Bilingual Poetics* 3–25). What interests me most in Cocozzella's analysis is his definition of "derecho juizio," whose special bond with truth he relates to Boethius's *Consolation*:

Dios se quexan porque no ay otra causa salvo la voluntad de Dios a ciertos y inmutables fines, los mejores que pueden ser" (184).

[158] "Cuyas reglas [de la Sabiduría] son que los que fama desean por ella misma desvían del hito porque las obras virtuosas toman la perfición de la Caridad, de la qual careçen si no adreçan sus autos del amor a Dios intenço y herviente" (189).

On the one hand, *juizio* underscores the cognitive faculty of reason and the ratiocinating powers of the intellect; on the other
hand, *derecho* has to do, etymologically, with straight direction,
and, thus, spells out the efficacy of reason in leading the individual —specifically the poet's persona— toward the contemplation
of the Divine Being, whose prime epiphany in Moner's thought is
precisely Truth or, less frequently, the Supreme Good. (*Bilingual
Poetics* 8)

What Barutell had in mind when speaking of Moner's *juicio* may
be surmised from the Saplana-Ginebreda exposition of *The Consolation*'s book IV, meter II ("et incipit 'Puro clarum lumine'"). The
commentary interprets the poem to signify that the clarity of divine
understanding outshines the natural sun ("el entendimiento divinal
sin toda comparación es más claro que el sol natural") and expatiates
on the four types of knowledge available to men and women according to their free will ("franco arbitrio o franca voluntad, más propiamente fablando, franco juyzio"), which is influenced by human
desire ("la dicha franqueza de juyzio sea en diversas maneras en las
criaturas según que dessean"). The highest degree of contemplation
is available only to men of learning who, by rejecting the world, are
able to launch their intellect toward God.[159] A more imperfect understanding is granted to the virtuous, who must remain engaged in
the temporal needs of others.[160] Those who *imagine* and *desire* what
pleases the body belong to an inferior stage of chaotic uncertainty,
barely saved by shame from complete ignorance.[161] Bestial irrational-

---

[159] "La primera e la más excelente e soberana de la dicha franqueza es quando
el ombre se da a conoscer e a contemplar las cosas divinales desmamparando tanto
quanto puede las cosas terrenales e a lançar el su pensamiento en alto contra Dios.
Este grado es llamado por los philósofos entendimiento ganado, ca por el su estudio
e por el su ingenio lo ganan los que han tal entendimiento, e han ganada la cosa que
es propia al entendimiento, ca su obra propia es entender las cosas celestiales de su
poder" (Se1).
   [160] "La segunda manera es de los que biven teniendo vida activa, e ya sea que
buena vida e virtuosa, empero hanse mucho de ocupar en las cosas temporales e sen-
sibles, las quales son ordenadas a necessidad de su vida e de los otros. E por tal como
se abaxan de la franqueza del entendimiento e no son tan francos como los primeros,
e por esto tal entendimiento es dicho alivianado, ca aliviánase de la propia franqueza
e abáxase a las cosas terrenales" (Se1).
   [161] "La tercera manera es de los que no tan solamente se alivianan aviendo pensamiento de las cosas terrenales que son necessarias a la vida, antes aun ymaginan e
después dessean e después consienten las cosas que son plazientes a las partes del
su cuerpo, por que offrescen las sus ánimas a algunos peccados e por esta razón han
muchos malos pensamientos. Empero non se dexan vencer del todo que lo culpan

ity, the fourth type, is the consequence of fleshly desires imprisoning the will.[162]

Barutell's qualification of Moner's *juizio* as *derecho* alludes to Augustine's *recta voluntas* and the Boethian straightening of the strong emotions that color memories and the process of continuous study that transforms mad Orpheus into wise Tiresias. However, contrary to Saplana-Ginebreda's Dominican intellectualism, *La noche* problematizes rationality from Razón's very first appearance. The protagonist sees her covered by a dazzling white cloud, which, according to Cocozzella, alludes to "the mist that beclouds the beholder's eyes in *De consolatione*" (*Bilingual Poetics* 86). However, Boethian Philosophy comes to clear the mist from the prisoner's eyes; she is not obscured by it; and she guides him until the end of his journey. Here, Razón disappears with Prudence when the protagonist is about to reach the top of the keep. As he struggles to enter the turret where the theological virtues of Faith, Hope, and Charity guard Truth, an eagle grabs him, lofts him, and lets him drop.

Attempting to explain this unexpected fall, Cocozzella notes the contrast between Razón and the personification of Cuydado [Care]. In the eagle's grasp, the protagonist complains to Care, which morphs into a frightening skeleton. Care and Reason represent the two complementary sides of cognition, "the conscious and the unconscious, order and chaos, perfectibility and utter perdition, hope and despair, optimism and pessimism." The eagle functions as an emissary of the order ruled by Divine Providence and illustrates the fallibility of reason (*Bilingual Poetics* 118–22, 127).

Clerical tradition supports a more precise interpretation of *La noche*'s eagle as an embodiment of the rational appetite that Razón's beneficial teachings elicit in the protagonist, transforming his infatuation —Desseo's dark wings— into a faculty of the soul: the will to know. An eagle's keen vision and high flight were allegorized in medieval expositions as the height of reason and the act of contempla-

---

por obra, ca algunos se abstienen por vergüença de Dios e de hombres, e otros por miedo de Dios [46r] e de gentes, otros por diversas razones. Éstos, ya sea que no lo cumplan por obra, esto es que fazen el pecado en pensar e desear, empero no fazen su poder de alcançar ni ganar las joyas de virtud, mas la su vida es turbada e pensosa; e por esto el su entendimiento es dicho atado por el cuerpo" (Se1).

[162] "La quarta manera es de las personas que se dan a pecados, en las quales no tan solamente es mengua de su propia voluntad, mas aun fecha cativa, e la han perdida por su culpa, e biven más bestialmente que humanal e han cativado el su entendimiento e sometido a la propia carne" (Se1).

tion, and, along the same line, the myth of Ganymede was expounded in Berchorius's *Ovidius moralizatus* as a contemplative symbol.[163]
The *Comedy* commentator Jacopo della Lana interprets the image of
a soaring eagle that appears in Canto IX of *Purgatorio* as the intellect, and Chaucer implicitly associates it with Boethian Philosophy in
the *House of Fame*, "fusing two familiar symbols of contemplation"
(Steadman 158–59). Leyerle also notes that eagles carved in brass
or wood, symbolizing Saint John, were such prevalent ornaments in
reading stands that Du Cange's *Glossarium* lists *lectern* as one meaning of the term *aquila* (Leyerle 253).

   Moner's misgivings about human reason must be framed within
Franciscan voluntarism. I mentioned the order's pervasive political
and cultural pull in the Crown of Aragon, and its sway was no less
encompassing in Castile. Darbord's classic study noted how devotional poetry composed at the court of the Catholic Monarchs was
deeply influenced by Franciscan meditation, and Dolz aptly demonstrated its narrative impact in explaining *Siervo*'s Sindéresis.[164] Summarized in Saint Bonaventure's *Itinerarium mentis ad Deum*, it prepares the soul for divine grace by first examining the facts available
to the senses in order to tear the veil of the flesh. It then searches for
God in nature, a mirror that preserves his trace (*vestigia*) without
awareness of it. Finally, it explores the interior of one's soul, created
in God's image.[165] Philosophic speculation gives way to mysticism in
the restoration of the divine image made possible by the theological
virtues (Darbord 20).

   La noche elucidates the divergence of intellectual and affective
perception by emphasizing the volitional aspects of consciousness.
The platonic orientation of Boethius's *Consolation* poses the body as
an obstacle to seeing the divine, which is the goal of human existence,
according to Augustine. To the contrary, Franciscan theologians

> gave a new expression to the Dionysian account of how eros-driv-
> en intellect surpasses and folds its own power in the supra-intel-

---

[163] See Steadman's "Chaucer's Eagle" for the full exposition of the eagle's medieval interpretations that I summarize here. Other remarks focusing on Chaucer
appear in Leyerle's "Chaucer's Windy Eagle."
    [164] Dolz explains in detail the connection pointed out by Cátedra (*Amor y peda-
gogía*). Cortijo Ocaña insists on that connection when comparing the phenomenology of love in *Siervo* and Boncompagno da Signa's treatise on friendship, *De amicitia*
("'De amicitia'").
    [165] Saint John of the Cross (1542–1591) details the process in his poetry of divine
love.

lectual union with God. According to these theologians, at the
highest stages of the mystical ascent, *affectus* and the associated
spiritual senses of touch and taste supersede and in some ways
subsume *intellectus* and the associated spiritual sense of sight thus
suggesting the notion of affective cognition. (Gavrilyuk and Coakley 15)

La noche's strong emphasis on vision and emotions derives from
the old inventive tecnhique of using rhetorical ornament, either
verbal or pictorial, to signal mood. It also points to Franciscan affective spirituality and devotion. Razón succeeds in transforming
Costumbre's natural inclination toward material needs into rational
appetite, but in searching for truth, the intellect must abstract the
species from the image produced by fantasy, and, as a consequence,
"individual reality is known only by reflection" (O'Donnell 401). Poetry is a confusing reflection, as illustrated by the mirror that Desesperaçión holds to the protagonist's face. He watches himself inside
the floundering boat, both as a lover and a poet, setting sail "en les
baixes antenes," as Roís de Corella defined "vulgar poesia." Allegorical personifications are also confusing reflections —the paradox that
another personification critiques Fortune's classical images is not
lost on Moner— and *La noche* underlines the impossibility of the
intellectual mirror reflecting truth and speculation's flight reaching
the mystical encounter. Instead, it repeatedly urges the protagonist
to direct his erotic appetite to emotional identification and affective
cognition.

A different kind of empathy is asked from the unnamed "Illustrious Lady" ("Egregia Señora") to whom *La noche* is addressed.
The 1528 edition identifies her as Joana de Cardona, adding that she
was Duchess of Nájera at the time of the printing.[166] As the daughter
of his patron, she offered Moner a thrifty dedication opportunity;
he might simply have praised her lineage, but his encomium of the
lady's virtues recalls both Amor's ecphrasis and Razón's personification in a disquieting counterpoint to my interpretation —and Cocozzella's— of the protagonist's philosophical and spiritual quest.

Joana's soul is clad with a beauty embroidered in gold, and her
virtuous life is the paradigm for those of her state. Her moral radiance both blinds Moner and guides his writing, ultimately left to her
to complete:

---

[166] "[Q]ue oy es Duquesa de Najera" (Cocozzella, *The Two Major* 67–68, 68n1).

These virtues possessed by Your Ladyship blind me, if I, presuming to praise them, look at them; but if I lower my eyes I find those virtues guide me just like the sun. Under the tutelage of your virtues I venture to write to Your Ladyship of an event which I cannot keep secret. And since in all things the intention gives perfection, I beg your Ladyship to finish this little work so long as you tell me that you forgive me. This would make me happy just as I would grieve if you were to deny me such a favor. (206)[167]

Is this dedication proof of Moner's fateful love affair? Did Joana cause him to enter the Franciscan Observance in his late twenties? Is she the crisis that Barutell mentions in his biography, *la belle dame sans merci* whose wit was "so sublime and so keen that it disdains more by nature than by artifice" (205)?[168] If so, what is the point of *La noche*'s elaborate construct?

In a previous article, I related the practice of patrons who asked to be depicted within the devotional paintings they commissioned to the economy of dedication and the *topica* of the *exordium* ("Reimagining"). Cultural historian Roger Chartier explains that the dedication does not simply represent an exchange between author and patron; "it is also a figure by means of which the prince seems himself praised as the primordial inspiration and the first author of the book that is being presented to him, as if the writer or the scholar were offering him a work that was in fact his own" (42). Religious paintings often encourage affective identification by setting the devotional scene against the local landscape of the donor's place of residence. In *La noche*, Moner exploits both conventions. The allegorical account begins on a precise Tuesday, after the Count and Countess, Joana's parents, "left Torá for Terroja," and the protagonist "had to remain in the house of their Lordships' two days." The place is obviously familiar to both correspondents.[169] The whole allegorical journey that

---

[167] "Estas gracias en Vuestra Señoría, si con presunpción de alaballa las miro, me ciegan; pero si baxo los ojos, bien como el sol hallo que me guían; en cuyo favor m'atrevo a escrevir a Vuestra Señoría un caso que encubrir no puedo. Y porque en todas las cosas el fin de la perfeción, la suplico acabe esta obresilla con tal que digo que me perdona, y haráme tan alegre como quedaría arrepentido si tal mercé me negasse" (72).

[168] "[E]ntendimiento tan alto y tan limplio que de su natural más es lo que desdeña que lo que por artificio podría faltarle" (72).

[169] "El llunes que los muy illustres Señores —el Conde y la Condeça, mys Señores— partieron de Torá para Teroja, tuve de quedar en casa de su Señoría dos días. Y como por la susencia de tales y tantos me pareciesse la vida robada, el seguiente día, martes, poco antes de que anochessiesse, sallíme por la puerta" (73–75).

follows is presented as part of the letter to the unnamed Joana, and he addresses her repeatedly as he meanders through the allegorical fortress. However, this strategy prevents her contemplative empathy; she remains a distant observer of the contrite protagonist's travails, not a participant.

According to the game of mirrors that Boethian interpretation of the Orphic myth suggested, fruitfully appropriated by Franciscan meditation on the life of Christ, penitential fictions encourage male readers to fully identify with the sufferings of their main actors. In *L'Ánima*, addressed to Moner's cousin, Mossén Francesch de Blanes, the journey begins in an equally familar landscape, "the nearby Valley of Saint Jerome of Hebron" (353), but the narration proceeds without further reference to the addressee until the end, prompting its reader to empathize with the protagonist and his desire for enlightment. In contrast, *La noche* accentuates the proemial convention of the patron as source of inspiration; the dazzling clarity of her virtues and her role as *mediatrix* of poetic inspiration cast Joana in terms very close to Dante's Beatrice or Petrarch's "Vergine bella, che di sol vestita." Perhaps *La noche* is a convoluted gloss on *Vita nuova*'s last poem, "Oltre la spera che più larga gira," where, as Dante explains in the commentary, the thought is a pilgrim who raises to the spiritual contemplation of a lady he cannot comprehend because his intellect fails him like a feeble eye staring at the sun ("come l'occhio debole a lo sole" Dante 116). Rather than building a claim for *Vita nuova* as a direct source, more likely we are dealing with a *cancionero* cliché. Joana, unlike Beatrice, was alive and well, and the intellect's failure to reach understanding may represent a more mundane request for carnal knowledge, once sight failed its mission.

Did Moner erect this elaborate apparatus only to claim his service in the religion of courtly love, as an ostentatious celebration of the beloved, or a plea of sexual *gloria*? Was Joana supposed to imagine herself atop the fortress's keep as the source of grace, poetic inspiration, and —God willing— sensual pleasure? Whinnom's classic study on the erotic wordplay of *cancioneros* (*La poesía amatoria*) points in this direction as does Cátedra's analysis of the Aristotelian naturalism that pervades it (*Amor y pedagogía*). Lacking better aristocratic credentials, Moner proudly displays the feathers of his extensive learning for his lady's benefit in exchange for a spark of her very human grace. Without any record of the lady's response, we may only speculate whether she understood *La noche* as a compliment, as MacPherson reads erotic puns ("Secret Language"), or just rolled her eyes at such a self-congratulatory parade of male learning.

Ingenious as any *cancionero* poet worth his salt, Moner does offer a choice to the lady's "entendimiento." To perfect its intention, she may read *La noche* as either her own courtly celebration or a recantation of the author's misdirected devotion for which he seems to apologize. At no point does he extend to her the option he offered his cousin —occupying a male contemplative *locus*. The lady, like God, is a silent spectator.

CHAPTER 3

ORPHEUS IN HELL: CONTRAFACTA AND *NOVELNESS*

A FRIEND at court differs greatly from a friend at school. Fernández de Madrigal's *Libro de amor y amicicia* calls attention to the
dangers of seeking camaraderie in a place characterized by intrigue
and dissemblance:

> And because seeking friends must not be done lightly but with
> great care and diligence, it is not advisable to look for a friend in
> the palace where all put on display a friendly heart but few have
> it; it is more appropriate seeking a friend with care and diligence
> where he can be found. So says Seneca in the *Epistles* book 1,
> 3: "Errs he who seeks the friend in the palace and tests him in
> the banquet because very few in these places show a friendly
> heart."[1]

However, both noblemen and bureaucrats were "nourished"
from early childhood at patrician courts and royal palaces, as Metge
fondly remembers. Trained in the rhetorical and moral constraints of
pietas litterata, young men formed close circles and composed poe-

---

[1] "Et porque el buscar de los amjgos non ha de seer ligero mas con grande cujdado & diligençia non conujene que alguno busque amjgo en el palaçio onde todos
muestran coraçon de amjgos et muy pocos lo tienen mas ende es buscar el amjgo
onde avnque con grande cujdado et diligençia se pueda fallar. De esto dize Seneca
en el primero libro de las Epistolas en la epistola terçera: yerra quien busca el amjgo
en el palaçio & lo prueua en el conujte ca en estos logares muy pocos son que non
muestren coraçon de amjgos" (fol. 23v–24r). As Heusch points out, the quotation is
not from Seneca but appears in Luca Manelli's *Tabula et expositio Senecae*, translated
and glossed by Alonso de Cartagena (*La philosophie* 340n63).

try. In his introduction to *Poesía cortesana (Siglo XV)*, Beltran offers a significant piece of evidence by a poet at the Isabelline court. Pedro de Gratia Dei describes a scene of courtly instruction ("docencia cortesana"):

> Entré [en] una sala do vi enseñar
> todos los pages a un grand maestro
> porque fuese cada uno diestro
> de ser enseñado y saber enseñar
> en leer, escribir, tañer y cantar,
> danzar y nadar, luchar, esgrimir
> arco e ballesta,
> llatinar y dezir,
> xedrez y pelota saber bien jugar. (xx)

> I entered a hall where I saw a master teaching all the pages so that each would be capable of learning and teaching the following skills: reading, writing, playing an instrument and singing, dancing and swimming, fighting, wielding bow and crossbow, reading and writing in Latin (*llatinar*), poetizing, being equally skilled at playing chess and playing ball.

As Beltran points out, in these halls, composing verses so easily dismissed as occasional ("poesía de circunstancias"), courtiers learned the art of poetry, which was so tightly bound to social standing ("inseparable de cualquier intento de distinción social" xxi). Powerful aristocrats, like Santillana, also commissioned the translations of old and new classics as a way to increase their prestige, while for individuals of more humble origins, poetry was a means of social legitimation. This paradigm may be extended to the great Aragonese cities, where wealthy merchants and oligarchies gathered to imitate courtly customs.[2] *Cancionero/cançoner* poetry, which deals with love *and* doctrinal topics, is fundamentally a speech genre, not only because it was meant to be delivered orally, but because it stresses ideological difference —the defense of, or attack on, women as a sign of courtliness or clerisy, respectively— or variance in power and knowledge —the whole genre of *preguntas* and *respuestas,* where *caballeros sçientes* displayed their learning to wrestle influence away

---

[2] Pérez Bosch comments, citing Martín de Riquer, that for the Valencian *tertulias* of Bernat Fenollar, poetry is a form of dialogue among friends (*Los valencianos* 51).

from the professional class. In chapter 2, we saw that, as poets aged, they morphed from Orpheus to Tiresias, intoning wisdom by commenting, like Dante, on their past experience in love and literature.

By the midfifteenth century, a hybrid form emerges, a mixture of voices and registers that alters the triangular balance of consolation. Its fictional mechanisms are those of penitential consolations adapted to the rhetorical environment of an author in love within a courtly setting. Like the penitential genre, it is articulated around male friendship, but women intervene as fictional addressees and characters with a distinctive voice. I call these fictions sentimental because they bear penitential generic markers —first-person narrative, dream vision, *altercatio* between Reason and Will— but, following the path broken by *Lo somni*, they exploit the lover's reluctance to accept a soothing moral balm when his flaw, innate desire, causes his downfall. Their deliberate rejection of conversion drives the plot. The triumph of erotic desire transforms sentimental heroes into madmen and explores the possibilities of the imagination. Orpheus enters Hell and refuses to leave; Boethius settles in with the common strumpets. The new genre suits the masculine courtly subject, a *vir geminus*, as Weiss labels it, "structured by a rhetoric of display and dissimulation" ("¿Qué demandamos?" 248).

The examples we will consider include Pedro de Portugal's *Sátira de infelice e felice vida* (c. 1453); *Triste deleytaçión* (c. 1458–1467), composed by the enigmatic F.A.D.C.; Francesc Alegre's *Somni* (c. 1475) and *Rehonament* (c. 1472–1486); and three canonical works: Diego de San Pedro's *Arnalte y Lucenda* and *Cárcel de Amor* and Juan de Flores's *Grimalte y Gradisa*, all published in the last decade of the fifteenth century but probably composed around the same time as Alegre's pieces. Pedro de Portugal was a contemporary of Rodríguez del Padrón with whom, Folger rightly notes, he shared reading habits (*Images in Mind* 134). He was the addressee of Santillana's *Proemio e carta*, and his glossing activity has much in common with the intellectual pursuits of his older friend's clique, of which he was a member. The dissonances of his *Sátira* express the birth pangs attendant on bearing the consolatory genre into the rhetorical environment of court.

Triste deleytaçión and the two short pieces by Alegre offer new perspectives on the canonical works of Flores and San Pedro. They were composed during roughly the last thirty years of the century, when the Catalan sentimental fad studied by Pellisa Prades was in flower. Bringing them into the discussion, along with Torroella's activity as *magister amoris*, highlights the cultural continuity of the Aragonese and Castilian courts. I shall refer to other texts with sentimental content but not visionary form that delineate the genre's boundaries and cultural environment, also discussing the logic of allegorical gaze and contemplative lay practices.

PEDRO DE PORTUGAL'S *NOVELAR DESINTERESADO*

Pedro, *Condestável* de Portugal, (1429–1466), was related by blood to the ruling houses of Portugal, Castile, and Aragon and deeply entangled in their dynastic disputes. *Sátira* was first composed in Portuguese around 1445 and 1449, but after 1453, Pedro decided to translate it into the language of Castile, where he spent seven years in exile.[3] The final Castilian version is the first-person dream vision of a tormented lover to which the author adds many lengthy glosses and a prefatory letter dedicating it to Queen Isabel of Portugal, his sister.[4] Montero deduces from her analysis of Portuguese chronicles and historical documents that *Sátira* was intended for both Castilian and Portuguese audiences, but the close familial ties among the courts of the peninsular Christian kingdoms make it more apt to speak of an aristocratic audience ("Imagen femenina").

Critics spotted *Sátira*'s similarities with, and intertextual references to, *Siervo*,[5] and Folger, who deems Pedro *Siervo*'s "earliest known reader," infers from them that he "expected his readers to be familiar" with it (*Images in Mind* 137). Serés calls attention to *Sátira*'s dictaminal background and demonstrates the glosses' debt to Fernández de Madrigal's *Las diez qüestiones vulgares*, which safely dates *Sátira*'s composition after 1453, when Fernández de Madrigal declared he was at work on his mythological treatise ("Don Pedro;" "La llamada; "Estudio introductorio"). Serés concludes that while Pedro cannot be conclusively identified, the "cavallero" who requested Fernández

---

   [3] On Pedro's life, see Gascón Vera.
   [4] A description of Mss. M (BNE 4023) and B (in a private collection) is found in Fonseca (x–xiv). Hawkins adds to them a review of Ms. L housed at the Museu Nacional de Arqueologia in Lisbon (76–87).
   [5] Castro Lingl, for instance, understands *Sátira* as a commentary that answers many questions *Siervo* leaves open ("The Constable" 78). See also Krause (*La novela*), Lida de Malkiel ("La tradición clásica"), Gerli ("Toward a Poetics"), Folger (*Images in Mind*), and Montero ("Imagen femenina").

de Madrigal's work, it was commissioned by someone in Santillana's circle ("Don Pedro" 978). Serés also qualifies Pedro's erudition as the bookishness typical of courtly dilettanti, lettered, but with limited knowledge of Latin, so they depended on vernacular *compendia* to enhance their writings ("La elegía" 982).

Pedro's liberal pilfering from the Salamanca professor's tract is a consequence, no doubt, of the practice of glossing so common to Santillana and his well-read friends. As we saw in chapter 2, the Castilian translation of Bruni's *Vite di Dante e del Petrarca*, housed in Santillana's magnificent library, holds that a poet should embellish his verse with the wisdom found in *los estudios*. Villena amply annotated his translation of Virgil's *Aeneid* under the trite pretext that the poem was obscure. Juan de Mena adduced the same reasons in adding a long commentary to his own poem, *La coronación del Marqués de Santillana*. He felt the need for no less than four preambles to showcase his command of literary theory, expounding on the nature of tragedy, comedy, and satire. His combination of poem and gloss is an instance of *tractado* whose moral purpose —"la voluntad del tractante" recording the misery of the wicked and the glory of the virtuous— aligns *La coronación* with satire.[6] Santillana himself, in his *Proverbios*, a collection of traditional moral maxims composed in 1437 at the request of Juan II for the edification of his son, the future Enrique IV of Castile, passionately defends the *caballero sçiente* by presenting learned display ("sçiencia") as an attribute that, contrary to clerical charges, does not blunt the sword's blade nor put a damper on the knightly hand (*Obras* 218–19).

In *Sátira*'s prefatory letter, Pedro offers "el primero fruto de mis estudios," the first harvest of his learning, to his sister Isabel de Portugal. The letter boasts of the joyful intellectual urge that motivated the glosses ("tanto mi mano con mayor gozo escrebía, e con mayor afección e estudio" 77), resorting to the binary slogan of the vernacular poet, "affección e estudio."[7] The glosses' drive to supersede the text is analogous to Villena's commentary on the *Aeneid* as reflected in one of its manuscript witnesses (see fig. 2).

---

    [6] "E aqueste nombre [i.e. calamicleos] da a entender que en el presente tractado la voluntad del tractante fue de escribir de aquestos dos fines, es a saber de la miserios de los malos e de la gloria de los buenos" (107). See Weiss for an insightful explanation of *La coronación*'s satirical intent in its ethical context ("Juan de Mena's").
    [7] I cite from Serés's 2008 edition.

Figure 2. Translation of the *Aeneid*, Enrique de Villena. Biblioteca Nacional de España, Mss/17975, fol. 157v. The translation becomes progressively dwarfed by commentary.

In *Sátira*'s three extant witnesses, the dream vision occupies the center of the page, surrounded by glosses that constantly threaten to engulf it (see fig. 3). To the modern reader, *Sátira*'s glosses may feel like useless appendages. Paz y Meliá excluded them from his 1892 edition, but Lida de Malkiel's remarkable intuition saw them as "novelar desinteresado," a lavish, unrestrained, undisciplined abandonment to novelizing. Later editions —Fonseca and Serés—

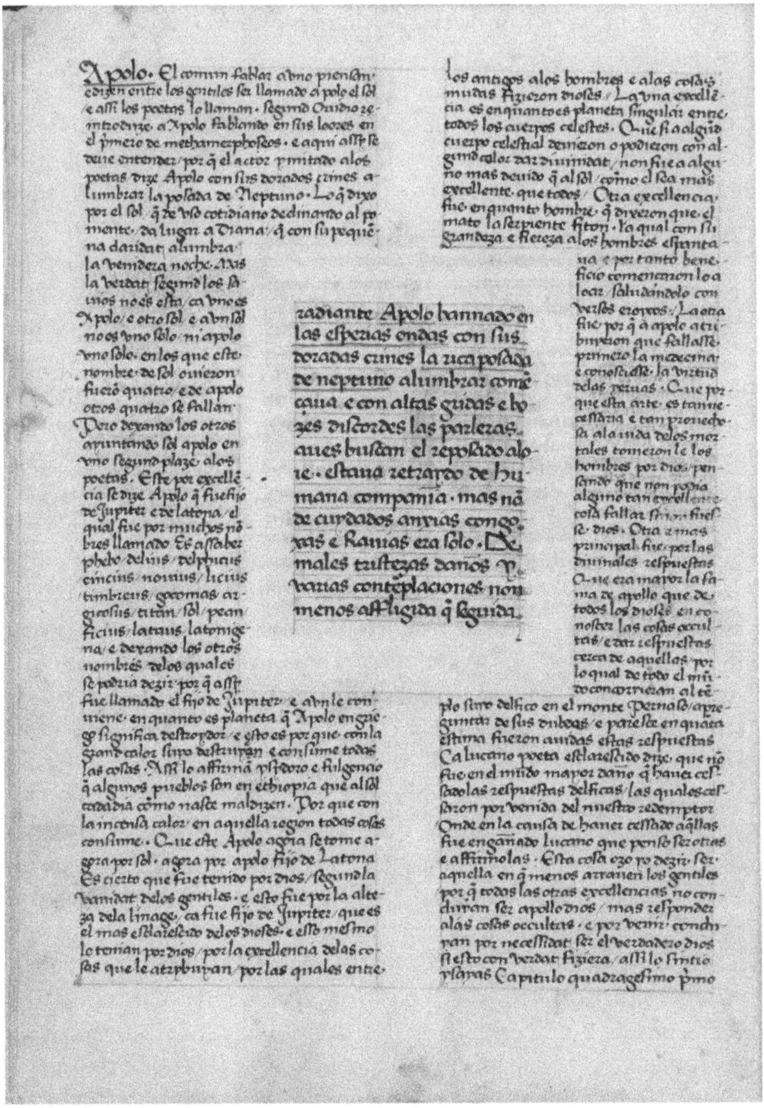

Figure 3. *Sátira de infelice e felice vida*. Pedro, Constable of Portugal. Biblioteca Nacional de España, Mss/4023, fol. 5v. Glosses engulf the text.

include the glosses, but as Hawkins rightly complains in her unpublished dissertation, the typographical constraints imposed by book printing utterly transform *Sátira*'s understanding; text and glosses appear to merge on the page, disorienting the reader (9). Hawkins's edition —a transcription of Ms. *M* with a *collatio* of Ms. *L*— solves this problem, which afflicts all contemporary editions of glossed manuscripts.[8]

Weiss (*The Poet's Art*; "Las 'fermosas'") was the first to pay sustained critical attention to the glosses' decidedly narrative character. In comparing the autobiographical standpoint of the desolate lover and the glosses' third-person voice, Lakarra noticed many instances when the glosses switch to the first person and identify with the lover, eliding their distance ("Los discursos"). The courtly and scientific discourses that Lakarra associates with those two voices are, Serés claims, impeccably interwoven: the glosses' scholarly voice authorizes the love narrative, whose protagonist, or actor, is the glosses' unifying thread ("Estudio introductorio" 17). The tension between the two may be clarified by considering *sátira*, the rhetorical exercise that Pedro chooses for the title, in its dictaminal context. Pedro's contemporaries, explains Serés, understood the term as praise (*laus*) of virtues and condemnation (*vituperium*) of vices, and he cites as evidence Santillana's *Carta a doña Violante de Prades*, Villena's *Doce trabajos de Hércules*, and Diego de Valera's *Tratado en defensa de las virtuosas mugeres* [Treatise in Defense of Virtuous Women]. Pedro vituperates against his sad life, *infelice vida*, while extolling his lady's happy existence, or *felice vida* (*Sátira* 22–25). While Serés is on the right track, and Mena's four prefaces to *La coronación* support his interpretation, Villena's use of the term in *Doce trabajos* has a subtler connection with *Sátira*'s peculiar structure.

Dictaminal theory classed both tragedy and satire as historical narratives with exemplary aims, but tragedy conceals its message under a poetic veil, while satire strips poetic myths to reveal the naked truth. Hence, Villena claims that his treatise on the labors of Hercules is a satire of the story told by tragic poets.[9] Drawing on a similar *tractandi* practice, Pedro digs out from the tragedy of a young male lover's misery a universal truth: his lady's excellence as synecdoche for womankind's. The lover's age, an adolescent between the ages of 14 and 16, positions *Sátira*'s narrative in its proper rhetorical environment: the infatuated poet in opposition to the discourse *in mulieres* of aged moralists. Diego de Valera, whom Serés mentions as a source of Pedro's understanding of satire, wrote that its courtly use

---

   [8]   See, for instance, Cátedra's 1994 edition of Villena's translation of, and commentary on, the *Aeneid*. Hawkins's edition is part of her dissertation and is available online.
   [9]   See chapter 1: 82.

involves "praising the virtues of noblewomen and denigrating the vicious nature of those who slander all of them, ignoring the difference between light and darkness."[10] The lover's account begins with the intellectual agitation that precedes any dream vision. He is alone ("retraído de humana compañía"), mulling over his melancholy life ("mas non de cuidados, anxias, congoxas e rabias era solo; de males, tristezas, daños e varias contemplaciones no menos afligida que seguida veía la triste vida mía" 84). He pedantically mythologizes the sunset as "the hour when radiant Apollo, bathed in the Hesperides's waves, with his golden mane, began to illumine Neptune's rich dwelling."[11] As in all dream visions, his restlessness is a consequence of both love's toxicity and a memorial recollection demonstrated by these mythological references and allusions to famous men harmed by Fortune's turns (Nero, Aníbal, Sila). Like Santillana at the beginning of *El sueño*, this lover is reading the classics. He seems to be investigating the courtly view of the debate about Woman: "How or why did fate determine that you [Fortune] inhabit the best woman in the universe?" ("¿Cómo o por qué quisieron los fados que tú habitases en la mejor del universo?" 93). Tears help with memorial work toward an answer and quiet the senses:

> In such state, I spoke at times, other times I was in silence, other times I remembered how miserable my life was —more than Cain's. My senses already benumbed, my mind and understanding tired of those continuous torments reprimanded my free will, which wanted my misfortune and eventual downfall.[12]

The lover is not asleep, but his senses are benumbed ("enmortecidos"), initiating a vision: Discreción, as both rhetorical decorum

---

[10] "[S]e refiere en loar virtudes de las nobles mugeres e denostar la viciosa condición de aquellos que de todas generalmente maldicen, no sabiendo faser diferencia entre la lus e las tiniebras" (qtd. in Serés, "Estudio introductorio" 24). On the connection between epideictic rhetoric, poetic slander at court, and authorship, see Gómez-Bravo (*Textual Agencies*).

[11] "[A] la hora que el radiante Apolo, bañado en las esperias ondas, con sus doradas crines, la rica posada de Neptuno alumbrar començava" (81 and 84). The odd pagination in this edition is due to placement of the glosses immediately after the term they comment on, so part of this short quote appears on p. 81 and part on p. 84 with the gloss on Apollo on pp. 82–83.

[12] "Así estando, a horas fablaba, a horas callaba, a horas redusía a la memoria cómo, con gran esparsimiento de mis lágrimas, mi vida más triste que fue la de Caín pasaba. Ya mis sentidos enmortecidos, ya mi seso, ya mi entendimiento, cansando de tan continuos males, me reprehender mi libre voluntad en contra de cuantos viven, deseaba mi mal e mi final perdimiento" (93–94).

and sound judgment, who has been wearing a blindfold for five years, reminds him about famous lovers and encourages him to fight his will: "Fight, fight against your will, I tell you yet again, fight, and not against someone else but against yourself" ("¡Pelea, pelea con tu voluntad e, otra ves te digo, pelea, e non con otro, sinon contigo mesmo!" 98). Following her advice, he returns to a *competens silentium* ("pensoso silencio"), the disciplined cognitive activity of meditation, although in it, he is riding a horse through steep, icy mountains. He remembers his love captivity *and* his readings to compare this passage to that of sailors who, attracted by the sirens' sweet songs, neglect their ship and wreck in a drunken stupor.[13] He finally arrives at a grove, where he encounters the theological and cardinal virtues, who come, not to save him from his infatuation, but to extol the lady's beauty and moral excellence. First, Prudencia, distinguishing right from wrong, delivers an "oración" (139) mustering the trite catalog of classical goddesses and legendary and biblical heroines in defense of women. Most of the examples died defending their virginity or chastity. As Montero points out, the ethical discourse centers on the practice of specifically feminine virtues, illustrated by women who stoically accepted martyrdom and death, and fits within the parameters of the defense of women ("'¿Durmiendo con el enemigo?'").

Prudencia closes her argument by mentioning "the three paths through which this our perfect lady follows her journey toward the Empyrean Heaven" ("fablaré de aquellas tres sendas, por las cuales fasta el empíreo cielo aquesta toda perfecta señora nuestra sigue su viaje" 149). Given *Sátira*'s references to *Siervo* and its author's familiarity with Fernández de Madrigal's work, we would expect the paths to correspond to friendship, love, and contemplative life, but the academic sources of comfort against life's perils —the enjoyment of friendship and intellectual speculation— are not within the lady's reach; her only consolation is the pursuit of the theological virtues: charity, faith, and hope.

The protagonist remains unmoved. Piedad [Compassion] makes the last attempt to exculpate the lady. "Do not blame her," she admonishes, "but complain instead to your own will which took you into captivity, turning a free man into a lifelong prisoner" ("quéxate

---

[13] "Tal parecía como los navegantes por la mar de las Serenas, que oyendo el dulce e melodioso canto de aquéllas, desamparado todo el gobierno de sus naos, embriagados e adormescidos, allí fallan la su postrimería" (100)

contra tu voluntad, que, de libre, captivo e perpetuo prisionero te fizo" 174). Like her colleagues, Piedad fails. *Sátira*'s narrative concludes with the prisoner cursing the day he fell in love and proclaiming his perseverance. He composes a love letter in verse, restating his desire for mercy, and, in a Joban mood, accepts the enduring torment of the lady's loveliness and great worth:

> I beg you to read the following couplets that I shall compose without leaving this solitary place, and fulfill my honest and licit request. I shall take it as a sign of your favor and compensation for my unremitting desire, unrequited longing, and pestilential suffering, which I patiently suffer for your great beauty and no lesser virtue.[14]

After the couplets, night finds the protagonist with the color drained from his face, staring at a sword in his right hand.

Folger explains that from a Lacanian perspective, fantasizing over a desired female body "effects a masculinized speaking 'I'," while the symptoms of *amor hereos* —weakness, lack of sound judgment— "effects a gradual loss of masculinity which menaces the culturally sanctioned gender hierarchy" ("*Cárceles*" 632).[15] The threat is solved, both in *Sátira* and its model *Siervo*, with a narrative closing that "sublimates the destructive force of *amor hereos*" and transforms "reprehensible silent despair and oblivion into praiseworthy literature and memory" and "pathologic amatory servitude into male power" (*Images in Mind* 146). Here, *Siervo* and *Sátira* take very different directions. *Siervo* offers the choice of channeling erotic energy into moral allegory. *Sátira* performs the opposite move. The debate with the virtues leads to despair, not solace; the lover's tragic story is not allegorized but expanded in lengthy, markedly narrative glosses. He willingly keeps company with the treacherous poetic muses.

Brownlee considers Pedro's glossing a dramatic inversion of medieval practice that anticipates the Renaissance use of *descriptio* "merely to give pleasure, like a picture" (*The Severed Word* 112).

---

[14] "[L]as coplas siguientes que, sin me partir d'este solitario lugar faré, por merced singular suplico que veáis e fagáis mi honesta e lícita demanda. La cual tomaré por merced sin estima e complido salario del continuo deseo, desigual ansia e dolor pestilencial que, por vuestra mucha fermosura e no menos virtud, se lieva e pacientemente se sufre" (185).

[15] See the fully developed argument in Folger's monograph *Escape from the Prison of Love* (2009).

However, he is not writing academic commentary but dictaminal invention in which reference to classical myths signals a lover's irrationality. Pedro performs in the rhetorical environment appropriate to his age and station as an Orpheus who forgets his *integumentum*. He treats the margin as the "creative space" in which to spin his tales and display his "conceptual and rhetorical virtuosity," Agnew notes; he cleverly remarks that "what Serés has characterized as the Constable's servile aping of his source texts (principally the bishop-professor Fernández de Madrigal's *Diez qüestiones*)" feels almost like parody. Pedro enjoys narrating outside the margins, particularly in relating some lurid comic tales associated with Vulcan that recall the apes that populate the borders of illuminated manuscripts (304, 307, 309).[16]

Sátira's love tragedy may poetically conceal a political intent, as Agnew and more recently Montero claim. It may have been meant to uphold "the sanctity of [Pedro's] genealogy" and to reaffirm "his threatened political authority in the face of exile" (Agnew 315). In that line, Montero believes that it was conceived with propagandistic intent as a mirror of princesses, emphasizing the virtue of clemency. She claims that the anonymous *belle dame sans merci* is Pedro's sister, and his own stance, a social game that had little to do with reality —he may well have taken a vow of chastity as master of the order of Avís ("Imagen femenina" 381, 391). Montero is correct in her qualification of *Sátira*'s autobiographical component, and any political intention does not detract from *Sátira*'s *novelness*. Following the practice of Santillana's courtly circle, Pedro claims authorial status by playing poet in love and commenting on it in glosses that display his *estudios* and do not moralize or recant. Instead, he consciously engages in *curiositas*, *fabula*'s "mental fornication," deliberately muddling the voices of mad lover and wise teacher and distorting the rhetoric of *exemplum* and consolation, narrativity and allegory, the wills of the flesh and the spirit. He acknowledges in the preface that *Sátira* is "the first harvest" of his learning and addresses it to, not a male friend, but a woman, offering her the portrait of the *caballero sçiente* as a young man, pained by desire, and proudly wielding his rhetorical power in the courtly defense of women's worth.

Pedro continued to reap the moral fruits of *estudios* in his *Coplas del menesprecio e contempto de las cosas fermosas mundo* (Stanzas on the Contempt for Worldly Beauties), composed between 1453 and

---

[16] On the ape as sinner, see Janson (*Apes and Ape-Lore*). Domínguez studies the association of apes and *luxuria* in *Carajicomedia* ("Monkey Business;" *Carajicomedia*).

1455, while he was at a fair in Medina del Campo. In more than one hundred and twenty *octavas*, he summarizes moral doctrine and his own experience. *Coplas* illustrates Fortune's treacherous gifts with the expected compendium of *exempla*, and Pedro cites Boethius's *Consolation* in the appended glosses. He tactfully declines to adduce examples of duplicitous friends ("Coplas" 252) and rejects the sweet poison of the muses in favor of the *santa musa* or, as a gloss expounds, moral philosophy: "*Musa* means science, and by *holy muse* he meant moral philosophy, which, being so beneficial to the soul's well-being, can appropriately be called holy wisdom."[17]

Both *Sátira* and *Coplas* function as moral mirrors, but *Coplas* reflects a man, Pedro's cousin and brother-in-law King Afonso V of Portugal, which alters the authorial stance. *Sátira* performs the courtly lover addressing a woman but, in teaching an ethical lesson to a powerful king, Pedro positions himself as the learned moralist. In the dedication to King Afonso, he preempts criticism by citing Seneca's *Ad Lucilium*:

> My hand began to dye the white paper without fearing what perchance some, biting with a poisonous mouth and using their natural and customary habit, shall say about me, that I forget what is written about our Redeemer, the most high Jesus: "Cepit Jesus façere et doçere," claiming that I have dared to castigate others with uncontrollable impudence and arrogance without having first castigated myself. My answer to them is that of Seneca to his Lucilium: "I speak with you, he said, of the common illness, like one who suffers the same malady as you, and discuss the remedies; therefore, listen to me as if I were speaking to myself in solitary retreat." And certainly, most wise and serene king, in my opinion, even if dissoluteness is castigated by the dissolute and greed by the greedy, one must pay attention to their fruitful and useful words.[18]

---

[17] "*Musa* tanto quiere desir como sçiencia, e disiendo en el verso *santa musa* entendio por la moral philosophia, la qual, segund es provechosa a la salud de la anima, bien se puede e deve llamar santa sabiduria" ("Coplas" 256).

[18] "Movido mi mano, começo de teñir el blanco papel, sin espanto ni temor de lo que, por aventura, algunos, mordiendo con boca venenosa, usando de su natural e acostumbrado offiçio, diran yo non haver sey rrecordado de aquello que de nuestro Redemptor, el muy alto Jesu, se escribe: 'Cepit Jesus façere et doçere,' e que yo me he atrevido, con osadia e altives no ordenada a querer reprehender a los otros, no haviendo primero reprehendido a mi. A los quales yo do por respuesta aquello que al moral Seneca al su Luçilo escribe: 'yo fablo, dixo el, contigo de la comun enfermedat, assi como aquel quejase contigo de usa dolençia mesma, e tracto contigo de los remedios, e, por tanto, oyeme assi como si yo fablasse apartada e secretamente a mi mesmo.'

Coplas does not concede righteousness to Afonso V; rather, that both king and author suffer the same moral malady and offers friendship as a shield against Fortune's whims. What may seem a transgression of rhetorical boundaries —assuming a role reserved for older men— masquerades as a display of modesty in a well-crafted exordium that hints at the fierce competition for status in the king's inner circle. The content is cliché, a courtly display of erudition on Fortune's capriciousness, and its recourse to the pompous *arte mayor* recalls Mena's *Laberinto de Fortuna*.

More transgressive is what Agnew calls the "concoction of hybrids, mingling different registers and genres" in *Sátira*. We heard the dissonance in *Lo somni* when Metge transferred the penitential component to court. As Montero remarks, *Sátira* filters and reshapes penitential elements from *Siervo*, a trend found in later sentimental fictions ("Imagen femenina" 382). This kind of "intentional dialogized hybrid" —"the crossing of two styles, two linguistic points of view, and in the final analysis two speaking subjects"— is, according to Bakhtin, the trademark of medieval parody and *novelness*, or prenovelistic discourse (76). However, Bakhtin's contention that parody and popular culture are opposed to official discourse and high culture's aesthetic canon ignores the fact that hybridity "seems to have been both a verbal and a visual fashion for élite audiences," as Agnew asserts in citing Camille's analysis of marginal illuminations (315). The reliefs embellishing the misericords of cathedral choirs, the illuminated margins of manuscripts, and the archivolts and borders of sepulchral spaces exhibit a grotesque mixture that implies *enarratio*'s authorizing discourses of *integumentum* and satire, as Villaseñor Sebastián's study of marginal iconography in Castile in the last half of the fifteenth century notes (*Iconografía marginal* 27). In the next two sections, I focus on a specific type of dialogic interaction at work in Gothic visual programs and illuminated devotional texts.

THE RHETORIC OF THE MARGIN

The manuscript as material interface between text and reader implies what Mortensen calls "the rhetoric of the page:" a multidi-

---

Ca ciertamente muy sabio e serenissimo rey, segund mi creyer, aunque la dissuluçion nos sea reprehendida por el dissuluto, e la cobdiçia por el cobdiçioso, nin por esso de debe dexar de dar orejas a las sus fructuosas e utiles palabras" ("Coplas" 183–84).

mensional space that encompasses "not just the voice of an orator
or the text of an author, but the handiwork of the scribe and printer as well," as Foster elaborates in reviewing Mortensen's chapter.
The role of marginal drolleries in richly illuminated fifteenth-century
manuscripts is often merely ornamental, although swirling acanthus
leaves, fruits, and flowers may suggest the old Pauline association of
springtime and resurrection. Sánchez Ameijeiras notes that Bonaventure and the Franciscans in general never quite abandoned the metaphor and quotes the introduction to *Historia naturalis* by Juan Gil
de Zamora (1240–1320), which aptly summarizes how nature's joyful
spectacle arouses a sensual love that lifts the contemplative mind.[19]

Bosch's analysis of the miniatures in a group of liturgical manuscripts housed in the Toledo cathedral may clarify the rhetorical
strategies of prayer books. The manuscripts were commissioned by
Alfonso Carrillo de Acuña, Archbishop of Toledo (1442–1482), and
his successor, Pedro González de Mendoza, appointed by the Catholic Monarchs, who remained in the post until his death in 1495.
Both were members of the royal courts of Enrique IV and Isabel of
Castile and blood relatives of Santillana. The stylistic harmony found
in these manuscripts, inspired by the northern Renaissance, reflects
the unity of taste among Castilian aristocracy —what Bosch calls "*caballero* style." They include no books of hours, which were reserved
for the laity, but only the liturgical books required for the celebration
of the Mass, the divine office, and other sacerdotal rites: breviaries,
choir books, diurnals, lectionaries, sacramentaries, missals, and pontificals (Bosch 137–38).

Bosch is stunned by the "contrapuntal dissonance" between
their historiated initials and marginalia. Her description of a Roman
missal made by Cano de Aranda for Archbishop Carrillo after his
appointment in 1446 spells out the cause of her perplexity:

> The marginalia of the page bearing the Last Supper are decorated
> with beguiling putti, who crouch in mock menace as they startle a
> horselike creature (bottom), while other putti laze or poke among
> the acanthus branches in an implicitly sexual way. This indicates a

---

[19] "Contempla la tierra, que recobra la vida con las flores, ¡qué espectáculo tan
agradable ofrece, cómo alegra la vista, cómo provoca el amor! Y, por encima de toda
hermosura, el verdor arrebata el alma contemplativa cuando en primavera brotan
las semillas que parecían muertas en invierno, a semejanza de la futura resurrección,
estallan simultáneamente y se abren a la luz" (qtd. in Sánchez Ameijeiras, *Los rostros
de las palabras* 123).

more than slightly irreverent attitude on the artist's part, because a vignette like this *appears at first glance inappropriate in the decoration of a liturgical book*. On the Pentecost page, this more than marginally impious element becomes even bawdier, as one putto fighting with another kicks him in the testicles (bottom left). In the upper border, a nude pregnant woman stands displaying her body, while directly below her at the foot of the page, another putto squats in a pose suggestive of a visit to the latrine. (143; my emphasis)

She concludes that devotional texts harbor two dissonant representational modes. The historiated initials are "peacefully conceived" in a "prosaic" mode that sharply contrasts with the "fantastic" representation of the borders, which "possess a spirit of vitality, fantasy, and limbic eroticism" (148–59).

Her description of a Pontifical also commissioned by Carrillo details the erotic nature of the marginal fantasies:

On fol, 4, on either side of the group of angels who hold the shield, there appears, on the right, a nude half-torso of a woman who looks across at a pair of putti who play with a fantastic monster that defies classification. ... Fol. 8's *bas-de-page* reveals a nude woman looking across at a man whose garments have fallen around his feet, leaving him equally nude. ... [A] clothed courtier advances toward a nude woman who turns her face and body away from him while holding her arms invitingly open. Behind them, on the right, a monkish figure gazes at them as he extends his hands toward them; balancing him on the left, a clothed aristocratic woman spins, while a putto dangles from the spindle she holds on her right hand. The motif of the clothed courtier and the nude woman repeats on the left bottom part of the border. (159–60)

Carrillo's interest in alchemy may explain the bizarre imagery in the books he commissioned, and Cardinal Mendoza's aversion to it may account for the gradual disappearance of these vivacious, raunchy borders at the end of the century (Lappin).

As an art historian, Bosch focuses on identifying the miniatures' artistic school, casting aside a revealing distinction she noticed earlier: the choir books and Roman missals were required for celebration of the Mass, while pontificals, breviaries, and diurnals were small books intended for private use. According to her own descriptions, the dissonance that so impresses her is limited to a small breviary (Ms. 33.9; 225 X 160 mm); a medium-sized Roman pontifical (Ms.

56.24; 340 X 260 mm); and a medium-sized Roman missal (Res. 4; 365 X 260 mm). The illuminations in choir books and missals —with the exception of the medium-sized Res. 4— are an assortment of acanthus leaves, birds, and floral motifs with the occasional naked figure or putti, whose supposed eroticism Lappin questions: the put-to that appears in a choir book bordering an image of Saint John *ante portam latinam* is not masturbating "but engaging in a puttesque pee" (Lappin 117).

The Toledan manuscripts support Greenia's assertion that "the smaller the book, the more marginalia or drolleries might be includ-ed if space were available for them in the margins" (732). Their more private use permitted the voyeurism Saenger identified. Bosch ac-knowledges that the Toledan texts have fewer bawdy images than the Anglo-French illuminations studied by Camille in his influential *Image on the Edge: The Margins of Medieval Art*, but they distinguish a static mode in the center from the marginal fantasies.

Bosch does not mention the Horas Alfonso (New York, Pierpont Morgan Library, Ms M.854), commissioned by Isabel of Castile on the death of her younger brother at fifteen in 1468 (Planas Badenas, "Lecturas pías" 465–66).[20] The margins display no trace of impro-priety; still, Wieck notices a clear disparity between the motionless, calm dignity of a central scene depicting the Adoration of the Magi and the narrative activity on the edge (fol. 90v), "where the Magi's grooms attend the horses or kill time while awaiting their masters" (70). While Wieck is not concerned with other images, his remarks apply to the border of fol. 100v, the Massacre of the Innocents, which glances at the mourning mothers, and of fol. 135v, the Last Judgment, where devils and nude figures are inexorably drawn by an invisible current toward the Maw of Hell, teeth already crunching on half a body. Other borders are more inscrutable. In one surrounding the Miracle of Raising Lazarus, a nude hybrid man rides a bird, while other sits astride a man, also nude, on all fours.[21]

The tendency to use narrative imagery in the borders is undoubt-edly related to Franciscan strategies using everyday scenes, rich in vernacular imagery and anecdotes, to present the life of Christ. For

---

[20] The date is uncertain. Villaseñor surmises that the manuscript was commis-sioned when Alfonso was proclaimed king (April 27, 1465) and completed after his death and Isabel's coronation in 1474 ("El Libro de Horas").

[21] The images can be viewed in CORSAIR, the Pierpont Morgan Library Online Collection Catalog.

instance, in the Libro de Horas de los Retablos (Biblioteca Nacional de España, Vit. 25–3, fol. 38r), the still representation of Joseph, Mary, and the child in the manger is bordered by a lively scene of farmers dancing in a circle (see fig. 4). A few pages earlier, the visitation of the Virgin Mary with her cousin Elizabeth is surrounded by several scenes: Mary washing the newborn John the Baptist, while Elizabeth rests in bed; an adult John preaching to an audience, one of whom is disturbingly headless in typological allusion to the saint's own beheading; and John surrounded by lambs in the wilderness (fol. 24r). The same pattern appears on a page showing the martyrdom of Saint Apollonia (fol. 184v), her life visually narrated in the background.

The depiction of daily rural life in the margins of the calendar, the first section of a book of hours, points in the same direction.[22] On the page corresponding to January in the Hours of Juana I de Castilla, or London Rothschild Hours, (British Library, Add Ms 35313), dated c. 1500, four medallions representing Jesus's circumcision, the Epiphany, Saint Vincent martyr, and Saint Paul's conversion contrast with a bas-de-page scene in which a woman sets the table, while a man warms his hands by the fireplace. For May, the medallions include Saint Philip, Saint James the Minor, and the discovery of the True Cross, while the bas-de-page depicts an amorous encounter in the *locus amoenus* and a group of noblemen hunting in the background. The religious medallions imitate the somber stiffness of a woodcarving in clear contrast to the liveliness and brilliant colors of the everyday scenes.

These examples support Bosch's critique of Camille's contention; the margin as a space for transgression and parody is an academic construct. Instead, she proposes "considering the margin as an alternative space employed to supplement the text to which it is related by placement" and that allegory, "with its veiled language encrypted for the elite," is "one possible tool that can break the code of the margins" (204, 202). However, the key is not, as Bosch suggests, a hierarchy of center and margin but their symbiosis. Gothic portals, for instance, make ample use of narrative scenes, sometimes with a typological meaning, as in the nativity vignette at the Cathedral of León, where Mary lies on a rumpled bed after giving birth, her pain prefiguring her son's passion (Sánchez Ameijeras, *Los rostros de las palabras* 153–54).

---

[22] See Villaseñor Sebastián's detailed description, history, and analysis of calendars and zodiacs in fifteenth-century manuscripts (*Iconografía marginal* 197–250).

Figure 4. Libro de Horas de los Retablos. Biblioteca Nacional de España,
Vit. 25–3, fol. 38r).

Robertson cites the doctrine of charity, which impels all Christian creations to either blame or satirize *cupiditas*, to explain marginal
representations of the monstrous, bestial, and absurd: "this is exactly

what we should expect of Christian authors" ("The Doctrine" 46).
The images' emotional content prompts meditation on their meaning
(*A Preface* 216). Similarly, Kessler notes that the margins and frames
of thirteenth- and fourteenth-century manuscripts "were often the
site of fanciful combats between animals representing the body de-
void of reason or grace" in contrast to "the sacred words and main
pictures" (*Seeing Medieval Art* 103). However, many of the manuscripts Camille reviews support neither typological reading nor Augustinian moralization of marginalia as negative examples of sinful
behavior. The reader must be kept in mind while assessing the images'
significance (*Image on the Edge* 116–17). The meanings and values of
Christian moral discourse on love shape Gothic art, but Gothic art —
like introspection— is also rooted in "the conflicted life of the body
with all its somatic as well as spiritual possibilities" (*Image on the Edge*
160). This tension reaches its full potential in the penitential process.

Marginal representations are what Bryson calls "high–deixis images;" they stress carnality because they point directly back to the artist's body (89, 122). The calligraphic doodles in an otherwise sparsely
decorated breviary (BNE Mss/9694) will serve to illustrate my point.
The red and blue capitals mark sections and stages and direct the
reader's attention; the proliferation of points around the squiggles
that grow out of the capitals —see, for instance, fol. 64r— reflect
the practice of *punctare*, the punctuation or wounding of memory in
the *compunctio cordis*, "the emotion-filled imagining as one recites or
chants the Psalms, the Passion, or other suitable texts" (Carruthers,
The Craft of Thought 103). A whimsical face in the shape of a heart
pierced by a blood-dripping sword in fol. 64v expresses the emotional and intellectual demands of prayer. This drollery frames the
word *inimici* (enemies), a call identifying the next folio, which begins
with that word. The drawing sprouts from the blue capital that begins a traditional prayer for compline begging the Lord to visit the
devout's dwelling and drive from it all the snares of the enemy.[23] In
the context of a prayer to be delivered at night, the emotional associations brought forth by the choice of a bleeding heart enclosing the
word *enemies* manifest the bodily cravings from which the prayer is
supposed to protect (see fig. 5). The copyist's indulgence in lavish

---

[23] The whole prayer reads: "Visita, quaesumus, Domine, habitationem istam, et
omnes insidias inimici ab ea longe repelle. Angeli tui sancti habitantes in ea nos in
pace custodiant; et benedictio tua sit super nos semper. Salva nos Omnipotens Deus,
et lucem tuam nobis concede perpetuam. Dominum nostrum. Amen."

Figure 5. *Breviary*. Biblioteca Nacional de España, Mss/9694, fol. 64v.

doodles, sometimes clearly anthropomorphic, tends to human time in the same way as the marginal glosses in Pedro de Portugal's *Sátira*. Margins as the site of temporalia, fantasy, and eroticism point backward to the flesh and upward to the serene stillness of allegorical representations and prayers. We saw this *intentio* embodied by the weeping Boethius, who sees himself in Orpheus's love for Eurydice, which then drives his gaze toward Lady Philosophy. The fictional Metge is equally mesmerized by the Orphic tale but he willfully rejects its moralization.

Bodies at work fill the margins of missals and books of hours, the floors and walls of churches, the lateral posts of altarpieces, the misericords in choirs, while the hieratic image addresses the viewing subject "liturgically, as a member of the faith, and communally as a generalized choric presence," to borrow Bryson's description of Gothic art. In this sense, Bosch raises an interesting point: "the Middle Ages and the Renaissance did not use the word *marginalia* to denote the decoration of what we identify as the margins of a manuscript" but called the typical figures *fabula*, curiosities, or babewyins (204–5). These terms indicate their narrative function and service of the uninhibited desire to know so chastised by moralists.

THE "PRAYER-BOOK" MENTALITY

Originally restricted to a religious elite, mnemonic techniques for contemplation were made available to the laity through preaching and affective private devotion. As a consequence of the reforms brought about by the Fourth Lateran Council (1215), regular canons and the newly founded mendicant orders revived oral rhetoric for homiletic purposes (Carruthers and Ziolkowski 21–22). The friars popularized the Victorines' great iconographic schemes, such as Hugh of Saint Victor's *Didascalicon*, and the Franciscans in particular adopted the craft to contemplate the life of Christ visually —that is, silently. The pictorial aspects of monastic meditation coincided in many ways with the old memorial system described in the pseudo-Ciceronian *Rhetorica ad Herennium*, or *Rhetorica nova*, as it was known. Villena translated it into Castilian, demonstrating its popularity among *caballeros sçientes*.

At the core of the contemplative process were illuminated devotional books and the visual programs of altarpieces and Gothic cathedrals that followed the rhetorical guidelines of the *artes praedicandi*, as Sánchez Ameijeiras demonstrates (*Los rostros de las palabras*). Devotional texts and books of hours were the primary vehicles for personal and communal reading. Their images "emphasized the need for a direct, vivid, visual re-enactment of Christ's life on earth ... [and] encouraged the devout to focus their attention so that they might truly be present at certain moments of Christ's life." They often show an inviting, open prayer book in the foreground and a scene from Christ's life in the background (Harbison 87, 95).

In Aragon and Castile, monarchs customarily appear in their personal altarpieces. For instance, in the central post of the *retablo* of the *Virgen de la Leche*, commissioned by Enrique II of Castile for the sanctuary of Tobed in Zaragoza, the king, his wife Juana Manuel, and their children Juan and Leonor kneel at the feet of the lactating Mary. Enrique's grandson, Fernando de Antequera, the first Trastámara King of Aragón, kneels in prayer with Sancho Rojas, Archbishop of Toledo, at the feet of the Virgin and child in one of the three main posts of a large, multipaneled altarpiece now at the Museo Nacional del Prado (Inv. 1.321). I borrowed these two references from a 2013 article by Muñoz Gómez, who assigns a political intent to the Trastámaras' piety ("De Medina del Campo"). Fernando de Antequera emphasized his Marian devoutness to support his right to the throne; he is praised in a biographical sketch by Pérez de Guzmán for steadily praying the Hours of Our Lady (Muñoz Gómez, "De Medina del Campo" 385). In the *retablo* of the Capilla de los Corporales [Chapel of the Corporals] in the colegiata de Daroca in Zaragoza, the Catholic Monarchs Isabel and Fernando with their children, Juan and Isabel, appear in a side panel, praying and staring at the miracle of the Eucharist depicted in the central post (Yarza Luaces, *Los Reyes Católicos* 79).

A portrait now at the Museo Nacional del Prado indicates that this practice was not restricted to the monarchy. Part of the Sopetrán altarpiece, dated after 1460, it purports to show the powerful Duque del Infantado, kneeling at his prie-dieu, where a small book lies open. His gaze is directed toward an altarpiece depicting a Crucifixion scene in the *banco*, or predella, as well as the Virgin and child surrounded by smaller panels impossible to identify (Yarza Luaces, *Los Reyes Católicos* 253). The prie-dieu, prayer book, and small altarpiece constitute the apparatus of private devotion designed for use in a personal chapel or oratory, outside the liturgical setting of a church's main altar (Williamson 380).

The devotions of members of the clergy and the wealthy classes were also depicted. Two panels of particular interest for my argument represent Mary's fifth sorrow, known later as a *Piedad*: Fernando Gallego's *Piedad* of uncertain date, now at El Prado, and Bartolomé Bermejo's *Pietà* (1490) at the cathedral of Barcelona. The subject was a feast, newly established by the Church in 1423, as Mary's Seven Sorrows, or the Seven Swords or Knives, matched to her Seven Joys. Fernando Gallego's *Piedad* depicts the traditional group of Virgin, dead son, and, kneeling to their left, the two donors, a woman and a man who utters the initial words of Psalm 50, "Miserere mei Domine," the greatest of the penitential psalms, believed to have been written by David after sinning with Bathsheba (Yarza Luaces, *Los Reyes Católicos* 151). Note that it verbalizes the *compunctio cordis* that initiates any meditation. Bermejo's *Pietà* is different. Finished in 1490, the painting was commissioned by Archdeacon Lluis Desplà, canon of the Barcelona Cathedral, for his private oratory.[24] He was cultivated, frequented latinist circles and collected Roman antiquities, and his taste was as refined as that of the *enamorada generació*. Although no evidence confirms that he actually read

---

[24] All the information about the Desplà *Pietà* comes from Joan Molina i Figueras (*Arte, devoción*) and John F. Moffit.

any sentimental works, his choice of iconography may demonstrate the artistic consequences of "the prayer-book mentality," a phrase coined by Harbison to describe the mindset of Flemish patrons and donors so avid to participate imaginatively in the Passion of Christ that they commissioned panel paintings recording their own visionary experiences.

Bermejo's large panel depicts "a grief-torn Mary lamenting over the stiffly rigid, gruesomely bloodied, body of her martyred son." Desplà kneels on the right, and "at the Virgin's right hand is St. Jerome, seemingly searching through his Vulgate translation of the Bible for consolation and inspiration" (Moffit 72–73). Molina i Figueras explains that the scene is a highly intellectualized meditation. It represents a private devotional act in which Desplà imagines, contemplates on, and finally revives the Passion through Saint Jerome's text (*Arte, devoción* 143). In this very private meditation, his presence at Calvary is more than mere convention. It reveals a common, late-medieval meditational praxis that blurs the lines between the contemplated site and personal experience —what Michael Camille, analyzing the glorious visions of Gothic art, calls the "spectacular interpenetration of image and viewer" that was lost with Renaissance perspective (*Gothic Art* 180–81). Moffit notes that the scene is set against the landscape of Catalunya, which becomes Calvary through typological transference, the same mechanism that converts Desplà into Saint Francis at Monte Alverna ("Bartolomé Bermejo's Pietà" 75). The old method of figural reading expounded the events narrated in the Old Testament as foreshadowings, or types, of the New, but in affective piety, exegetical similitude is expanded into a timeless and intimate identification with Christ through emotional remembrance. Moffit quotes Saint Francis's *Fioretti*, the popular fourteenth-century hagiographic anthology, where Monte Alverna becomes the landscape of Christ's last hours "because the Passion of our Lord Jesus Christ was to be renewed *through love and pity in the soul* of St. Francis" ("Bartolomé Bermejo's Pietà" 74; emphasis added).

Depicting the donors within their devout visions animates the autobiographical component of penitential fictions, while another important tool of devotion, the *retablos*, were designed to elicit the same affective journeys and open-ended associative processesing which penitential protagonists search for consolation. In Carrós's *Regoneixença*, the ecphrasis of a *retablo* of the *Virgo lactans* surrounded by panels depicting the martyrdoms of Saint Ursula and

Saint Agnes marks the protagonist's progress from literary fiction to divine love.[25]

Books of hours, *retablos*, and Gothic religious edifices all juxtapose grotesque images and sacred allegories. In her studies of Alfonso Martínez de Toledo's *Corbacho*, Sanmartín Bastida, following Harpham, suggests that the mixture of carnality and spirituality characteristic of the grotesque reflects an increasing tendency to value the human body, very much in line with the new devotional trend of the *imitatio Christi* (23).

From a contemplative perspective, the grotesque performs a much more important theological and philosophical role. Both monastic meditation and the *Ad Herennium* recommend the construction of architectural sites, real or imaginary, and placing inside them *imagines agentes*, shocking, active images with a theatrical quality, to trigger recollection. Marvelous devotional images were tools to encourage religious curiosity and lead to a vision of heaven (Carruthers, *The Craft of Thought* 195). According to Bynum, "marveling and astonishment as reactions seem to be triggered most frequently and violently by what Bernard of Clairvaux called *admirabiles mixturae*: events or phenomena in which ontological and moral boundaries are crossed, confused, and erased" (21). She cites Julian of Norwich, for whom human beings are a miraculous mixture of sin and grace because of the Incarnation, the supreme paradox of God made man. The grotesque in Gothic art graphically represents this miracle, which has profound implications for human salvation (21–22). The ritual practice of contemplating such images suggests, like the dictaminal reading of Ovid's *Metamormophoses*, the presence of the eternal in *temporalia* as distinctly human.

The proliferation of portable prayer books used in affective devotion is closely related to the advent of silent reading, which had profound cultural ramifications (Saenger, "Books of Hours" 142). "The new privacy gained through silent reading . . . intensified orthodox devotional and spiritual experiences ... [and] played an important role in the spirituality of the reformed mendicants in the Fifteenth century" (401).[26] By century's end, thanks to the new privacy afforded by silent reading, "artists decorated books of hours with increasingly suggestive erotic scenes, often ostensibly depicting the vices for which penance was required but consciously intended to excite

---

[25] See chapter 2: 154–59.
[26] This article is reproduced in Saenger's *Space Between Words*.

the voyeur of the book" (Saenger, "Books of Hours" 156).[27] After 1480 and coinciding with this voyeuristic tendency, Costley identifies a change in the illuminations decorating the section dedicated to the penitential psalms. They cease to depict King David's contrition and focus on Bathsheba's bath, turning illicit sex into a symbol of every sin. "The astonishing proliferation of images of David and Bathsheba in sixteenth-century Books of Hours," Costley claims, signals "a new development that organized penitential practice around sexuality." This development supports Foucault's argument that "by the end of the Middle Ages penance and sex were inextricably related via the procedures of confession" (1252).

A truly grotesque grouping of carnality and devotion in a different kind of illuminated text and its contemporary analysis warrant pause. Whinnom mentions the drawings of naked couples and copulating animals that surround the poems in a midfifteenth-century manuscript, the *Cancionero de Palacio* (Ms. 2653 of the Biblioteca Histórica de la Universidad de Salamanca), to support courtly poetry's eroticism (San Pedro, *Obras completas II*). Following his lead, Gerli concludes from the surprisingly lewd illustrations in the margins around Juan de Agraz's elegy on the tragic death of the young Conde de Mayorga that the "decorated folio and its intellectual content require the presumption of the presence of an active public educated not only in Juan Ruiz's themes, but in the textual strategies of his work" ("On the Edge" 7). His strong analysis supports what I have been arguing: marginal images make manifest the authorizing discourses of literature.

However, in adopting Bakhtin's understanding of the obscene as subversive and Camille's of the margin as parody, Gerli places too much weight on the dynamics of inversion, challenge, and irony: "In the synthesis of the libidinal images of love with the solemn language of Christian penitence, the illustrator *inverts* the message contained in the poem, *challenges* it from the margin, and reveals the implicit *ambivalence* and sublimations of piety, which in the medieval mind can never free itself from desire" ("On the Edge" 6; emphasis added). Camille's later critique identifies one problem in modern approaches to the obscene in medieval art: the "assumption, following Bakhtin,

---

[27] Saenger indicates that "erotic scenes developed particularly as frontispieces to Book IX of the French translation of Valerius Maximus, *Facta et dicta memorabilia*" (Saenger, "Books of Hours" 156), a manuscript frequently listed in the inventories of Castilian nobles' libraries.

that the obscene is marginal and other to the sacred." In fact, "so-called 'profane' church art demonstrates instead that obscenity was produced from within the sacred and not always in opposition to it." He concludes that "much of what we now call obscenity in medieval sculpture is, rather, an integral part of the intended, official programme" ("Dr. Witkowski's" 36). Affective devotion, like *enarratio*, does not reject or seek to be free of the body but exploits its energy to instigate spiritual progress. As Villaseñor Sebastián acknowledges, the overlapping of erotic images and sacred texts implies a culture that views them on a continuum (*Iconografía marginal*).

Meditation freezes the mind's ceaseless flow in what Bakhtin terms the "logic of the vertical chronotrope," or "the coexistence of everything in eternity" (157). Violence is imposed on the body to extract a moral meaning; flesh and spirit become indivisible components of a single truth. As a discipline, penance reshapes carnality and temporality into the eternal stillness and virtue of the hieratic gaze. The prose prologue and paratexts of Juan Ruiz's *Libro* document the complexity of this ethical approach to texts and images whose value is contingent on individual will.

The powerful association of sex and confession that Costley identifies in later prayer books can be traced back to the rich production of school parodies and penitential fictions articulated around male friendship and consolation that we saw in chapters 1 and 2. The next section focuses on several burlesques that Cátedra subsumes in the wider category of *tratados de amor*. Not surprisingly, he believes their first instance was Fernández de Madrigal's doctrinal text on love, *Libro de amor y amicicia*, although he suspects their seeds may lie in the jokes of Juan Ruiz's *Libro de buen amor* (*Poesía de Pasión* 277–79). These fifteenth-century burlesques further elucidate the *letrado* context of later sentimental fictions.

PARODY AND MALE RITES OF PASSAGE

In chapter 1, we saw two Ovidian narratives, Boncompagno's *Rota Veneris* and Juan Ruiz's *Libro de buen amor*, that use dictaminal compositional techniques —dream vision, pseudo-autobiography, and epistolary exchange or debate— to bind an anthology of school exercises under the guidance of a *magister amoris*. In the *Libro de buen amor*, later paratexts, in particular manuscript S's prologue, invite readers to direct the *intentio* of the book into either immoral fabulation or reprobation of carnal love. In this expected moral choice, the major authorizing discourses of Ovid, *integumentum* and satire, which alter the aim of the will and attentiveness, are applied to the *Libro*. Manuscript S's prose prologue shares with Fernández de Madrigal's *Libro de amor y amicicia* a concern over mental disorder; both locate the affliction in fantasy, although the prologue attributes it to general human imperfection, while Fernández de Madrigal puts the blame squarely on erotic desire.[28] The Archpriest's *Libro* illustrates the dangers of meditation noted in the introductory sermon: the weakness of *memoria*, mental laziness, and unholy curiosity that penitential consolations aim to reverse. Its protagonist is a babewyn, one of the monkeys mocking piety, church rituals, schoolwork, and preaching that populate the margins of manuscripts.

A similar leaning toward the margin arises in the brief verse narratives that Martín de Riquer called "contes plaents," such as the *Llibre de fra Bernat* [Friar Bernat's Book], composed by Francesc de la Via, royal clerk between 1405 and 1408; and the *Col·loqui de dames* [Colloquium of Ladies] copied by Narcís Gual in his compilation *Jardinet d'orats* and therefore datable to c. 1485. Méndez Cabrera studies them as concretions of late-medieval grotesque realism in Bakhtin's sense, as popular culture's system of images expressing the joyfulness of materiality and the body in action. In the *Llibre de fra Bernat*, a character named Francesc de la Via tells the story of a degenerate friar infatuated with a nun. It is a funny take on both biblical commentary —Genesis's "crescite et multiplicamini" justifies fra Bernat's debauchery— and courtly love rituals —the friar offers his penis to the nun as a present worthy of her favors. In the anonymous *Col·loqui*, the ferocious misogyny does not emphasize moral reproof but the jubilant display of insults, blasphemy, vulgarity, and obscenity, verbal equivalents of lively, erotic marginal illuminations.

This tendency toward *curiositas* and narrative is at play in another spoof of academic exercises, the anonymous *Tratado de cómo al hombre le es necesario amar*. It was originally attributed to Fernández de Madrigal, but Cátedra tentatively credits it to Juan de Mena, which dates it to around the same time as Fernández de Madrigal's

---

[28] As Haywood remarks, "in the *Libro* the Augustinian belief that disordered love, *cupiditas*, subverts the priorities of will and leads to the misdirection of appetite towards sin is substituted for the view that it is not so much desire but the flawed nature of human mind, particularly memory, that is an obstacle to salvation" (Haywood and Vasvári, eds. 29).

Libro (*Poesía de Pasión*). Lampooning notions about the determinis-
tic effect of desire on reason to excuse random sex in a carnivalesque
world of insane lovers, it must be analyzed within the context of university initiation rituals, as Weissberger analyzed Lucena's *Repetición
de amores* (c.1497), a mock *repetitio*, or school lecture, that draws
heavily on the *Tratado*.[29]
    The University of Salamanca had a long tradition of poking fun
at institutional practices and rituals. Egido and Madroñal studied it
in the sixteenth and seventeenth centuries, and Campo Tejedor documented its pervasiveness in his examination of the banquets, danc-
es, and mock sermons that accompanied a cleric's celebration of his
first mass. Karras showed that such rituals constructed a model of
masculinity in which young men, although actively engaged in sexual relations, repudiated the "uncontrolled, animal lasciviousness
... associated ... with femininity" to form a bond with their peers.
Being a man meant having power over sexual impulses (108).[30] Penitential fictions use the process of silent composition and prayer to
keep the sexual drive in check with the help of the intellect and
free will. The *Tratado* creates a masculine bond through subversive
joking.
    Heusch follows Cátedra's argument that the *Tratado* is an expur-
gate letter ("epístola expurgativa"), a self-defense in scholastic terms;
its autobiographical tone recalls the sentimental fictions popular at
the time (Alvar and Lucía Mejías, eds. 965). In fact, it inverts *Siervo*'s
power dynamic. Instead of a work written at the request of an older
man who demands to know his younger friend's "case," the *Tratado*
is addressed to a friend of tender age —"tu hedad es tierna" (55)—
who reprimanded the older author for falling in love. It resorts to the
customary medley (Ovid's *Metamorphoses*, Boethius's *Consolation*,
the Bible, and sapiential *compendia*) to prove two arguments: first,
the Aristotelian principle that for men to love is natural and inevitable; second, all lovers lose their minds. In misrepresenting love's
destructive potential as a universal truth, the second argument is a
fallacy. Classical *auctoritates* are invoked, not to admonish against
sex, but to excuse the protagonist's behavior as inevitable. The comic
conclusion to be drawn from this warped logic is the innate foolishness of all men. Is the younger friend a freshman, recently initiated

---

[29] I draw many of the ideas presented here on misogyny and male bonding from
Weissberger's analysis of *Repetición* (*Isabel Rules* 140–48).
[30] See also chapter 1: 42–54.

into the masculine model, rebuking a sexually active older man? If
so, the treatise is practical proof of a lover's foolishness. Perhaps the
joke is on the freshman since the older man demonstrates full control of his intellectual powers by writing a hilarious tract that only
a fool would take seriously. Like Juan Ruiz's *Libro*, the anonymous
Tratado presents a world of men deprived of reason and free will by
their lust; it manipulates and morally sullies the classics for devious
purposes in another instance of "monkeying around." It stages the
death of reason and, therefore, masculinity.

Grotesque realism and parody, then, are not the exclusive domain of popular culture, as Méndez Cabrera claims in analyzing
the virulent misogyny and mocking of courtly poetry in the "contes
plaents." Both Deyermond and Minnis remind us that parody, even
in its crudest forms, does not imply hostility or rejection.[31] As Minnis proposes for the *Roman de la rose*, humorous parodies were not
addressed to those on the margins of society, but the "recreational
activities of pillars of the establishment." Their humor is "characteristic of a world without women, wherein the hardships of enforced
celibacy are often relieved by elaborate sexual fantasies and sometimes express themselves through an interest in virility." The comic
climax is closely linked to the performance of masculinity (*Magister
amoris* 192–94).

The conflation of *ars amandi* and *ars dictandi*, the assimilation of
acts of love to dictaminal textuality, is at work in Roís de Corella's
Tragèdia de Caldesa (c. 1458), a funny rant on the evils that sexual
desire brings on men. The title led early critics to Isidore and Boethius, who define *tragedy* as lamentation over the destruction of happiness (Cortijo Ocaña, "Religious Parody" 15), but Cocozzella cleverly
points out that this *Tragèdia* has nothing to do with the fall of princes
but with "an ordinary individual's mourning over his personal crisis" (*Text, Translation* 186). Roís de Corella does not resort to classical myths and examples as he will later in *Parlament*. Instead, he
composes a supposedly historical narrative about great crimes and
injustices; that is, a tragedy, according to Nicholas Trevet's definition.[32]

---

[31] Deyermond cites *The Lore and Language of Schoolchildren*: "Parody, that most
refined form of jeering, gives an intelligent child a way of showing independence
without having to rebel … [They] are not necessarily irreverent. It is just a thing they
do. It is as if children know instinctively that anything wholly solemn, without a smile
behind it, is only half alive" ("Some Aspects" 76).

[32] See chapter 1: 82.

The protagonist is an idiotic lover who relates how a hussy deceives him. Cortijo Ocaña ponders its religious dynamic —the dialectic of sin and redemption— and its burlesque elements —the mockery of courtly customs— without choosing the dominant register ("Religious Parody"). However, *Tragèdia de Caldesa* exhibits all the trademarks of a dictaminal jest *à la* Boncompagno or Juan Ruiz: a comical assortment of biblical echoes, mythological *horae*, courtly love banalities, and colloquial expressions peers would easily recognize. Cortijo Ocaña relates its prosimetric form to Dante's *Vita nuova* ("Religious Parody"), but its extravagant pathos and ostentatious rhetoric bring to mind the lacrimose excesses of young Pedro de Portugal's *Sátira*, composed just a few years earlier. While I am not claiming that *Tràgedia* is a parody of Pedro's work, it undeniably caricatures any aspiring Orpheus.

Rico diagnoses *Tràgedia*'s blend of high and low styles as "indeterminación," addressing a problem of rhetoric and literary history, not two fools' dalliance.[33] In other words, it is a product of dictaminal training. If he wonders what moves Caldesa to accept the narrator as her suitor and, at the same time, give herself to a boorish lover, to feign joy with one and deep sorrow with the other, he uses the vapid pretext of indetermination to shrug off answering ("Imágenes del Prerrenacimiento" 19–20). What would an author gain from such indetermination? In the context of dictaminal jests, Caldesa literalizes the discourse *in mulieres* —the association of Fortune's fickleness and female wantonness with worldly disorder and sin. The adjective *afortunat* in the subtitle ("Raonant un cas afortunat que ab una dama li esdevenc") points to those connections as does the qualification of Caldesa's behavior as "wanton to the extreme, offensive to all common decency."[34] Very little separates this siren from those calling to untrained youths involved in meditation, the easiest path to deviate from and the hardest to follow. The joke here is on the dumb lover, restless and vexed by unhappy thoughts, unable to see until the end that Caldesa's sex appeal hides Fortune's deceitful and faithless will. *Tragèdia de Caldesa* caricatures the hazards along a young man's intellectual journey.[35] It mocks the

---

[33] "Así, la intriga, la anécdota de la obra, se cifra en un problema de retórica e historia de la literatura" ("Imágenes del Prerrenacimiento" 19).

[34] I cite from Cocozzella's study, which offers an edition and English translation: "ab altres mostres d'amor extrema, d'honestat enemigues" (*Text, Translation* 192; trans. 200).

[35] Cortijo Ocaña is "tempted to find a parallel with the mockery of the courtly male lover that appears in many Castilian compositions that belong to the genre of

grandiose style, exhibition of bookish learning, frequent exclama-
tions, and abuse of pathetic fallacies. Above all, it makes fun of the
moment of recollection that dream visions figure as the entrance to
memoria's inner chamber. In *Tràgedia de Caldesa*, the protagonist is
admitted to his lover's room and realizes the ugly truth. The work's
main innovation is not the locker-room crack but telling a story that,
because of its "indeterminacies," feels real. Years later, in *Parlament,*
Roís de Corella will put female wickedness on trial under the cover
of the Ovidian stories told by aging friends. Although we never hear
her voice, Caldesa moves, kisses, and laughs like the very physical
floozies roaming school corridors and palatial halls or living down
the street, like one of Celestina's girls from "las tenerías del río."

Torró studied the enormous success of *Tragèdia de Caldesa*; its
dissolute heroine became a literary type appropriated by other authors ("El mite de Caldesa"). To understand her realism, we must
not forget Woods's caveat that "what passes in medieval literature
for feminine psychology ... was a standard part of the medieval as
well as the classical boy's schoolroom repertoire, a creative exercise
bounded by extremely long-lasting conventions and topoi" ("Rape
and the Pedagogical" 71). Juan de Flores achieved a similar realism
through similar means in *Grisel y Mirabella*, which became a European bestseller. *Tragèdia de Caldesa*'s original readership was comparable in many ways to that of *Grisel y Mirabella*: an all male audience
"of sophisticated readers of national and international literature."
Later readers "misunderstood its parodic nuances and interpreted
it as a serious take on love" (Severin, *Religious Parody* 10–11). We
must include among them contemporary critics who routinely categorize *Grisel y Mirabella* as a sentimental novel because it recounts a
doomed love affair. In fact, the narrative component is a coat hanger.
Although she extends the analysis to the whole sentimental genre,
Rohland de Langbehn perceptively notices that in *Grisel y Mirabella*,
the characters' only mission is to set forth a particular core of opinions, and their action is limited to the influence they exert through
argument. A reader cannot discern their personalities from their
speeches, which are structured according to the argument (*La unidad genérica* 70).[36] Their purpose is to draw attention to the author's

---

sentimental romance" and understands the whole narrative as "an *amplificatio* of a
serious lyric motif: that of the injured/rejected lover" ("Religious Parody" 13).

[36] Or as Francomano points out in *Three Spanish Querelle Texts*, "oratory out-
weighs action" (34).

mastery of all sides of the *querella de las mugeres*, and the work's ghastly conclusion is nothing but a clever take on Ovidian myths.[37] Juan de Flores, whose university background is now beyond doubt —he was at some point rector at Salamanca— executes the piece, Metge-style, as a *magister amoris* fully acquainted with the *enarratio* of classical myths.[38]

Braçayda's eloquent and impassioned defense of women's worth, which refutes Torroella's deriding arguments, led critics to consider Flores a champion of women. More cautiously, Francomano acknowledges the work's *indeterminacy* —notice the term's recurrence to describe this kind of dictaminal exercise— "which invites readers to continue the debate and question when the book is closed" (*Three Spanish Querelle Texts* 43). She rightly points out that Braçayda is a stock character in medieval retellings of the Trojan war. Rodríguez del Padrón turned her into one of the correspondents in *Bursario,* his, adaptation of Ovid's *Heroides* (Francomano, *Three Spanish Querelle Texts* 36–37). In *Grisel y Mirabella,* her heroic attempts to champion her gender with no other weapons than her attacker's arguments is a testament to Flores's rhetorical skill; she appears painfully aware of her powerlessness in a world where, always, "men are in the right, since they are judges, litigants, and lawyers in the same case" (Francomano, *Three Spanish Querelle Texts* 141). No wonder readers mistook her for the actual female voice since her logic rings so true even now.

From a dictaminal point of view, the most interesting character is Torroella, a funny synecdoche of a poet's two ages. Read alongside Metge's retelling of both myths in *Lo somni, Grisel y Mirabella* fictionalizes Torroella as an Orpheus, oddly in love with his opponent Braçayda, and a wise Tiresias. They are both destroyed by raging viragos for ignoring other women or telling the truth about them. In *Lo somni,* Tiresias tells Metge that he knows about women firsthand because he was transformed into one for seven years. Based on this experience, he is forced to settle Juno and Jupiter's debate on sexual appetite and attests that female lust is three times greater than

---

[37] As Severin points out, "any temptation to take the tragic death of the lovers too seriously is soon dispelled by the grotesque death of Torrellas at the hand of the queen and her ladies, in a scene reminiscent of the Bacchae" (*Religious Parody* 11).

[38] On the identity of Juan de Flores, see Gwara's two parts of "The Identity of Juan de Flores" and Parrilla's "Un cronista olvidado".

men's.[39] The enraged Juno takes out his eyes.[40] In *Grisel y Mirabe-lla*, Torroella endures comparable tortures at the hands of affronted ladies for similar reasons. Whether Flores knew Metge's *Lo somni* is uncertain, but both authors most certainly knew Ovid. *Grisel y Mirabella* closes on a binary cliché on women's cruelty: "out of their *wickedness* and *indignation*, women cruelly murdered Torroella with their own hands."[41] In *Lo somni,* before the maenads murder Orpheus, the narrator says, "Seeing and hearing this, one of a great multitude of women, whose *wrath* and *hatred* I had incurred, began to speak."[42] Metge's vocabulary is more precise; *ira* conveys the original Latin sense of uncontrolled and violent vengeance, fueled by extreme aversion (*oy*), a distinctively feminine behavior. In *Parlament*, Roís de Corella illustrates it in Philomela's hideous murder of her own son. The more academic Flores pairs strong displeasure (*indignación*) with moral depravity (*malicia*).

Flores addresses his *tractado* to an unnamed "amiga." Critics speculate she may have been Queen Isabel because the introductory letter identifies Flores as the *amiga*'s scribe, and he served as official chronicler to the Catholic Monarchs (Francomano *Three Spanish Querelle Texts* 174n1). However, given the queen's pious disposition and serious attitude —Severin notes that love poetry fell from grace in the 1480s and 1490s as a consequence (*Del manuscrito* 6)— I wonder what she would have made of a work introduced to her as "folly" ("loco ensayo") and concluding with an enactment of women's bestiality. In addition, *amiga* rarely means friend but lover. If the letter was part of the original redaction —and dictaminal exercises were often part of epistolary correspondence between friends— the use

---

[39] Tiresias tells his story in *Lo somni*, book 3 (Metge, '*The Dream*' 122–25).

[40] After a long dispute was held between [Juno and Jupiter] about this subject, they agreed that since I had experienced each nature, I was to be the judge of the aforementioned question, since I ought to know it better than anyone else. After hearing the reasons of each party, I said that the lust of females surpasses three times that of men. Immediately Juno, becoming very outraged by it, and recurring to her characteristic iniquity, took from me not only my sight, but also my eyes (Metge, '*The Dream*' 124). Haüda entre [Júpiter e Juno] gran discepció sobre açò, concordaren ensemps que per tal com jo havia experimentat cascuna natura, fos jutge de la qüestió dessús dita, axí com aquell qui mils ho devia saber que altre. Oÿdes les rahons de cascuna part, diguí que la luxúria de la fembra suprepuge tres vegades aquella de l'hom. Tantost Juno, mol irada d'açò, usant de la sua acostumada iniquitat, tolgué'm no solament la vista, mas los ulls (125).

[41] "con su *indignación* y *malicia* por sus manos dieron cruel muerte al triste de Torrellas" (Francomano, *Three Spanish Querelle Texts* 172–73).

[42] "Veyent e oynt açò gran multitud de dones, la ira e *oy* de les quals encorreguí, una d'aquelles comença a parlar" (Metge, '*The Dream*' 108–09).

of the feminine form may place the work in a very specific rhetorical context, referencing one of the three forms of friendship outlined by Fernández de Madrigal's *Libro*: the lowly erotic passion that goes against reason.

The letter's ambiguities present a serious challenge to the reader; "Flores's dedication," Francomano complains when translating it, "is confusing to the point of illegibility" (*Three Spanish Querelle Texts* 174n2). It may simply be wisecracking, intended for a close circle of male friends, but more meaning can be gleaned when considering it against the discourse *in mulieres* implied in Flores's rhetorical execution of Orpheus and Tiresias: women are lustful and vindictive beasts. Couched in the pleasantries of dedication, praising his *amiga* as the work's inspiration, Flores claims that readers must thank her because he could not have composed the treatise without her "esfuerço." A few lines later, he repeats that "sin esfuerço de vuestra ayuda no podiera hazer cosa que razonable fuesse" (*Three Spanish Querelle Texts* 86). Francomano translates the two instances as "urging" and "fortitude," respectively, but I wonder whether the term is a euphemism in a letter ripe with innuendos about sexual performance. Might Flores be presenting his knowledge of female truth as based on personal experience and his humble stance as nothing less than poorly disguised fear of his *amiga*'s rancor if displeased?

Despite its dictaminal capture of women as signs of irrationality and chaos, *Grisel y Mirabella* differs greatly from *Siervo libre de amor* and the other penitential fictions analyzed in chapter 2. It is not the dream vision of a male protagonist who explores his own desires and fears through the process of writing. It does not offer the soothing balm of consolation but a conventional, if clever, display of extensive learning. It conveys the main tenets of the discourse *in mulieres* as articulated by Torroella's famous slander and the Salamancan burlesques: love inevitably leads all men to destruction. It playfully fictionalizes the death of reason and masculinity at the hands of courtly ladies.

In chapter 2, we saw the efforts exerted by Roís de Corella's friends in *Parlament* to rein in their imagination and moralize the Ovidian tales they so much enjoyed. Instead of the comic relief provided by Caldesa as a source of solidarity among young men, the violence of allegory prevails, and, in a mirror image of *enarratio*, at least one heroine's body is savagely penetrated and silenced before it is made to symbolize female perversion. The friends know their *integumentum* but can barely disguise their interest in the emotions so lovingly described, the episodes so minutely retold that they see themselves reflected, and tears spring to their eyes. *Grisel y Mirabella* shares dictaminal techniques with Roís de Corella's interpretations of classical myths,[43] although different social occasions call for different textual strategies. Flores's *auctoritas* relies on unveiling, not an Ovidian tale, but Woman. The tone of his dedication signals a jest easily lost on those ignorant of the web of Ovidian reminiscences that the training in *pietas litterata* immediately triggered in his schoolmates and courtly comrades. He exerts his power in a most courtly way: hiding slander under the pretense of praise. He is winking at friends.

MAN'S NATURAL INCLINATION

The philosophical inquiry into the phenomenology of erotic drive and the role of free will in the context of Aristotelian naturalism that found vernacular expression in Alonso Fernández de Madrigal's *Libro de amor y amicicia* is also present throughout the Crown of Aragon, as Cátedra demonstrated (*Amor y pedagogía*). Through the lively exchange of letters among authors who addressed the topic in poems, *tractatus*, and parodic sermons, it reached courtiers and wealthy merchants. In his edition of Torroella's works, Rodríguez Risquete points to the dissemination of sacro-profane texts —love masses, profane *lectiones*, love's commandments and joys— that endowed the discourse with its own laws and prophets.

One of the most famous prophets was none other than Pere Torroella (ca. 1425–c. 1492). He is charged with provoking the Castilian *querelle* with his scandalous "Maldezir de mugeres" [Slander against Women], a catalog of women's vices commonly decried in Catalan-Occitan poetry as well as Metge's *Lo somni* but "unprecedented in Castilian *cancioneros*, where individual women were sometimes made the targets of vituperation, but never in the context of courtly love itself" (Francomano, *Three Spanish Querelle Texts* 17). Torroella's slander was built on his authority on womanly nature, but his strategy of paradox and ambiguity, designed to set his lady and himself above other courtiers, backfired, according to Weiss, because he misread the social context ("¿Qué demandamos?"). Had he

---

[43] *Lamentació de Biblis, La història de Leànder i Hero*, or *Parlament*, discussed in chapter 2.

composed the slander in Catalan, it would have been nothing new. He also penned a prose retraction, "Razonamiento en defensa de les dones" [Defense of Ladies against Slanderers], which, Weiss notes, was not unique: Andreas Capellanus and several Castilian poets who were Torroella's contemporaries "chose to play both sides of the debate" ("¿Qué demandamos?" 247). Flores, we saw, followed this trend.

Up to this point, women's nature was discussed in prose treatises meant "for the individual private reader, who engages the material in a distanced, meditative, and rational manner." Weiss mentions defenses, such as Álvaro de Luna's *Libro de las claras e virtuosas mugeres* (1446), Rodríguez del Padrón's *Triunfo de las donas* (1445), and Valera's treatise, that appropriated learned discourse to articulate an aristocratic, cultural view outside the clerical domain ("¿Qué demandamos?" 250–51). Such defenses were courtly responses to the arguments carried out in the penitential consolations studied in chapter 2, and we saw Pedro de Portugal's manipulation of satire to celebrate his lady presented as a courtly attribute. Both penitential consolations and their sentimental contrafacta required mastering and rereading literary tradition, which, as Weiss states, located the debate in the past. However, the ahistorical look, the engagement with "the eternal verities in the philosophical arguments and copious accumulation of historical exempla" did not "solve the problems of the here and now" ("¿Qué demandamos?" 251). The dissonances of these practices sound early in the debate between *Lo somni*'s fictional Metge, an Orpheus in love, and his wise counselor Tiresias. In the end, Tiresias's allegorical aim fails to elevate Metge's backward glances from either his sexual desire or its literary mirror, and, as critics point out, *Lo somni* is a consolation that ends with a disconsolate protagonist.

Torroella's mastery of the literary past led him into a *faux pas*, not only in his choice of language, but more specifically in articulating his own rhetorical stance. In *Lo somni,* Tiresias, the wise counselor, exploits the slander to encourage penitential conversion. In contrast, Torroella invents his authorial position by conflating Orpheus's undying love for Eurydice and subsequent rejection of women with Tiresias's penitential discourse; that is, he resorts to defamation, not to console the male lover, but to praise his lady. No wonder Juan de Flores, who knew his field —and his Ovid— has courtly maenads murder him at the end of *Grisel y Mirabella*. This connection was not lost on readers since, as Rodríguez Risquete documents, a manuscript from the first half of the sixteenth century lists a fragment of *Grisel y Mirabella* along with Torroella's slander (vol. 1, 123).

Beyond his reputation as slanderer, Torroella was the center of an extensive circle of friends and poets, as Pellisa Prades demonstrates. His reply to a letter, now lost, by Bernat Hug de Rocabertí, Knight Commander of Montsó, composed at some point between 1458 and 1462, encapsulates the prevalent discourse on love.[44] Three manuscripts attest to the letter's popularity, one of them the *Jardinet d'orats*. The fact that *Jardinet*'s copyist, the notary Narcís Gual, felt the need to draw attention to Torroella's letter, pointing a manicula to its title twice —in the table of contents and the text page— and glossing love-related terms, speaks to its significance. Furthermore, textual transmission proves the extent of Torroella's reach across a significant social network of bilingual authors in Naples, Barcelona, Zaragoza, Navarre, and Valencia, who were related at some point to the courts of Carlos de Viana, Alfons the Magnanimous, and his successor Joan II (Pellisa Prades, "La transmissió" 58–59, 71–72).

Torroella's response to Bernat Hug de Rocabertí's inquiry into the nature and workings of hope is a rereading of the *Consolation*'s arguments on Fortune's unpredictable nature and habits. The seventh meter that closes the *Consolation*'s first book outlines the relationship of hope and understanding. Pedro de Valladolid's version of Saplana-Ginebreda translated it into Castilian as follows:

> Si tú quieres aver clara conosçencia de las cosas que te quiero mostrar, es menester que eches de ti los cuidados mundanales, conuiene saber, gozo & tristura desordenados, & esperança de las cosas mundanales & dolor de la pérdida de aquellos. Ca aquestas quatro cosas, conuiene saber, gozo & tristura, esperança & dolor contesçen a la persona por los bienes o por los males presentes o por venir. Ca el bien quando es presente da e trae gozo & pagament al omne; quando el bien es por venir trae al ombre en esperança & mueuele el coraçon ha aquella.E por el contrario es del mal. Ca si es presente da al omne dolor & si es por venir da ha omne temor & pauor. E todas las dichas cosas turban el entendimiento de la persona que non puede conoscer claramente la verdat de las cosas. (N 21r)

---

[44] For the dating, see Rodríguez Risquete's introduction to Pere Torroella's *Obra completa* (vol. 1, 59–60), which includes the letter, a useful introduction, and ample notes (vol. 2, 215–21). All my quotations are from this edition.

If you wish to have lucid understanding, you must rid yourself of mundane imaginings, which are disorderly enjoyment and melancholy, hope of worldly things, and suffering for their loss. Because these four things, enjoyment and melancholy, hope and suffering for their loss, happen to a person as a consequence of misfortunes and opportunities, present and future. Because a present good brings and gives enjoyment; if it lies in the future, it moves man to hope. The same applies to the opposite: evil when present causes suffering, in the future it causes worry and fear. And all the aforementioned things cloud understanding.

The translation-commentary ignores Boethius's striking metaphors of dark clouds and raging winds that obscure understanding and rocks breaking off cliffs to block one's path. It focuses on moral amplification of the final mandate: to follow the right road by casting off all joy and fear and fleeing hope and sorrow. It recalls the mistaken path —the error— in penitential and sentimental topification of a lover's inner conflict.[45]

The translation's move to identify Fortune's uncertainty with erotic passion and woman as its cause is fully accomplished in Torroella's courtly argumentation. He conflates Boethian moral arguments on Fortune's fickleness with Aristotelian naturalism, transforming amatory instinct into an irresistible force. He defends lovers' hope by arguing for the righteousness of its object, delight, while detailing the stages of infatuation:

> Vul sapiau que·ls ulls sols, acompanyats del altres senys, sollen representar a la imaginació la belleza e disposició de la dona; en la stimació de la qual, migensant natural atracció, se cauze una passible aprobació nomenade grat, e per consegüent se figure delit. E perquè delit no és altre cosa sinó aplicació de hun covinent ab lo seu convenible, parteix del sperit sensibla un cobagós talent en la pocessió de la cosa agradable que s'entitule desig; per adquisició de la qual, investiguant la fi, resulte de la part opinative una fianzose crehense de l'advenidor bé nomanade pròpiamente speransa. (vol. 2, 216)

> You must know that the eyes only, in the company of the internal senses, represent to the imagination woman's beauty and bodily

---

[45] Also in Manrique's *Coplas*, where the world is a path one should walk "sin errar."

features; when considering them, mixed with natural attraction, a passible agreement named *grat* is caused, and as a consequence, delight appears. And because delight is nothing else but the connection of a suitable thing and what suits it, a concupiscent appetite to possess the pleasant thing, named desire, is born from the sensible spirit; in order to acquire such a thing, expecting its conclusion, a supposition about the future good, properly called hope, results from the *aestimativa*.

Torroella differentiates *grat* from delight as the *primus motus*, although, as Rodríguez Risquete notes, they were commonly understood as synonyms.[46] Hope of future enjoyment, not the erotic sting, is what causes love. Hope stimulates all human initiatives: farmers, sailors, and merchants endanger their station in life; courtiers suffer the outbursts, anger, and disfavor of arrogant lords; soldiers risk their lives; and even Christians are moved by the hope of paradise.[47] Torroella spells out the courtly discourse on hope as the will's *intentio,* motivating both courtly love and social advancement.

In *Jardinet d'orats,* Narcís Gual's marginal glosses call attention to key terms in Torroella's letter: "enteniment" (understanding), "voluntat" [will], "goig" [joy], "cobegança" [desire], "dolor," and "temor," which correspond word-for-word with Saplana-Ginebreda's translation of, and commentary on, the seventh meter. Furthermore, *Jardinet* is a compilation of texts that support the letter's contentions, as Pellisa Prades cleverly notes.[48] Francesc Alegre's *Rehonament* includes an allegory of Hope that coincides with Torroella's argument, and Narcís Gual uses a manicule to call attention to a line in Roís de Corella's *Lamentació de Biblis*: "virtuosa cosa és portar a fi lo comen-

---

[46] Rodríguez Risquete cites Arnau de Vilanova's *Tractatus de amore heroico*: "gratum seu delectabile" (vol.2, 219n23–24).

[47] "Aquesta causa als lauredors ab excessiva e molesta afflicció coltivar la fatiguoza terra. Per aqueste los navigants induïts, súlcan perillant les naufraguoses aygües. En aquesta los mercaders confiant, entre los strany comercis peregrinant, comanen son estat a fortuna. De aquesta los cortezans consellats, soffrint opprobres, anuigs e desfavors, los ingrats e superbos senyors servir se disponen. Ab aquesta los militans sforzats, entre molts strems e perilosos afanys, acompenyats de la mort, seguexen lo militar axercici. E dich, per no més dilatar, que si la speransa de paradís no·s representàs a nosaltres, se atroberie Déu ab tant pochs servidors que poque satisfecció bastaria" (vol. 2, 217).

[48] Following the work by Martos on the *cançoners* that include sentimental pieces, Pellisa Prades argues that in *Jardinet d'orats*, theoretical texts on the phenomenology of love are closely linked to sentimental compositions, both in verse and prose, that act as models or examples ("La transmissió" 63).

sat e més com fortuna hi constrasta" [finishing what one begins is a virtuous thing especially when fortune is against it]. This amplification on courtly hope is further expanded in the final advice Antoni Vidal provides to the protagonist of Francesc Alegre's *Somni* (58), which will be the subject of my next section. But before analyzing Francesc Alegre's *Somni*, the anonymous *Triste deleytaçión*, another compilation of a more narrative nature, illustrates hope's conflicting discourse with the tribulations of an author in love.

In the Company of Ladies: *Triste deleytaçión*

The muddling of narrative voices, allegory, and realistic narrative, its Castilian-Catalan diglossia, and the complexity of its plot drive Folger to label the prosimetrum *Triste deleytaçión* "a messy piece of literature" (*Images in Mind* 149).[49] Preserved in a single manuscript (Biblioteca de Catalunya Ms. 770), it was composed after 1458, if we take the author's remark that the events narrated occurred at that time ("tiempo de cinquenta y ocho") at face value. Along with *Siervo* and *Sátira*, it is considered one of the earliest monuments of sentimental fiction, although this dating relies on the early reading *à clé* by Martín de Riquer, who identified the enigmatic F.A.D.C. mentioned in the prologue as Fra Artal de Claramunt, Knight Commander of La Guardia (Lérida) ("Triste deleytación"). Martín de Riquer retracted his opinion later and even questioned the anonymous author's nationality; he could have been an Aragonese fluent in Catalan ("Elements comuns"). Most critics today accept that he was a Catalan speaker, perhaps attached to the itinerant court of Carlos, Príncipe de Viana, a multilingual atmosphere, like that of his uncle Alfons the Magnanimous at Naples, that makes such distinctions irrelevant. Deyermond ("El punto de vista narrativo"), Blay Manzanera ("La dinámica"), and Impey ("*Contraria*") date *Triste deleytaçión* to the 1470s, much closer to the works of Diego de San Pedro and Juan de Flores, but all critics agree that it occupies an intermediate position between *Siervo libre de amor* and *Sátira de infelice e felice vida* on the one hand and later sentimental texts in Castile and Aragon on the other.

---

[49] On *Triste deleytaçión's* temporal-spatial dynamics, see Blay Manzanera ("La dinámica").

F.A.D.C. builds on the courtly canon by including Rodríguez del Padrón in the lovers' paradise and mentioning the protagonists of *Siervo*'s interpolated *Estoria,* which supports a connection between their fictional mechanisms. Both prologues declare that the work concerns a love affair, although in *Triste deleytación,* it is not the author's but a double "auto de amores" involving a virtuous lady (a *señora,* indicated later in the text by the cypher S^a), a young gentleman (*enamorado,* or E°), his friend (*amigo,* or A°), and the lady's stepmother (*madrastra,* or M^a). F.A.D.C. claims to know about it by indirect means ("por via jndirecta" 1).[50] As in most of this demanding work, the hint is unclear, especially since a few lines later, he states that the affair is not yet over and goes into a long, convoluted explanation for leaving the story unfinished.[51] Both Gerli (ed., *Triste deleytacion*) and Rohland de Langbehn (ed., *Triste deleytación*) sidestep a key fact in summarizing the passage in the introductions to their editions: the narrator and the young man are friends. F.A.D.C. claims that he wishes to avoid fiction and will not praise his friend unduly by attributing to him a greater role in the affair than he actually played; if he did so, his friend and those who in due course came to know the truth would deem it mere flattery.

Unlike *Siervo,* the prologue in *Triste deleytación* is not addressed to a male friend but to the narrator's estranged lady. His ulterior motive in recounting the love affair, he confesses, is to deliver her —and other ladies who may read the work— from feeling ungrateful toward men and convincing them that all lovers are constant. Folger cautiously "venture[s] that E°'s and S^a's authentic passionate love appealed to F.A.D.C.; the exemplarity of their realistic story is founded in their realistic suffering from lovesickness" (*Images in Mind* 160). Without denying the twin plots' exemplary nature, note that the narrator confesses that he cannot stop thinking about both S^a's determination and a happy ending to the affair.[52] His alignment with one of the male participants and his strong desire for a certain outcome

---

[50] I cite from Rohland de Langbehn's 1983 edition.

[51] "[L]a causa fue no aplicar fiçion, por ser mas obligado en tal caso a la verdat que al amigo. Que loandolo el auer hauido mas parte en ella del que huuo, me seria atribuydo a lisonja mas que a buena amistat, en la hopinyon no solo d'aquel, mas ahun de todos aquellos que por delante de la verdat fuesen informados, si bien la strema voluntat de la senyora donzella y del enamorado ajuntamiento de gran amor el pensamiento mio siempre me representaua" (1).

[52] "La strema voluntat de la *senyora* donzella y del *enamorado* ajuntamiento de gran amor el pensamiento mio siempre me representaua" (1).

seem to drive the narrative and call his reliability and realistic intent into question. Is he telling his own story? As most critics have noted, *Triste deleytaçión* blurs the lines between imagination and experience. This blurring acquires full meaning when we understand *Triste deleytaçión* as F.A.D.C.'s affective meditation on a lover's trials and tribulations with which he fully identifies.

F.A.D.C. labels his work *jnuençion* ("sta jnuençion como propio bien le quise narar en suma" 1–2), with a dictaminal understanding of the term as literary creation based on recollection of authoritative texts and personal experience. Pere Torroella intends the same meaning in his "Tant mon voler s'és dat a Amors" [My Will Surrendered to Love], a so-called "collective poem" that explains love sufferings by quoting fragments from Catalan, Castilian, French, and Provençal poets as *auctoritates*.[53] Addressed to the young, the poem's structure is barely narrative and works by contrafaction of a wise adult's moralizing stance in instructing the novice (Torroella, vol. 1, 375n20). Torroella uses *invensions* to describe the original poems by troubadors;[54] in them, he finds proof to support the verities of his existence ("refermar les veritats de mon esser") but also the strange pleasure ("strany pler") of not being alone in his sorrow ("com trob no sol esser en mas dolors").

> Lurs rahons tròban actoritats
> en refermar les veritats
>   de mon esser,
> e no dupteu quin strany pler
> trobe com trob no sol esser
>   en mas dolors. (vol. 1, 351 vv. 10–15)

This feeling is echoed in F.A.D.C.'s choice of title for his *jnuençion*, *Triste deleytaçión*, the paradoxical sad delight of knowing that the unfulfilled desire —"mi deseo trasposado en aquella senyora" (1)— propelling his writing is shared with, and explained by, an extensive literary tradition. His friend's case and his own are simply instances of man's natural inclination. F.A.D.C.'s emotionally driven account fits

---

[53] The information on "Tant mon voler" comes from Rodríguez Risquete's introduction and substantial notes to his edition of the poem in Torroella's *Obra completa* (vol. 1, 349–94).

[54] "*Invensions* remet al tecnicisme *inventio*, 'troballa d'un tema, obra original,' al qual sembla que Torroella equipara l'activitat dels 'trobadors' que 'tròban auctoritats' (v. 10) mitjançant el seus poemes" (Torroella, vol. 1, 376n41).

within the parameters of affective piety, which asks the devout reader
to actively participate in the events of Christ's life the text describes.

In the context of contemporary theory on erotic phenomenology and dictaminal *inventio* as practiced by the rhetorical poets,
the "trobadors studiosos," who fill the pages of Catalan *cançoners*,
Triste deleytaçión is an anthology held together by a narrative about
people affected by recurrent imaginings. As Impey (1986) noticed,
the prologue gives no details about the plot's twofold love affairs
but instead calls the reader's attention to the theoretical pieces that
take up most of the pages: an ecphrasis of the palace of Love, the
disputation of Reason and Will, and the *querella de las mugeres* disguised as advice given to S^a by a character named Madrina (god-
mother). F.A.D.C. does not mention the final allegorical dream
vision in which E° journeys through Hell, Paradise, and Heaven
in search of his lady. According to Impey ("Un doctrinal") and Folger (*Images in Mind*), love, or more specifically the discourse on
amor hereos, is the only connection among these disparate pieces.
Blay Manzanera ("El más allá"), after Martín de Riquer ("Triste
deleytación"), suggests that the final dream vision may have been
conceived independently and added later. All these questions seem
uncannily similar to those raised by Juan Ruiz's *Libro de buen amor*,
another work in which pseudo-autobiographical narration, with
abrupt changes in voice, binds a love anthology. First-person narrative and dream vision, as we have seen in penitential consolations
and school parodies, are tools to appropriate the literary past; they
are also common practice among "trobadors studiosos," the rhetorical poets like Pere Torroella or Jordi de Sant Jordi in his *Passio
amoris secundum Ovidium*.

The name chosen for love's palace, "el palacio Aborintio," supports my interpretation. Rohland de Langbehn (ed. *Triste deleytaçión*) and Impey ("*Contraria*") relate it to labyrinth without further
explanation, but it may be a pun on Eberhard the German's labyrinth
of learning, whose title, *Laborintus*, is "devised from *labor habens intus* 'having misery in it'" (Murphy 180). This thirteenth-century *ars
poetriae* is "a delightful maze of verse, grammar, and rhetoric, a labyrinth of learning containing an allegorical account of grammar, poesy, and rhetoric" (Purcell 95). *Triste deleytaçión* is, in Gerli's words,
"an anthology of the medieval literature of love written with tongue
very often firmly in cheek" (ed. *Triste deleytacion* xiv). However, unlike Boncompagno's *Rota*, Juan Ruiz's *Libro,* and later Salamancan
spoofs, it is addressed to inconstant ladies, not school peers. Like

Pedro de Portugal in *Sátira,* F.A.D.C. adapts *inventio,* a tool aging clerks use to moralize, to narrate desire, which explains the challenging structure of the resulting work.

The first-person account begins in the most conventional manner. A young man, ignorant of the pleasures of love, goes riding and happens to see a lovely lady in a window. Love-struck, he retreats to his chamber to mull over and assuage the conflicting feelings the image of beauty has sparked ("My coraçon gozoso y triste de aquella nueua vista" 4).[55] After a sleepless night, he composes the expected debate between Lady Reason (Razón) and Lady Will (Voluntad). Razon sternly reprimands Voluntad: "your recent exposure to love greatly endangers your virtuous living" ("la nueua speriençia de amor al vuestro virtuoso biuir graue jnpedimiento pone" 4), conflating the voices of Voluntad and the lover. Razón must repeat her rebuke before Voluntad, red with shame, finally lowers her eyes ("con el jesto colorado abaxo los oios" 5); she remains in this position for a while before fearfully replying ("por hun rato / con la cabeça baxa stado auia, con cara temerosa y voz scura alço los oios y empeço de faular" 5). Their physical stances at the beginning of the dialogue and Voluntad's reluctance to contend clearly allude to Saplana-Ginebreda's translation of the *Consolation*'s initial scene.

Furthermore, their arguments emphasize free will, but now Voluntad misrepresents Boethian arguments to justify the lover's infatuation. She fully accepts Fortune's capriciousness, although she identifies it with human inconstancy ("nuestra natura ser jncostante" 6); conflates joy and hope; and embraces sorrows and fears as part of a gentleman's training on his path to fame and love —*glory* is a code word for love's ultimate reward.[56] She echoes naturalistic arguments on the inevitability of erotic passion and states that God gave men free will, so they could choose the woman who best answers their desire. Razón's words, she argues, are not compelling enough to thwart nature's powerful drive.[57]

---

[55] Cortijo Ocaña relates the scene to Dante's *Vita nuova* (*La evolución genérica* 117).

[56] On the double meanings of words in *cancionero* poetry, see Whinnom (*La poesía amatoria*); MacPherson ("Secret Language"); and Cátedra's study of Aristotelian naturalism (*Amor y pedagogía*).

[57] "Antes, libre la nuestra voluntat, dio poder de scoger aquella que mas agradable fuese al querer suyo ... ¿como presumis vos que solo palabras fuesen sufiçientes defender ni quitar lo que natural condiçion jnclina e fuerça?" (5).

Manipulating Boethian arguments in the service of false conclusions may impart a parodic tone, but I argue for a different approach, following Heinrichs's study of "lovers' consolations." These
lovers are not sarcastic; they speak in character as examples of "will-
ful moral blindness." They enunciate Boethian arguments but cannot carry them to their proper conclusion because "an act of will
… has entrapped them in servitude to Fortune and … they believe
they cannot, or must not, reverse" it ("'Lovers' Consolations" 112).
Razón is fully aware of her opponent's deviousness ("vuestras fengi-
das razones, con alguna color de verdat reçitadas" 6; "con disimula-
das palabras y fictas parençerias trabaias a vuestro preposito venir"
11). She implies that Voluntad's faulty reasoning is a consequence of
her distressed mental state and lists the symptoms of her ailment: her
heart has been hooked by the sweet delightful principle promised
by hope, and love's subtle nets snare human freedom and, in place
of restful joy, offer sadness, dragging the sick along a narrow path
between crags, strewn with thorns (6). Razón's words expound on
Saplana-Ginebreda's translation of the seventh meter that ends the
Consolation's first book.

As in Torroella's reply to Bernat Hug de Rocabertí, Voluntad turns
hope into the courage that proves a lover's steadfastness. She argues
that when the goal is so salubrious, the transition from desire to hope braces love's determination, and no travail seems too dangerous:

> 's posible representarse algun bien tan exçelente a los nuestro sen-
> timientos, aprouado por el entendimiento, ser tal que el grado al
> deseo y el deseo al esperança dan tal sfuerço <a> amor, que por al-
> cançar la possesion de la fin qualquiere cosa acometer no le pareçe
> peligroso. (10)

> It is possible to picture a good so adequate to one's feelings, sanc-
> tioned by understanding, that the move from pleasure to desire
> and from desire to hope endows love with such determination that
> no travail seems dangerous to attain possession of it.

Unlike Torroella, Voluntad does not distinguish two degrees of
desire —*grat* and *delit*— but the progress from first sight to hope
is identical. Significant delight ("deleytaçion") —and not only that
attendant on loving women— overcomes freedom (11). The deviousness of Voluntad's argument on the workings of joy, fear, hope,
and sorrow deserves to be quoted in full:

El corazon enlazado y ençendido de las lamas de amor no cabe en
libertat suya alcaçar, sino con gran afan, aquella agua que mata las
fuerças suyas, que la enamorada voluntat, reçebiendo de la sperança sus delytosos frutos, con demasiado querer sigue los fines
de aquella. E con este tan justo sperar sus dulçes pensamientos
creçen, y reçiben por aquel sus sentimientos vn nueuo gozo que
dispone el corazon en poder poseer lo que sus deseos desean ...
Que el que por el temor de jinconuenientes dexa su bentura seguir,
aquel tal / antes de ser muerto lo tienen la verguença y desonrra
enterrado, pues viue aconortado de no dexar mas honrra ny mas
bienes en el mundo de quanto truxo en el, antes asi desnudo como
vino le plaze lo pongan sota la tierra. La qual error y opinyon tiene
enganyado el gentil honbre por el stado en que es, que lo obliga y
fuerça con animo verill los peligros y temores hosarlos enprender,
porque el tal sufrimiento lo ponga en esperiençia de bien y fama,
la qual con discreçion y sin banagloria fuera reçebida por alcaçar
eterna gloria; que sto por manifiesto tenemos, que la buena ny la
mala ventura no puede star con firmeza ... Que de Amor quere
mudar sus condiçiones seria gran / fantasia, como tengamos por
cierto que a de condenar a muchos y otros tantos dar vida. E con
sta sperança de ser de los scogidos se ponen a la ventura aquelos
que suyos se dizen, y avn yo conformarm'e con ellos, quando mi
voluntat terna por bien pasar con deleyte las penas que su merçet
por prouar mi firmeza me dare. (12–13)

The heart, ensnared and burning with love's flames, cannot freely
attain, except with great determination, the water that puts out
combustion, because a lover's will, receiving from hope its delightful fruits, follows hope's aspirations with extreme appetite. And
with this fair hope the heart's sweet imaginings increase and receive
a new joy that prepares the heart to possess what its desires desire
... He who does not seek his fortune for fear of inconvenience, he
who, before dying, shame and dishonor have already buried, lives
with the only consolation of not leaving behind more honor and
wealth than those he brought into this world and is pleased to be
laid to rest as naked as he came. This erroneous opinion deceives
the gentleman because his station forcefully compels him to face
dangers and fears with virile determination so that by enduring
them he may experience worldly goods and fame, which he can receive with prudence and without arrogance to attain eternal glory;
because this we know for sure, that good and bad fortune cannot
be steady ... Trying to change Love's terms would be presumptu-
ous as we know for certain that it will condemn many and bring

life to many others. And with the hope of being the chosen ones
many seek their fortunes, among them myself, when my will shall
endure with delight all the sorrows that her mercy shall give me to
prove my faithfulness.

The Aristotelian naturalism that justifies the spoof *De cómo al
hombre le es necesario amar* is fully articulated here for the benefit
of courtiers and gentlemen: erotic drive paired with hope becomes
virtus. Petrarch, directly or indirectly, could very well be the source
for Voluntad's ideas on fame and glory. In a letter on the education of
princes, he exorted Francesco da Carrara "to undertake such tasks
as will bring you a share of glory that your ancestors never attained"
and to "lust after a form of greediness that is generous and beyond
reproach: a greediness to obtain the treasure of *virtus* and the outstanding attribute of fame" (Skinner 414).

Unable to reorient Voluntad's aim, Razón turns to great lovers
for examples of frightful deaths. She cites the expected Ovidian lore
along with the courtly canon of Boccaccio's heroes —Fiammetta,
Ghismonda, and Guiscardus— and the protagonists of *Siervo*'s "Estoria," Ardanlier and Liessa. Voluntad rejects moralization ("la delicada sentençia") and opposes her own inventory of blissful devotees
who accepted Love's primacy. The list is taken almost exclusively
from the *Decameron* but includes the expected biblical and mythological characters along with wise Aristotle and Virgil. According to
Gerli, it is "a standard list of learned and famous men destroyed by
love, variants of which can often be found in fifteenth century Castilian antifeminist works" (ed. *Triste deleytacion* 126n26). The statement that "sta fuerça incomparable pudieron jamás registir" (17)
seems to point to a parodic treatment in line with *De cómo al hombre
le es necesario amar*. While burlesques consciously misappropriate
school forms and themes for laughter, parading their authors' dictaminal skill in interpreting a text from opposing perspectives, Voluntad's humorous intent is less clear. She is characterized as a determined lover, who craftily counterfeits Boethian arguments to defend
her point. From Razón's point of view, her understanding is clouded
by the pleasurable love stories in which she sees herself mirrored,
like *Lo somni*'s fictional Metge, declining their "delicada sentençia."

Razón feels indebted to her friend, and in a final attempt to cure
her of her error, resorts to a detailed description of a lovers' paradise, the Palacio Aborintio, to demonstrate the falsity of its earthly
pleasures and joys ("sabe que todo es falso y sufistiquo, que no es

mas obligado el amigo a su amigo, si no lo por venir azerle a saber"
23). Its circular tower, Impey remarks, connotes spiritual elevation
and perfection, but it is also a phallic image: Cupid of the multihued
wings and gold arrows, whose power never fails, lives in it (*"Contraria"*). A flaming door leads to a stairway and a fabulous hall on whose
walls are represented "jnfinitos autos pasados y presentes d'amor"
(22); Venus, surrounded by her court, sits among sensual enjoyments
—"flores odorificas de jnnumerables colores ... arbolles muy deley-
tosos, con vozes de aves con multitud de tenores, ali tanta cantidat de
plazeres / y alegrias, que ser ali el parayso judicarias" (23). Breçayda,
traditional symbol of infidelity, and other modern ladies, of whom
Razón says, "I have written in my fantasy" ("en companya de otras
senyoras modernas, *las quales no aqui, mas en mi fantasia tengo es-
critas"* 23, emphasis added), advance to receive the lover. At Venus's
command, Adriana [Ariadne] offers him a drink that predictably
transforms sensual paradise into horrid landscape.

Notable in this otherwise cliché scene is that the transformation
results from a voluntarily ingested venom. This departure acquires
full meaning when read alongside Jorge Manrique's *Coplas,* in which
he rejects the fictions of famous poets and orators because their
sweet flavors are laced with secret poisons ("trahen yeruas secretas
sus sabores"). In Venus's hall, the lover finds, not actual people, but
textual memories, phantasms, and pictorial representations. The allegorical Palacio Aborintio is not so much a warning against love as
a more general indictment of fictions —in art or infatuation— that
resist the rigors of moralization. As a memory structure, it is also
the *imago agens* that initiates the twin plots' *inventio,* although, unlike *Siervo,* no warship will arrive at the end, demanding its ethical
due. Instead, *Triste deleytaçión*'s story of star-crossed lovers comes
to an inconclusive end: E° walks alone. His emotional restlessness
resembles that of the awakening protagonist-narrator in *Siervo*'s last
section. In *Triste deleytaçión,* the moment of creative energy is articulated as counterfaction of the Boethian sea of Fortune:

> Como mitiguar ny refrenar las pasiones d'amor nuestra libertad no
> tiene tal fuerça, que, alagada la voluntad de los pensamientos de-
> leytosos, nuestro querer con mayor fe sino en ser suyo se conoçe,
> que forcado d'aqueste poder que qualquiere otro vençe, *en todo
> otro auto fuera d'este bolber las spaldas.* Y asy no fue marabilla el
> diligente enamorado ... la terçera quiso tentar por ver si la suerte
> le cupiera por sus afetados trauajos acoger sus deseos, y siguiendo

tal proposito, fue causa poner la proa de su sperança en parte que razon ninguna la fin del que tanto queria le consentia; y en tal forma nauegando en el tempestuoso mar de amor, qu'en / seguro puerto de la aduersa fortuna casy o no ninguno con propera anquoras sorgir puede, le fue supliendo al demasiado querer suyo la tal ventura, como aquí por las syguientes coplas se aze mincion presentada. (141; emphasis added)

Our freedom does not have the strength to assuage or restrain love passion; when the will is gratified with delightful thoughts, our desire works with greater determination so that, compelled by such force that overpowers everything, it cannot turn ("bolber") as it would in any other work. Therefore, it was not surprising that the resolute lover ... for the third time tried his luck and oriented the prow of his hope in the direction blocked by reason; navigating love's tempestuous sea, where nobody can drop anchor in the port of adverse fortune, he supplied to his unrestrained desire this poem titled *ventura* here presented in the following *coplas*.

My translation is admittedly free but covers the main points of Eº's predicament: man's natural inclination prevents him from *bolber*, from reorienting his desire and effecting a moral conversion of the story. Voluntad made that point, but it acquires full meaning when juxtaposed to *Siervo*, specifically, the narrator's injunction to his free will to change direction ("buelta, buelta mi esquivo pensar") after he finishes "Estoria" and wakes up. At that point, he composes a few poems rejecting passional servitude and encouraging conversion while journeying through the hills and valleys of his meditations until he is assisted by the warship of Christian education. In *Triste deleytaçión,* Eº's uncompromising hope keeps his literary boat bound toward the dangerous sea of fictional narrative. The result is an allegorical vision of lovers' hell, purgatory, and paradise that bears a close resemblance to Santillana's *Sueño,* not just because the protagonist runs into Tiresias ("vn honbre muy ançiano / con vn baston en la mano" 158, lines 18–19) but rejects his advice, moved by a force comparable to that of Orpheus ("con mas amor que Orfeo ... me complia / por la fuerça del deseo" 160, lines 22 and 25). These verses, titled *Ventura* (another term for fortune), first and foremost describe a sea journey through the texts and motifs of love literature, mostly Dante and Boccaccio, as Gerli points out (ed. *Triste deleytacion* xii).

Its intention may be clarified by a similar narrative poem, *Glòria de amor* [Love's Glory], composed by Bernat Hug de Rocabertí around 1459–1461. Rocabertí adopts a very different stance, renouncing his past follies: in the prose prologue, he addresses the account of his pain ("narrar la mia dolor") to an audience as young as that of F.A.D.C. ("youths and maidens ... whose hearts are ever filled with love" 49).[58] Wounded by love one last time, the protagonist entered the garden of love and its castle only to find that some "were enjoying eternal happiness, while others were denied love's joys" (16-17). The prologue ends on a melancholy note by advising "young maidens and ladies" to resist Cupid's arrows and be happy while they are young "for time passes like a stream of running water, never to turn back." His poem will make them "aware of the rewarding of the good and the punishment of the bad" (17) —in effect, it seeks revenge against a cruel lady— but will also provide consolation, teaching protagonist and audience that "those who abstained from love profited most" (41). E°'s sea journey explores similar geographies but lacks a moralizing or retaliatory intent.

The perplexing *coplas de disparates* [nonsensical couplets] provide another key to unlock the meaning of his last visionary journey. In them, the seafarer is insulted by a group of "vellacos" [scoundrels]. Blay Manzanera notices that their semantic inversions express a topsy-turvy universe. Worldly and textual madness, she concludes, run together, opening the way for fantasy ("El humor" 71). The final dream vision, moving from hell to purgatory to heaven, is a specular image that inverts the lover's journey to Palacio Aborintio, another space defined by *contraria*, as Impey demonstrates (*"Contraria"*). Whether the piece was composed as an integral part of *Triste deleytaçión* or added as an afterthought, it affords the lover no closure or solace. Lost in his imagination, he continues writing to his lady.

In its counterfaction of penitential discourse, *Triste deleytaçión* perverts Boethian ethical principles, not only in the debate of Razón and Voluntad, but also in another long theoretical piece that breaks the plot's dynamics. In the "doctrinal of ladies," as Impey classifies it ("Un doctrinal"), Madrina instructs S^a in the ways of love. The very old woman ("vna duenya muy antigua" 58) appears when S^a has withdrawn to her chamber in tears, tormented by love and undecided whether to heed the advice given by Vergüenza [Shame]. Madrina's consolation to mitigate Love's absolute power spends no time on dissuading S^a but explains in very practical terms how to succeed

---

[58] I cite from Heaton's edition and translation of the poem.

in erotic pursuits. She advises choosing a mature lover, wealthy and discreet, who can satisfy sexual needs, and considers the advantages of loyalty to a single man. After a debate on the deceptions of men and women, she provides more specific advice on how to keep a lover. Impey is shocked by her emphasis on wealth, contrary to Christian morals, and notes her similarity to the "balia, di anni antica" who comes to console Fiammetta ("Un doctrinal" 198, 222). As in Boccaccio's tale, the old counselor is a counterfeit Lady Philosophy, who instructs her charge on, not the evanescence of worldly goods, but the desirability of taking full advantage of them because life is short and human nature unstable. Madrina's doctrine shares only an admonitory tone with *Castigos e documentos para bien vivir*, the *Disciplina clericalis,* or *El conde Lucanor*. Instead, it is an *ars amandi* that promotes wealth and erotic energy and, as Impey notes, the amatory practices attributed to the classical world ("Un doctrinal" 227). It is not addressed to a learned audience, like Juan Ruiz's *Libro*, or a courtly lover, like Andreas Capellanus's *De amore*, but to a maiden tormented by erotic visions ("Un doctrinal" 221). Impey takes it as a sign of a new amatory mentality prompted by changing economic conditions, particularly in Catalonia: the emergence of a social class centered on material wellbeing (231–32). While I do not disagree with her conclusion, emphasized by Blay Manzanera ("El más allá"), we both recognize that female greed is a favorite subject of moralists.[59]

Sexual vigor and wealth, the two attributes that Madrina most values in a male lover, are viewed very differently in women. Roís de Corella's *Tragèdia de Caldesa*, we have seen, incarnates lust as female. Francesc Alegre's *Faula de Neptuno i Diana*, penned under the name Claudiano and included, like *Caldesa*, in the *Jardinet d'orats*, is a dream vision of Venus's court in which a character named Diana, illustrating female greed, is put on trial.[60] She is transformed into a black rock as punishment, which, as Pellisa Prades proves (*La ficció sentimental*), is Alegre's fictional take on Aglauros's myth of the *Metamorphosis*, which he translated into Catalan in his youth. In both cases, Pellisa Prades cleverly notices, a voyeur exposes the

---

[59] The connection with Alfonso Martínez de Toledo's *Corbacho* is also noted by Gerli (ed. *Triste deleytacion* 126n29) and Cortijo Ocaña (*La evolución genérica* 123)

[60] The complete title is *Faula de les amors de Neptuno i Dyana ab la transfformació de aquella en rocha per la ira de Cupido feta per Claudiano* [Fable of the Love of Neptune and Diana with Her Transformation into a Rock by Cupid's Wrath Composed by Claudiano].

lady's deception: the narrator-protagonist silences the woman's voice (*La ficció sentimental* 143). The violent impulse of the allegorical gaze, the camera obscura of moral discourse, flattens the two female characters into symbols of depravity.[61] Madrina, by contrast, presents female appetites as the counterpart of manly *virtus* to succeed in society.

F.A.D.C.'s explanation of the enigmatic term "Verbino" in the prologue places *Triste deleytaçión* firmly in the sentimental genre.[62] Blay Manzanera looks for a source in Servius's commentary on Virgil, where Verbino is ambiguously identified with Hippolytus, who was killed by his own horses, revived by Asclepius, and transported by Artemis to Italy; his rebirth might explain why F.A.D.C. uses the expression "dos veces hombre" [twice the man] ("El más allá" 139). F.A.D.C. may have borrowed the term from dictaminal *enarratio,* but the connection with Hippolytus is tenuous at best. The context in which the first instance of "Verbino" occurs suggests a different reading.

The only plot-related event that F.A.D.C. mentions in the prologue is Fortune's appearance to E° during the night, when she calls him "Verbino." The name's meaning, "twice the man," is said to indicate that he is both unfortunate and fortunate ("la vna significa ser mal aventurado, y la otra, ser bien aventurado" 3). The paradox recalls the title, *Triste deleytaçión,* as well as Pedro de Portugal's use of *sátira* to define his personal experience —a sad life extoling the lady's happy life— and his *usus tractandi* and *intentio* —uncovering the universal truth of women's worth inside his own misery.

However, "Verbino" acquires full force from Torroella's insult to slanderers as "hombre no hombre" [man who is not a man] in his retraction (vol. 2, 182, line 223). According to Rodríguez Risquete in a footnote to the expression, Torroella is able to transform his earlier slander into praise because virility, identified with moral perfection, is as easily attained as lost (vol. 2, 201n223). More to the point, moral righteousness and love madness are the rhetorical choices of penitential Tiresias and sentimental Orpheus, respectively. They determine, not only a character's behavior, but an author's

---

[61] Cocozzella's clever reading of the dark chamber where the lover comes to understand Caldesa's treason as a psychic space related to literary creation inspires my understanding of allegory as camera oscura (*Text, Translation*).

[62] The term appears two other times in *Triste deleytaçión* but its explanation occurs only in the prologue.

usus tractandi. Fortuna calls E° "Verbino" because he is in love, but so is F.A.D.C. The only choice for a gentleman, Voluntad argues, is accepting the natural urge, driven by hope, to which his station forcefully compels him. That same urge guides F.A.D.C.'s hand away from moral conversion. *Triste deleytaçión* is autobiographical in the sense of a game of mirrors reflecting an author in love writing about a lover who writes.

Unlike those lover's consolations in which a lonely writer addresses a male friend, F.A.D.C.'s rhetorical stance and *Triste deleytaçión*'s textual form address the company of ladies and desire to please them. F.A.D.C.'s comments immediately following his explanation of Verbino elaborate on this point:

> Y mas, como en el razonamiento de las tres senyoras quexosas, la vna llorando manifestaua / el grande sujuzgamiento en que las magnificas senyoras por los honbres stauan, mostrandolo ella, y confirmandolo la madrina por viuas razones, ser ellas mas perfetas y nobles que los onbres; y como reçitaua la madrina que ellos por autos de virtuosos onbres pasados se defendian, y afirmauan ellos ser mas eccelentes que las donas, y de aqui les venia amar mas perfectamente por ser ellos mas nobles y la virtut del amor mas prinçipal de todas; y como la madrina demostraua con otros tantos viçiosos autos ser el contrario. (3)

> And more [is added] in the argument of the three plaintive ladies; one declared in tears how men subjugated excellent ladies, of which she was an example; and Madrina confirmed with clever arguments that women were more perfect and noble than men; as Madrina explained, men defended themselves by citing the tales of past virtuous males and maintaining that they were more excellent than women, and from this they inferred that they loved more perfectly because they were more noble and the virtue of love was the most important of all; and Madrina demonstrated the contrary with as many enjoyable tales.

This passage is notable in connecting personal experience with the debate on women, two features that Cortijo Ocaña (*La evolución genérica*) identifies with the sentimental genre, but I want to call attention to the striking association of the debate and literary enjoyment. Men and Madrina support their arguments with "viçiosos autos," delightful stories whose purpose, we may assume, is to amuse. The camera obscura of penitential consolation, operated in company of ladies, becomes the Orphic mirror, the shared thrill of reading for entertainment.

The last couplets of the final dream vision, *Ventura,* fully articulate the motif of desire, rather than reason, as guide. Cortijo Ocaña believes that E° enters religious life after he finds that Sª has entered a convent, but his final words, cited in support, are unclear (*La evolución genérica* 128):

> Aunque mi querer libre
> con voto y sagramento
> yo jamas no le quite
> de donde primero fue
> con primero complimiento (196, couplet 157)

The concessive clause and its subjunctive mood ("aunque mi querer libre") locate E°'s religious vows in the realm of the possible. Even if he took them, he remains adamant ("jamas") in his commitment to the lady. In the couplets immediately preceding E°'s request for a letter from Sª, the nautical metaphors that initiated the vision change. In a state of captivity ("catiuo"), neither dead nor alive ("muerto ni biuo"), E° is no longer captain of his ship; he is an oarsman stirred by the boatswain's whip ("puesto en el cruel banco / sintiendo diuersas bregas") and without a compass ("sin ti no tiene compas").[63]

---

[63] Pues vale a tu catiuo
mas de los triste penado
que no es muerto ni biuo
con tanto pensar squiuo,
qu'es animal jnsensado
puesto en el cruel banco
sientiendo diuersas bregas,
con el tu coraçon franco,
l'envies vn campo blanco
grande, con las armas negras.

Pues sabes que mi valer
sin ti no trae compas
ni el mi simple saber
no tiene otro poder
de quanto tu le daras,
pues sera mi vençimiento
la fuerça grande, tu ffe,
y tanbien mi perdimiento
sy tu gran contrenymiento
basta vençer tu merçe. (196, couplets 155 and 156. Emphasis added)

Following earlier critics like Gerli, Brownlee, and Blay Manzanera, Folger argues that "in the 'realistic' story of *Triste deleytaçión* no
endeavor is made to sublimate carnal love, resulting in an uninten-
tional subversion of earlier amatory fiction and prefiguring the works
of Flores and San Pedro" (*Images in Mind* 151). I argue against any
subversion and for a fully intentional distancing. F.A.D.C.'s first-person account —his friend's *auto de amores* with which he emotionally
identifies— is powered by a conscious, if irrepressible, act of will
that directs the prow of his literary boat away from moral allegory to
explore, at leisure, the *auctoritates* with whom he shares the sad delight of man's natural inclination to narrate in the company of ladies.

Pedro de Portugal had already revealed a pernicious drift to the
margin that *Triste deleytaçión* fully explores in a complex plot that
conflates the voices of author and character and binds theoretical
pieces in what Folger, following Blay Manzanera's analysis of the
work's temporal-spatial dynamics ("La dinámica"), calls the "blurring of the border between allegorical and 'realistic' chronotropes"
(*Images in Mind* 151). That such blurring is not a literary innovation
but a common practice in affective meditation need not be restat-
ed. More significantly, as Cortijo Ocaña affirms, *Triste deleytaçión*
introduces a woman's perspective (*La evolución genérica*). Madrina
may be a counterfaction of Lady Philosophy, but Sª speaks with the
moving candor of Fiammetta, even if her needs and fears remain
secondary to those of a male author-protagonist resolved to uphold
the far-reaching tradition of literary friends with whom he shares the
grief of passional inclination and the urge to tell about it. Comparison
with a much simpler piece will illustrate the importance of friends in
reading literary tradition to configure the sentimental genre.

"A True and Binding Law to Indulge a Friend:" Francesc
Alegre's *Somni*

Composed around the same time as *Triste deleytaçión* or shortly
thereafter, *Somni de Francesch Alegre recitant lo procés de una qüestió
anemorade* [Francesc Alegre's Dream, Narrating the Trial of a Love
Case, c. 1475] resorts to the legal language of Catalan merchants
to craft a defense and texts in support of the first-person narrator's
claim to a lady's favor. Born in Barcelona around 1450 to a family of the urban aristocracy of wealthy merchants, Alegre studied
in Palermo with Jacopo della Mirabella, a humanist related to the

courts of Carlos, Príncipe de Viana, and his half-brother, the future Ferran II. Alegre probably translated Ovid's *Metamorphoses* in his youth, although it appeared in print in 1492.[64] He belongs to the generation of bilingual Catalan-Castilian authors in the Crown of Aragon who maintained frequent epistolary contact.[65] At some point between 1479 and 1482, he corresponded with Torroella, and a reply to Romeu Llull, who requested from his two friends a representation, or *figura*, of the concept of honor, sheds light on the rhetorical context that determines an author's choice of literary form.[66]

While Pere Torroella resorts to etymology to clarify the essence of the term, Alegre develops a mental diagram similar to polymath Ramon Llull's tree of knowledge. I am not concerned here with its philosophical underpinnings so much as the fact that Alegre replies with a moral discussion. His definition of honor as due reverence for virtue, Rodríguez Risquete notes, is identical to that provided in the Catalan translation of the *Consolation* (Torroella, vol. 2, 251n9–10). As a result, Honor is figured as the outcome of a journey through the branches of all the virtues —theological, intellectual, moral, and cardinal. As a courtly attribute, Honor depends on perseverance ("Perseverança"), which is the counterpart of amorous Hope in the search for *glòria*. If a lover's hope is fueled by desire for a woman, Honor's tree is nourished by true divine love that sets human actions straight.[67]

As the logical outcome of virtuous living, Alegre's definition strikingly resembles Fernández de Madrigal's characterization of male friendship. Friendship, unlike love, is a rational act and, as Alegre states at the beginning of his letter, indulging a friend's just request is a true and binding law.[68] The desire to satisfy Romeu Llull gives way to a *summa*, or compilation, on the workings of allegory and memory. His intellect invents the design of honor's *figura* by fantasizing ("mon entendre trobe fantesiant per fingir tal figura" Torroella, vol. 2, 251). Upon receiving the letter, Romeu Llull praised

---

[64] For Alegre's biography, see Pellisa Prades (*La ficció sentimental* 123–25) and Badia (ed. *Història*, vol. 3, 202–05).

[65] See Pellisa Prades ("La transmissió").

[66] The dating comes from Rodríguez Risquete's edition of Torroella's works, which includes Romeu Llull's and Alegre's letters.

[67] "Axí com lo sol material amoleix, scalfa e conforta, la vera amor divina per set raixs infundix en nosaltres gràcia endressant nostres actes per attènyer honor" (Torroella, vol. 2, 250).

[68] "La verdadera y ferma ley de amistat a complaura los amichs de coses justes nos força" (Torroella, vol. 2, 248).

its "eximplis e auctoritats" and Alegre's philosophical and natural reasons ("philosòphicas e naturals rehons"), which fully satisfied his queries ("satisfent a mosts duptes"). He was nonetheless put off by the argument's complexity and requested a drawing of the memorial architecture ("la forma del xiprer pintada segons vostre fantasia és en la letre fantasiada" 253).

A similar desire to please a friend moves the character Antoni Vidal when Alegre, *Somni*'s narrator-protagonist, sends him a dream vision he composed with a request for advice. However, *Somni* is a fictional narrative, not a real epistolary exchange, and the desire that drives its composition is a lady's refusal to accept the protagonist's devotion. It is included in Narcís Gual's *Jardinet* where Alegre is well represented with *Rehonament fingit entre Ffrancesch Alegre y Speransa tramès per ell a una dama* [Debate of Francesc Alegre and Hope, Which He Sent to a Lady], *Faula de Neptuno i Diana*, a *Sermó d'amor* [Love Sermon], and *Requesta d'amor recitant una altercació entre la Voluntad y la Raó* [Love Request with a Debate between Will and Reason], which dates their composition to between 1472 and 1486. *Faula* (1482–1486) is closer in time to Alegre's religious works, *Passió de Jesucrist* (1488), and the lost *Vida de Nostra Dona* and *Vida de Sant Josafat* (1494).[69]

Somni, *Rehonament*, and *Faula* are characteristic dream visions initiated by the intellectual agitation identified with love's tumultuous thoughts, but *Faula* eschews any epistolary context as Alegre's penitential performance on an Ovidian myth. Its first-person narrator, an exhausted man of considerable experience, is no longer enslaved by love's false hopes and frenzied imaginings.[70] He journeys through Love's palace where Diana is put on trial; her allegorical capture by an act of consolation turns her into a black rock, a symbol of female greed and malice.[71]

Somni and *Rehonament*, on the other hand, are addressed to the "Senyora de ma vida," as the narrator calls her in *Rehonament* (46). In *Rehonament*, the lover's fatigue and desire for relief lead him to complain, not about Fortune, but Speransa [Hope] —"cruel, ficta, malvada!"— who appears covered in a woolen blanket lined with

---

[69] See Badia (ed. *Història*, vol. 3 202).

[70] "Cansat de sostenir los contínuus treballs que sota lo jou de Amor me ha fet tan conèxer la largue experiència, ja tenia en oy les falses speranses, y les folles crehenses ja menys no m'enlassaven" (Pellisa Prades, *La ficció sentimental* 173).

[71] Torró points out the similarity with Roís de Corella's *Tràgedia de Caldesa* but beyond depicting infidelity and greed, traits commonly attributed to women, the works are formally quite different ("'Officium poetae'").

green sateen. Other than its symbolic color, no explanation is given for such odd attire.[72] Speransa's anger at Alegre's insults and his humble demeanor recall the primordial scene of Boethius's *Consolation* as refashioned by Torroella's network of friends. Her argument follows a similar line of thought. Life's instability makes some things possible with little effort, while others are so difficult, they often appear unattainable, and, therefore, virtue resides in steadfastness. She demands a record of Alegre's sufferings to take to the lady as a sign of his commitment ("done'm algun recort perquè li pugua fer present l'anuig que has pessat" 49). When Speransa takes her leave, fictional Alegre composes a *cançó* in Castilian ("Mi dolor es de tal mena"). Speransa is no Lady Philosophy who comes to console the lover but a poetic muse at whose prompt Alegre happily remains writing. The encounter is so condensed, it seems like a gloss to the *cançó*, but the clever conceit fully illustrates the generative role of desire and hope in literary creation.

Compared to *Rehonament*, *Somni*'s plot is more developed. Alegre reminds his lady of the day he fell captive ("vós singular me cativàs" 93). Wearied by her aloofness, he tells her how he went to bed, and his unremitting imaginings took him to a marvelous garden square ornamented with tapestries ("draps") depicting the travails of classical love heroes; its striking porphyry pavement signified their faithfulness.[73] He saw a flaming oven on a cart, continuously generating arrows made of gold and unpolished iron in equal parts. Many were following the cart, among them, Petrarch, reciting the first of his *Trionfi*. He guided the way into the court of Love, not a winged youth with his traditional weapons, but, to Alegre's surprise, a grave old man carrying a scepter in his capacity as judge, Petrarch explained.

Alegre then files a written complaint against his lady's cruelty. King Cupid mandates hearing both sides. The lady appears in the company of Laura, and Petrarch takes Alegre's defense. Alegre states his claim, that his desire be satisfied as promised. In her rejoinder, the lady accepts condemnation if and when Alegre's claim is proven

---

[72] I translate "drap burell" as *woolen* based on the regalia worn at his coronation by James I of England: "Item le drape de laine Burrell sur qui le Roy et Royne passe de le port occidental du Esglise" (Wickham Legg lxix)

[73] "Lo peÿment de aquella noble plassa era d'un porfi bell, designant la firmesa dels qui lealment amen" (94). Orazi construes that scenes are depicted in the pavement ("sul pavimento sono istoriati esempi di amore leale" 292), but the text clearly supports my reading of porphyry as symbol of loyalty.

true. The passage's language is obscure, and critics disregard it so that it seems as if *Somni* silences the lady's voice, but she speaks loud and clear. She objects that Alegre has not forgotten the fictions ("les ficcions") about love's countless evils. In them, she alleges, he hides the sting of love's wounds whenever the opportunity arises; in them, he takes pleasure in extolling love but combines its glory with mendacity, slandering those women who do not wish to accept love's disorders. She asks Cupid to free her from defamation and discharge her of any obligation toward her suitor.[74]

Alegre reacts by accusing the lady of a wrathful passion that has subverted her judgment ("Qual irada passió subverteix vostre juý" 101) and prevents her from understanding his services. He has tried to please her and to protect her reputation, not smear it, and demands a formal declaration of her rejection if she really wants him to stop loving her. Petrarch's defense generalizes the lady's arguments as "femenils rehons," so he implicitly accuses all womankind of mental weakness and misguided willpower. Her reasons —"la presumtuosa cuydar de una flaqua dona"— are unsubstantiated opinions, and her behavior perplexing —"ella adés mostra li plau ésser seguida, ara desdenyosa de si l'aparta" (101). In the event of a ruling favorable to the lady, Petrarch requests that no one be allowed to fall in love with her ever again.

Laura's retort deems Petrarch's arguments pretentious —"affectat rehonar"— and adduces the cases of cruel Theseus and Jason, whose fabrications —"ficcions," "fictes rehons"— deceived Ariadne and Medea. Petrarch repeats his appeal to reason —"si per rehó, com acustuma, és goverbada aquesta noble cort"— that Alegre should not be punished on account of a few men's fault. He has perpetrated no crimes —"no devem per la culpa de pochs tan justs condempnats ésser," "cessau de dar-li culpa de crim no perpetrat" (103).

All critics have ignored this revealing section of *Somni*, focusing instead on the humanist background of the characters who come forward to express their expert opinion on the case.[75] Clearly, it pro-

---

[74] "Mas veig no té oblidades les ficcions, senyalants tans mals que, del menor, Samsó sobrat seria, los quals amaga lo fibló ab què pica, quan veu avinentesa. No sol li plau lo ver gloriejar [234r], ans ab aquell bé sovint lo fals mesclant, tant trihumfo de moltes qui, son desorde complaura no volent, són per ell diffamades. Si donchns, justíssim senyor, tanta gràcia puc en vós haver trobada, que·m fassau quítia de encórrer tal blasme, sentenciau de ses rehons sia jo deslliurade" (100).

[75] See, for instance, Orazi and Quarti. Cortijo Ocaña simply relates it to formal *disputatio* (*La evolución genérica* 188). A more detailed study in Pellisa Prades edition

vides a basic script for the aggressive arguments that suitors wield against the lady in fictions by Flores and San Pedro. *Somni*'s lady is granted a voice, but her arguments are dismissed as nonsense, and her defender's reading of classical myths as partial. The opposition of womanly opinion to male argument underlines the fight for cultural capital waged with unequal arsenals of rhetorical prowess. The male author may exercise his rationality by arranging texts in a pattern that demonstrates the point, if not the truth. In other words, an individual case cannot support a conclusion; their relationship to one another —the mental *ratio* arranged by an author's craft— constructs the valid argument. In *Somni*, the contingent of heroic lovers who make up Love's tribunal is meant to offset Laura's biased interpretation, and sincerity.

The catalog, as Cortijo Ocaña notes, reflects peninsular tradition, appearing in more or less similar form in Santillana's narrative poems, especially *Triumphete*; Rocabertí's *Glòria d'amor*; and *Triste deleytaçió* (*La evolución genérica* 189–90). Biblical characters (Jacob, David, Solomon, and Samson), classical myths (Phoebus, Aeneas, Achilles, and Demophon), and courtly lovers, both fictional and historical (Lancelot, King Pere I of Aragon, Paris, and Macías) are mustered in formation to uphold the courtly view that women are bound to satisfy a lover's desire as a reward for his services ("sia forçade la acusada satisfer a qui l'ame," says Macías, 110). Even Lancelot, who takes the lady's side, implicitly supports Alegre's case by recollecting his unfailing determination to conquer Guinevere's heart ("venint-me a recort los perills grans e scampaments de sanch sostenguts per alcansar Ginebre" 108).

At that point, Alegre wakes up. He fears that his lawsuit has displeased the lady and writes to his friend Antoni Vidal for advice. The older man accepts the merit of the legal complaint, and his response renders the ruling that Cupid could not.[76] Remarkably, he adjudges, not Alegre's right to the lady's favors, which is taken for granted, but his fictions' *ratio* ("diré de les ficcions"). His young friend, Vidal notes approvingly, has composed a learned piece ("lo ymaginar de la fantesia dormint en sopmni passa *en molts delicats passos y de gran sentència*," emphasis added). However, its impartiality ("del ver y

---

of Alegre's works where she traces *Somni*'s love trial motif and mysogynistic elements (Alegre).

[76] Cortijo Ocaña states: "Vidal juega un papel como juez similar al del personaje Amor en su tribunal" (*La evolución genérica* 186).

fals gloriar desigant" 113) is counterproductive, and Vidal instructs Alegre to convey his desire more directly, dodging those arguments that could harm his case, so the lady may feel only his anxiety and passion.[77] She must understand, Vidal continues, that Alegre values her honor above everything else ("après conegue que desigant honra sua, mé que de la que cosa que estimeu"), so he must stay away from slanderers and point out their errors ("apartant-vos los qui maldients són creguts ésser"). Words must be accompanied by deeds showing that love is his only motivation ("vege amor sol ésser lo moviment qui vostre voler li dóna" 113–14). In Vidal's summary, Alegre may deliver his *somni* to the lady but should limit it to Petrarch's biased defense of his legal claim and the supporting votes, without mentioning any arguments that might weaken it:

> Recitau lo que dormint seguí, cridant congoxat *la parcial de-ffenció* de Patrarcha, e mostrant los vots dels qui per Cupido de les deurades totes tocats, justament en favor de vós parlaren; *no mencioneu los que foren contraris*, perquè fallits de aquelles coses que·s demanen a tal servir, fora de bon juý votaren. (115; emphasis added)

Cortijo Ocaña reads Vidal's response as an *ars amandi* inspired by Andreas Capellanus's *De amore* and love *jugements* like those that appear in Chartier's *La belle dame sans merci*, a work of unquestionable influence on Iberian sentimentality.[78] It is remarkable for the clarity with which it spells out a courtly lover's rhetorical stance as an Orpheus who willingly ignores *integumentum* (the "gran sentència"), not because of his madness and grief, but to attain his goal.

Somni's epistolary frame and discourse on love are similar to *Siervo*'s, but the occasions that motivated them and their intended purposes determine two very different genres. *Siervo* is a consolation that demands the moral conversion of a fictive tale; *Somni* is a sentimental fiction that upholds deliberate manipulation of textual

---

[77] "Per apartar-vos ço qui de son recort damnar vos pot, me semble camí tenir deveu que lo dit [242r] sentiment, vostres rehons veritat affermant, tal repòs pretica que l'anugat de vós, lo dupte qui lo delit vos deté senta, amant sol lo que veritat sperimenta" (113).

[78] See Cortijo Ocaña (*La evolución genérica* 187–88). For the influence of Chartier's work, see Pellisa Prades, who includes the translation into Catalan by Francesc Oliver in her catalog of sentimental fictions (*La ficció sentimental*); Rocabertí's *Glòria de amor* circulated in manuscript along with this translation (112).

tradition to conquer the lady. Both works point to communities of readers. *Siervo* speaks of the reciprocal affection between its narrator and the Mondoñedo judge; their friendship, the time to love and be loved ("el tiempo que bien amó y fue amado"), motivates the writing of a consolation as a shield against uncontrolled imaginings. A similar aim motivates Romeu Llull's petition to Torroella and Alegre to provide him with a memorial aid, a *figura*. In *Somni*, amorous hope ("el tiempo que bien amó y no fue amado") guides the protagonist's hand, and the lady's voice meddles in the conversation. It is not her real voice, granted, but Antoni Vidal's voice is not real either. Notable in *Somni*'s fictional colloquy is a woman's perspective, articulated by the lady and Petrarch's Laura. It clearly formulates the impasse staged by the discourse on love: women are coldblooded murderers or signs of depravity. The lady sensibly petitions Cupid to be released from Alegre's attentions and refuses to continue being their target. Unlike penitential fictions, *Somni* and *Triste deleytaçión* reveal a subtle sensitivity to women's needs and predicament, albeit only to uphold masculine truth.

I agree with Cortijo Ocaña (*La evolución genérica*) that *Somni* may best fit in the "marco referencial" or, as Deyermond put it, on the frontier of sentimental fiction. It is an experiment that does not quite reach the narrative intricacy of *Triste deleytaçión*. On the other hand, it lays the foundation for a buttress of later sentimental fiction: the triangle formed by a woman, her suitor, and his friend.

LOVE TRIANGLES

Dictaminal training did not ignore the powerful female voices that pervade the works of Virgil and Ovid but used them to illustrate immoderate passions. Woods examined glosses to a 1469 manuscript of the *Rhetorica ad Herennium* explaining how to act out Dido's two famous speeches in the *Aeneid*. The commentator considers them fine examples of lament (*conquestio*) and wrath (*iracundia*) and advises that their highly emotional tone "necessitated an expanded repertoire of performative techniques," which his glosses provide ("Performing Dido" 265).

While we have no comparable comments in the Iberian context, the popularity of the *Rhetorica ad Herennium* and the proliferation of letters ascribed to mythical heroines abandoned by their unfaithful lovers reveal vernacular writers' similar interest in the expression of extreme emotion that the pseudo-Ciceronian treatise disdained. Rodríguez del Padrón added three letters of his own invention to the collection in *Bursario*, his personal take on Ovid's *Heroides*, and the translations that Alfonso X included in his *General Estoria* and *Crónica General* are a much earlier example in Castile.[79] Impey was the first to call attention to such letters' novelistic ferment and deemed the Alphonsine versions "the beginnings of Spanish senti-mental prose" ("The Literary;" "Ovid, Alfonso X;" "Un dechado").

In the Catalan-speaking world, intensely sentimental prose let-ters are included in *Frondino e Brisona* (c. 1400), a compilation of poetic styles and a model of *exercitatio* in the *ars dictaminis* as prac-ticed in Catalan courts and society from the time of Pere IV (Cortijo Ocaña, *La evolución genérica* 29). Pellisa Prades notes that *Frondi-no e Brisona*'s epistolary correspondence is part of a larger narrative (*La ficció sentimental* 43), just as in the Alphonsine workshop, the translations of the *Heroides* perform a double role as reliable source and narrative support for the more encompassing accounts. Roís de Corella's *Escriu Medea a les dones la ingratitud e desconeixença de Jeson, per dar-lo exemple de honestament viure* [Medea's Letter to Women on Jason's Ingratitude and Disregard as an Example En-couraging Chastity], composed c. 1456–1458, follows the same trend as a moral warning, like Boccaccio's *Fiammetta* (Pellisa Prades, *La ficció sentimental* 101).

Thus, the integration of feminine voices in the plots of *Triste de-leytaçión* and *Somni* should come as no surprise, even if not confined to letters, although Boccaccio's influence must be qualified. Without denying Roís de Corella's acquaintance with the *Elegia di Madon-na Fiammetta,* the Alphonsine translations of the *Heroides* exhibit similar ethical intent. As Salvo García demonstrates, by appropriat-ing non-Ovidian materials from medieval *accessus*, these texts sub-tly moralized female characters. The translation of Phyllis's letter to Demophon ("la epistola que Fillis enbio a Demofon") closes with a chapter on Ovid's intention:

> La entençion de Ouidio en esta epistola fue dar enxemplo e cas-tigo a las doncellas de alta guisa, e avn a quales quier otras que su castigo quisieren tomar que non sean ligeras de mouer se para

---

[79] For a quick overview of the *Heroides's* popularity in medieval Castile, see Saquero Suárez-Somonte and González Rolán's introduction to their 2010 edition of *Bursario*.

creer luego los dichos de los entendedores, por que se non fallen
dello después commo fizo esta Fillis que creyo a este Demofon,
e la enarto el, e se fallo ende muy mal por que se fue e finco ella
desamparada. (qtd. in Salvo García 226)

Ovid's intention in this letter was to warn high-born maidens, and
any other who may profit from his advice, that they must not be
easily moved and willing to believe a suitor's words so that they do
not find themselves in the same situation as Phyllis, who believed
Demophon; he deceived and abandoned her, leaving her exposed.

Fiammetta voices this intention in Boccaccio's tale, but, as Deyermond notes, Castilian and Catalan sentimental texts consistently
ignore her narrator-protagonist model ("La ficción sentimental" 27–
28). Their oversight is insufficiently noted by scholarship, according
to Weissberger, who asserts that these penitential and sentimental
writers "eliminate what makes the *Heroides* aesthetically innovative
and politically subversive: first-person female narration" ("Resisting
Readers" 182). In penitential consolations, only personifications of
vices and virtues are allowed to speak in debates between a disciple
and a wise teacher who offers advice on channeling desire toward its
proper spiritual end. In school parodies of the penitential triangle,
randy authors journey through the *pietas litterata* curriculum toward
an aberrant interpretation that sustains their madness. In both cases,
the lady is silent; the story is about, not her, but the affirmation of
male desire and male bonding through the rhetoric of rationality or,
in the case of spoofs, mockery and laughter.

Luis de Lucena's youthful *Repetición de amores* took root in this
context, as Weissberger demonstrates. Originally composed for an
all-male audience at Salamanca, it lampoons a university lecture.
The topic is not a legal or philosophical text but Torroella's famous
slander, and the argument is "a patchwork of contradictory passages
borrowed more or less verbatim from other treatises and romances
on love and fortune" (*Isabel Rules* 141). Lucena's repertoire includes
mock treatises, such as *Tratado de cómo al hombre es necesario amar*,
and sentimental narratives, such as Pedro de Portugal's *Sátira*. Weissberger's most interesting insight is her reading of *Repetición* alongside *Arte de axedrez* [Chess Rules], which was included in a portfolio
supporting Lucena's application for a curial position at a court ruled
by the most powerful woman of the time: "By pairing *Repetición de
amores* and *Arte de axedrez*, Lucena expresses his awareness that the

'rules of the game' for masculine advancement have changed" (*Isabel Rules* 157). Weissberger's analysis of male anxiety at Isabel's court is indisputable, but I would like to explore it more generally to explain the impact of the love triangle on the articulation of the male gaze and narrative form.

Weissberger cites 1992 Finucci's psychoanalytical interpretation of Castiglione's *The Courtier,* triangulating the effect of jokes on women to elucidate the homosocial bonding at the University of Salamanca that excluded women from the symbolic order (*Isabel Rules* 144). However, Finucci's analysis of the male gaze cannot be restricted to jokes; it fully conveys the violence of allegorical silencing in both penitential consolations and courtly adoration:

> The male voice is hegemonic throughout because it has control of representation while the female voice, even when heard, is obfuscated, for it is assimilated to the authoritative, and always male voice, appointed to create civilized courtly masculine and feminine identities. This process constructs woman as indispensable to the courtier's being and well-being; it also keeps her in her place through both a linguistic tour de force of minimization and desexualization, and an aesthetic process of idolization and iconization. (Finucci 53)

As we saw in Alegre's *Somni,* the lady's arguments are consistently rejected as irrational, fickle, incomprehensible. The first-person narrator and his friend Antoni Vidal attack them with a specific grouping of texts to prove their insignificance. The desire that propels *Somni*'s writing depends on hope to achieve two goals: glory, in *cancionero* poetry's meaning of sexual conquest, and, more to point, honor in the eyes of his peers through public exercise of the gentlemanly virtue of determination in the face of opposition. *Somni* rests on the proto-narrative of suffering Boethius, Lady Philosophy, and the strumpet muses, but Antoni Vidal consoles the lover-writer intent on remaining subject to the virile hope that guides his hand.

Stripping the metafictional dream to its triangular struts begs the question: What kind of vision does the triangle aid? *Vision and Painting*, Bryson's study of the logic of the gaze in Western oil painting, will serve as the theoretical frame to explore how the transfer of moral *enarratio* from a school or school-like homosocial setting to the public halls of court profoundly altered the dream vision's way of seeing and its form.

Penitential dream vision, having evolved from the application of the principles of eloquence to interpretation and composition, maintains, like marginal doodles and art, a deictic reference, a call back to the writer's body. As a rhetorical performance on literary tradition, the author-narrator's most natural desire is on permanent display, and his work of *inventio* unfolds through time as the dreamer roams his memorial landscapes and composes. Moral metamorphosis aims to abstract his agitated imaginings into meaning, to smother them in allegory. Conversely, the epistolary context that frames the vision places the reader in a position identical to that of the author-narrator, dramatically transforming his desires into disembodied symbols. Like in Western oil painting, the transcendent moment of the gaze obliterates the duration of the creative process and the temporality of the depicted scene; they are reduced to "on the one hand, the moment of origin, of the founding perception; and on the other, the moment of closure, of receptive passivity" (Bryson 93).

The violent capture and triangular dynamics moral allegory demands is nowhere better represented than in Peter Paul Rubens's allegory of Fortuna (1636–1638), commissioned by agents of Philip IV to decorate the king's hunting lodge at El Pardo. The description in the catalog of a 2016 exhibit at the Clark Art Institute, "Splendor, Myth, and Vision: Nudes from the Prado," articulates the logic of the gaze, transforming erotic desire and male anxiety in the representation of a woman isolated from any context except the vertical axis of eternity:

> Unlike many of the narrative images in the series, this work depicts a single, full-length woman in a tightly constructed vertical composition, removed from any narrative context. Instead, she represents the allegorical figure of Fortune, which embodies the varied chances of life. Rubens depicted this conceit as a nude female figure, resembling the tradition of the birth of Venus, emerging, full-grown, from the sea. Choosing to emphasize Fortuna's solid, fleshy form, Rubens departed from such idealized models of Venus, however, and executed a figure that has the tangible presence to occupy our world. ... As she gazes obliquely beyond the canvas, she engages the viewer and creates an eroticized tension between the real and pictorial space. This nude figure can be recognized by her allegorical attributes and her instability. Not only does she bestride tumultuous ocean waves during a storm, but she is poised unsteadily on a crystal globe at the bottom center of the canvas. Her billowing veil and wet, stringy hair underscore

the force of the gale in which she advances. (Loughman et al. 125–26).

Notice the coincidence of this critic's suggestive description and moral allegory. Rubens's illusion —woman as Fortuna— mirrors the viewer's gaze: his desire for the soft, appealing young woman —"the tangible presence to occupy our world"— and fear of a symbolic order in constant flux.

That some 150 years separate Rubens's Fortuna from sentimental production does not undermine my argument. By the midfifteenth century, painting and fiction take different paths. Western oil painting, Bryson argues, is predicated on disavowal of the body and freezing of temporal duration: the image appears to have been painted by no one, and the viewing subject it proposes is a point (116). Sentimental fiction peaked precisely when what Camille calls the "spectacular interpenetration of subject and viewer" was replaced by the image as illusion, arresting "the possibility of painting as vision" (*Image on the Edge* 183). In contrast, in sentimental fictions, marginal *fabula* will erode the power of allegory.[80] The dialogic interaction of the rhetorics of the center (the vertical logic of moral allegory) and the margin (temporality, laughter, the body) produces a hybrid, intertextual, self-referential genre. The genre takes shape when the penitential dream vision based exclusively on male interaction moved to the mixed world of the court. In that social setting, the triangular interaction that supports the vertical progression of Augustinian *caritas* —two men and Fortune's embodiment— is compromised by actual women who, as Whetnall ("Isabel González;" "Lírica femenina") and Gómez-Bravo ("'A huma senhora'") among others have compellingly demonstrated, actively participated in the composition of *cancionero* lyrics, moving far beyond their imposed status as commodities in the economies of courtly power.

Male angst cannot be restricted to the Isabelline court, which perceived a monarch "who does not know or keep her place as either woman or wife, and who furthermore appropriates and redirects patriarchal norms and institutions to further her own political goals" (Weissberger, *Isabel Rules* xv). Bernat Metge had to contend with Queen Maria de Luna during the succession crisis generated by Joan I's untimely death in a hunting accident. San Pedro's poet-

---

[80] In this sense, paintings by Hieronymus Bosch are closer to sentimental fiction.

ry offers a glimpse of some humiliating incidents in which damsels were not the distant goddesses worshiped by courtly lovers but witty, even foul-mouthed contenders in the ruthless social games of courtly life. However, not until the last quarter of the century —coinciding roughly with Isabel's reign— did sentimental contrafacta begin to introduce strong, highly eloquent heroines, not Ovidian types. As Gómez Bravo notes, Isabel and Fernando embellished their centralized monarchic power with visual symbols and spectacles, while courtly speech adopted a literary register. The standard of feminine discourse changed from silence to the eloquence needed to participate in the rhetorical exercises of courtly life ("'A huma senhora'" 46–47).

The triangular dynamics of penitential consolation and school spoofs recalls jokes between two courtiers where the butt is consistently a woman; her image, Finucci points out, is not the ideal offered as a spectacle and object of desire; instead, "the glance that surveys her is more often than not one of violation" (53). In dream visions like Alegre's *Somni* and *Triste deleytaçión* in which the fictional reader is a woman, the tension between the allegorical gaze that "attempts to extract the enduring form from fleeting process" and the glance, "a furtive look whose attention is always elsewhere" (Bryson 93–94), explains the dialogic fluctuation that both sustains and escapes the violence of moralization.

In *Somni*, the lady's needs are ignored; the lover, intent on sustaining the hope that guides his hand, is consoled by a friend, and the two perform the model of masculinity based on rhetorical dominance. In *Triste deleytaçión,* F.A.D.C. offers the narrative to the ladies in the hope of moving them to compassion. In both cases, the allegorical gaze fails to capture women because the rhetorical stance places the author-in-love in the realm of hope —that is, the wheel of fortune— forced to praise and to please, in real time, the object of his inborn desire, which can never be satisfied without altering his social self. Therefore, the penitential gaze is displaced by a glance that "shifts to conceal its own existence, and [carries] unofficial messages of hostility, collusion, rebellion, and lust" (Bryson 94). The furtive male look explains the tendency toward the margins and narrative temporality. At court, where lovers exchange secret glances, gossips whisper; plots develop.

In her analysis of the rhetoric of Ovidian eroticism that affects Petrarch's portrait of himself in love, Enterline argues for a constantly changing subjectivity poised between language and *eros*. From a dictaminal perspective, the articulation of an author's stances —Orpheus or Tiresias— signals a similar state of flux in the practice of *enarratio* and contemplation. In fifteenth-century Aragon and Castile, those practices were inextricably interwoven with "a redefinition of what constituted cultural and symbolic capital at court" (Weiss, "¿Qué demandamos?" 238). As Weissberger notes, the rules of the game of love changed in a court where a woman held real power, further roiling gender roles and relations (*Isabel Rules*). The concept of nobility was also destabilized by new lineages; bureaucrats, a little over 10 percent of whom were university graduates, functioned as another nobility (Gómez-Bravo, *Textual Agencies* 23–24).

These new courtly dynamics were articulated in the triangle formed by two men facing an unreadable, unpredictable woman in a hybrid genre that shuttled between a failed moral gaze and the curious glance. The author's position in relation to the narrative content and his public also became unstable. Pictorial art will demand that viewers adopt the interpretive position of the gaze, the "transcendent point of view that exists only as a disembodied *punctum*" (Bryson 106). In Rubens's Fortuna, woman, as in the *enarratio* of Ovidian myths, is a mere sign. In sentimental contrafacta, on the other hand, the glance lacks "some essential formal and generic mask that could serve to define the position from which [it] views life, as well as the position from which [it] makes that life public." Bakhtin identifies this lack of immanent authorial position as a defining characteristic of the novel (160–61). This impasse receives full narrative treatment in the sentimental contrafacta of Diego de San Pedro and Juan de Flores.

FOOLS AND MARTYRS: DIEGO DE SAN PEDRO'S *TRACTADO DE AMORES DE ARNALTE Y LUCENDA* AND *CÁRCEL DE AMOR*

Diego de San Pedro is without doubt one of the most famous writers of the period; his books were European best-sellers, and he was an accomplished poet whose *Pasión trovada* enjoyed huge popularity in Spain for four centuries. However, as his biographer Whinnom states, there are few authors of his status about whom we know so little.[81] He most certainly belonged to the group of *letrados*,

---

[81] "Habrá pocos autores de la categoría de Diego de San Pedro de quienes sepamos menos" (San Pedro, *Obras completas I* 34).

as his service to Juan Téllez-Girón, Count of Urueña, indicates,[82] but his connection to the University of Salamanca, unlike that of Juan de Flores, has yet to be documented beyond his latinizing style and occupation as some kind of secretary. His name does not appear among the poets who engaged in the *preguntas* and *respuestas* of the *Cancionero general* of 1511, which leads Whinnom to assert that he remained on the fringes of the royal court (*Diego de San Pedro*; San Pedro, *Obras completas III*), yet San Pedro dedicated *Arnalte y Lucenda* to the ladies of the queen, and his minor poetry reveals a social context that, if not the royal court itself, was quite like it.

The male anxiety that Weissberger studies at the Isabelline court is manifest in San Pedro's extreme lack of confidence and almost obsessive inclination to please his patrons. His supposed *converso* origin cannot be proven, and if he was an *hidalgo*, Whinnom notes, he was still a servant. Some episodes in his poetry seem to confirm that he was regarded as a buffoon: a lady snubs his request for a kiss with an obscene remark; another mocks his love note before the court (San Pedro, *Obras completas III* 80–81). San Pedro's marginal position and servile attitude make his *Tractado de amores de Arnalte y Lucenda* a perfect test case for analyzing the triangular dynamic that supports visionary contrafacta.

Although addressed to a general courtly readership ("por mis razones fazer al palacio" 87), *Tractado de amores de Arnalte y Lucenda* is dedicated specifically to the powerful "virtuosas señoras" of Isabel's entourage. The print version appeared in 1491 (Burgos, by Fadrique de Basilea), but Whinnom convincingly argues for its composition in the early 1480s (San Pedro, *Obras completas I* 43–47), which makes it contemporaneous with the work of Roís de Corella and Alegre and a little later than *Triste deleytaçión*. As in *Triste deleytaçión*, the epistolary frame has given way to the public hall of the royal and nobiliary courts. San Diego morphs into "el autor," the narrator, who, during a trip from Castile the previous summer, hears Arnalte's direct account of his efforts to conquer the love of Lucenda. The narrative is inexplicably interrupted, once by the 210 stanzas of a panegyric on Queen Isabel, and once by "Las siete angustias de Nuestra Señora" [The Seven Sorrows of Our Lady], which Arnalte oddly compares to his own suffering. These sections could easily be removed without altering the narrative. Their convoluted, latinate

---

[82] See Whinnom (*Diego de San Pedro*; San Pedro, *Obras completas I*).

style and the accumulation of set pieces —letters, *carteles* [challenges], speeches, *planctus*— throughout the work suggest a rhetorical compilation barely held together by a thin narrative thread, again like *Triste deleytaçión*. A panegyric is included based on Arnalte's insipid justification that he wanted to see if "el autor" could do the Queen justice.

The memorial journey that generates the composition of a dream vision takes a more realistic form, but its main traits can still be discerned. *El autor* gets lost in the wilderness at dusk and finds a black palace where a group of gentlemen, dressed in black, invite him in. He passes through a door with a sign that reads, "Ésta es la triste morada / del que muere / porque muerte no le quiere" (91) [This is the sad dwelling / of one who is dying / because death does not want him].[83] *El autor* spends a sleepless night, agitated by the events he has witnessed and the noisy lamentations of Arnalte, whose tale he hears at daybreak.

Unlike previous dream visions and more in tune with Francesc Moner's *La noche* —another nobiliary servant writing for a lady— *el autor* is reading and inventing on, not the canon of *auctores,* but *cancionero* poetry and courtly behavior. The protagonist's actions are completely inappropiate. Arnalte falls in love with a grief-torn Lucenda at her father's funeral. He confides in his friend Elierso, who takes the opportunity to marry her. Arnalte then kills Elierso in a duel and sends the widow a condolence letter that is also a marriage proposal. The whole *tractado* is an anthology of nonsensical episodes. Whinnom, citing Rohland de Langbehn's dissertation, wonders whether the work's humor lies in the absurd contrast of Arnalte's silly behavior, lofty ideals, and the dissonance between prosaic details and sublime style but maintains a healthy suspicion that San Pedro was not aware of it (San Pedro, *Obras completas I* 59). Severin affirms that it is "lampooning a courtly lover so inept that he manages to break all tenets of courtly love" and sees the ludicrous episodes and the exaggerated final penance in a living tomb as parody (*Religious Parody* 68–70). I would like to explore these dissonances in terms of the hybrid form that the dialogue of penitential form and courtly voices provokes.

The presence of women, we saw, alters the subtle balance of two men gazing at an embodiment of Fortune, whether she is a flesh-

---

[83] I cite from Whinnom's edition (San Pedro, *Obras completas I* 87–171).

and-blood woman or culled from the extensive inventory of literary samples. In *Tractado de amores*, *el autor*'s position as a first-person narrator in love who demands that readers identify with his sufferings is compromised by the dedication to the virtuous ladies, so he dons a mask that observes and reflects —indeed, relates— Arnalte's deeds and feelings. He does so and shares the result specifically with women at Arnalte's request:

> [M]e dixo que todo lo que comigo fablase, en poder de mugeres no menos sentidas que discretas lo pusiese, porque mugeres supiesen lo que muger le hizo; e porque su condición más que [la] de los hombres piadosa sea, culpando a ella, dél se doliesen. (100)

> [Arnalte] asked me to transmit all that he was going to tell me to women as sensitive as discreet, so that women would know what a woman did to him; and because women's nature is more compassionate than men's, they would take pity on him and blame her.

Arnalte is demanding that Lucenda be frozen into a stereotype of cruelty, *la belle dame sans merci*, in the conventional register of *integumentum* and satire, but *el autor* gives the account to the "virtuosas señoras" as "pasatiempo," something to be enjoyed in the merry company of the young men at court:

> Pero vuestras mercedes no a las razones mas a la intención mire[n], pues por vuestro servicio mi condenación quise, haviendo gana de algund pasatiempo darvos, y porque cuando cansadas de oír y fablar discretas razones estéis, a burlar de las mías vos retrayáis, y para que a mi costa los cavalleros mancebos de la corte vuestras mercedes festejen, a cuya virtud mis faltas remito. (170)

> But your ladyships should consider my intention and not my arguments since I accepted my condemnation so that I could serve you, wishing to offer you a pastime so that when you are tired of hearing and speaking prudent arguments, you may withdraw to mock mine, and at my expense young men at court may amuse your ladyships, whose virtue I ask to pardon my faults.

This conclusion is remarkable in the articulation of what Bakhtin calls "the chronotrope of the public square." *El autor* concedes he is an outsider to the interactions of young men and women at court. The fool and the clown are essential figures in the public square who can exploit its theatrical trappings to assume any position they choose and expose human behavior to parodic laughter. In a novel, the author can resort to these figures to express the incomprehensibility of conventions, to explore subjectivity in real life, not allegory. The "device of 'not understanding'," Bakhtin asserts, "always takes on great organizing potential when an exposure of vulgar conventionality is involved" (164). In *Tractado de amores de Arnalte y Lucenda* the fictional San Pedro who addresses the ladies adopts the rhetorical stance, not of an author in love, but an astounded observer of Arnalte's foolish excesses. The failed identification of female readers with first-person narrator and the dissociation required by the device of "not understanding" put the text at a distance, prevents interiorization. By ignoring his protagonist's request, *el autor* moves to the margin, the space of laughter and *fabula*, and offers the ladies a glance at the realities of daily life through the distorted glass of humor, laying bare the artificiality of courtly mores.

An intriguing feature at the conclusion is the author's request for the ladies "to withdraw." The invitation, "A burlar de las mías vos retrayáis," may be a humble plea that they refrain from mocking his work, but the context so emphasizes his role as entertainer, it precludes this interpretation. The verb *retraerse* seems to refer to the habits of reading; he is asking the ladies to retire to their chambers to read the *tractado* and laugh and then share the fun with young men. Silent reading, Saenger argues in *Space Between Words*, afforded a new privacy, which could stimulate erotic fantasies but also intensify lay religious experience. While in *Tractado de amores,* the narrator adopts a more autonomous, distant —hence, novelistic— perspective, in another work, *Cárcel de Amor*, he will exploit the conventions of contemplative silent reading to portray its protagonist, Leriano, as a martyr of love.

Cárcel de Amor is also a *tractado,* but it was composed at the explicit request of an aristocrat related to the Téllez-Girón family, Diego Hernandes, *alcaide de los donzeles*, leader of a light cavalry troop composed of young palace noblemen. It was published in 1492 and because of its dedication, scholars agree that it must have been composed after 1483, when Diego took King Boabdil prisoner at the battle of Lucena.

Its story echoes, to some extent, the beginning of *Tractado de amores.* A character named *el auctor*, returning home through the Sierra Morena after the summer's fighting, suddenly finds himself in

Macedonia, where he encounters Leriano, son of a duke, who will tell him about his love tribulations with Princess Laureola. The similarities end here. A number of allegories are developed in full detail, and *el auctor* abandons his position as observer to become a critical actor in the development of *Cárcel's* plot. The device of not understanding is applied only to Laureola's behavior, not courtly interactions, and *el auctor* identifies with Leriano's sufferings by shedding abundant tears. The tale he brings back to Diego Hernandes after Leriano's suicide is a deeply emotional account of his own involvement: "With sighs I set out on my journey; with tears I departed; with moans I spoke; and so I passed the time until I arrived here in Peñafiel, where I remain your lordship's humble servant" (San Pedro, *Prison of Love* 82).[84] Whinnom's translation obscures the fact that *el auctor* describes his display of passions with the same word, *pasatiempo*, he used to convey entertainment at the conclusion of *Tractado de amores*. In *Cárcel,* it signifies the male pursuit of honor through perseverance.

Comparing *Cárcel* to Carrós's *Regoneixença* calls attention to its deployment of a narrative voice that, as in affective meditations, channels the emotions of the tale's protagonist and male readers in a counterfaction of penitential consolation. In *Regoneixença,* the first-person narrator —also called Actor— recants past errors after the conventional debate of Reason and Will. At that point, he engages in the ecphrasis of an altarpiece in which, located underneath a Man of Sorrows, he sees a lactating Mary whose sweet milk has replaced the classics as inspiration. In *Cárcel*, the initial disorientation provoked by desire occurs when *el auctor* meets a fearsome knight named Desire, who carries on his left arm a steel shield and secures with his right a striking stone carving representing a beautiful woman radiating fire. The flames are dragging a man to the prison of love; he begs *el auctor* to help him. The pair disappears, and *el auctor* spends a sleepless night in sad contemplation ("And I spent the whole night in sad and troubled meditation" 6).[85]

The next morning, he sees a three-cornered tower on a mountain peak. It stands on four pillars with an eagle perched on its roof. He

---

[84] Parrilla's 1995 edition reads: "[C]on sospiros caminé; con lágrimas partí; con gemidos hablé; y con tales pasatiempos llegué aquí a Peñafiel, donde quedo besando las manos de vuestra merced" (79). I cite from this edition and Whinnom's translation, which have identical pagination.

[85] "[Y] assí estuve toda la noche en triste y trabajosas contemplaciones" (6)

climbs the tower, enters, and sees the prisoner ceaselessly burning in a chair of fire, subjected to all kinds of torture. Two weeping ladies wait on the wretched figure, crowning him with metal spikes. Although the tableau takes place in complete darkness, an intense light emanating from the prisoner's heart enables *el auctor* to see. The prisoner, who identifies himself as Leriano, explains the meaning of the odd scene.

In the conventional image of the castle where love dwells, San Pedro installs, not Love, but the lover, whose demeanor is very similar to the devotional image of the Man of Sorrows. Like the central symbolic images of a retable, the allegory paints an image in the reader's heart and, more important, San Pedro crafts an architecture within which to recall other texts on which to build the narration of Leriano and Laureola's unhappy love affair. This central image is flanked by narrative panels in which Leriano asks *el auctor* for help in winning over Laureola's heart, Laureola and Leriano exchange letters, the traitorous Persio makes false accusations, and duels and assaults take place. In a secondary allegory, *el auctor*, with a battalion comprised of "Contentamiento y Esperança y Descanso y Plazer y Alegría y Holgança" [Content and Hope and Ease and Pleasure and Mirth and Bliss] (29), puts up a fight to liberate Leriano from his jailers, highly reminiscent of a psychomachia.

Sharrer identifies the statuette that Deseo carries as an image of Mary transformed into Venus ("La *Cárcel de Amor*"). The use of a single image to symbolize different, even contradictory terms, is common to biblical exegesis —a lion may refer to the vices of arrogance and wrath or to Jesus the Messiah. In *Cárcel*, the choice of Venus indicates an opposite move from *Regoneixença*'s *intentio* in which the vision of divine truth and the *reprobatio amoris* are accomplished with the help of reason and Mary surrounded by eleven thousand virgins who are enemies of the world and love ("enemigues del mon y de amor viciosa," 146). *Cárcel*'s Deseo also addresses *el auctor* as "caminante," indicating meditation as a walk about memorial places. Throughout the work, *el auctor* emotionally reflects on his role as an observer of a story lived by others. He moves along the scenes or sites of Leriano's life as if passing by the panels of an altarpiece or the scenes of Christ's life.

Unlike *Tractado de amores*'s narrator, *Cárcel*'s *el auctor* is not a passive listener. His triple role as *auctor*, narrator, and a character who mediates between Leriano and Laureola has been the subject of numerous critical inquiries. James Mandrell questions *el auctor*'s reliability in spite of his authorial voice, but Haywood warns against *Cár-*

cel's illusion, conflating the historical San Pedro with the character ("Apuntes"). She sides with Alfonso Rey's proposal to split *el auctor*'s role into "character witness" and "omniscient narrator" as a strategy that allows him to narrate his own experiences and to evaluate them. Torrego considers *Cárcel* a literary oration but still underscores San Pedro's novel use of *el auctor* as a narrative tool to balance the contradictory effects of fiction and explicit moral teaching (331). I contend that *Cárcel* depicts a visionary experience like that of Actor in Carrós's *Regoneixença* but instead of a personal vision, resorts to the conventions of affective devotion to narrate the male courtly practice of desire as unremitting hope and perseverance in the face of defeat.

Leriano's torments are articulated in terms of a Passion of Christ. *Cárcel* depicts the visionary experience of Diego Hernandes, who petitions San Pedro to write the work for his pleasure and that of the other gentlemen of the court also mentioned in the dedication: "el siguiente tractado fue hecho a pedimiento del señor don Diego Hernandes, alcaide de los donzeles, y otros cavalleros cortesanos" (3). *El auctor*'s vision is one and the same as that of the young aristocrat and his friends. Like the donors' representation in the paintings they commission, emotion colors every memorial site —letters, challenges, the debate on women, and the mother's lament— into a journey through a mock Passion that, in a meditation, would be supposed to stimulate devotion. It does not relate a personal vision of Mary burning with divine love as a source of wisdom and inspiration, like the one Actor contemplates in *Regoneixença*, but young men's experience of libidinal desire with which *Cárcel*'s *el auctor* fully identifies. The combined images of fierce Deseo and tortured Leriano remind the beholder of past infatuations, and *el auctor* acknowledges that he was able to understand the imagery in the past when he was in love.[86] They also encourage him to show compassion and emotionally participate in a scene that illustrates the eternal truth of the power of physical desire over man.

While *Tractado de amores* is offered for the amusement of the ladies, in *Cárcel,* beginning with the *exordium* in which a patron is praised as the work's first inspiration, San Pedro transfers to Diego

---

[86] "La moralidad de todas estas figuras me ha plazido saber, puesto diversas vezes las vi, mas como no las pueda ver sino coraçón cativo, quando le tenía tal conoscíalas, y agora que estava libre dubdávalas" (12). [To know the meaning of all these allegories is a pleasure. Although I have seen them before on diverse occasions, nevertheless, since they are perceptible only to a captive heart, when my heart was held prisoner I recognized them, and now that it is free, they perplexed me, 11].

Hernandes both responsibility for the work ("In truth, so far as the present work is concerned, I am the less to blame in that I embarked upon it more because of my duty of obedience than because of my desire to write") and its final authorship ("I resolve further to dedicate it to your lordship, so that it might receive the favour of your patronage and benefit from the emendations dictated by your cultured judgment," 3).[87] The convention is carried on in the narrative. Diego Hernandes is not only co-creator of *Cárcel* as instigator and editor but appears in it as *Auctor,* just as Archdeacon Desplà appears at the right hand of Mary in a very intimate vision that is nonetheless painted by Bartolomé Bermejo.

Unlike *Regoneixença's* Actor, whose contemplation of Mary's burning love leads him to reject love literature in favor of the divine wisdom that flows through her milk, *Cárcel's* protagonist gulps the poison. In the final scene, Leriano, rejected by Laureola for the last time, mixes her letters with water, drinks the concoction, and dies. Its irreverent tone as a sacramental communion has puzzled critics. Chorpenning finds a link between the scene and Ezekiel's "eating of the precious scrolls, which he found as sweet as honey" ("Leriano's Consumption") but Gerli objects that this precedent "could not have been widely known" (qtd. in in Whinnom, "Cardona" 212). I agree that the biblical reference may have gone unnoticed among courtly readers but wonder if a subtler irony aimed at readers from more professional settings. In scholastic circles, the link between remembering and digesting was commonplace. Carruthers mentions "the motif, found in both Ezequiel and John's Apocalypse, of the visionary 'eating the book' as a prelude to a vision of heaven, [and] Ezequiel also became ill ... when he experienced his visions" (*The Craft of Thought* 180). Leriano's consumption of Laureola's letters could be a literal dramatization meant for readers tearfully consuming San Pedro's work as a prelude to their own inventions. The sweetness of the letters, in spite of their lethal content, hints at their memorial role as "food for thought," the old monastic metaphor for invention, and as pleasant poetic activity.

The voluntary consumption of the letters, when read in the context of sentimental contrafacta like *Triste deleytación*, where drinking

---

[87] "[V]erdad es que en la presente obra no tengo tanto cargo, pues me puse en ella más por necesidad de obedecer que por voluntar de escribir" ... "acordé endereçarla a vuestra merced porque la favorezca como señor y la emiende como discreto" (3).

the poison served by Adriana initiates the plot, also signals a clear intention away from moralization. Before drinking Laureola's letters, a friend named Tefeo attempts to cure Leriano by slandering women. The moribund hero responds with an eloquent tirade —surprisingly long given his overall weakness— against slanderers. It is followed by twenty reasons why men are indebted to women and a substantial list of classical, biblical, and contemporary women as examples. Leriano rejects interpreting his captivity as a symbol of Laureola's cruelty, but the arguments he advances are a defense of, not women, but male honor.

> Every nobleman is obliged to occupy himself in noble deeds, in his words no less than in his actions, and so if foul language is an offence against purity, those who spend their lives in such talk expose their honour to disrepute ... Noblemen of former times so exalted virtuous actions and regarded goodness so highly that they feared nothing more than leaving a memory of infamy, and I cannot think that they believe so, who place foulness before virtue and soil their own reputation with their tongues, for people judge what a man is by what he says. (68)[88]

The traditional controversy between reason and will gives way to Leriano's impassioned defense of a lover's steadfastness as courtly *virtus*. Such behavior, announced in Leriano's initial moan that "in the constancy of my love, all suffering can be borne" ["en mi fe se sufre todo"] (4) as he is dragged along by Sir Desire, attests to his unshakable hope understood as courage. If *Triste deleytaçión*'s E° remains stubbornly writing to his Sᵃ, Leriano keeps reading —in fact, digesting— Laureola's letters, poisoning himself with them in a counterfaction of sacramental communion and moral reading. He embodies *lletraferit*.

Cárcel calls for its male readers to identify emotionally with suffering Leriano via *el auctor,* but Laureola's behavior is deemed incomprehensible. She is highly eloquent and expresses herself di-

---

[88] "Todo noble es obligado a ocuparse en autos virtuosos, assí en los hechos como en las hablas, pues si las palabras torpes ensuzian la linpieza, muy a peligro de infamia tienen la onrra de los que en tales pláticas gastan su vida ... los antiguos nobles tanto adelgazavan las cosas de bondad y en tanto las tenían, que no avían mayor miedo de cosa que de memoria culpada, lo que no me parece que guardan los que anteponen la fealdad a la virtud, poniendo mácula con su lengua en su fama, que cualquiera se juzga lo que es en lo que habla" (66).

rectly and clearly, without the affectation of her suitor and his go-between. Even so, *el auctor* unfailingly misreads her. *Cárcel*'s auctor/
donor experiences the confusion of any passionate lover who faces
feminine irrationality and capriciousness:

> Laureola's behaviour created such confusion in my mind that just
> when I thought I understood her best, I realized I knew nothing
> of her real feelings; just as I held the greatest hopes, she withdrew
> them furthest from me; just as I gained confidence, she gave me
> greatest reason to be afraid. The inconsistency of her behaviour
> baffled my understanding. (22)[89]

In spite of Leriano's deathbed defense of women, his conventional arguments cannot overcome the feelings of puzzlement and
extreme anxiety that Laureola's supposed indecisiveness in granting
her favors creates throughout the work. *El auctor* summarizes that
emotion early on in an elegant parallel clause redolent of *cancionero*
lyrics: "en el recibir la carta me satisfizo; en el fin de su habla me
desesperó" ["in accepting the letter she fulfilled my highest hopes;
in concluding her speech she thrust me into the deepest despair"]
(22). *El auctor* misjudges Laureola because, like fictional Petrarch in
Alegre's *Somni*, he dismisses her words as irrational feminine nonsense. Gilkinson cleverly notes that Laureola has no ownership of
her voice: "she is in the eyes of Leriano, the Auctor, Persio, The
King, even the critic, what they choose to make of her" (120). *Cárcel*
resorts to the traditional dynamic of two men facing a volatile woman. The desire to capture Laureola, frustrated by the lover's rhetorical stance, is reoriented toward episodic narrative —the glance at the
margins of the court.

Weissberger has expertly argued that many women were resisting readers, who did not accept the male stance of *Cárcel* and identified with Laureola. In Juan de Flores's *Grimalte y Gradisa*, the female
protagonist is a competent reader of Boccaccio's *Elegia di madonna
Fiammetta.* Grimalte offers her the work to seduce her, but she uses
it to her own benefit —to forestall his advances ("Resisting Readers"
181).

---

[89] "Tanta confusión me ponían las cosas de Laureola, que quando pensava que
más la entendía, menos sabía de su voluntad; quando tenía más esperança, me dava
mayor desvío; quando estava seguro, me ponía mayores miedos; sus desatinos cega-
van mi conocimiento" (22)

FIAMMETTA'S FEMALE READERS AT WORK: JUAN DE FLORES'S *GRIMAL-TE Y GRADISA*

Contrary to the international success enjoyed by *Grisel y Mira-bella*, translated into English, Italian, and French, *Grimalte y Gra-disa* had a much more limited circulation.[90] Two manuscripts from the last quarter of the fifteenth century, one of them fragmentary, and a 1495 print edition survive. In the introduction to her 2008 edition, Parrilla notes that these three witnesses are independent; their examination suggests a process of revision and adaption that Flores may have undertaken after his colaboration with an Alonso de Córdoba, a common name in Aragon and Castile, but probably referring to a music professor at the University of Salamanca in the 1480s. According to the witnesses, *Grimalte y Gradisa* circulated with and without poetry. *M* (Ms. 22.018) and incunabulum *L* (I382), both at the Biblioteca Nacional de España, contain the 42 poems, while the fragments included in *S* (Ms. 5-3-20 Biblioteca Colombina de Sevilla) are limited to prose. Severin surmises that in the last stage of adaptation from an all-male university setting to court, it "could be read by four readers and sung by individuals or even be given a choral setting" ("Audience and Interpretation" 68). Parrilla denies that textual clues support this hypothesis; furthermore, Catalan and Italian *cancioneros* contain some of the poems, and others are incor-porated into Arthurian texts (Flores, *Grimalte y Gradisa* 57).

The Catalan *cançoner* in which two of *Grimalte y Gradisa*'s poems appear is none other than Narcís Gual's 1486 *Jardinet d'orats*, which points to earlier dissemination of the story outside Castile. As in the print version, the poems are introduced under the rubric "Phiame-ta a Grimalte dezia la seguent coble" [Fiameta recited to Grimalte the following couplets], but in manuscript *M*, Grimalte recites them to Fiameta (Flores, *Grimalte y Gradisa* 16, 66).[91] In manuscript *S*, which includes sections from Flores's *Grisel y Mirabella* and *Triunfo de amor*, the fragments of *Grimalte y Gradisa* are referenced in the index as "Cartas de Grimalte y Frometa que escrivió Juan de Flores" [Letters of Grimalte and Fiometa written by Juan de Flores] (Flores, *Grimalte y Gradisa* 64). These variations reflect the practice of com-

---

[90] The poet Maurice Scève translated it into French as *La deplourable fin de Fla-mete, elegante invention de Jehan de Flores*, printed in 1535 and 1536.
[91] Fiameta (or Grimalte) recites a *dezir*, a type of poem related to the French *dit* or *ditié*.

piling rhetorical set pieces. They are given narrative treatment in the full version of *Grimalte y Gradisa* by fictionalizing the patron-author relationship.

Flores lays bare the metafictional conceit from the beginning: "comiença un breve tractado compuesto por Johan de Flores, el cual por la siguiente obra mudó su nombre en Grimalte, la invençión del cual es sobre la Fiometa" (90) [Here begins a brief *tractatus* composed by Juan de Flores who in this work changed his name into Grimalte; it is an *inventio* on Fiometa].[92] The creative process is placed within the parameters of rhetorical *inventio* on a literary source, Boccaccio's *Elegia di madonna Fiammetta,* here Fiometa. The invention is performed in a fictional courtly setting: the lady Gradisa, deeply moved by Fiometa's fate after reading the book that Grimalte gave her, asks him to bring together the heroine and her lover, Pánfilo, so they may reconcile. All critics agree that Flores's *usus scribendi* is highly experimental. By inserting himself as a character into Boccaccio's work, he almost erases the line between fiction and reality. As Martínez Morán notes, Juan de Flores becomes a Castilian literary character (149).

Grimalte y Gradisa seems to lack the essential components of the dream vision beyond its first-person, pseudo-autobiographical narration, but as Folger notes, "the techniques used by Flores reflect traditional reading habits and modes of composition" (*Images in Mind* 178). On closer inspection, Flores counterfeits the fictional mechanisms of dream vision into an entertaining tale that seems to defend women but in fact, like *Grisel y Mirabella,* upholds the main tenet of the discourse *in mulieres*: a naturalistic understanding of erotic desire as an inescapable force that brings only destruction.[93] Grimalte's journey to find Fiometa is memorial work: he crosses mountains and forests until he arrives at the crossing of several paths where he finally finds his narrative subject. After a debate between Fiometa and Pánfilo, Fiometa's death, and Gradisa's definitive rejection of her suitor, the *tractado* closes with a dream vision of a lover's hell.

Waley compared *Grimalte y Gradisa* to *Grisel y Mirabella* as "a sort of debate between the sexes, here between man as a rational, and woman as an emotional, being" (269). In *Grimalte y Gradisa,*

---

[92] I cite from Parrilla's 2008 edition. The treatise's self-referential nature attracted the interest of such critics as Gerli ("Metafiction"), Brownlee ("The Counterfeit Muse;" *The Severed Word*), Weissberger ("Authors, Characters;" "Resisting Readers"), Grieve, Haywood ("Gradissa"), and others.

[93] For Folger, only the tale of Fiometa, not the whole *tractado*, presents an example of love's power (*Images in Mind* 187).

Waley contrasts Fiometa, whose "emotional behaviour is continually stressed," to Pánfilo, whose "concrete and logical" reasons
clash with Fiometa's "persuasive" speeches (270). Grieve reverses
the dichotomy in the case of the title characters: "of the two lovers,
Grimalte and Gradissa, she is the one more readily associated with
razón ... Grimalte ... represents *voluntad*" (85–86). Without denying these contrasts, I contend that Flores's ingenuity consists in using
the debate of will and reason to examine the two types of reading the
eponymous characters represent.

The idea that *Grimalte y Gradisa* is about reading is not new.
Haywood ("Gradissa") and Weissberger ("Resisting Readers") make
a strong case for Gradisa as a reader resisting patriarchal norms.
Haywood posits that her emotional reading prompts her request for
both the lovers' reconciliation and Grimalte's written account of it.
Flores questions textual limits and traditional gender roles by opposing the dominant part Boccaccio assigns Fiammetta to the passive
role assigned sentimental heroines; the tension "results in the break-
down of generic and diegetic barriers" ("Gradissa" 95). As we have
seen, it is not specific to this work. I would like to compare Gradisa's
reading of the "Libro de Fiometa" —the fact that she reads like a
woman— with the rational, or patriarchal, reading that the "tractado
de Fiometa y Pánfilo" Grimalte sends her finally effects.[94]

Grieve considers Gradisa "the ideal moral reader, one who benefits from the example of another's misfortune" (92). She fully empa-
thizes with Fiometa's plight:

> Pues son notorias las quexas grandes que con justa causa Fiome-
> ta de Pánfilo escribe, yo, por cierto, en sus males pensando, casi
> como ella las siento, en especial que muchas vezes me veo teme-
> rosa que, si por vuesta me diese, que yo misma me daría al peligro
> que ella tiene. (92)

> Since the complaints that Fiometa writes of Pánfilo with just cause
> are publicly known, I, certainly, thinking of her torments, expe-
> rience them almost as strongly as she does, especially because I
> often fear that, if I became yours, I would face the danger of her
> destiny.

---

[94] Walde Moheno aptly differentiates "el libro de Fiometa" read by Grimalte and
Gradisa and "el tractado de Fiometa y Pánfilo" that Grimalte composes ("Experimentación literaria").

Like the lady to whom Alegre addresses his *Somni,* Gradisa fears desertion by a lover, but why is male infidelity such a terrible danger? What are the consequences for a woman? Flores's choice of Boccaccio's work offers a clue. As Parrilla reminds us, citing Segre, Boccaccio's *Fiammetta* belongs to the genre of the *Heroides* ("Estudio introductorio" 20). It is no concidence that when Laura defends the lady in Alegre's *Somni,* she adduces as proof two of Ovid's *epistulae,* the cases of Ariadne and Medea. They represent instances of male ingratitude but, more important, a warning against female lust, as Roís de Corella's descriptive title for his Catalan version reveals: *Escriu Medea a les dones la ingratitud e desconeixença de Jeson, per dar-lo exemple de honestament viure* [Medea's Letter to Women on Jason's Ingratitude and Disregard as an Example Encouraging Chastity]. Gradisa's request implies her rejection of a moral reading in favor of a narrative with a happy ending that will make Fiometa a mirror to guide her actions ("Así que ella me será un espejo de doctrina con que vea lo que con vos a mí convien fazer" 95). Gradisa's literary competence, Parrilla notes, is confirmed when she outlines the basics of the desired plot: two lovers and a go-between ("Estudio introductorio" 43).

The idea that women were interested in sentimental literature while men preferred chilvalric exploits is long discredited.[95] Queen Isabel's library contained at least three Arthurian romances —*Historia de Lanzarote, Baladro de Merlín,* and *La demanda del Santo Grial*— and Teresa de Ávila inherited her well-known youthful fondness for chivalric tales from her mother. Moralists disparaged their interest. In his 1528 *Instrucción de la mujer cristiana* [Education of the Christian Woman], Juan Luis Vives testified that chivalric romances were a serious danger to chastity ("¿Oy qué lugar seguro puede tener entre las armas la flaca y desarmada castedad?"); he believed that when women drank their poison ("la muger que estas cosas piensa beve poco a poco la ponçoña"), they became infected by a deathly disease ("mortal es esta infición;" Marín Pina 135). More than a century earlier, Tiresias's penitential tirade in Metge's *Lo somni* expressed similar concerns, commenting explicitly on the literary expertise of courtly ladies. He warned the fictional Metge that:

> [Women] consider themselves very happy for having a lot of luxury and comfort, and being able to speak diverse languag-

---

[95] See, for instance, Marín Pina's "La mujer y los libros de caballerías."

es, remembering many songs and rhymed tales, quoting verses
from troubadours and the *Epistles* of Ovid, reciting the stories of
Lancelot, Tristan, King Arthur and of all the lovers that lived in
their time: for arguing, attacking, defending and reasoning upon a
fact, knowing how to answer well those who speak to them of love,
having rosy and full cheeks, as well as large hips and breasts. (142)

Elles entenen ésser en gran felicitat haver molt delicament e loça-
nia, saber parlar diverses lenguatges, recordar moltes cançons e
noves rimades, al·legar dits de trobadors, e les *Epístoles* de Ovidi, reçitar les istòries de Lançelot, de Tristany, del rey Artús e de
quants amorosos són stats a lur temps; argumentar, ofrendre, defendre e rahonar un fet, saber bé respondre a aquells qui d'amor
les enqueren, haver les galtes ben plenes e vermelles, e grosses an-
ques e grossos pits. (143)

Tiresias equates women's literary skills with flaunting their sexuality. If, as Weiss argues, the games of courtly love aligned literary
composition with sexual prowess ("La *Affección* Poetal" 255), Metge
provides early testimony of how sexually charged courtly interactions could be. Moreover, in consoling the fictional Metge, Tiresias
contrasts women's fondness for story telling with the learned practice of *integumentum* and satire. The pernicious effects of fiction can
be reversed by both exegetical and personal conversion of erotic
yearning into ethical teaching and love for God.

Gradisa is very specific: she wants a tale that skips the moral plat-
itudes and narrates the here-and-now. Like Metge's eloquent ladies,
she wants help in dealing with a suitor who, we sense, keeps pester-
ing her. From a moralist's perspective, her request for a tale reuniting
a couple who have so openly betrayed the marital bond, is highly
questionable.[96]

Grimalte's reading of the "libro de Fiometa" differs radically
from Gradisa's. He gave her the book, "not as an example prov-
ing that men must be generally mistrusted, but as an *exemplum ex
negativo* for his case." Unlike Pánfilo, he is a faithful lover (Folger, *Images in Mind* 186–87). His desire for Gradisa, Walde Moheno
notes, drives the plot and tries to bring about the sentimental reconciliation that Gradisa demands to prove her fear of male infidelity

---

[96] Note that in the prologue to *Triste deleytaçión*, F.A.D.C. mentions that he cannot stop thinking about a happy ending to the love affair told in his *tratado* as a
logical outcome of S[a]'s determination.

wrong ("Experimentación literaria"). This last service to his lady, the acceptance of her "tricky request to resolve Fiometa's problems is the definite proof of his valor as a lover" (Folger, *Images in Mind* 187). Grimalte's writing is another exercise in the courtly virtue of determined hope in the face of opposition. However, the mission proves problematic, destabilizing the triangular dynamic that supports dream-vision logic.

No matter how hard he tries, Grimalte cannot sympathize with Fiometa like Gradisa does. When she regrets having consented to Pánfilo's advances so easily, she confirms Gradisa's worst fears. Grimalte attempts to excuse her behavior by blaming Love's deadly arrows but grows impatient with her obstinacy ("pues a vos ni tiempo largo ni chico no veo que ponga calma" 119). Within *Grimalte y Gradisa*'s metafictional structure, Grimalte composes Fiometa's speeches and letters as part of the *tractado* requested by his lady. In them, Fiometa accepts precisely what Gradisa rejects: her passion is disorderly ("a mi Pánfilo con tanto desorden amo" 114), and because of it, she has become a symbol of immorality ("así ha plaçido a Dios que sea que otras en mi maldad se castiguen" 114). Fiometa's final recrimination of Pánfilo is a superb rhetorical exercise of female *iracundia*, described by Grimalte as "mortal ira" (162) and "furiosa saña" (166). It exposes the extent of her sins:

> ¡O malaventurada de ti Fiometa, infamia de castas mugeres, derribamiento de nobles famas, ensuziamiento de limpios coraçones, enbargo de los castos lechos, enxemplo de tales males, inclinaçión de las que a malos usos las voluntades disponen! ¿Con qué graves penas puedes justamente punirte? Pues que tus errores no solamente ofenden a ti, mas aun de tu vergüença padescen las nobles dueñas. (163)

> Woe betide Fiometa, disgrace of chaste women, wrecker of noble reputations, blemish of untainted hearts, obstacle to chastity, example of such sins, model for those women who wilfully act with impropriety! Which severe punishment would be commensurate? Indeed, your errors not only defile you but also noble ladies suffer on account of your shame.

Grimalte knows his Ovid well; Fiometa's words so clearly recall Dido's suicide motives. He describes her agony in purely physical terms but with extreme pathos:

Que tal fue la basca de su tormento que como de po<n>çoña feri-
da, con ravias de la sensible y muy afincada muerte, dando mil
bueltas a unas partes y a otras, con espantables señales en la disfi-
gurada cara, dio fin a su triste vida. (178)

The vomit and convulsions caused by her torment were as if she
had been poisoned, with the rattle of a predictable death, her head
spinning with a thousand thoughts, her disfigured face horribly
contorted, she ended her sad life.

Whether Fiometa kills herself or is done in by her passion is unclear. In either case, she is a distinct instance of the intense madness
brought about by love passion.[97]

Grimalte also does not empathize with Pánfilo. He considers his
behavior toward Fiometa boorish: "más paresce que por la grand
conversaçión suya vos enseñó rústicas leyes" (118) [it seems that his
company taught you rustic laws], he fusses to Fiometa. When he finally meets Pánfilo, Grimalte is captivated by his good looks ("jamás
una persona de tan gentil parescer no nasció" 133) but confounded
by his laidback approach to sex. Love, Pánfilo explains bluntly,

should not last more than one year of courtship and half year of
possession. Women are fully aware that nature makes men unfaithful but they are still willing to surrender for this brief time,
even if it were shorter. Such time is way passed for me and Fiometa. So, what does Fiometa demand? When a man is attractive and
willing, the sensible thing is sharing his favors with many, not just
with one.[98]

After Fiometa's death, Grimalte unsuccessfully challenges Pánfilo to a duel. His letter of challenge again expresses incomprehension
of Pánfilo's "nuevas leyes" that tolerate Fiometa's death, completely
rejecting the courtly ideal: "raçonable cosa es, como suele acaescer,
a nosotros por las mugeres morir" (192) [the sensible and accept-

---

[97] In the *Bursarii super Ovidios*, the *accessus* to Dido's *epistula* states: "intencio
auctoris est reprehendere eam a stulto amor" (Rodríguez del Padrón, *Bursario* 149).

[98] "Amor no devría más tener término de un año de seguimiento y medio de
possesión. Y las mugeres, segund la condición de los hombres, <bien conoscen> que
es este caso de poca firmeza, pero por este pequeño tiempo que dura, aunque fuese
menos, se dexan vencer. Pues este tiempo ya yo y muy más tengo passado. Y por esto
Fiometa, ¿qué me demanda? El hombre que gracioso y dispuesto se conosce, razón
es querer partir sus gracias por muchas, no es razón que sólo una lo goze" (140).

ed behavior is that we die for women]. Courageously following his determination to its last consequences is the expected performance of manly *virtus*, what Weissberger calls "the kind of superior sense and sensibility that the aristocracy used to set itself apart from and legitimize its dominance over the lower classes" ("The Politics" 320). Fernández de Madrigal's *Libro de amor y amicicia* states that those moved exclusively by physical pleasure cannot be called lovers but belong in the category of brutes. Grimalte aligns with his class in calling Pánfilo's mores "rústicas leyes."

Walde Moheno is astonished by the work's abundance of ridiculous characters, cynics, and hypocrites ("Experimentación" 82). Grimalte observes them with suspicion, although Waley considers him "querulous and unheroic" (267). Unable to identify with Gradisa's desire and approach the "Libro de Fiometa" from her perspective, Grimalte adopts the mask of the fool to narrate the story. No wonder Gradisa dislikes the "tractado de Fiometa y Pánfilo" he eventually sends her: she asked for a love story and receives instead a scathing satire. It is exactly the opposite of what she requested: Grimalte's participation fails to reconcile Fiometa and Pánfilo; his narration so deftly weaves the rhetorical pieces that it subtly moralizes the characters as symbols of depravity. If the *tractado* ended at this point, Gradisa could interpret it as an entertainment like that San Pedro sent to the ladies of the queen, but Grimalte's *planctus* after Fiometa's death makes clear the tale's moral aim:

> ¡O engañoso Amor! ¿Por qué en la tormenta de tus alterados mares aniegas aquellos que más te sirven? Tú casi como en la Fortuna abrazado, las sus opiniones sigues. No sé de qué po<n>çoñosa forma eres compuesta, pues los que te fuyen viven y los que te esperan mueren. (180)

> O deceitful Love! Why do you drown your most faithful servants in the storms of your ever-changing seas? You, as if in Fortune's tight embrace, follow her opinions. I do not know of what poisonous form you are made that those who escape you live and those who trust you die.

In the end, Grimalte's desire leads to a very penitential capture of Fiometa's story as an allegory of Fortune.

Why would Grimalte offer Gradisa a patriarchal *enarratio* that so blatantly contradicts her wishes? Folger claims that Gradisa certainly understands the *tractado* as "a demonstration of the fatal and inescapable force of passionate love" but that Grimalte hopes that the hardships he endured prove that she will not suffer Fiometa's fate (*Images in Mind* 187). However, Grimalte's conflation of a lover's rhetorical stance and moral *enarratio* is problematic. Gradisa's fictionalization as internal reader is such a powerful device that it obscures the fact that *Grimalte y Gradisa*, not the "tractado de Fiometa y Pánfilo" within it, is narrated by an aging Grimalte, twenty-seven years after Fiometa's death. He spent all those years searching for Pánfilo's retreat yet remains loyal to Gradisa. His rhetorical stance as a steadfast lover is shaded by the humorous undertones of university spoofs.

Grimalte's faithfulness has turned him into a victim of what Ovid termed "turpe senilis amor" [disgraceful elderly love, *Amores* 1.9]. The Pánfilo he eventually finds is as feral as the crude manners of his youth would predict: he cannot speak. Grimalte needs the help of some hounds to dislodge him from his burrow. At night, Fiometa appears in the company of deformed figures whose mouths and eyes exhale fire. She is fully clothed ("de diversos vestidos cubierta" 218–19) and complains of the torments that Pánfilo's cruelty still cause her. When she breaks off, she climbs into a frightful chariot, and her now-naked figure no longer reflects her renowned beauty but a tortured soul in hell. Notice her penitential undressing; the vision slowly removes the outer layers of both woman and her tale to reveal the final truth: Love's fires —the embrace of Fortune— destroy us all, as the couplet that closes the appearance of Fiometa's wraith sings:

> Amor, tu cárcel y casa,
> para quien más bien tenemos
> es fuego mortal y brasa
> donde su fin padescemos. (220)

The final vision has a distinct air of mockery. Folger diagnoses Pánfilo with melancholy, a mental disease that causes hallucinations similar to those of the *amor hereos*, which he never suffered (*Images in Mind* 191). Waley and Grieve deem his arguments rejecting the emotional Fiometa highly rational; they certainly resemble the Aristotelian naturalism put forward by university *letrados*. Is Flores-Grimalte making fun of allegorical conversion as another form of delusion? In Grimalte's case, the vision fails to produce a conversion or relieve his desire for Gradisa. Instead, he willingly becomes Pánfilo's "legítimo heredero" [rightful heir], a naked beast in the wilderness contemplating Fiometa's horrific visitations three times a week —like a regular schedule of university lectures? In a final letter to Gradisa, he refuses to forget her and surrenders his right to choose —his *libertad*— to remain her servant:

> Y si hay alguno que, medroso de ver mi mal, me reprenda de simple por conportar tan estremado dolor, las causas de tu beldad y valer me desculpan, las cuales, si me vencieron, no siento fuerte omenaje que delante de tu vista defienda su libertad. (224)

> And if there is anyone who, frightened by my suffering, reprehends my foolishness for tolerating such acute pain, your beauty and worth vindicate me because if they won over me, my freedom to serve was forfeited when I saw you.

The wilting of Gradisa's beauty after a quarter of a century is another joke that could not have gone unnoticed. Grimalte's foolishness is patent: he is an elderly Orpheus who chooses to remain in hell.

CONVERTING DESIRE,
NARRATING DESIRE

THE SPREAD of lay literacy in Aragon and Castile at the turn of the fourteenth century enabled the knightly class to become *caballeros sçientes* by performing their love poems as acts of literary and sexual prowess. They wielded them against both noble foes and professional men of letters, who, like the learned Bishop of Cartagena, fought and lost a Herculean battle to restrict the field to a clerical minority. The rising class of university-trained *letrados* who populated royal and urban administrations joined the battle. Aristocrats and clerks actively constructed the discourse of lay cultural literacy.[1] The love of learning and desire for God are rendered in the vernacular as sexual and intellectual desire, not only in narrative poems and letters, but also in sentimental and penitential fictions.

In composing amorous works, *caballeros* and *letrados* deploy the fictional mechanisms of the *ars dictaminis*: autobiographical stance, *altercatio* between Reason and Will, descent into Hell or ascent into Heaven, and, most important, the dream vision sparked by an inventive image. The most productive images are either the old architectonic trope of love prisons and castles of perseverance or taken from Boethius's opening scene in *The Consolation*. A miniature of

---

[1] Weiss studies the fictions of masculine power by Constable Alvaro de Luna, an upstart who rose to be "the greatest man uncrowned" under Juan II of Castile before Santillana and other aristocrats maneuvered him to the gallows; the royal secretary of Latin letters Juan de Mena ("Alvaro de Luna, Juan de Mena"); and Mosén Fernando de la Torre ("What Every Noblewoman"). *The Greatest Man Uncrowned* is the title of Luna's biography by Round (1986).

the triangle formed by the lachrymose Boethius, the Muses, and Philosophy decorated a manuscript of Pere Borró's Catalan version, according to the book inventory of King Alfons, the Magnanimous.[2] This iconography is common on manuscripts and, as Astell showed, configures *The Consolation*'s argument as a love story to hook it into memory (*Job, Boethius* 128).[3] A second Boethian icon of lasting impact is Fortune at her wheel. Besides its rhetorical energy, the proliferation of debates over Fortune and the taste for the *materia de amore* reveals a deep concern with contingency and change embodied as "woman" and told in the Ovidian amatory tradition, a repository of life's arbitrary happenings, whose ultimate value was teaching the young to heal their minds by converting carnal desire into spiritual love.

Exegetical, medical, and penitential discourses on sex identify Fortune with erotic burning and swelling —the smart of a bee sting, the agony of a poisonous snake bite— triggered by either seeing beauty or reading a suggestive text. The liberal arts were meant to train the intellect and free will to change the emotional color of these dangerous images; *letrados* and *caballeros sçientes* deploy their power to disguise their various courtly self-images. Weiss illustrates with Mena's *Tratado de amor* in which the poet "records the conventional Ovidian love-cure whereby the lover heals his sickness by the power of his own imagination: 'todo aquel que podrá fingir de sano, sano será'" [he who is able to feign health shall be cured] ("La *Affección Poetal*" 255). They also use their power of ratiocination to perfect the intentions of their courtly disguises. While feigning *amor hereos* to play the power games of courtly love as both subjects and masters, they later composed consolations renouncing youthful cravings, privileging the male *pietas litterata* —the cultivation of rational masculinity— in structuring the authorial position of old age. They construct the contemplative stance of a private subject who recants earlier errors and a similarly private reading *locus* that demands empathy with the protagonist's sufferings. Writer and readers are meant to benefit from the intellectual and emotional journey.

Penitential consolations presuppose the exclusively masculine social interactions typical of the schools' homosocial setting and conforming to the triangular dynamics that Sedgwick theorized in

---

[2] ".I. altre gran estratges e dins aquel jau Boeci en. i. lit e a l'una part de lit es pintade philosophia e en l'altre costat. jjj. donzelles" (qtd. in Briesemeister 64).

[3] Astell refers to Courcelle's study for reproductions of some illuminations.

Between Men. Cortijo Ocaña noted that *Siervo*'s dream vision is framed by the epistolary exchange —an *epístola marco*— between two friends; he reads *Siervo* as a warning against untrustworthy companions, both male and female, as a source of blindness, chaos, and disorder ("'De amicitia'"). Against them, Boncompagno da Signa's *De amicitia* —an index of common dictaminal practices— proposed the soothing bond among rational men as the site of virtue, equilibrium, and happiness. In Castile, Fernández de Madrigal's *Libro de amor y amicicia* deemed friendship a rational act, a shield against Fortune. This relationship, claims Cortijo Ocaña, supports *Siervo*'s correspondents.

Epistolary exchanges also frame Carrós's *Regoneixença* and Moner's *L'Ánima d'Oliver*, while Roís de Corella's *Parlament* promotes the positive effect of networks of friends. All of them make a point of displaying the *sapientia* acquired in the process, as Santillana did when sending his *Proemio e carta* to Pedro de Portugal. In all of them, a vertigo of specular reflections and translations morphs the original Boethian triangle of prisoner, Lady Philosophy, and the meretricious Muses into the interactions of a young Orpheus and an aged Tiresias, who instructs the poet on the inconstancy of Fortune, figured as either a silent or silenced woman —her tongue cut off— in a project of allegorical capture.

Two penitential fictions not framed by a letter —the last two books of Metge's *Lo somni* and Romeu Llull's *Lo despropiament*— appear to address the more mixed public of, respectively, the royal court and Barcelonian elite social gatherings that mimicked courtly practices. In the latter, the male body is captured as a poetic text that can be dressed and undressed, expounded and moralized; solace is found in marriage later in life. In Metge's learned display, the protagonist fails to achieve consolation.

The same unsatisfactory conclusion is reached in *La noche;* Moner, blending scholarly and courtly practices, seems to offer his physical body and body of knowledge to a silent, unnamed lady in exchange for erotic relief. The offending Muses, unlike trusted friends, offer nothing but poison. The failure to find moral relief is the consequence of a more profound dissonance, the attempt to transfer the penitential component to court; in *Lo somni*'s case, it heralds sentimental contrafaction.

Gerli's analysis of *Siervo*'s metafictional artifice can be safely applied to the whole genre, but I must stress that the act of writing depicted in penitential fictions is the meditation on, and moral in-

terpretation of, an author's own past and poetry, either read or composed. Tears, moans, and laments gesture toward the agitated mood
that precedes inventive recollection. The initial mental disposition
—their *affectio*— is identified with erotic desire and *curiositas*, which
drive the protagonists to the darkest recesses of their minds —the
memorial hells of Ovidian myths, passionate feelings, and love poems— in search of subject matter. They emerge from darkness and
chaos to find an allegorical personification who teaches them how
to turn —*bolver*— their material away from disorder and into focus
by painting it in a different emotional hue and redirecting their creative energy. For these clerks and courtly dilettantes, dream vision is
the chosen form for probing their feelings and exploring their soul.
Augustinian conversion proceeds inward, then upward, mirroring
Orpheus's journey through Hell and Boethius's intellectual journey.
The dream vision also becomes a tool to read and to appropriate
poetic tradition.

If the arguments on the role of sexual appetite, free will, and
moral responsibility sound familiar to those versed in the great poets
of the fourteenth century —Jean de Meun, Petrarch, Chaucer— it
is because they are. Penitential fictions do not offer profound philosophical discussions on those traditional Christian topics but rather
the rhetoric of display on the main points of *pietas litterata* and dissimulation of a taste for literature. The consecutive stages of school
training provide the model for a young man's entrance to maturity;
Ovid and Orpheus follow the course of Boethius's *Consolation,* read,
in the most medieval way, with Augustine's *De libero arbitrio,* as we
saw in Petrus Compostellanus's *De consolatione Rationis.* Augustine
and Boethius provide more than philosophical underpinning; as
Stock points out about Augustine, they model the reader who withdraws into a private inner space to scrutinize his own past ("Reading,
Ethics" 7).

Those scholarly models were revamped or energized by contact with Dante, Petrarch, and other fourteenth-century authors for
whom, Stock said, "the philosophical understanding of the soul or
self is complemented by literary understanding" ("Reading, Writing"
725). Butiñá ("El humanismo") underscored how Italian humanism
stimulated Catalan letters, and Serés ("La llamada") proposed a
close connection between the widespread appetite for translations
and the emergence of the sentimental genre in Aragon and Castile.
Cultural contact and exchange between the two crowns enriched
penitential consolations. Besides "extrapeninsular" and "intrapen-

insular" translations —I am using Cátedra's terms ("Presentación" 13)— two other types of *translatio* had a lasting influence. We saw in chapter 1 how Saplana-Ginebreda's version of William of Aragon's commentary discovered a *dictator*'s rhetorical and penitential course in Boethius's *Consolation*, prompting Villena's exegetical feat on the twelve deeds of Hercules and Virgil's *Aeneid*. Penitential fictions add French and Italian texts and their motifs to the memorial repository of classical myths and themes. Metge dared to correct Petrarch and Boccaccio, while Haywood suspects that the *novella* that Rodríguez del Padrón inserts in *Siervo* may be a translation ("On the Frontiers" 74), perhaps from the French, as Impey suggested. This ethical allegoresis must be understood as a type of secondary translation that cannot be accomplished without a more fundamental *translatio*, the metamorphosis of erotic drive into *caritas*.

Boethian-Augustinian *contemptus mundi* provides the template for the recantation of material pleasures and sensual deceits, particularly by sight and hearing, typified by women and poetry. However, the recurrent mention of Cupid's multicolored attire, the sirens' enticing songs, the white sails of seafaring love reveal a deep attraction and enjoyment barely hidden behind the composed middle-aged melancholy. Conversely, shipwrecks and battleships project allegorical violence to focus errant thoughts and misguided inquisitiveness, to control imagination and garrulity, to transfix the fluidity of life into silent symbol. Franciscan spirituality encouraged a healthy curiosity when meditating on the life of Christ, but a worldlier attraction to the "virtualità della trama" pervades the penitential genre from the very first moment —fictional Metge's reluctance to stop listening to Orpheus.

The practice of *pietas litterata* fixes the powerful gaze of moral allegory on the realm of Fortune, sliding temporal change along the vertical axis of eternity through a progression of *intentiones*, or emotional tracks. As its engine, desire generates a consolatory form that purges both the temptations of the flesh and an image's narrative possibilities by freezing temporal existence into ageless symbol, the logic of moral allegory and the vertical chronotrope that Bakhtin identifies in Dante's *Commedia*.

Auctores undergo a similarly violent transmutation. In the spurious *De vetula*, Ovid metamorphoses into an aging Augustine, articulating the two ages of the poet: Orpheus in love and reflective old Tiresias. The influence on Catalan and Castilian *materia de amore* Cortijo Ocaña imputes to Dante's *Vita nuova* may be found, not in

its prosimetric form or its clever fusion of poetic experience and exegetical techniques: many a *dictator* tried his hand at them (for example, Boncompagno da Signa and Juan Ruiz). Less obviously, Dante
modeled *auctoritas* as a vernacular *magister amoris*, a modern Ovid,
victim and teacher, whose extensive *estudios* helped him to *bolver* his
youthful *affecçión* into love of wisdom later in life, as the Castilian
translation of Bruni's *Vite di Dante e del Petrarca* explained. Suffering a milder poetic fever than Orpheus or Saint Francis, Dante was
still inspired by the assiduous learning he so magnificently explained
and later translated into Christian ethics.

The influence of another *magister amoris* runs much deeper than
direct borrowings. In the preface to the *Secretum*, Petrarch reenacts
the initial Boethian scene, clearly framed as a dream vision. He is visited by Truth, *Veritas*, a lady of blinding splendor, accompanied by
Augustine, the most excellent physician of his own youthful passions.
Petrarch complains to Augustine that he has been cast on a stormy
ocean, and his deployment of the marine metaphor informs penitential and sentimental literature, not so much as direct quotation —the
image's pedigree is too extensive to point to a single source— but
to question Augustinian confidence. A sensitive twentieth-century
reader of the *Secretum* poignantly echoes our authors' stance:

> If the *Confessions* are the memoirs of the retired sea captain,
> written in the warmth and security of his house overlooking the
> harbor, the *Secretum* is the daily log of a mariner in the midst of
> stormy and dubious voyage. To long for the calming of the waves
> and for the beacon of a friendly shore is not the same as to have
> them. ... Augustine gives us conflict, decisive resolution, definitive
> conversion. Petrarch gives conflict, equivocal volition, and rhetor-
> ically empathic indecision. (Fleming 147)

Penitential authors enter —they *labor intus*— the labyrinth of
their dream visions and private hells. They impart order by pointing
their *affecçión* in the direction of charity: their free will frantically
steers the helm of the little boat away from the whirlpools of love and
stories. Safely ashore, the reflective gaze cast on past experience and
imagination attempts to control mutability and proliferation through
sheer force of moralization.

If penitential consolations are intended for a masculine readership, circles of friends whose bonds are meant to safeguard against
feminine chaos, a very different web of habits and expectations arises from the gallant, vernacular world of royal and nobiliary courts.

Courtly social interactions lead to the sentimental form, which implies a very different way of seeing: the allegorical gaze of consolation gives way to narrative glance.

Sentimental fictions share most of the formal traits of penitential consolations —pseudo-autobiographical narrative, dream vision, *altercatio* of Reason and Will, and fictionalization of readership, but the ritual performance of courtly love demands the lover assume an Orphic stance that conflates erotic desire, rhetorical choice, and hope as social destiny; it guides virile enterprises and manly *virtus*. In the courtly arena, although closely related to the mental distress caused by *aegritudo amoris*, desire becomes *voluntad*, both volition and rhetorical aim, which determines a text's formal design. The success of an author's *voluntad* is no mere *cancionero* motif but drives the subject matter away from moral allegory. It dismantles *enarratio*'s authorizing discourses, *integumentum* and satire. The steadiness of the lover's faith orients his will to invent a praise of woman and a defamation of her slanderers in the vernacular curriculum of *pietas litterata*.

This rhetorical choice and authorial stance are shared with *cancionero* poetry, but poets, as in a school *disputatio*, stress the difference of their oral genre. They attempt to wrestle knowledge and power in a public ritual. In contrast, sentimental fiction is a hybrid genre that distorts the penitential performance of silent affective contemplation, examining the incongruous voices of courtly social interactions in private reading.

Extending the range of classics on which to invent penitential journeys to chivalry tales —as Rodríguez del Padrón did and, we may assume, the incomplete Catalan *Tragèdia de Lançalot*— explains the misguided aim of sentimental contrafacta: their pernicious curiosity about plot. Moner's *La noche* and San Pedro's *Cárcel de Amor* begin with a similar topification of a lover's psychological turmoil and analogous emphasis on its poetic shades, but *La noche* aims at conversion, even if it turns out to be an extravagant plea to a lady, while *Cárcel* rows right into the perilous waves of narrative, allegory's Other.

The flesh-and-blood, not allegorical, women to whom sentimental fictions are addressed unbalance the consolatory equilibrium based on the gaze of two men facing a representation of Fortune and inscribed in the letters that often frame penitential consolation. The enigmatic F.A.D.C. and Alegre offer their works as testimony of their fidelity in resolute hope that their ladies will desist from their cruelty. Instead of moralizing their stories and moving on, they are writers in love forever writing.

San Pedro presents his *Arnalte y Lucenda* to the ladies of the queen but not as a love service. The presence of a narrative voice distinct from the lover-protagonist, which views the story's characters from outside, alters the sentimental form. *El autor*'s detached perspective and Arnalte's foolishness are two sides of the novelistic device of "not understanding" that portray the nonsensical excesses of courtly male cliques playing the love game. Arnalte finishes his days as a forlorn Orpheus, but he is not alone in the wilderness; in the company of all his retinue, he inhabits a black dwelling built to mirror Lucenda's merciless behavior. The narrator ignores Arnalte's request to deliver his story to the ladies as a symbol of their cruelty, handing it over as some "nuevas" to entertain their leisure time.

Cárcel de Amor is not only dedicated to, but requested by, the same circle whose bizarre actions *Arnalte y Lucenda* exposes, the "caballeros cortesanos" in young Diego Hernandes's entourage. San Pedro adapts the techniques of affective devotion, and *el auctor* assumes the mask of the devout who contemplates and shares a lover's suffering, to portray the collective experience of a clique to which he does not fully belong. Consistent with the logic of the patron's request, the device of "not-understanding" is applied to the lady's, not young men's behavior. Like the painter who depicts a sitter inside his own visionary experience, *el auctor*'s deferential kissing of his patron's hand at the end conveys a sense of distance: the emotive account he has just told is not really his own but a commission he has professionally executed.

If San Pedro invents *Cárcel* by taking advantage of his patron's devotional literacy, Flores's *Grimalte y Gradisa* casts an ironic look on courtly life through Grimalte's inability to understand the ladies' taste for, and understanding of, storytelling. By focusing on the rituals of courtship, we forget that sentimental authors and their public contended with another love —for stories. How can they reconcile their beautiful narratives with slanderous moralizations when daily exchanges present them with the very tangible reality of female delights? We saw in chapter 2 how the married friends in *Parlament* cry when retelling Orpheus's loss; the comforts of conjugal life disturb their *enarratio* of classical myths. *Triste deleytación* calls attention to an aspect of *la querella de las mugeres* that critics neglect in their analysis of gender ideologies and power economics: both sexes thoroughly enjoyed the pastime. Its lover-narrator, rowing his literary boat away from moralization, keeps writing, presumably as a service to his lady's hunger for love stories.

That same hunger motivates Gradisa's request for a happy ending to Boccaccio's *Fiammetta,* but Grimalte, the fool Flores chooses as a narrative mask, fails to identify with her reading and insists, contrary to her wishes, on traditional *enarratio,* casting Fiometa as the symbol of love's depravity. Grimalte's ludicrous destiny, a life in the wilderness contemplating hell's visions in the company of a brutish Pánfilo, presents school life as an unpleasant counterpart to the court.

San Pedro also references reading in *Cárcel* when Leriano literally drinks Laureola's letters to suggest the muscular physical process involved in solitary meditation. Dream vision and the allegory of Love's prison still initiate composition, but, as Martín notes, allegory's ultimate attempt to capture Leriano's subjectivity fails and is supplanted by a Christological model. Allegory still takes a stab at Laureola and leaves a "trace" in the physical imprisonment from which Leriano frees her ("Love's Subjects" 402).

The collapse of allegory is a consequence of its strong connection to memory and the narrative potential at the core of its powerful images. *El auctor*'s curiosity when he enters the allegorical prison of Love is partly satisfied by Leriano's outline of the plot that is going to develop: "Who I am I shall tell you; about the mysteries you see here I mean to enlighten you; the cause of my captivity I wish you to know; and I would beseech you to liberate me, if you think it right to do so" (8).[4] San Pedro struggled with the demands of the sentimental form, and his choice of the Christological model represents the last attempt to solve the old dynamic of the center and the margin, to reconcile the eternal and the contingent in the God made man. However, Leriano keeps escaping from the prison of Love in the company of Hope and Contentment —that is, he is driven by *virtus*— to find a real woman who suffers real incarceration at peril of death: real, of course, in a fictional, narrative sense. Laureola, like Gradisa on behalf of Fiometa, actively resists Leriano and *el auctor*'s attempts to reduce her to another iteration of "woman," a symbol of cruelty. She is a full-fledged human being, daughter of King Gaulo and his Queen; she lives at the Macedonian court with other restless characters whose individual paths continually cross. She speaks, writes, chooses her silences, experiences fears, and makes hard, life-turning decisions. Leriano must die because such a vibrant,

---

4 "Quien yo soy quiero dezirte; de los misterios que vees quiero informarte; la causa de mi prisión quiero que sepas; que me deliberes quiero pedirte si por bien lo tovieres" (8).

complex, ever-changing world has no place for his static character. In drinking Laureola's letters to commit suicide, he is the last gasp of moral allegory, gobbling, but not assimilating, life.

It is not an insignificant detail that *el auctor* always prompts Leriano's breakouts from his atemporal prison. When *el auctor* visits, the materiality of the here-and-now encroaches on allegory as his glance scrutinizes courtly interactions, rivalries, gossip, fears, and expectations. The narrative distance elicited by "the device of not understanding" breaks down the illusion of solace and the permanence of the unified visionary world afforded by the gaze of moral allegory. Pedro de Portugal's "novelar desinteresado" winds up in the center by the end of the century, and, by altering the rhetoric of the margin, the sentimental genre discovers its *novelness*. A narrator's glance observes the variety and multiplicity of human existence and interprets its mutability in plot form. This experience drives the form and content of the novel.

BIBLIOGRAPHY

Accorsi, Federica. "A vueltas con San Agustín y el *Libro de buen amor*: estado de la cuestión." *Juan Ruiz, Arcipreste de Hita y el "Libro de buen amor:" Congreso Homenaje a Jacques Joset*, edited by Francisco Toro Ceballos and Isabel Godinas, Ayuntamiento de Alcalá la Real, 2011. Centro Virtual Cervantes. cvc.cervantes.es.

Adams, James Noel. *The Latin Sexual Vocabulary*. The Johns Hopkins UP, 1982.

Agnew, Michael. "The 'Comedieta' of the Satira: Dom Pedro de Portugal's Monkeys in the Margins." *Modern Languages Notes*, vol. 118, no. 2, 2003, pp. 298–317.

Akbari, Suzanne Conklin. *Seeing through the Veil: Optical Theory and Medieval Allegory*. U of Toronto P, 2004.

Alanus de Insulis. *Anticlaudianus: or The Good and Perfect Man*. Edited by James J. Sheridan, Pontifical Institute of Medieval Studies, 1973.

Albesano, Silvia. *Consolatio Philosophiae Volgare: Volgarizzamenti e Tradizioni Discorsive Nel Trecento Italiano*. Universitätsverlag Winter, 2006.

Alegre, Francesc. *Obres de ficció sentimental*. Edited by Gemma Pellisa Prades, Edizioni dell'Orso, 2016.

Alemany Ferrer, Rafael. "Tres reescrituras del mito de Orfeo en las letras catalanas medievales: Bernat Metge, Joan Roís de Corella y Francesc Alegre." *Actas del VIII Congreso Internacional de la Asociación Hispánica de Literatura Medieval*, vol. 1, Consejería de Cultura del Gobierno de Cantabria, 2000, pp. 117–27. Biblioteca Virtual Joan Lluís Vives, 2013.

Allen, Judson Boyce. *The Ethical Poetic of the Later Middle Ages*. U of Toronto P, 1982.

Alton, D. Ernest Henry, and D. E. W. Wormell. "Ovid in the Mediaeval Schoolroom." *Hermathena*, vol. 95, 1961, pp. 67–82.

Alvar, Carlos. "Acerca de la traducción en Castilla en el siglo XV." *Traducciones y traductores: materiales para una historia de la traducción en Castilla durante la Edad Media*, Centro de Estudios Cervantinos, 2010, pp. 257–89.

Alvar, Carlos, and José Manuel Lucía Mejías. "Repertorio de traductores del siglo XV: tercera veintena." *Traducción y práctica literaria en la Edad Media románica*, edited by Rosanna Cantavella, et al., U de València, 2003, pp. 1–40.

Alvar, Carlos, and José Manuel Lucía Mejías, editors. *Diccionario filológico de literatura medieval española*. Castalia, 2002.

Amasuno Sárraga, Marcelino V. *La escuela de medicina del estudio salmantino (siglos XIII–XV)*. U de Salamanca, 1990.

Andrachuk, Gregory Peter. "The Function of the 'Estoria de dos amadores' in *Siervo libre de amor.*" *Revista Canadiense de Estudios Hispánicos*, vol. 2, 1977–1978, pp. 27–38.

---. "A Further Look at the Italian Influence in the *Siervo libre de amor.*" *Journal of Hispanic Philology*, vol. 6, no. 82, 1981–1982, pp. 45–56.

---. "On the Missing Third Part of *Siervo Libre de Amor.*" *Hispanic Review*, vol. 45, 1977, pp. 1971–80.

---. "Prosa y poesía en el *Siervo libre de amor.*" *Actas del Sexto Congreso Internacional de Hispanistas, celebrado en Toronto del 22 al 26 de agosto de 1977*, edited by Alan M. Rugg and Evelyn Gordon, Asociación Internacional de Hispanistas, 1980, pp. 60–62.

---. "A Re-examination of the Poetry of Juan Rodríguez del Padrón." *Bulletin of Hispanic Studies*, vol. 57, 1980, pp. 299–308.

Annicchiarico, Annamaria. *'Narracions en vers' catalane medievali: apunti e materiali per una guida bibliografica.* Edizioni di Storia e Letteratura, 2003.

Archer, Robert. *The Problem of Woman in Late-Medieval Hispanic Literature.* Tamesis, 2005.

Arizaga Castro. "La caracterización del enamorado en la poesía amorosa del *Cancionero de Baena* y del *Cancionero de Palacio.*" *Iberia cantat: estudios sobre la poesía ibérica medieval*, edited by Juan Díaz Martínez and Eva María Casas Rigall, U de Santiago de Compostela, 2002, pp. 321–34.

Arnau de Vilanova. *Tractat sobre l'amor heroic.* Edited by Michael McVaugh and translated by Sebastià Giralt, Barcino, 2011.

Arronis Llopis, Carme, and Fernando Baños Vallejo. "Las vidas de María en el ámbito peninsular pretridentino." *Estudios Humanísticos: Filología*, vol. 36, 2014, pp. 65–105.

Astell, Ann W. *Job, Boethius, and Epic Truth.* Cornell UP, 1994.

---. "Visualizing Boethius's *Consolation* as Romance." *New Directions in Boethian Studies*, edited by Noel Harold Kaylor and Philip Edward Phillips, Medieval Institute Publications, 2007, pp. 111–24.

Augustine, Bishop of Hippo. *The City of God.* Translated by Marcus Dods, Hafner Publishing Co., 1948.

Avenoza, Gemma. "Traducciones, público y mecenazgo en Castilla (siglo XV)." *Romania*, vol. 128, 2010, pp. 452–500.

Aybar Ramírez, María Fernanda. *La ficción sentimental del siglo XVI.* 1994. U Complutense de Madrid, PhD dissertation.

Azcarate, José María. "El tema iconográfico del salvaje." *Archivo Español de Arte*, vol. 82, 1948, pp. 81–99.

Badia, Lola. "De la 'reverenda letradura' en el *Curial e Güelfa.*" *De Bernat Metge a Joan Roís de Corella: estudis sobre la cultura literària de la tardor medieval catalana*, Quaderns Crema, 1988, pp. 121–43.

---. "'En les baixes antenes de la vulgar poesia': Corella, els mites y l'amor." *De Bernat Metge a Joan Roís de Corella: estudis sobre la cultura literària de la tardor medieval catalana*, Quaderns Crema, 1988, pp. 145–80.

---, editor. *Història de la literatura catalana. Vol. 1: Literatura medieval (I). Dels orígens al segle XIV*, Barcino, 2013.

---, editor. *Història de la literatura catalana. Vol. 2: Literatura medieval (II). Segles XIV–XV.* Barcino, 2014.

---, editor. *Història de la literatura catalana. Vol. 3: Literatura medieval (III). Segle XV.* Barcino, 2015.

---. "*Lo somni* di Bernat Metge e coloro 'che l'anima col corpo morta fanno' (*Inferno*, X.15)." *Fourteenth-Century Classicism: Petrarch and Bernat Metge*, edited by Lluís Cabré, Warburg Institute, 2012, pp. 69–83.

Badia, Lola, et al., editors. *Els manuscrits, el saber i les lletres a la Corona d'Aragó, 1250–1500.* Publicacions de l'Abadia de Montserrat, 2016.

Badia, Lola, and Albert Soler, editors. *Intel·lectuals i escriptors a la baixa edad mitjana*. Curial, 1994.

Bakhtin, Mikhail. *The Dialogic Imagination: Four Essays*. Translated by Michael Holquist, U of Texas P, 1981.

Balint, Bridget K. *Ordering Chaos: The Self and the Cosmos in Twelfth-Century Latin Prosimetrum*. Brill, 2009.

Barletta, Vincent. "Trotaconventos and the Mora: Grammar, Gender and Verbal Interaction in the *Libro de buen amor*." *La corónica*, vol. 37, 2008, pp. 339–64.

Bassegoda, Enric. *Vida i obra de Fra Bernat Hug de Rocabertí*. U de Girona, 2011.

Beard, Ana. "*El sueño*, del Marqués de Santillana: géneros y realidad." *Palabras e imagen en la Edad Media. Actas de las IV Jornadas Medievales*, edited by Aurelio González and Lillian von der Walde Moheno, UNAM, 1995, pp. 317–25.

Beaujouan, Guy. *Manuscrits scientifiques médiévaux de L'Université de Salamanque et des ses "colegios mayores."* Féret, 1962.

Beceiro Pita, Isabel. "De las peregrinaciones al viaje interior: las transformaciones en la religiosidad nobiliar castellana." *Cahiers d'Études Hispaniques Médiévales*, vol. 30, 2007, pp. 109–25.

---. "La educación: un derecho y un deber del cortesano." *La enseñanza en la Edad Media: X Semana de Estudios Medievales, Nájera 1999*, edited by José Ignacio de la Iglesia Duarte, Gobierno de la Rioja, 2000, pp. 175–206.

---. "Educación y cultura en la nobleza (siglos XIII–XV)." *Anuario de Estudios Medievales*, 1991, pp. 775–806.

---. "Entre el ámbito privado y las competencias públicas: la educación en el reino de Castilla (siglos XIII–XV)." *Pensamiento medieval hispano: homenaje a Horacio Santiago-Otero*, edited by José María Soto Rábanos, vol. 1, Consejo Superior de Investigaciones Científicas, 1998, pp. 861–86.

---. *Libros, lectores y bibliotecas en la España medieval*. Nausicaä, 2007.

---. "Los libros que pertenecieron a los condes de Benavente, entre 1434 y 1530." *Hispania. Revista Española de Historia*, vol. 154, 1983, pp. 237–80.

Beceiro Pita, Isabel and Alfonso Franco Silva. "Cultura nobiliar y bibliotecas: cinco ejemplos, de las postrimerías del siglo XIV a mediados del XVI." *Historia, Instituciones, Documentos*, vol. 12, 1986, pp. 277–350.

Beltran, Vicenç, editor. *Poesía cortesana (siglo XV)*. Biblioteca Castro, 2009.

Beresford, Andrew M, et al., editors. *Medieval Hispanic Studies in Memory of Alan Deyermond*. Tamesis, 2013.

Berlin, Henry. "Alfonso de Madrigal, el Tostado, on the Politics of Friendship." *Hispanic Review*, vol. 84, no. 2, 2016, pp. 147–69.

Blanco Soto, Pedro. "Petri Compostellani de consolatione rationis libri duo." *Beiträge zur Geschichte der Philosophie des Mittelalters*, vol. 8, no. 4, 1912, pp. 1–151.

Blay Manzanera, Vicenta. "La conciencia genérica en la ficción sentimental. (Planteamiento de una problemática)." *Historias y ficciones. Coloquio sobre la literatura del Siglo XV*, edited by Rafael Beltrán, et al., Servei de Publicacions de la U de València, 1992, pp. 205–25.

---. "Las cualidades dramáticas de *Triste deleytación*: su relación con *Celestina* y con las llamadas 'Artes de amores.'" *Revista de Literatura Medieval*, vol. 9, 1997, pp. 61–96.

---. "La dinámica espacio-temporal como elemento estructural en *Triste deleytación*." *Actas de III Congreso de la Asociación Hispánica de Literatura Medieval*, edited by María Isabel Pascua Toro, vol. 1, Biblioteca Española del Siglo XV, 1994, pp. 187–96.

---. "Espectáculos cortesanos y parateatralidad en la ficción sentimental." *Bulletin of Hispanic Studies*, vol. 74, 1997, pp. 61–91.

---. "El humor en Triste deleytaçión: sobre unas originales coplas de disparates." *Revista de Literatura Medieval*, vol. 6, 1994, pp. 45–78.

---. "El más allá de Triste deleytaçión y el mito de Verbino." *Bulletin of Hispanic Studies*, vol. 75, 1998, pp. 137–52.

Blecua, Alberto. "Los problemas textuales del *Libro de buen amor.*" *Estudios de crítica textual*, Gredos, 2012, pp. 67–120. Biblioteca Virtual Miguel de Cervantes. www.cervantesvirtual.com.

Bliss, J., editor. *Sir Orfeo.* Clarendon P, 1966.

Blumenberg, Hans. *Shipwreck with Spectator: Paradigm of a Metaphor for Existence.* MIT P, 1997.

Boccaccio, Giovanni. *Filocolo. Tutte le opera*, edited by E. Quaglio, vol. 1, Mondadori, 1967.

Boethius, Anicius Manlius Severinus. "Boecio de consolación." 1497. Edited by Antonio Doñas, *Memorabilia*, vol. 8, 2004–2005. parnaseo.uv.es/Memorabilia/memorabilia8/boecio/index.htm.

---. *The Consolation of Philosophy.* Edited and translated by Hugh Fraser Stewart, E. K. Rand, and S. J. Tester, Harvard UP, 1973.

---. *Libre de consolacio de philosophia ... transladat en romanç catalanesch. Estampat novament amb la Moral consideració contra les persuassions, vicis e forces de amor de don Francesch Carroç Pardo de la Casta; a cura de don Bartolomeu Muntaner; ... notes bibliogràfiques del Àngel Aguiló.* Biblioteca Virtual Joan Lluís Vives, 2001, www.lluisvives.com.

Bofarull y Mascaró, Próspero. *Documentos literarios en antigua lengua catalana.* Barcelona, Imprenta del Archivo, 1857.

Bolgar, R. R. *The Classical Heritage and its Beneficiaries.* Cambridge UP, 1954.

Boncompagno da Signa. *La rueda del amor. Los males de la vejez y la senectud. La amistad.* Edited by Antonio Cortijo Ocaña and Luisa Blecua, Gredos, 2005.

---. *El Tratado de amor carnal o rueda de Venus: motivos literarios en la tradición sentimental y celestinesca (ss. XIII–XV).* Edited and translated by Antonio Cortijo Ocaña, Ediciones U de Navarra, 2002.

Boro, Joyce. "Multilingualism, Romance, and Language Pedagogy; or, Why Were So Many Sentimental Romances Printed as Polyglot Texts?" *Tudor Translation*, edited by Fred Schurink, Palgrave MacMillan, 2011, pp. 18–38.

Bosch, Lynette M. F. *Art, Liturgy, and Legend in Renaissance Toledo.* The Pennsylvania State UP, 2000.

Brandenberger, Tobias. *La muerte de la ficción sentimental: transformaciones de un género iberorrománico.* Verbum, 2012.

Briesemeister, Dietrich. "The *Consolatio Philosophiae* of Boethius in Medieval Spain." *Journal of the Warburg and Courtauld Institutes*, vol. 53, 1990, pp. 61–70.

Brownlee, Marina Scordilis. "The Counterfeit Muse: Ovid, Boccaccio, Juan de Flores." *Discourse of Authority in Medieval and Renaissance Literature*, edited Kevin Brownlee and Walter Stephens, UP of New England for Darthmouth College, 1989, pp. 109–27.

---. "The Generic Status of the *Siervo libre de amor*: Rodríguez del Padrón's Reworking of Dante." *Poetics Today*, vol. 5, 1984, pp. 629–43.

---. "Genre, History, and the *Novela sentimental.*" *La corónica*, vol. 31, no. 2, 2003, pp. 239–44.

---. *The Severed Word: Ovid's "Heroides" and the "Novela Sentimental."* Princeton UP, 1990.

---. *The Status of the Reading Subject in the 'Libro de buen amor.'* Department of Romance Studies at the University of North Carolina at Chapel Hill, 1985. North Carolina Studies in the Romance Languages and Literatures, 224.

Bruni, Leonardo. "Vidas de Dante e de Petrarca." Ca. 1401–1500. Biblioteca Nacional de España. MSS/10171, ff 25–62.

Bryson, Norman. *Vision and Painting: The Logic of the Gaze.* Macmillan, 1983.

Bultot, Robert. "La *Chartula* et l'enseignement du mépris du monde dans les écoles et les universités médiévales." *Studi Medievali*, vol. 7, 1967, pp. 787–834.

Burke, James F. "The *Libro de buen amor* and the Medieval Meditative Tradition." *La corónica*, vol. 9, 1981, pp. 122–27.

Butiñá, Julia. "De Metge a Petrarca pasando por Boccaccio." *Epos*, vol. 9, 1993, pp. 217–29.

---. "El humanismo catalán en el contexto hispánico." *La corónica*, vol. 37, 2008, pp. 27–71.

Bynum, Caroline Walker. "Wonder." *American Historical Review*, vol. 102, 1997, pp. 1–17.

Cabré, Lluís. "Bernat Metge." *Història de la literatura catalana. Vol. 2: Literatura medieval (II). Segles XIV–XV*, edited by Lola Badia, Barcino, 2014, pp. 192–238.

---. "Comentaris sobre Bernat Metge i la seva primera consolació: el *Llibre de fortuna e prudència.*" *Intel·lectuals i escriptors a la baixa edad mitjana*, edited by Lola Badia, Curial, 1994, pp. 95–108.

---. "Petrarch's *Griseldis* from Philippe de Mezières to Bernat Metge." *Fourteenth-Century Classicism: Petrarch and Bernat Metge*, edited by Lluís Cabré, The Warburg Institute, 2012, pp. 29–42.

Cabré, Miriam. *Cerverí de Girona and His Poetic Traditions*. Tamesis, 1999.

Cabré, Miriam, and Sadurní Martí. "Per a una base de dades dels cançoners catalans medievals. L'exemple de SG." *Actes del 13è col·loqui internacional de l'AILLC (Girona, 2003)*, edited by Sadurní Martí, et al., vol. 3, Publicacions de l'Abadia de Montserrat, 2007, pp. 171–86.

Cacho Blecua, Juan Manuel. "Los grabados de la *Cárcel de Amor* (Zaragoza, 1493, Barcelona, 1493, y Burgos, 1496): La muerte de Leriano." *Actas del XI Congreso Internacional de la Asociación Hispánica de Literatura Medieval*, edited by Amando López Castro and María Luzdivina Cuesta Torre, vol. 1, U de León, 2007, pp. 367–79.

Camargo, Martin. *Ars dictaminis, Ars dictandi*. Brepols, 1991.

---. "Toward a Comprehensive Art of Written Discourse: Geoffrey of Vinsauf and the *Ars Dictaminis.*" *Rhetoric: A Journal of History of Rhetoric*, vol. 2, 1988, pp. 167–94.

---. "Were Medieval Letter Writers Trained in Performance?" *Rhetoric Beyond Words: Delight and Persuasion in the Arts of the Middle Ages*, edited by Mary Carruthers, Cambridge UP, 2010, pp. 173–89.

Camille, Michael. "Before the Gaze: The Internal Senses and Late Medieval Practices of Seeing." *Visuality Before and Beyond the Renaissance: Seeing as Others Saw*, edited by Robert S. Nelson, Cambridge UP, 2000, pp. 197–223.

---. "Dr. Witkowski's Anus: French Doctors, German Homosexuals and the Obscene in Medieval Church Art." *Medieval Obscenities*, edited by Nicola McDonald, York Medieval Press, 2006, pp. 17–38.

---. *Gothic Art: Glorious Visions*. Harry N. Abrams, 1996.

---. "The Image and the Self: Unwriting Late Medieval Bodies." *Framing Medieval Bodies*, edited by Sara Kay and Miri Rubin, Manchester UP, 1994.

---. *Image on the Edge: The Margins of Medieval Art*. Reaktion Books, 1992.

---. *The Medieval Art of Love*. Lawrence King Publishing, 1998.

---. "Mimetic Identification and Passion Devotion in the Later Middle Ages: A Double-Sided Panel by Meister Francke." *The Broken Body: Passion Devotion in Late Medieval Culture*, edited by Alasdair A. MacDonald, et al., Egbert Forsten, 1998.

---. "Seeing and Reading: Some Visual Implications of Medieval Literacy and Illiteracy." *Art History*, vol. 8, 1985, pp. 26–49.

Campo Tejedor, Alberto del. "Diversiones clericales burlescas en los siglos XIII a XVI: las misas nuevas." *La corónica*, vol. 38, 2009, pp. 55–95.

Cancel, Christine. *Résurgences de la Consolation de la Philosophie de Boèce au quatorzième siècle*. 2009. U de Versailles-Saint-Quentin-en-Yvelines, PhD dissertation.

Cantavella, Rosanna. *Els cards i ell llir: una lectura de l'"espill" de Jaume Roig*. Quaderns Crema, 1992.

Carlos, Helena de. "Poetry and Parody: Boethius and Gestures in the Letters of Godfrey of Rheims." *Essays in Medieval Studies*, vol. 18, 2001, pp. 18–30.

Carr, Derek C. "A Fifteenth-Century Castilian Translation and Commentary of a Petrarchan Sonnet: Biblioteca Nacional Ms. 10186 ff 196r–199r." *Revista Canadiense de Estudios Hispánicos*, vol. 5, 1981, pp. 123–43.

Carrós Pardo de la Casta, Francesc. *Las obras de Francesch Carroç Pardo de la Casta*. Edited by José Enrique Reyes-Tudela, Albatros Hispanófila, 1987.

Carruthers, Mary. *The Book of Memory: A Study of Memory in Medieval Culture*. Cambridge UP, 1990.

---. *The Craft of Thought. Meditation, Rhetoric, and the Making of Images, 400–1200*. Cambridge UP, 1998.

Carruthers, Mary, and Jan M. Ziolkowski. *The Medieval Craft of Memory: An Anthology of Texts and Pictures*. U of Pennsylvania P, 2002.

Cartagena, Alonso de. *La rethórica de M. Tullio Cicerón*. Edited by Rosalba Mascagna, Liguori, 1969.

Casas Rigall, Juan. *Agudeza y retórica en la poesía amorosa de cancionero*. U de Santiago de Compostela, 1995.

---. "'Género literario,' 'novela' y narrativa sentimental." *La corónica*, vol. 31, 2003, pp. 245–49.

Castro, Américo. *España en su historia. Cristianos, moros y judíos*. Editorial Losada, 1948.

Castro Lingl, Vera. "Back to the Text: Another Look at Juan Rodríguez del Padrón's *Siervo libre de amor*." *Romanische Forschungen*, vol. 106, 1994, pp. 48–60.

---. "The Constable of Portugal's *Sátira de infelice e felice vida*: A Reworking of Juan Rodríguez del Padrón's *Siervo libre de amor*." *Revista de Estudios Hispánicos*, vol. 32, 1998, pp. 75–100.

Cátedra, Pedro M. "Algunas obras perdidas de Enrique de Villena con consideraciones sobre su obra y su biblioteca." *El Crotalón. Anuario de Filología Española*, vol. 2, 1985, pp. 53–75.

---. *Amor y pedagogía en la Edad Media. (Estudios de doctrina amorosa y práctica literaria)*. U de Salamanca, 1989.

---. "Un aspecto de la difusión del escrito en la Edad Media: la autotraducción al romance." *Atalaya*, vol. 2, 1992, pp. 67–84.

---. "Creación y lectura: sobre el género consolatorio en el siglo XV: la *Epístola de consolaçión embiada al reverendo señor Prothonotario de Çigüença, con su respuesta* (c.1469)." *Studies on Medieval Spanish Literature in Honor of Charles F. Fraker*, edited by Mercedes Vaquero and Alan D. Deyermond, Hispanic Seminary of Medieval Studies, 1995, pp. 35–61.

---. *Del Tostado sobre el amor*. Estelle dell'Orsa, 1986.

---. "La literatura funcionarial en tiempos de los Reyes Católicos." *Siempre soy quien ser solía: estudios de literatura española medieval en homenaje a Carmen Parrilla*, edited by Antonio Chas Aguión and Cleofé Tato, U da Coruña, 2009, pp. 57–82.

---. *Poesía de Pasión en la Edad Media. El "cancionero" de Pero Gómez de Ferrol*. SEMYR (Seminario de Estudios Medievales y Renacentistas), 2001.

---. "Presentación." *Modelos intelectuales, nuevos textos y nuevos lectores en el siglo XV: contextos literarios, cortesanos y administrativos*, edited by Pedro M. Cátedra, SEMYR, 2012, pp. 11–25.

---. "Prospección sobre el género consolatorio en el siglo XV." *Letters and Society in Fifteenth-Century Spain. Studies Presented to P. E. Russell on his Eightieth Birthday*, edited by Alan D. Deyermond and J. N. H Lawrance, The Dolphin Book Co., 1993, pp. 1–16.

---. "Sobre la biblioteca del Marqués de Santillana: *La Ilíada* y Pier Candido Decembrio." *Hispanic Review*, vol. 51, 1983, pp. 23–28.

---. "Sobre la obra catalana de Enrique de Villena." *Homenaje a Eugenio Asensio*, Gredos, 1988, pp. 127–40.

Cátedra, Pedro M., et al. *Tratados de amor en el entorno de Celestina (Siglos XV–XVI)*. Sociedad Estatal España Nuevo Milenio, 2001.

Cátedra, Pedro M., and Derek C. Carr. "Datos para la biografía de Enrique de Villena." *La corónica*, vol. 11, no. 2, 1983, pp. 293–99.

---. *Epistolario de Enrique de Villena*. Department of Hispanic Studies, Queen Mary and Westfield College, 2001.

Chartier, Roger. *Forms and Meanings: Texts, Performances, and Audiences from Codex to Computer*. U of Pennsylvania P, 1995.

Chartier, Roger, and J. A González. "Laborers and Voyagers: From the Text to the Reader." *Diacritics*, vol. 22, 1992, pp. 49–61.

Chas Aguión, Antonio. *Amor y corte: la materia sentimental en las cuestiones poéticas del siglo XV*. Toxosoutos, 2000.

---. *Categorías poéticas minoritarias en el cancionero castellano del siglo XV*. Edizioni dell'Orso, 2012.

Cherchi, Paolo. "Los *Doce trabajos de Hércules* y la *Istoria fiorita* de Guido da Pisa." *Los doce trabajos de Hércules*, edited by Pedro M. Cátedra, vol. 2, U de Cantabria, 2007, p. 115–31.

Chiner Gimeno, Jaume J. "Joan Roís de Corella, la seua vida i el seu entorn: noves dades per a la història de la cultura en la València del segle XV." *Magníficat. Literatura i Cultura Medieval*, vol. 1, 2014, pp. 111–377.

Chorpenning, Joseph F. "Leriano's Consumption of Laureola's Letters in the *Cárcel de Amor*." *Modern Languages Notes*, vol. 95, 1980, pp. 442–45.

---. "The Monastery, Paradise, and the Castle: Literary Images and Spiritual Development in St Teresa of Ávila." *Bulletin of Hispanic Studies*, vol. 62, 1985, pp. 245–57.

Cicero. *On Invention. The Best Kind of Orator. Topics*. Translated by Harry Mortimer Hubbell, Harvard UP, 1949.

Cifuentes, Lluís. "La promoció intellectual i social dels barbers-cirurgians a la Barcelona medieval: l'obrador, la biblioteca i els béns de Joan Vicenç (*fl.* 1421–1464)." *Arxiu de Textos Catalans Antics*, vol. 19, 2000, pp. 429–79.

---. "Traduccions i traductors." *Història de la literatura catalana. Vol. 2: Literatura medieval (II). Segles XIV–XV*. Edited by Lola Badia, Barcino, 2014, pp. 117–83.

---. "L'Université de Médecine de Montpellier et son Rayonnement (XIIIe–XVe siècles)." *Actes du Colloque International de Montpellier, organizé par le Centre Historioque de Recherches et d'Études Médiévales sur la Mediterranée Occidentale*, edited by Daniel Le Blévec, Brepols, 2004.

---. "Vernacularization as an Intellectual and Social Bridge: The Catalan Translations of Teodorico's *Chirurgia* and of Arnau de Vilanova's *Regimen sanitatis*." *Early Science and Medicine*, vol. 4, 1999, pp. 127–48.

Cingolani, Stefano Maria. "Bernat Metge e gli *auctores*: da Cicerone a Petrarca, passando per Virgilio, Boezio e Boccaccio." *Fourteenth-Century Classicism: Petrarch and Bernat Metge*, edited by Lluís Cabré, Warburg Institute, 2012, pp. 109–24.

---. *Joan Roís de Corella: La impòrtancia de dir-se honest*. Ediciones 3 i 4, 1998.

Cocozzella, Peter. "Ausiàs March Text of Subjectivity and Francesc Moner's *Auto de Amores* of the Early Spanish Renaissance." *Renaissance du Théâtre Médiéval: XII Colloque de La Société Internationale du Théâtre Médiéval, Lille 2–7 Juillet 2007*, edited by Véronique Dominguez, PU de Louvain, 2009, pp. 19–41.

---. "Fra Francesc Moner y el auto de amores en el dominio del catalán y del castellano a finales del siglo XV." *Estudios sobre el teatro medieval*, edited by Josep Lluís Sirera, Universitat de València, 2008, pp. 57–80.

---. *Fra Francesc Moner's Bilingual Poetics of Love and Reason: The "Wisdom Text" by a Catalan Writer of the Early Renaissance*. Peter Lang, 2010.

---. "Fra Francesc Moner's Psychic Space / Soulful Place." *Caplletra*, vol. 53, 2012, pp. 9–34.

---. "Pere Torroella i Francesc Moner: aspectes del bilingüisme catalan literari (català-castellano) a la segona meitad del segle XV." *Llengua i Literatura*, vol. 2, 1987, pp. 155–72.

---. *Text, Translation, and Critical Interpretation of Joan Roís de Corella's Tragèdia de Caldesa, a Fifteenth-Century Spanish Tragedy of Gender Reversal.* Edwin Mellen P, 2012.

---. "The Thematic Unity of Juan Rodríguez del Padrón's *Siervo libre de amor.*" *Hispania*, vol. 64, 1981, pp. 188–98.

---. *The Two Major Prose Works of Francisco Moner: A Critical Edition and Translation.* 1966. St. Louis U, PhD dissertation.

Colomer Amat, Emilia. "Libros de horas impresos en España en el primer tercio del siglo XVI." *Locus Amoenus*, vol. 4, 1998–1999, pp. 127–35.

Concina, Chiara. "Il trattamento dei miti nelle traduzioni catalane (Saplana e Ginebreda) della *Consolatio Philosophiae* di Boezio." *eHumanista/IVITRA*, vol. 7, 2015, pp. 42–65.

Conde, Juan-Carlos. "De las fuentes y los modelos del *Siervo libre de amor*: algunas conexiones con la literatura medieval francesa de índole penitencial y confesional." *Atalaya*, vol. 11, 2009. atalaya.revues.org/399.

---. "Ensayo bibliográfico sobre la traducción en la Castilla del siglo XV: 1980–2005." *Lemir*, vol. 10, 2006. parnaseo.uv.es/lemir/Revista/Revista10/Conde/Traduccion_siglo_xv.htm.

---, editor. "Ottavio di Camillo's *El humanismo castellano del siglo XV*, Thirty-Five Years Later." *La corónica*, vol. 39, No. 1, 2010.

Copeland, Rita. *Rhetoric, Hermeneutics, and Translation in the Middle Ages: Academic Traditions and Vernacular Texts.* Cambridge UP, 1991.

Corfis, Ivy A. "Sentimental Lore and Irony in the Fifteenth-Century Romances and *Celestina.*" *Studies on the Spanish Sentimental Romance (1440–1550): Redefining a Genre*, edited by Joseph J. Gwara and E. Michael Gerli, Tamesis, 1997, pp. 153–71.

Cornelius, Roberta D. *The Figurative Castle: A Study in the Mediaeval Allegory of the Edifice with Especial Reference to Religious Writings.* 1930. Bryn Mawr, PhD dissertation.

Cortijo Ocaña, Antonio. "'De amicitia, amore et rationis discretione.' Breves notas a propósito de Boncompagno da Signa y el 'Siervo libre de amor.'" *Revista de Poética Medieval*, vol. 16, 2006, pp. 23–52.

---. *La evolución genérica de la ficción sentimental de los siglos XV y XVI: género literario y contexto social.* Tamesis, 2001.

---. "La ficción sentimental ¿un género imposible?" *La corónica*, vol. 29, 2000, pp. 5–13.

---. "Hacia la ficción sentimental: La *Rota Veneris* de Boncompagno da Signa." *La corónica*, vol. 29, 2000, pp. 53–74.

---. "El libro VI de la *Confessio Amantis.*" *eHumanista*, vol. 7, 2007, pp. 38–72.

---. "Religious Parody or Courtly Mockery?" *Multilingual Joan Roís de Corella: The Relevance of a Fifteenth-Century Classic of the Crown of Aragon*, edited by Antonio Cortijo Ocaña and Vicent Martines, Publications of eHumanista, 2013, pp. 11–25.

---, editor and translator. *La rueda del amor.* www.scrineum.it/scrineum/wight/rvcortijo.htm

---. "El *Siervo libre de amor* y Petrarca: a propósito del motivo de la nave." *Revista de Poética Medieval*, vol. 18, 2007, pp. 133–54.

---. "Notas sobre el Tostado *de amore.*" *La corónica*, vol. 33, 2004, pp. 67–83.

Cortijo Ocaña, Antonio, and Teresa Jiménez Calvente. "Humanismo español latino: breve nota introductoria. Critical Cluster 'Salió buen latino:' Los ideales de la cultura española tardomedieval y protorrenacentista." *La corónica*, vol. 37, 2008, pp. 5–25.

Costley, Clare L. "David, Bathsheba, and the Penitential Psalms." *Renaissance Quarterly*, vol. 57, 2004, pp. 1235–77.

Coulson, Frank T. *The 'Vulgate' Commentary on Ovid's Metamorphoses: The Creation Myth and the Story of Orpheus.* Centre for Medieval Studies, 1991.

Courcelle, Pierre. La *Consolation de Philosophie dans la tradition littéraire: Antécédents et postérité de Boèce.* Études Augustiniennes, 1967.

Covarrubias, Pedro. *Memorial de pecados y aviso de la vida cristiana*. Sevilla: Jacobo Cromberger, 1516. Banco de datos (CORDE). *Corpus diacrónico del español*, Real Academia Española. corpus.rae.es/cordenet.html.

Covarrubias, Sebastián de. *Tesoro de la lengua castellana*. Madrid: Luis Sánchez, 1611. ntlle.rae.es.

Cristóbal, Vicente. "Ovid in Medieval Spain." *Ovid in the Middle Ages*, edited by James G. Clark, et al., Cambridge UP, 2011, pp. 231–56.

Crosbie, John. "Medieval 'Contrafacta': A Spanish Anomaly Reconsidered." *The Modern Language Review*, vol. 78, 1983, pp. 61–67.

Crossley, Paul. "The Man from Inner Space: Architecture and Meditation in the Choir of St Laurence in Nuremberg." *Medieval Art, Recent Perspectives: A Memorial Tribute to C.R. Dodwell*, edited by Gale R. Graham and Timothy Owen-Crocker, St. Martin's P, 1988, pp. 165–82.

Curtis, Florence. "Punning on the Mind as *çela* in the *Libro de buen amor*." *La corónica*, vol. 44, 2016, pp. 29–47.

Curtius, Ernst Robert. *Literatura europea y edad media latina*. 2 vols. Fondo de Cultura Económica, 1984.

Dagenais, John. *The Ethics of Reading in Manuscript Culture: Glossing the* Libro de buen amor. Princeton UP, 1994.

---. "A Further Source for the Literary Ideas in Juan Ruiz's Prologue." *Journal of Hispanic Philology*, vol. 11, 1986, pp. 23–52.

---. "Juan Rodríguez del Padrón's Translation of the Latin *Bursarii*: New Light on the Meaning of 'Tra(c)tado.'" *Journal of Hispanic Philology*, vol. 10, 1986, pp. 117–39.

Damiani, Bruno. "The Didactic Intention of the "Cárcel de Amor.'" *Hispanófila*, vol. 56, 1976, pp. 29–43.

Dante Alighieri. *La vida nueva*. Edited by Carlos Alvar, translated by Julio Martínez Mesanza, Siruela, 1985.

Darbord, Michel. *La poésie religieuse espagnole des Rois Catholiques à Philippe II*. Centre de Recherches de l'Institut d'Études Hispaniques, 1965.

Davidoff, Judith M. *Beginning Well: Framing Fictions in Late Middle English Poetry*. Fairleigh Dickinson UP, 1988.

De Looze, Laurence. *Pseudo-Autobiography in the Fourteenth Century: Juan Ruiz, Guillaume de Machaut, Jean Froissart, and Geoffrey Chaucer*. UP of Florida, 1997.

---. "Text, Author, Reader, Reception: The Reflections of Theory and the *Libro de Buen Amor*." *A Companion to the* Libro de buen amor, edited by Louise M. Haywood and Louise O. Vasvári, Tamesis, 2004, pp. 131–50.

Delgado Criado, Buenaventura, editor. *Historia de la Educación en España y América. Vol. 1: La educación en la Hispania antigua y medieval*. Fundación Santa María, 1994.

Deyermond, Alan D. "Estudio de la ficción sentimental: balance de los últimos años y vislumbre de los que vienen." *Ínsula*, vol. 651, 2001, pp. 3–9.

---. "The Female Narrator in Sentimental Fiction: 'Menina e Moça' and 'Clareo y Florisea.'" *Portuguese Studies*, vol. 1, 1985, pp. 47–57.

---. "La ficción sentimental: origen, desarrollo y pervivencia." *Cárcel de Amor con la continuación de Nicolás Núñez*, edited by Carmen Parrilla, Crítica, 1995, pp. ix–xxxiii.

---. "El hombre salvaje en la novela sentimental." *Filología*, vol. 10, 1964, pp. 97–111.

---. "The Lost Genre of Medieval Spanish Literature." *Hispanic Review*, vol. 43, 1975, pp. 231–59.

---. "On the Frontier of the Sentimental Romance: The Dream-Allegories of James I and Santillana." *La corónica*, vol. 29, 2000, pp. 89–112.

---. "El punto de vista narrativo en la ficción sentimental del siglo XV." *Tradiciones y puntos de vista en la ficción sentimental*, U Nacional Autónoma de México, 1993, pp. 65–88.

---. "Las relaciones genéricas de la ficción sentimental española." *Symposium in Honorem prof. M. de Riquer*, edited by Carlos Alvar, U de Barcelona and Quaderns Crema, 1986, pp. 75–92.

---. "Santillana's Love-Allegories: Structure, Relation and Message." *Studies in Honor of Bruce W. Wardropper*, edited by Dian Fox, et al., Juan de la Cuesta, 1989, pp. 75–90.

---. "Sentimental Romance, the Problem of Genre, and the Regula Rohland de Langbehn's 'Lanza.'" *La corónica*, vol. 31, 2003, pp. 266–73.

---. "Some Aspects of Parody in the *Libro de buen amor*." *'Libro de buen amor' Studies*, edited by G. B. Gybbon-Monypenny, Tamesis Books, 1979, pp. 53–78.

---. *Tradiciones y puntos de vista en la ficción sentimental*. U Nacional Autónoma de México, 1993.

---. "Was It a Vision or a Waking Dream?: The Anomalous Don Amor and Doña Endrina Episodes Reconsidered." *A Companion to the* Libro de buen amor, edited by Louise M. Haywood and Louise O. Vasvári, Tamesis, 2004, pp. 107–22.

---. "The Woodcuts of Diego de San Pedro's *Cárcel de Amor*, 1492–1496." *Bulletin Hispanique*, vol. 104, 2002, pp. 511–28.

Deyermond, Alan D., et al., editors. *Juan Rodríguez del Padrón: Studies in Honour of Olga Tudorica Impey*. Department of Hispanic Studies, Queen Mary, U of London, 2005.

Di Camillo, Ottavio. "Humanism in Spain." *Renaissance Humanism*, edited by Albert Rabil, Jr., vol. 2: *Foundations, Forms, and Legacy*, U of Philadelphia P, 1988, pp. 55–108.

---. *El humanismo castellano del siglo XV*. Fernando Torres, 1976.

---. "*Libro de buen amor* 70a: What Are the *Libro*'s Instruments?" *Viator*, vol. 21, 1990, pp. 239–71.

Dolz, Enric. "*Siervo libre de amor*: entre la alegoría y la anagogía." *"Quien hubiese tal ventura:" Medieval Hispanic Studies in Honour of Alan Deyermond*, edited by Andrew Beresford and Alan D. Deyermond, Department of Hispanic Studies, Queen Mary and Westfield College, 1997, pp. 247–57. "El simbolismo de los colores y la estructura del *Siervo libre de amor*." *La corónica*, vol. 35, 2006, pp. 109–36.

---. "El vocabulario del alma en el *Siervo libre de amor*." *Revista de Poética Medieval*, vol. 16, 2006, pp. 79–122.

Domínguez, Frank A. "The Burlesque, the Parodic and the Satiric: A Brief Preface." *La corónica*, vol. 38, 2009, pp. 43–53.

---. *Carajicomedia: Parody and Satire in Early Modern Spain*. Tamesis, 2015.

---. *Love and Remembrance: The Poetry of Jorge Manrique*. UP of Kentucky, 1988.

---. "Monkey Business in *Carajicomedia*: The Parody of Fray Ambrosio Montesino as 'Fray Bugeo.'" *eHumanista*, vol. 7, 2006, pp. 1–27.

Domínguez Rodríguez, Ana. "Libros de horas de la Corona de Castilla. Hacia un estado de la cuestión." *Anales de la Historia del Arte*, vol. 10, 2000, pp. 9–54.

Domínguez Rodríguez, Ana, et al. "El Libro de Horas de Isabel la Católica de la Biblioteca de Palacio." *Reales Sitios*, vol. 110, 1991, pp. 21–31.

Doñas, Antonio. "La *Consolación de la filosofía* de Boecio en traducción anónima (1497)." Biblioteca Virtual Miguel de Cervantes, 2012. www.cervantesvirtual.com

---. "Introducción." *Boecio de consolación (Sevilla: Meinardo Ungut y Estanislao Polono, 1497)*." *Memorabilia*, vol. 8, 2004–2005, parnaseo.uv.es/Memorabilia/memorabilia8/boecio/index.htm.

---. "Versiones hispánicas de la *Consolatio Philosophiae* de Boecio: testimonios." *Revista de Literatura Medieval*, vol. 19, 2007, pp. 295–312.

Dumas, Geneviève. *Santé et société à Montpellier à la fin du Moyen Âge*. Brill, 2015.

Dwyer, Richard A. *Boethian Fictions: Narratives in the Medieval French Versions of the Consolation Philosophiae*. The Medieval Academy of America, 1976.

Early, Nicholas. "The Poet at the Mirror: René d'Anjou and Authorial Doubling in the *Livre au Coeur d'Amour épris*." *Fifteenth-Century Studies*, vol. 37, 2012, pp. 17–45.

Egido, Aurora. "De ludo vitando. Gallos aúlicos en la universidad de Salamanca." *El Crotalón. Anuario de Filología Española*, vol. 1, 1984, pp. 609–48.

Elliott, Elizabeth. *Remembering Boethius: Writing Aristocratic Identity in Late Medieval French and English Literatures*. Ashgate, 2012.

Enterline, Lynn. "Embodied Voices: Petrarchan Reading (Himself Reading) Ovid." *Desire in the Renaissance: Psychoanalysis and Literature*, edited by Valeria Finucci and Regina M. Schwartz, Princeton UP, 1994, pp. 120–45.

Fàbrega i Escatllar, Valentí. "La *Consolació de la Filosofia* en la versió catalana de Pere Saplana i Antoni Genebreda (1358/1352)." *Zeitschrift Für Katalanistik*, vol. 3, 1990, pp. 33–49.

Faulhaber, Charles B. "Las bibliotecas españolas medievales." *Pensamiento medieval hispano: homenaje a Horacio Santiago-Otero*, edited by José María Soto Rábanos, vol. 1, Consejo Superior de Investigaciones Científicas, 1998, pp. 785–800.

---. *Latin Rhetorical Theory in Thirteenth and Fourteenth Century Castile*. U of California P, 1972.

---. *Libros y bibliotecas en la España medieval: una bibliografía de fuentes impresas*. Grant & Cutler, 1987.

---. "Rhetoric in Medieval Catalonia: The Evidence of Library Catalogs." *Studies in Honor of Gustavo Correa*, edited by Charles B. Faulhaber, et al., Scripta Humanistica, 1986, pp. 92–126.

Fernández de Madrigal, Alonso. *Del Tostado sobre el amor*. Edited by Pedro M. Cátedra, Stelle dell'Orsa, 1985.

---. "Libro de amor y amicicia (Bib. Univ. Salamanca 2178)." *Textos Medievales misceláneos [Archivo de Ordenador]: (Textos y Concordancias)*, edited by María Nieves Sánchez, et al., Hispanic Seminary of Medieval Studies, 2003.

Fernández Jiménez, Juan. "La estructura de *Siervo libre de amor* y la crítica reciente." *Cuadernos Hispanoamericanos*, vol. 388, 1982, pp. 178–90.

---. "*Siervo libre de amor*: ¿novela incompleta?" *Hispanófila*, vol. 75, 1982, pp. 1–7.

Ferreiro Alemparte, Jaime. *La leyenda de las once mil vírgenes: sus reliquias, culto e iconografía*. U de Murcia, 1991.

Finucci, Valeria. "Jokes on Women: Triangular Pleasures in Castiglione and Freud." *Exemplaria*, vol. 4, 1992, pp. 51–77.

Fleming, John V. *Reason and the Lover*. Princeton UP, 1984.

Flores, Juan de. *Grimalte y Gradisa*. Edited by Carmen Parrilla, Centro de Estudios Cervantinos, 2008.

---. "Grisel y Mirabella." *Three Spanish Querelle Texts: Grisel and Mirabella, The Slander against Women, and The Defense of Ladies against Slanderers*, edited and translated by Emily C. Francomano, Centre for Reformation and Renaissance Studies, 2013.

Folger, Robert. "Alfonso de Paradinas, ¿carcelero del Arcipreste de Hita? El *Libro de buen amor*, MS. S, como narrativa (anti) boeciana." *Revista de Estudios Hispánicos*, vol. 30, 2003, pp. 61–73.

---. "*Cárceles de amor*: 'Gender Trouble' and Male Fantasies in 15th-Century Castile." *Bulletin of Spanish Studies*, vol. 83, 2006, pp. 617–35.

---. *Escape from the Prison of Love: Caloric Identities and Writing Subjects in Fifteenth-Century Spain*. Department of Romance Studies at the University of North Carolina at Chapel Hill, 2009. North Carolina Studies in the Romance Languages and Literatures, 292.

---. *Images in Mind. Lovesickness, Spanish Sentimental Fiction and Don Quijote*. Department of Romance Studies at the University of North Carolina at Chapel Hill, 2002. North Carolina Studies in the Romance Languages and Literatures, 274.

---. "Memoria en *Siervo libre de amor*: El papel de la psicología medieval en la ficción sentimental." *La corónica*, vol. 26, 1998, pp. 197–210.

Fonseca, Luís Adão da, editor. *Obras completas do Condestável Dom Pedro de Portugal*. Fundação Calouste Gulbenkian, 1975.

Foster, David William. "The Misunderstanding of Dante in Fifteenth-Century Spanish Poetry." *Comparative Literature*, vol. 16, 1964, pp. 338–47.

Framiñán, María Jesús. "El *Memorial de pecados* de Pedro de Covarrubias (151): texto y ámbito literario." *Actas del IV Congreso de la Asociación Internacional Siglo de Oro*, edited by María Cruz García de Enterría and Alicia Cordón Mesa, vol. 1, U de Alcalá, 1996, pp. 599–609.

Franco, Gustavo Cambraia, and Ricardo da Costa. "A *sapientia christiana* e a analogia das artes liberais em um Sermão de São Vicente Ferrer (1350–1419)." *Mirabilia/ MedTrans*, vol. 4, 2016, pp. 1–26.

Francomano, Emily C. "Manuscript Matrix and the Meaning of *Siervo libre de amor*." Open Session of the Division on Spanish Medieval Language and Literature, MLA Conference, 28 December, 2006, Loews Hotel, Philadelphia, PA. Conference Presentation.

---. *The Prison of Love: Romance, Translation, and the Book in the Sixteenth-Century*. U of Toronto P, 2018.

---. "'Puse un sobreescripto' I Wrote a New Cover: Print, Manuscript, and the Material Epistolarity of 'Cárcel de Amor.'" *Fifteenth-Century Studies*, vol. 36, 2011, pp. 24–48.

---. "Reversing the Tapestry: *Prison of Love* in Text, Image, and Textile." *Renaissance Quarterly*, vol. 64, 2011, pp. 1059–105.

---, editor and translator. *Three Spanish Querelle Texts: Grisel and Mirabella, The Slander against Women, and The Defense of Ladies against Slanderers*. Centre for Reformation and Renaissance Studies, 2013.

---. *Wisdom and Her Lovers in Medieval and Early Modern Hispanic Literature*. Palgrave, 2008.

Fraxanet Salas, María Rosa. "Estudio sobre los grabados de la novela *La Cárcel de Amor* de Diego de San Pedro." *Estudios de iconografía medieval española*, edited by Joaquín Yarza Luaces, U Autónoma de Barcelona, 1984, pp. 429–82.

Freccero, John. "Infernal Inversion and Christian Convention (*Inferno XXXIV*)." *Dante: The Poetics of Conversion*, edited by Rachel Jacoff, Cambridge UP, 1986, pp. 180–94.

Friedlein, Roger. "A Tale of Disconsolation: A Structural and Processual Reading of Bernat Metge's *Lo somni*." *Fourteenth-Century Classicism: Petrarch and Bernat Metge*, edited by Lluís Cabré, Warburg Institute, 2012, pp. 141–58.

Friedman, John Block. *Orpheus in the Middle Ages*. 1970. Harvard UP, 2000.

Fulgentius. *The Mythographer*. Translated by Leslie George Whitbread, The Ohio State UP, 1971.

Fuog, Karin E. C. "Placing Earth at the Center of the Cosmos: *The Kingis Quair* as Boethian Revision." *Studies in Scottish Literature*, vol. 32, 2001, pp. 140–49.

Garin, Eugenio. *L'Educazione in Europa*. Laterza, 1957.

Gascón Vera, Elena. *Don Pedro, Condestable de Portugal*. Fundación Universitaria Española, 1979.

Gavrilyuk, Paul L., and Sarah Coakley. *The Spiritual Senses: Perceiving God in Western Christianity*. Cambridge UP, 2012.

Gerli, E. Michael. "Fernán Pérez de Guzmán, *Cancionero de Baena* 119, and the *Libro de buen amor*." *Modern Language Notes*, vol. 105, 1990, pp. 367–72.

---. "Leriano and Lacan: The Mythological and Psychoanalitical Underpinnings of Leriano's Last Drink." *La corónica*, vol. 29, 2000, pp. 113–28.

---. "Metafiction in Spanish Sentimental Romance." *Age of the Catholic Monarchs, 1474–1516: Literary Studies in Memory of Keith Whinnom*, edited by Alan D. Deyermond and Ian Macpherson, Liverpool UP, 1989, pp. 57–63.

---. "The Old French Source of *Siervo libre de amor*." *Studies on the Spanish Sentimental Romance (1440–1550): Redefining a Genre*, edited by Joseph J. Gwara and E. Michael Gerli, Tamesis, 1997, pp. 3–19.

---. "On the Edge: Envisioning the *Libro de buen amor* in the *Cancionero de Palacio*." *eHumanista*, vol. 1, 2001, pp. 1–11.

---. "'Recta voluntas est bonus amor': St Augustine and the Didactic Structure of the *Libro de buen amor.*" *Romance Philology*, vol. 35, 1981–1982, pp. 500–08.

---. "*Siervo libre de amor* and the Penitential Tradition." *Journal of Hispanic Philology*, vol. 12, 1988, pp. 93–102.

---. "Toward a Poetics of the Spanish Sentimental Romance." *Hispania*, vol. 72, 1989, pp. 474–82.

---, editor. *Triste deleytacion: An Anonymous Fifteenth Century Castilian Romance.* Georgetown UP, 1982.

Gernert, Folke. *Parodia y 'contrafacta' en la literatura románica medieval y renacentista: historia, teoría y textos.* CiLengua, 2009.

Giles, Ryan D. "A Galen for Lovers: Medical Readings of Ovid in Medieval and Early Renaissance Spain." *Ovid in the Age of Cervantes*, edited by Frederick A. de Armas, U of Toronto P, 2010, pp. 3–19.

Gilkinson, Jean. "Language and Gender in Diego de San Pedro's *Cárcel de Amor.*" *Journal of Hispanic Research*, vol. 3, 1994–1995, pp. 113–24.

Gleason, Mark J. "Clearing the Fields: Towards a Reassessment of Chaucer's Use of Trevet in the *Boece.*" *The Medieval Boethius: Studies in the Vernacular Translations of De Consolatione Philosophiae*, edited by Alastair J. Minnis, D. S. Brewer, 1987, pp. 89–105.

Gómez, Jesús. "Las 'artes de amores', *Celestina* y el género literario de 'Penitencia de amor' de Urrea." *Celestinesca*, vol. 14, 1990, pp. 3–16.

Gómez-Bravo, Ana M. "'A huma senhora que lhe disse': Sobre la práctica social de la autoría y la noción de texto en el *Cancioneiro geral* de Resende y la lírica cancioneril ibérica." *La corónica*, vol. 32, no. 1, 2003, pp. 43–64.

---. "Cantar decires y decir canciones: género y lectura de la poesía cuatrocentista castellana." *Bulletin of Hispanic Studies*, vol. 76, 1999, pp. 169–87.

---. "Slander and the Right to Be an Author in Fifteenth-Century Spain." *Journal of Spanish Cultural Studies*, vol. 16, 2015, pp. 239–53.

---. *Textual Agencies: Writing Culture and Social Networks in Fifteenth-Century Spain.* Toronto UP, 2013.

Gómez Moreno, Ángel. *España y la Italia de los humanistas: primeros ecos.* Gredos, 1994.

---. *El Prohemio e carta del Marqués de Santillana y la teoría literaria del s. XV.* PPU, 1990.

---. "Revaluación de Juan de Valdés Leal: claves de *In ictu oculi.*" *Medievalia*, vol. 28, 2015, pp. 369–97.

Gómez Redondo, Fernando. "De Boccaccio a Caviceo: la conexión italiana de la ficción sentimental." *Cuadernos de Filología Italiana*, Volumen Extraordinario, 2010, pp. 109–28.

González-Haba, María. *La obra De consolatione Rationis de Petrus Compostellanus.* Bayerische Akademie del Wissenschaften, 1975.

González Rolán, Tomás, and Pilar Saquero Suárez-Somonte. "Boecio en el medievo hispánico. Las versiones catalana y castellana de la *Consolación* a la luz de sus fuentes latinas: los comentarios de Guillermo de Aragón y Nicolás de Trevet." *Humanitas in Honorem Antonio García Fontán*, Gredos, 1992, pp. 319–37.

---. "Las cartas originales de Juan Rodríguez del Padrón: edición, notas literarias y filológicas." *Dicenda: Cuadernos de Filología Española*, vol. 3, 1984, pp. 39–72.

---. *La tradición clásica en España (siglos XIII–XV). Bases conceptuales y bibliográficas.* Clásicas, 2002.

Green, Otis H. "*Fingen los poetas*: Notes on the Spanish Attitute toward Pagan Mythology." *The Literary Mind of Medieval and Renaissance Spain.* The UP of Kentucky, 1970, pp. 113–23.

Greenia, George D. "The Bigger the Book: On Oversize Medieval Manuscripts." *Révue Belge de Philologie et d'Histoire*, vol. 83, 2005, pp. 723–45.

Grendler, Paul F. *Schooling in Renaissance Italy: Literacy and Learning 1300–1600.* The Johns Hopkins UP, 1989.

Grieve, Patricia. *Desire and Death in the Spanish Sentimental Romance (1440–1550)*. Juan de la Cuesta, 1987.

Guinot, Salvador. *Parlament de casa Mercader i Tragedia de Caldesa: Nocela de J. Roiç de Corella, siglo XV*. Armengot, 1921.

Guynn, Noah D. "Authorship and Sexual/Allegorical Violence in Jean de Meun's *Roman de la Rose*." *Speculum*, vol. 79, 2004, pp. 628–59.

Gwara, Joseph J. "The Identity of Juan de Flores: The Evidence of the *Crónica incompleta de los Reyes Católicos*." *Journal of Hispanic Philology*, vol. 11, 1987, pp. 103–30.

---. "The Identity of Juan de Flores: The Evidence of the *Crónica incompleta de los Reyes Católicos* (Concluded)." *Journal of Hispanic Philology*, vol. 11, 1987, pp. 205–22.

---, editor. *Juan de Flores: Four Studies*. Department of Hispanic Studies Queen Mary, U of London, 2005.

Gwara, Joseph J, and E. Michael Gerli, editors. *Studies on the Spanish Sentimental Romance (1440–1550): Redefining a Genre*. Tamesis, 1997.

Hagen, Susan K. *Allegorical Remembrance: A Study of The Pilgrimage of The Life of Man as a Medieval Treatise on Seeing and Remembering*. U of Georgia P, 1990.

Hahn, Cynthia. "Picturing the Text: Narrative in the *Life* of Saints." *Art History*, vol. 13, 1990, pp. 1–33.

---. *Portrayed on the Heart: Narrative Effect in Pictorial Lives of Saints from the Tenth through the Thirteenth Century*. U of California P, 2001.

---. "*Visio Dei*: Changes in Medieval Visuality." *Visuality Before and Beyond the Renaissance: Seeing as Others Saw*, edited by Robert S. Nelson, Cambridge UP, 2000, pp. 169–96.

Hamilton, Michelle. "The Musical Book: Judeo-Andalusi Hermeutics in the *Libro de buen amor*." *La corónica*, vol. 37, 2009, pp. 35–59.

Harbison, C. "Visions and Meditations in Early Flemish Painting." *Simiolus*, vol. 15, 1985, pp. 87–118.

Haskins, Charles H. "The Life of Medieval Students as Illustrated by their Letters." *The American Historical Review*, vol. 3, 1898, pp. 203–29.

Hawkins, Kellye D. *Sátira de felice e infelice vida de Don Pedro, Condestable de Portugal (1429–1466): Edición crítica*. 2013. Temple U, PhD dissertation. digital.library.temple.edu/digital/collection/p245801coll10/id/214803/.

Haywood, Louise M. "Apuntes sobre la *Cárcel de Amor* de Diego de San Pedro: La estructura externa." *Ínsula*, vol. 633, 2003, pp. 17–19.

---, editor. *Cultural Contexts: Female Voices*. Department of Hispanic Studies Queen Mary and Westfield College, 2000.

---. "'La escura selva': Allegory in Early Sentimental Romance." *Hispanic Review*, vol. 68, 2000, pp. 415–28.

---. "Gradissa: A Fictional Reader in/of a Male Author's Text." *Medium Aevum*, vol. 64, 1995, pp. 85–99.

---. "Lyric and Other Verse Insertions in Sentimental Romances." *Studies on the Spanish Sentimental Romance (1440–1550): Redefining a Genre*, edited by Joseph J. Gwara and E. Michael Gerli, Tamesis, 1997, pp. 191–206.

---. "Narrative and Structural Strategies in Early Spanish Sentimental Romance." *Fifteenth-Century Studies*, vol. 25, 1999, pp. 11–24.

---. "On the Frontiers of Juan Rodríguez del Padrón's *Siervo libre de amor*." *Medieval Hispanic Studies in Memory of Alan Deyermond*, edited by Andrew Beresford, et al., Tamesis, 2013, pp. 71–90.

---. "Romance and Sentimental Romance as 'Cancionero'." *Cancionero Studies in Honour of Ian Macpherson*, edited by Alan D. Deyermond and Ian Macpherson, Queen Mary and Westfield College, Department of Hispanic Studies, 1998.

---. "What's in a Name." *La corónica*, vol. 31, 2003, pp. 282–91.

Haywood, Louise M., and Francisco Toro. *Juan Ruiz, Arcipreste de Hita y el "Libro de Buen Amor": Congreso Homenaje a Alan Deyermond*. Ayuntamiento de Alcalá la Real, 2008.

Haywood, Louise M., and Louise O. Vasvári, editors. *A Companion to the* Libro de buen amor. Tamesis, 2004.

Heaton, Harry Clifton. *The Gloria d'amor de Fra Rocabertí: A Catalan Vision Poem of the 15th Century.* Columbia UP, 1916.

Heinrichs, Katherine. "'Lovers' Consolations of Philosophy' in Boccaccio, Machaut, and Chaucer." *Studies in the Age of Chaucer*, vol. 11, 1989, pp. 93–116.

---. *The Myths of Love: Classical Lovers in Medieval Literature.* Pennsylvania State UP, 1990.

Herrero, Javier. "The Allegorical Structure of the *Siervo libre de amor.*" *Speculum*, vol. 55, 1980, pp. 751–64.

Heusch, Carlos. *La philosophie de l'amour dans l'Espagne du XVe siècle.* 1992. U de la Sorbonne, PhD dissertation. tel.archives-ouvertes.fr/tel-00734876.

---. "Los 'tiempos çiertos' del *Buen amor*: estructura y genética textual en la obra de Juan Ruiz." *Juan Ruiz, Arcipreste de Hita y el "Libro de buen amor." Congreso Homenaje a Jacques Joset*, edited by Francisco Toro Ceballos and Isabel Godinas, Ayuntamiento de Alcalá la Real, 2011. Centro Virtual Cervantes. cvc.cervantes.es.

Impey, Olga Tudorica. "*Contraria* en la *Triste deleytación*: materia fundamental del Aborintio de Amor y de Fortuna." *Proceedings of the Ninth Colloquium*, edited by Andrew Beresford and Alan D. Deyermond, Department of Hispanic Studies, Queen Mary and Westfield College, 2000, pp. 145–64.

---. "Un dechado de la prosa literaria alfonsí, el relato de los amores de Dido." *Romance Philology*, vol. 34, 1980, pp. 1–27.

---. "Un doctrinal para las doncellas enamoradas en la 'Triste deleytaçión'." *Boletín de La Real Academia Española*, vol. 66, 1986, pp. 191–234.

---. "En el crisol de la prosa literaria de Alfonso X, unas huellas de la preocupación estilística en las versiones del relato de Dido." *Bulletin Hispanique*, vol. 84, 1982, pp. 5–23.

---. "Los enigmas de *Siervo libre de amor.*" *Actas del XI Congreso de la Asociación Internacional de Hispanistas (1992)*, vol. 5, 1992, pp. 107–17. Centro Virtual Cervantes. cvc.cervantes.es

---. "The Literary Emancipation of Juan Rodríguez del Padrón: From the Fictional "Cartas" to the 'Siervo de amor.'" *Speculum*, vol. 55, 1980, pp. 305–16.

---. "Ovid, Alfonso X, and Juan Rodríguez del Padrón: Two Castilian Translations of the *Heroides* and the Beginnings of the Spanish Sentimental Prose." *Bulletin of Hispanic Studies*, vol. 57, 1980, pp. 283–97.

---. "La poesía y la prosa del *Siervo libre de amor*: ¿'aferramiento' a la tradición del *prosimetrum* y de la convención lírica?" *Medieval, Renaissance and Folklore Studies in Honor of John Esten Keller*, edited by Joseph R Jones, Juan de la Cuesta, 1980, pp. 171–87.

Irving, Singer. *The Philosophy of Love.* MIT P, 2009.

Ivers, Christina E. "Risky Collaboration in Fifteenth-Century Printing and *Cárcel de Amor.*" *La corónica*, vol. 43, 2015, pp. 85–109.

Izquierdo, Josep. "El segon llibre del *Memorial del pecador remut* de Felip de Malla." *Llengua & Literatura*, vol. 23, 2013, pp. 7–44.

Jacquart, Danielle, and Claudie Thomasset. "L'amour 'heroïque' à travers le traité d'Arnaud de Villeneuve." *La Folie et Le Corps*, edited by Jean Céard, 1985, pp. 143–58.

Jaeger, C. Stephen. *The Envy of Angels: Cathedral Schools and Social Ideals in Medieval Europe, 950–1200.* U of Pennsylvania P, 2000.

James I of Scotland. *The Kingis Quair and Other Prison Poems.* Translated by Linne R. Mooney and Mary-Jo Arn, Medieval Institute Publications, 2005. d.lib.rochester. edu/teams/publication/mooney-and-arn-kingis-quair-and-other-prison-poems

Janson, H. W. *Apes and Ape-Lore in the Middle Ages and the Renaissance.* U of London P, 1952.

Jeauneau, Édouard. "Le symbolisme de la mer chez Jean Scot Érigène." *Le Néoplatonisme,* Éditions du Centre National de la Reserche Scientifique, 1971, pp. 385–94.

Juan Ruiz, Archpriest of Hita. *The Book of True Love: A Bilingual Edition.* Edited and translated by Anthony N. Zahareas and Saralyn R. Daly, The Pennsylvania State UP, 1978.

Karras, Ruth Mazo. *From Boys to Men: Formations of Masculinity in Late Medieval Europe.* U of Pennsylvania P, 2003.

Kaylor, Noel Harold and Philip Edward Phillips, editors. *A Companion to Boethius in the Middle Ages.* Brill, 2012.

Keightley, Robert G. "Boethius in Spain: A Classified Checklist of Early Translation." *The Medieval Boethius: Studies in the Vernacular Translations of 'De consolatione Philosophiae,'* edited by Alastair J. Minnis, Cambridge UP, 1989, pp. 169–87.

---. "Boethius, Villena and Juan de Mena." *Bulletin of Hispanic Studies,* vol. 55, 1978, pp. 189–202.

---. "Enrique de Villena's *Los doze trabajos de Hércules*: A Reappraisal." *Journal of Hispanic Philology,* vol. 3, no. 79, 1978, pp. 49–68.

Kerkhof, Maximiliam P. A. M. "Sobre la transmisión textual de algunas obras del Marqués de Santillana: doble redacción y variantes del autor." *Revista de Literatura Medieval,* vol. 2, 1990, pp. 35–47.

Kessler, Herbert L. *Seeing Medieval Art.* U of Toronto P, 2011.

Kinkade, Richard P. "'Intellectum tibi dabo...': The Function of the Free Will in the *Libro de buen amor.*" *Bulletin of Hispanic Studies,* vol. 47, 1970, pp. 296–315.

Kohut, Karl. "El humanismo castellano del siglo XV: replanteamiento de la problemática." *Actas del VII Congreso de la Asociación Internacional de Hispanistas,* edited by Giuseppe Bellini, Bulzoni, 1982, pp. 639–47. Centro Virtual Cervantes. cvc.cervantes.es.

Krause, Anna. *La novela sentimental (1440–1513).* 1928. U of Chicago, PhD dissertation.

---. "El 'tractado' novelístico de Diego de San Pedro." *Bulletin Hispanique,* vol. 54, 1952, pp. 245–75.

Kress, Gunther. *Linguistic Processes in Sociocultural Practice.* 1985. Oxford UP, 1989.

Kurtz, Barbara E. "Diego de San Pedro's *Cárcel de Amor* and the Tradition of the Allegorical Edifice." *Journal of Hispanic Philology,* vol. 8, no. 84, 1983, pp. 123–38.

Lacarra, María Eugenia. "Juan de Flores y la ficción sentimental." *Actas del IX Congreso de la Asociación Internacional de Hispanistas,* edited by Sebastian Neumeister. Vervuert, 1989, pp. 223–33. Centro Virtual Cervantes. cvc.cervantes.es.

---. "Notes on Feminist Analysis of Medieval Spanish Literature and History." *La corónica,* vol. 17, 1988, pp. 14–22.

---. "La parodia de la ficción sentimental en la *Celestina.*" *Celestinesca,* vol. 13, 1989, pp. 11–29. parnaseo.uv.es/celestinesca.htm.

---. "Sobre la cuestión de la autobiografía en la ficción sentimental." *Actas del I Congreso de la Asociación Hispánica de Literatura Medieval, Santiago de Compostela, 2 al 6 de diciembre de 1985,* edited by Vicente Beltrán, PPU, 1988, pp. 359–68.

Ladero Quesada, M. A., and M. C. Quintanilla Raso. "Bibliotecas de la alta nobleza castellana en el siglo XV." *Livre et lecture en Espagne et en France sous l'ancien régime.* Éditions A.D.P.F, 1981, pp. 47–62.

Lakarra Lanz, Eukene. "Los discursos científico y amoroso en la *Sátira de felice e infelice vida* del Condestable D. Pedro de Portugal." *Never Ending Adventure: Studies in Medieval and Early Modern Spanish Literature in Honor of Peter N. Dunn,* edited by Edward Friedman and Harlan Sturm, Juan de la Cuesta, 2002, pp. 109–28.

---. "*Siervo libre de amor* ¿autobiografía espiritual?" *La corónica,* vol. 29, 2000, pp. 147–70.

Lama de la Cruz, Víctor de. "En torno al simbolismo de los colores en el *Cancionero general.*" *Estudios sobre el* Cancionero general *(Valencia, 1511),* edited by Marta Haro Cortés, U de València, 2012, pp. 265–84.

Lapesa, Rafael. *La obra literaria del Marqués de Santillana*. Ínsula, 1957.

Lappin, Anthony John. "Book review of Lynette Bosch's *Art, Liturgy, and Legend in Renaissance Toledo*." *Bulletin of Hispanic Studies*, vol. 83, 2006, pp. 116–17.

Lawrance, Jeremy. N. H. "The Audience of the *Libro de buen amor*." *Comparative Literature*, vol. 36, 1984, pp. 220–37.

---. "La autoridad de la letra: un aspecto de la lucha entre humanistas y escolásticos en la Castilla del siglo XV." *Atalaya*, vol. 2, 1991, pp. 85–105.

---. "Humanism in the Iberian Peninsula." *The Impact of Humanism in Western Europe*, edited by A. Goodman and A. Mackey, Longman, 1990, pp. 220–58.

---. "Nuño de Guzmán and Early Spanish Humanism: Some Reconsiderations." *Medium Aevum*, vol. 51, 1982, pp. 55–85.

---. "On Fifteenth-Century Spanish Vernacular Humanism." *Medieval and Renaissance Studies in Honour of R. B. Tate*, edited by Ian Michael and Richard A. Cadwell, Dolphin, 1986, pp. 63–79.

---. "The Spread of Lay Literacy in Late Medieval Castile." *Bulletin of Hispanic Studies*, vol. 62, 1985, pp. 79–94.

---. *Un tratado de Alonso de Cartagena sobre la Educación y los estudios literarios*. U Autónoma de Barcelona, 1977.

Lázaro Carreter, Fernando. *Teatro medieval*. Castalia, 1965.

Leclercq, Jean. *The Love of Learning and the Desire for God: A Study of Monastic Culture*. Fordham UP, 1961.

Léglu, Catherine E., and Stephen J. Milner, editors. *The Erotics of Consolation: Desire and Distance in the Late Middle Ages*. Palgrave, 2008.

Leyerle, John. "Chaucer's Windy Eagle." *University of Toronto Quarterly*, vol. 40, 1971, pp. 247–65.

Lida de Malkiel, María Rosa. *Juan de Mena: poeta del prerrenacimiento español*. Colegio de México, 1950.

---. "Juan Rodríguez del Padrón: vida y obras." *Nueva Revista de Filología Hispánica*, vol. 6, no. 4, 1952, pp. 313–51.

---. "Nuevas notas para la interpretación del *Libro de buen amor*." *Nueva Revista de Filología Hispánica*, vol. 13, 1959, pp. 17–82.

---. "La tradición clásica en España." *Nueva Revista de Filología Hispánica*, vol. 5, no. 2, 1951, pp. 183–223.

Llull, Ramon. "Libre d'intenció." *Obres de Ramon Lull, edició original feta en vista dels millors y més antichs manuscrits*, vol. 18, Editora Lulliana, 1935, pp. 3–66.

Llull, Romeu. *Obra completa*. Edited and translated by Jaume Turró, Barcino, 1996.

López Grigera, Luisa. "Notas sobre el Marqués de Santillana y el humanismo castellano." *Studies on Medieval Spanish Literature in Honor of Charles F. Fraker*, edited by Mercedes Vaquero and Alan D. Deyermond, Hispanic Seminary of Medieval Studies, 1995, pp. 211–18.

Loughman, Thomas J., et al., editors. *Splendor, Myth, and Vision: Nudes from the Prado*. Yale UP, 2016.

Lynch, Kathryn L. *The High Medieval Dream Vision*. Stanford UP, 1988.

MacPherson, Ian. *The invenciones y letras of the Cancionero general*. Department of Hispanic Studies, Queen Mary and Westfield College, 1998.

---. "Secret Language in the *Cancioneros*: Some Courtly Codes." *Bulletin of Hispanic Studies*, vol. 62, 1985, pp. 51–63.

Madroñal, Abraham. *"De grado y de gracias:" Vejámenes universitarios de los siglos de oro*. Consejo Superior de Investigaciones Científicas, 2005.

Malla, Felip de. *Memorial del pecador remut: manuscrit de Barcelona*. Edited by Manuel Balasch, Editorial Barcino, 1981.

Mandrell, James. "Author and Authority in *Cárcel de Amor*: The Role of El Auctor." *Journal of Hispanic Studies*, vol. 8, 1984, pp. 123–38.

Map, Walter. *De nugis curialium: Courtiers' Trifles*. Edited and translated by Christopher N. L. Brooke and R. A. B. Mynors, Oxford UP, 1983.

Maravall, José Antonio. "El pre-Renacimiento del siglo XV." *Nebrija y la introducción del Renacimiento en España: actas de la III Academia Literaria Renacentista*, edited by Víctor García de la Concha, Universidad, 1983, pp. 17–36.

Marín Pina, María Carmen. "La mujer y los libros de caballerías: notas para el estudio de la recepción del género caballeresco entre el público femenino." *Revista de Literatura Medieval*, vol. 3, 1991, pp. 129–48.

Martín, Óscar. "Allegory and the Spaces of Love." *Diacritics*, vol. 36, 2006, pp. 132–46.

---. "Love's Subjects: The Alhambra Ceilings, Sentimental Fiction and Allegory." *Medieval Encounters*, vol. 14, 2008, pp. 390–406.

Martín Baños, Pedro. *El arte epistolar en el Renacimiento europeo, 1400–1600*. U de Deusto, 2005.

Martínez Latre, María Pilar. "La evolución genérica de la ficción sentimental española: un replanteamiento." *Berceo*, vols. 116–117, 1989, pp. 7–22.

Martínez Morán, Francisco José. "Epístola, diálogo y poesía en *Grimalte y Gradisa* de Juan de Flores." *Revista de Poética Medieval*, vol. 16, 2006, pp. 147–69.

Martos Sánchez, Josep Lluís. *Les proses mitològiques de Joan Roís de Corella: estudi i edició*. 1999. U d'Alacant, PhD dissertation. 2 vols. rua.ua.es/dspace/handle/10045/3721?locale=en.

---. "La 'Vida de Sancta Bàrbara' del 'Jardinet d'orats': Joan Roís de Corella o la recepció de la seua obra." *Actas del VIII Congreso Internacional de la Asociación Hispánica de Literatura Medieval*, Biblioteca Virtual Miguel de Cervantes, 2013, pp. 1269–87. www.cervantesvirtual.com/nd/ark:/59851/bmc4b4s6

Matulka, Barbara. *The Novels of Juan de Flores and Their European Diffusion: A Study in Comparative Literature*. 1931. Columbia U, PhD dissertation.

Mazzochi, Giuseppe. "I manoscritti nella trasmissione della novela sentimental castigliana." *L'Europa Del Libro Nell'età Dell'Umanesimo: Atti Del XIV Convegno Internazionale, Chianciano, Firenze, Pienza 16–19 luglio 2002*, F. Cesati, 2004, pp. 365–80.

---. "Los manuscritos y la definición de un género: el caso de la novela sentimental." *Los códices literarios de la Edad Media: interpretación, técnicas y catalogación*, edited by Eva Belén Carro Carbajal and Javier Durán Barceló, Cilengua-Instituto de Historia del Libro y la Lectura, 2009, pp. 195–205.

---. "Un testimonio manuscrito antiguo de *Cárcel de Amor*." *Actas del IX congreso internacional de la Asociación Hispánica de Literatura Medieval, A Coruña, 18–22 de septiembre de 2001*, Toxoutos, 2005, pp. 167–75.

McKinley, Kathryn L. *Reading the Ovidian Heroine: "Metamorphoses" Commentaries 1100–1618*. Brill, 2001.

Mena, Juan de. *Obras completas*. Edited by Miguel Ángel Pérez Priego, Planeta, 1989.

Méndez Cabrera, Jerónimo. "El realismo grotesco en la narrativa breve catalana del siglo XV: la concepción burlesca de la cultura medieval." *La corónica*, vol. 38, 2009, pp. 211–30.

Mendoza Negrillo, Juan de Dios. *Fortuna y Providencia en la literatura castellana del siglo XV*. Anejos del Boletín de la Real Academia Española, 1973.

Menéndez Pelayo, Marcelino. *Bibliografía hispano-latina clásica*. 1902. Fundación Ignacio Larramendi-Fundación MAPFRE, 2009.

---. *Orígenes de la novela*. Vol. 1, Aldus, 1943.

Metge, Bernat. *Book of Fortune and Prudence*. Edited by David Barnett, Barcino, Tamesis, 2011.

---. *'The Dream' of Bernat Metge: Del Somni d'en Bernat Metge*. Edited and translated by Antonio Cortijo Ocaña and Elisabeth Lagresa, John Benjamins Publishing Co, 2013.

---. *Obras de Bernat Metge*. Edited by Martín de Riquer, U de Barcelona, 1959.

Michael, Ian. "Epic to Romance to Novel: Problems of Genre Identification." *Bulletin of the John Rylands Library*, vol. 68, 1985–1986, pp. 498–527.

---. "From Her Shall Read the Perfect Ways of Honour: Isabel of Castile and Chivalric Romance." *The Age of the Catholic Monarchs, 1474–1516: Literary Studies in Memory of Keith Whinnom*, edited by Alan D. Deyermond and Ian Macpherson, Liverpool UP, 1989, pp. 103–12.

Miguel-Prendes, Sol. *El espejo y el piélago: la Eneida castellana de Enrique de Villena.* Edition Reichenberger, 1998.

---. "Otra frontera de la ficción sentimental: la *Consolatio Philosophiae* de Boecio." *eHumanista*, vol. 28, 2014, pp. 511–35.

---. "Reimagining Diego de San Pedro's Readers at Work: *Cárcel de Amor.*" *La corónica*, vol. 32, 2004, pp. 7–44.

---. "La retórica del margen y la prehistoria de la novela." *eHumanista*, vol. 11, 2008, pp. 31–64.

---. "Tratar de amores: el espacio textual en la ficción sentimental." *"Recuerde el alma dormida:" Medieval and Early Modern Spanish Essays in Honor of Frank A. Domínguez*, edited by John K. Moore and Adriano Duque, Juan de la Cuesta, 2009, pp. 217–37.

Minervini, Vincenzo, and Maria Luisa Indini, editors. *Càrcer d'amor, Carcer d'amore: due traduzione della 'novela' di Diego de San Pedro.* Schena Editore, 1986.

Minnis, Alastair J. "The Author's Two Bodies? Authority and Fallibility in Late Medieval Textual Theory." *Of the Making of Books: Medieval Manuscripts, Their Scribes and Readers. Essays Presented to M. B. Parkes*, edited by Pamela Robinson and Rivkah Zim, Scholar P. Co, 1997, pp. 259–79.

---. "Authors in Love: The Self-Exegesis of Medieval Love Poets." *The Uses of Manuscripts in Literary Studies: Essays in Memory of Judson Boyce Allen*, edited by Charlotte C. Morse, et al., Western Michigan U, Medieval Institute Publications, 1992, pp. 161–91.

---. *Magister amoris: The Roman de la Rose and Vernacular Hermeneutics.* Oxford UP, 2001.

---, editor. *The Medieval Boethius: Studies in the Vernacular Translations of De* consolatione Philosophiae. D. S. Brewer, 1987.

---. *Medieval Theory of Authorship.* Scholar P, 1984.

Moffit, John F. "Bartolomé Bermejo's Pietà (1490) and the Invention of Expressionistic Landscape." *Gazette Des Beaux-Arts*, 1998, pp. 71–76.

Molina i Figueras, Joan. *Arte, devoción y poder en la pintura tardogótica catalana.* U de Murcia, 1999.

---. "La Virgen de los *consellers*: Metáfora mariana e imagen de poder." *Boletín del Museo e Instituto "Camón Aznar,"* vol. 77, 1999, pp. 111–51.

Moll, Francesc de B. "El 'Corbatxo' de Giovanni Boccaccio traduït en català per Narcís Franch (Segle XIV). 1935." *Textos i estudis medievals*, Associació de Llengua i Literatura Catalanes, 1982, pp. 43–119.

Moner, Francesc. *Obres catalanes.* Edited by Peter Cocozzella, Barcino, 1970.

Moner, Pedro. *Obras nueuamente imprimidas assi en prosa como en metro: las mas dellas en lengua castellana y algunas en su lengua natural catalana compuestas en diuersos tiempos y por diuersos y nobles motiuos: las quales son mas para conocer y aborrescer el mondo que para seguir sus lizonjas y engaños.* Facsimile edition by Antonio Pérez Gómez, C. Amorós, 1951.

Montero, Ana M. "*Cárcel de Amor* by Diego de San Pedro: An Analysis of Clemency, Cruelty, and Justice in Late Fifteenth-Century Castile." *Essays in Medieval Studies*, vol. 30, 2014, pp. 97–112.

---. "'¿Durmiendo con el enemigo?': La reina Isabel de Portugal en la obra literaria de su hermano Don Pedro, condestable de Portugal. Ficción e historia." *Erebea: Revista de Humanidades y Ciencias Sociales*, vol. 4, 2014, pp. 173–98.

---. "Imagen femenina, virtud y heroísmo: ficción sentimental e historia en *Sátira de felice et infelice vida* del condestable don Pedro." *eHumanista*, vol. 33, 2016, pp. 379–401.

---. "A New Reading of *Sátira de infelice e felice vida* by Don Pedro, Constable of Portugal: The Influence of Seneca's *On Clemency.*" *La corónica*, vol. 41, 2013, pp. 103–34.

Mooney, Linne R., and Mary-Jo Arn, editors. *The Kingis Quair and Other Prison Poems.* Medieval Institute Publications, 2005. d.lib.rochester.edu/teams/publication/mooney-and-arn-kingis-quair-and-other-prison-poems

Mortensen, Lars Boje. "The Rhetoric of the Latin Page: Authority, Persuasion and Latinity in Medieval and Renaissance Historiography." *Text and Voice: The Rhetoric of Authority in the Middle Ages*, edited by Marianne Borch, UP of Southern Denmark, 2004.

Munjic, Sanda. "Diego de San Pedro's *Cárcel de Amor*: Allegorizing the Role of Poets in a Well Ordered State." *Revista Hispánica Moderna*, vol. 65, 2012, pp. 81–99.

---. "How Love Took Reason to Court: Diego de San Pedro's Prison of Love." *Words of Love and Love of Words in the Middle Ages and the Renaissance*, edited by Albrecht Classen, University of Arizona, 2008, pp. 461–76.

---. "Leriano's Suffering Subjectivity, or, the Politics of Sentimentality in *Cárcel de Amor*." *Revista Canadiense de Estudios Hispánicos*, vol. 32, 2008, pp. 203–26.

---. "Vindication of King Gaulo: Anger Management in *Cárcel de Amor*." *Bulletin of Hispanic Studies*, vol. 91, 2014, pp. 331–45.

Muñoz Gómez, Víctor. "De Medina del Campo a Zaragoza: un periplo por las devociones 'políticas' de un príncipe castellano bajomedieval (el infante Fernando de Antequera, 1380–1416)." *eHumanista*, vol. 24, 2013, pp. 375–95.

Murphy, James J. *Rhetoric in the Middle Ages*. U of California P, 1974.

Muzzi, Luigi. *Fiore di Italia*. Bolonia, 1824.

Nalle, Sarah. "Literacy and Culture in Early Modern Castile." *Past and Present*, vol. 125, 1989, pp. 65–96.

Nauta, Lodi. "'Magis sit Platonicus quam Aristotelicus': Interpretations of Boethius's Platonism in the *Consolatio Philosophiae* From the Twelfth to the Seventeenth Century." *The Platonic Tradition in the Middle Ages: A Doxographic Approach*, edited by Stephen Gersh and Marteen J. F. M. Hoenen, de Gruyter, 2002, pp. 165–204.

Nepaulsing, Colbert. "Bernat Metge's *Libre de Fortuna e Prudència* and the Literary Tradition of Goddess Fortuna." *Catalan Studies in Memory of Josephine de Boer*, edited by Joseph Gulsoy and Josep Solá-Solé, 1977, pp. 203–12.

Newman, Barbara. "What Did It Mean to Say "I Saw"? The Clash between Theory and Practice in Medieval Visionary Culture." *Speculum*, vol. 80, 2005, pp. 1–43.

Newman, Jonathan M. "Dictators of Venus: Clerical Love Letters and Female Subjection in *Troilus and Criseyde* and the *Rota Veneris*." *Studies in the Age of Chaucer*, vol. 36, 2014, pp. 103–38.

O'Donnell, Clement. "Voluntarism in Franciscan Philosophy." *Franciscan Studies*, vol. 2, 1942, pp. 397–402.

Olmedilla Herrero, Carmen. "Comentarios a la *Consolatio Philosophiae* de Boecio: Guillermo de Aragón y la versión castellana anónima del comentario de Nicolás Trevet." *Cuadernos de Filología Clásica: Estudios Latinos*, vol. 2, 1992, pp. 277–88.

---. *Edición crítica de los comentarios de Guillermo de Aragón al* De consolatione philosophiae *de Boecio*. 1997. 2 vols. U Complutense, PhD dissertation.

Orazi, Veronica. "Il *Somni recitant lo procés d'una qüestió enamorada* di Francesc Alegre: Cornice onirica per un'allegoria di sapore humanistico nella Barcelona della fine del XV sec." *Sogno e scrittura nelle culture iberiche. Atti del XVII Convegno, Milano 24–25–26 ottobre 1996*. Bulzoni Editore, 1998, pp. 289–304.

Orth, Myra D. "*The Prison of Love*: A Medieval Romance in the French Renaissance and Its Illustrations (BN Ms. fr.2150)." *Journal of the Warburg and Courtauld Institutes*, vol. 46, 1983, pp. 211–21.

Pacheco, Arseni, editor. "L'anàlisi de la passió amorosa en alguns texts del segle XV. Anatomia d'un gènere en embrió." *Miscel·lània Pere Bohigas*, vol. 3, Publicacions de l'Abadia de Montserrat, 1983, pp. 25–38.

---. "La narració en primera persona en els segles XIV i XV: notes per a una reavaluació crítica." *Actes del Cinquè Col·loqui d'Estudis Catalans a Nord Amèrica*, edited by Curt Wittlin, Abadia de Montserrat, 1988, pp. 99–109.

---. *Novel·letes sentimentals del segles XIV i XV*. Editions 62, 1970.

Paetow, Louis John. *The Arts Course at Medieval Universities with Special Reference to Grammar and Rhetoric.* 1910. U of Pennsylvania, PhD dissertation. archive.org/details/artscourseatmed00goog.

Parrilla, Carmen. "Cantar y contar en *Siervo libre de amor.*" *Revista de Literatura Medieval,* vol. 22, 2010, pp. 217–40.

---. "Un cronista olvidado: Juan de Flores autor de la crónica incompleta de los Reyes Católicos." *The Age of the Catholic Monarchs, 1475–1516: Literary Studies in Memory of Keith Whinnom,* edited by Alan D. Deyermond and Ian Macpherson, Liverpool UP, 1989, pp. 123–33.

---. "Dos cartas inéditas en la Biblioteca Colombina." *Epos,* vol. 2, 1986, pp. 341–50.

---. "Estudio introductorio." *Grimalte y Gradisa.* Centro de Estudios Cervantinos, 2008, pp. 9–86.

---. "La ficción sentimental y sus lectores." *Ínsula,* vol. 675, 2003, pp. 21–24.

---. "La novela sentimental en el marco de la instruccion retorica." *Ínsula,* vol. 651, 2001, pp. 15–17.

---. "Qui scit, docere debet: acerca de Alfonso de Madrigal el Tostado." *Archivum: Revista de La Facultad de Filología,* vols. 54–55, 2005–2004, pp. 367–90.

Patch, Howard R. *The Goddess Fortuna in Medieval Literature.* Harvard UP, 1927.

---. *The Tradition of Boethius: A Study of His Presence in Medieval Culture.* 1935. Russell & Russell, 1970.

Pedro de Portugal. "Coplas del menesprecio e contempto de las cosas fermosas del mundo." *Obras completas do Condestável Dom Pedro de Portugal,* edited by Luís Adão da Fonseca, Fundação Calouste Gulbenkian, 1975, pp. 179–304.

---. "Sátira de infelice e felice vida." *Obras completas do Condestável Dom Pedro de Portugal,* edited by Luís Adão da Fonseca, Fundação Calouste Gulbenkian, 1975, pp. 15–175.

---. *Sátira de infelice e felice vida.* Edited by Guillermo Serés, Centro de Estudios Cervantinos, 2008.

Pedro de Valladolid. *Comentario de Boecio,* 1436. MSS/10193, Biblioteca Nacional de España.

Pellisa Prades, Gemma. *La ficció sentimental catalana de la segona meitat del s. XV.* 2013. U de Barcelona, PhD dissertation. diposit.ub.edu/dspace/bitstream/2445/53204/1/GPP_TESI.pdf.

---. "La transmissió manuscrita de la ficció sentimental catalana." *Els manuscrits, el saber i les lletres a la Corona d'Aragó, 1250–1500,* edited by Lola Badia, Publicacions de l'Abadia de Montserrat, 2016, pp. 57–76.

Percival, Richard. *Bibliothecae Hispanicae pars altera: Containing a Dictionarie in Spanish, English and Latine.* John Jackson and Richard Watkins, 1591. ntlle.rae.es.

Pérez Bosch, Estela. "Francés Carrós Pardo de la Casta: un humanista para el *Cancionero general.*" *Quaderns de Filologia: Estudis Literaris,* vol. 10, 2005, pp. 117–31.

---. *Los valencianos del* Cancionero general*: estudio de sus poesías.* PUV, 2009.

Pérez Bustamante, Rogelio, and José Manuel Calderón Ortega. *El Marqués de Santillana: biografía y documentación.* Taurus, 1983.

Pérez López, José Luis. *Temas del Libro de buen amor (el entorno catedralicio toledano).* Ediciones D. B., 2007.

Pérez Priego, Miguel Ángel. "Los infiernos de amor." *Iberia cantat: estudios sobre la poesía ibérica medieval,* edited by Juan Casas Rigall and Eva María Díaz Martínez, U de Santiago de Compostela, 2002, pp. 307–20.

Pérez Rosado, Miguel. "Dos notas sobre la *Consolación* de Boecio en la edad media castellana." *Cuadernos de Filología Clásica: Estudios Latinos,* vol. 4, 1993, pp. 113–26.

Planas Badenas, Josefina. "Lecturas pías de los reyes: el libro de uso devocional durante los siglos del gótico." *Maravillas de la España medieval: tesoro sagrado y monarquía,* edited by Isidro Gonzalo Bango Treviso, vol. 1, Junta de Castilla y León, 2000, pp. 461–73.

---. "Plegarias iluminadas: Libros de Horas conservados en bibliotecas catalanas." *De Arte: Revista de Historia del Arte*, vol. 6, 2007, pp. 75–106.

Post, Chandler R. *Mediaeval Spanish Allegory*. Harvard UP, 1915.

Pujol, Josep. "'Gaya vel gaudiosa, et alio nomine inveniendi sciencia:' les idees sobre la poesia en llengua vulgar als segles XIV i XV." *Intel·lectuals i escriptors a la baixa edad mitjana*, edited by Lola Badia, Curial, 1994, pp. 69–94.

---. "Les glosses de Guillem Nicolau a la seva traducció de les *Heroides* d'Ovidi (1390): una proposta d'identificació." *Caplletra*, vol. 39, 2005, pp. 129–229.

---. "The Hispanic Vernacular Reception of William of Orléans's *Bursarii ovidianorum*: The Translations of Ovid's *Heroides*." *The Journal of Medieval Latin*, vol. 21, 2011, pp. 17–34.

---. "Els 'trobadors estudiosos' segons Felip de Malla." *La cultura catalana tra l'umanesimo e il barocco. Atti del V Covegno dell'Associazione Italiana di Studi Catalani*, edited by Carlos Romero and Rossend Arqués, Programma, 1994, pp. 191–208.

Purcell, William M. "Eberhard the German and the Labyrinth of Learning: Grammar, Poesy, Rhetoric, and Pedagogy in Laborintus." *Rhetorica*, vol. 11, 1993, pp. 95–118.

Quadrado, José María. *Forenses y ciudadanos: historia de las disensiones civiles de Mallorca en el siglo XV*. Tipo-litografía de Amengual y Montaner Editores, 1895.

Quain, Edwin. "Medieval Accesus ad Auctores." *Traditio*, vol. 3, 1945, pp. 215–64.

Quarti, Lara. "Il Somni recitant lo procés d'una qüestió enamorada di Francesc Alegre: il mito al servizio dell'allegoria." *eHumanista*, vol. 7, 2015, pp. 78–85.

Quilligan, Maureen. "Allegory and Female Agency." *Thinking Allegory Otherwise*, edited by Brenda Machosky, Stanford UP, 2009, pp. 163–87.

---. *The Language of Allegory: Defining the Genre*. Cornell UP, 1979.

Recio, Roxana. "El humanismo italiano y las producciones catalanas: Carroç Pardo como modelo de adaptación y recreación." *Proceedings of the Ninth Colloquium: 'Papers on Medieval Hispanic Research Seminar,'* edited by Andrew Beresford and Alan D. Deyermond, Department of Hispanic Studies, Queen Mary and Westfield College, 2000, pp. 43–52.

---. "Intextuality in Carroç Pardo de la Casta." *Mediaevalia*, vol. 22, 2000, pp. 157–81.

---. *Petrarca y Alvar Gómez: la traducción del Triunfo de amor*. Peter Lang, 1996.

---. *Los Trionfi de Petrarca comentados en catalán: una edición de los manuscritos 534 de la Biblioteca Nacional de París y del Ateneu de Barcelona*. Department of Romance Studies at the University of North Carolina at Chapel Hill, 2009. North Carolina Studies in the Romance Languages and Literatures, 293.

René I, King of Naples and Jerusalem. *The Book of the Love-Smitten Heart*. Edited by Stephanie Vierek Gibbs and Kathryn Karczewska. Routledge, 2001.

Reyes-Tudela, José Enrique. *Las obras de Francesch Carroç Pardo de la Casta*. Albatros Hispanófila, 1987.

Richard of St Victor. "On the Four Degrees of Violent Love. Introduction and translation by Andrew B. Kraebel." *On Love: A Selection of Works of Hugh, Adam, Achard, Richard, and Godfrey of St Victor*, edited by Hugh Feiss, Brepols, 2011, pp. 263–300.

Rico, Francisco. "Imágenes del Prerrenacimiento español: Joan Roís de Corella y la Tragèdia de Caldesa." *Estudios de Literatura Española y Francesa. Siglos XVI y XVII. Homenaje a Horst Baader*, edited by Frauke Gewecke, Vervuert, 1984, pp. 15–28.

---. "Las letras latinas del siglo XII en Galicia, León y Castilla." *Abaco*, vol. 2, 1969, pp. 9–91.

---. "Petrarca y el humanismo catalán." *Actes del Sisè Col.Loqui Internacional de Llengua i Literatura Catalanes, Roma 28 setembre–2 octubre 1982*, edited by Giuseppe Tavani, Publicacions de l'Abadia de Montserrat, 1983, pp. 257–91.

---. "Por aver mantenencia. El aristotelismo heterodoxo en el *Libro de buen amor*." *El Crotalón. Anuario de Filología Española*, vol. 2, 1985, pp. 169–85.

---. "Sobre el origen de la autobiografía en el *Libro de buen amor*." *Anuario de Estudios Medievales*, vol. 4, 1967, pp. 301–25.

Riera i Sans, Jaume. "Sobre la difusió hispànica de la *Consolació* de Boeci." *El Crotalón. Anuario de Filología Española*, vol. 1, 1984, pp. 297–327.

Ríos, José Amador de los. *Historia crítica de la literatura española*. Imprenta de J. Rodríguez, 1861–1865.

Riquer, Isabel de. "Les poèmes narratifs catalans en noves rimades des XIV et XV siècles." *Revue des Langues Romanes*, vol. 96, 1992, pp. 327–50.

Riquer, Martín de. "Elements comuns en la cultura i en l'espiritualitat del món aragonès." *La Corona d'Aragona e il Mediterraneo. Aspetti e problemi comuni da Alfonso il Magnanimo a Ferdinandi il Cattolico (1416–1516). IX Congresso Di Storia Della Corona d'Aragona, Napoli, 11–15 Aprile 1973*, vol. 1, Società Storia Patria Napoli, 1982, pp. 211–32.

---. "Francesc Carros Pardo de la Casta." *Estudis de Literatura Catalana oferts a Jordi Rubió i Balaguer en elseu setanta-cinquè aniversari*. Institut d'Estudis Catalans, 1962, pp. 301–06.

---. *Història de la literatura catalana*. Ariel, 1964. 3 vols.

---, editor. *Obras de Bernat Metge*. U de Barcelona, 1959.

---. "La *Tragèdia de Lançalot*, texto artúrico catalán del siglo XV." *Filologia Romanza*, vol. 2, 1955, pp. 113–39.

---. "Triste deleytación, novela castellana del siglo XV." *Revista de Filología Española*, vol. 40, 1956, pp. 33–65.

Robathan, Dorothy M. *The pseudo-Ovidian* De vetula. A. M. Hakkert, 1968.

Robertson, D. W. "The Doctrine of Charity in Medieval Literary Gardens. A Topical Approach Through Symbolism and Allegory." *Speculum*, vol. 26, 1951, pp. 24–29.

---. *A Preface to Chaucer. Studies in Medieval Perspectives*. Princeton UP, 1962.

Rodríguez del Padrón, Juan. *Bursario*. Edited by Pilar Saquero Suárez-Somonte and Tomás González Rolán, Centro de Estudios Cervantinos, 2010.

---. *Siervo libre de amor*. 1976. Edited by Antonio Prieto, Castalia, 1980.

---. *Siervo libre de amor*. Edited by Enric Dolz, Anexos de la Revista Lemir, 2004.

Rodríguez Risquete, Francisco J. "La regoneixença de Francesc Carrós Pardo de la Casta." *Actes del X Congrés Internacional de l'Associació Hispànica de Literatura Medieval*, edited by Rafael Alemany, et al., vol. 3, Institut Interuniversitari de Filologia Valenciana, 2005, pp. 1379–89.

---. *Vida y obra de Pere Torroella*. 2003. U de Girona, PhD dissertation. www.tdx.cat/handle/10803/7825.

Roest, Bert. *Franciscan Learning, Preaching and Mission c. 1220–1650*. Brill, 2014.

Roffé, Mercedes. *La cuestión del género en Grisel y Mirabella*. Juan de la Cuesta, 1996.

Rohland de Langbehn, Regula. "Una lanza por el género sentimental ... ¿ficción o novela?" *La corónica*, vol. 31, 2002, pp. 137–41.

---. "Un mundo al revés: la mujer en las obras de ficción de Juan de Flores." *Studies on the Spanish Sentimental Romance (1440–1550). Redefining a Genre*, edited by Joseph J. Gwara and E. Michael Gerli, Tamesis, 1997, pp. 125–43.

---, editor. *Triste deleytaçión*. U de Morón, 1983.

---. *La unidad genérica de la novela sentimental española de los siglos XV y XVI*. Department of Hispanic Studies; Queen Mary and Westfield College, 1999.

Roís de Corella, Joan. "Parlament o collació que aprés de sopar sdevench en cassa de Berenguer Mercader entre alguns hòmens de stat." *Les proses mitològiques de Joan Roís de Corella*, edited by Josep Lluís Martos, U d'Alacant, 1999. www.narpan.net/ben/indexcorella.htm.

---. "Tragedia de Caldesa." *Multilingual Joan Roís de Corella. The Relevance of a Fifteenth-Century Classic of the Crown of Aragon*, edited by Antonio Cortijo Ocaña and Vicent Martines, Publications of eHumanista, 2013, pp. 225–30. www.ehumanista. ucsb.edu.

Ross, Jill. *Figuring the Feminine: The Rhetoric of Female Embodiment in Medieval Hispanic Literature*. U of Toronto P, 2008.

Round, Nicholas Greenville. *The Greatest Man Uncrowned: A Study of the Fall of Don Alvaro de Luna*. Tamesis, 1986.

---. *Libro llamado Fedron: Plato's Phaedo Translated by Pero Díaz de Toledo*. Tamesis, 1993.

---. "Renaissance Culture and Its Opponents in 15th-Century Castile." *Modern Languages Notes*, vol. 57, 1962, pp. 204–15.

Rubió i Balaguer, Jordi. *Estudis de literatura catalana*. Publicacions de l'Abadia de Montserrat, 1992.

Ruiz, Elisa. *Los libros de Isabel la Católica: arqueología de un patrimonio escrito*. Instituto de Historia del Libro y de la Lectura, 2004.

Ruiz-Gálvez Priego, Estrella. "*La noche de Moner*, más propiamente llamada *Vida humana*." *Cahiers d'Études Hispaniques Médiévales*, vol. 30, 2007, pp. 167–82.

Russell, Peter E. "Las armas contra las letras: para una definición del humanismo español del siglo XV." *Temas de* La Celestina *y otros estudios*. Ariel, 1978, pp. 207–39.

---. *Traducciones y traductores en la Península Ibérica (1400–1550)*. U Autónoma de Barcelona, 1985.

Saenger, Paul H. "Books of Hours and the Reading Habits of the Later Middle Ages." *The Culture of Print: Power and Uses of Print in Early Modern Europe*, edited by Roger Chartier, Princeton UP, 1989, pp. 143–73.

---. "Silent Reading: Its Impact on Medieval Script and Society." *Viator*, vol. 13, 1982, pp. 367–414.

---. *Space Between Words: The Origins of Silent Reading*. Stanford UP, 1997.

Salvo García, Irene. "Las *Heroidas* en la *General Estoria* de Alfonso X: texto y glosa en el proceso de traducción y resemantización de Ovidio." *Cahiers d'Études Hispaniques Médiévales*, vol. 32, 2009, pp. 205–28.

San Pedro, Diego de. *Cárcel de Amor. Arnalte y Lucenda. Sermón*. 1995. Edited by José Francisco Ruiz Casanova, Cátedra, 2005.

---. *Cárcel de Amor con la continuación de Nicolás Núñez*. Edited by Carmen Parrilla and Estudio preliminar by Alan D. Deyermond, Crítica, 1995.

---. *Obras completas I. Tractado de amores de Arnalte y Lucenda. Sermón*. Edited by Keith Whinnom, Castalia, 1979.

---. *Obras completas II. Cárcel de Amor*. Edited by Keith Whinnom, Castalia, 1979.

---. *Obras completas III. Poesías*. Edited by Keith Whinnom and Dorothy Sherman Severin, Castalia, 1979.

---. *Prison of Love, 1492, together with the Continuation by Nicolás Núñez, 1496*. Translated with an introduction and annotations by Keith Whinnom, Edinburg UP, 1979.

Sánchez Ameijeiras, Rocío. "Espiritualidad mendicante y arte gótico." *Las religiones en la historia de Galicia*, edited by Marco Virgilio García Quintela, U da Coruña, 1996, pp. 333–54.

---. "History and Stories of Love and Conversion in Fourteenth-Century Burgos." *Hispanic Research Journal: Iberian and Latin American Studies*, vol. 13, 2012, pp. 449–67.

---. *Los rostros de las palabras: imágenes y teoría literaria en el Occidente medieval*. Akal, 2014.

Sanmartín Bastida, Rebeca. "El *Corbacho* o el arte de la representación del Bajomedievo." *eHumanista*, vol. 3, 2003, pp. 19–29.

Santillana: López de Mendoza, Íñigo, Marqués de. *Obras completas*. Edited by Ángel Gómez Moreno and Maximilian P. A. M. Kerkhof, Planeta, 1988.

Santos Paz, José Carlos. "Nuevas cuestiones sobre Pedro Compostelano." *Actas do IV Congresso Internacional de Latim Medieval Hispánico. Lisboa, 12–15 de Outobro del 2005*. U de Lisboa, Centro de Estudos Clássicos, 2006, pp. 833–48.

Saquero Suárez-Somonte, Pilar, and Tomás González Rolán. "Las glosas de Nicolas de Trevet sobre los trabajos de Hércules vertidas al castellano: el códice 10.220 de la B. N. de Madrid y Enrique de Villena." *Epos*, vol. 6, 1990, pp. 177–97.

Saunders, Corinne. "'The thoughtful maladie': Madness and Vision in Medieval Writing." *Madness and Creativity in Literature and Culture*, Palgrave Macmillan, 2005, pp. 65–85.

Scheidegger, Jean R. "Couleurs, amour et fantaisie dans le *livre du cuer d'amours espris* de René d'Anjou." *Les couleurs au Moyen Age*, PU de Provence, 1988, pp. 387–99.
Schevill, Rudolph. *Ovid and the Renascence in Spain*. Berkeley, 1913.
Schiff, Mario. *La Bibliothèque du Marquis de Santillane*. E. Bouillon, 1905.
Schrock, Chad D. *Consolation in Medieval Narrative: Augustinian Authority and Open Form*. Palgrave MacMillan, 2015.
Sedgwick, Eve Kosofsky. *Between Men: English Literature and Male Homosocial Desire*. Columbia UP, 1985.
Seidenspinner-Nuñez, Dayle. *The Allegory of Good Love: Parodic Perspectivism in the Libro de Buen Amor*. U of California P, 1981.
Serés, Guillermo. "La autoridad literaria: círculos intelectuales y géneros en la Castilla del siglo XV." *Bulletin Hispanique*, vol. 2, 2007, pp. 335–83.
---. "Don Pedro de Portugal y el Tostado." *Actas del III Congreso de la Asociación Hispánica de Literatura Medieval (Salamanca, 3 al 6 de octubre de 1989)*, edited by María Isabel Toro Pascua, Biblioteca Española del Siglo XV, 1994, pp. 975–82.
---. "La elegía de Juan Rodríguez del Padrón." *Hispanic Review*, vol. 62, 1994, pp. 1–22.
---. "Estudio introductorio." *Sátira de infelice e felice vida*, Centro de Estudios Cervantinos, 2008, pp. 11–66.
---. "La llamada ficción sentimental y el humanismo vernáculo del siglo XV. Un ejemplo." *Ínsula*, vol. 651, 2001, pp. 12–14.
---. "La traducción en su contexto histórico y cultural." *La traducción en Italia y España durante el siglo XV. La "Ilíada en romance" y su contexto cultural*, U de Salamanca, 1997, pp. 233–61.
---. *La transformación de los amantes. Imágenes del amor de la Antigüedad al Siglo de Oro*. Crítica, 1996.
Severin, Dorothy Sherman. "Audience and Interpretation: Gradisa the Cruel and Fiometa the Rejected in Juan de Flores's *prosimetrum*, *Grimalte y Gradisa*." *Cultural Contexts/Female Voices*, edited by Louise M. Haywood, Department of Hispanic Studies Queen Mary and Westfield College, 2000, pp. 63–71.
---. *Del manuscrito a la imprenta en la época de Isabel la Católica*. Edition Reichenberger, 2004.
---, project director. *An Electronic Corpus of 15th Century Castilian Cancionero Manuscripts*, cancionerovirtual.liv.ac.uk.
---. *Religious Parody and the Spanish Sentimental Novel*. Juan de la Cuesta, 2005.
---. "The Sentimental Genre: Romance, Novel, or Parody?" *La corónica*, vol. 31, 2003, pp. 312–15.
Sharrer, Harvey L. "La *Cárcel de Amor* de Diego de San Pedro: la confluencia de lo sagrado y lo profano en la 'imagen femenil entallada en una piedra muy clara.'" *Actas del III Congreso de la Asociación Hispánica de Literatura Medieval (Salamanca, 3 al 6 de octubre de 1989)*, edited by Isabel Toro Pascua, vol. 2, Biblioteca Española del Siglo XV, 1994, pp. 983–96.
---. "La fusión de las novelas artúrica y sentimental a fines de la Edad Media." *El Crotalón. Anuario de Filología Española*, vol. 1, 1984–1985, pp. 147–57.
Silleras-Fernandez, Nuria. *Chariots of Ladies: Francesc Eiximenis and the Court Culture of Medieval and Early Modern Iberia*. Cornell UP, 2015
---. *Power, Piety, and Patronage in Late-Medieval Queenship*. Palgrave, 2008.
Singer, Julie. *Blindness and Therapy in Late Medieval French and Italian Poetry*. D. S. Brewer, 2011.
Skinner, Quentin. "Political Philosophy." *The Cambridge History of Renaissance Philosophy*, edited by Charles B. Schmitt, Cambridge UP, 1988, pp. 387–463.
Smith, Kathryn A. *Art, Identity and Devotion in Fourteenth-Century England. Three Women and Their Books of Hours*. British Library and U of Toronto P, 2004.
Sobré, Judith Berg. *Behind the Altar Table. The Development of the Painted Retable in Spain, 1350–1500*. U of Missouri P, 1989.

Sorthou Carreres, Carlos. *Iconografía mariana y patronatos de la Virgen*. Semana Gráfica, 1957.

Spitzer, Leo. "Note on the Poetic and the Empirical 'I' in Medieval Authors." *Traditio*, 1947, pp. 414–22.

Steadman, John M. "Chaucer's Eagle: A Contemplative Symbol." *PMLA*, vol. 75, no. 3, 1960, pp. 153–59.

Stock, Brian. "Reading, Ethics, and the Literary Imagination." *New Literary History*, vol. 34, 2003, pp. 1–17.

---. "Reading, Writing, and the Self: Petrarch and His Forerunners." *New Literary History*, vol. 26, 1995, pp. 717–30.

Summers, Joanna. *Late-Medieval Prison Writing and the Politics of Autobiography*. Oxford UP, 2004.

Tejerina-Canal, Santiago. "Unidad en *Cárcel de Amor*: El motivo de la tiranía." *Kentucky Romance Quarterly*, vol. 31, 1984, pp. 51–59.

Teskey, Gordon. *Allegory and Violence*. Cornell UP, 1996.

Torrego Esther. "Convención retórica y ficción narrativa en la *Cárcel de Amor*." *Nueva Revista de Filología Hispánica*, vol. 32, 1983, pp. 330–39.

Torró, Jaume. "Una cort a Barcelona per a la literatura del segle XV." *Revista de Catalunya*, 2001, pp. 97–123. www.narpan.net/documents/tirant.htm.

---. "El mite de Caldesa: Corella al 'Jardinet d'orats.'" *Atalaya*, vol. 7, 1996, pp. 103–16. www.lluisvives.com.

---. "El ms. 151 de la Biblioteca Universitària de Barcelona (Jardinet de orats): descripció i estudi codicològic." *Boletín Bibliográfico de la Asociación Hispánica de Literatura Medieval*, vol. 6, 1992, pp. 1–55.

---. "'Officium poetae est fingere': Francesc Alegre i la *Faula de Neptuno i Dyana*." *Intel·lectuals i escriptors a la baixa edad mitjana*, edited by Lola Badia and Albert Soler, Curial, 1994, pp. 221–41.

---. "Il *Secretum* di Petrarca e la confessione in sogno di Bernat Metge." *Fourteenth-Century Classicism: Petrarch and Bernat Metge*, edited by Lluís Cabré, Warburg Institute, 2012, pp. 57–68.

---, editor. *Sis poetes del regnat d'Alfons el Magnànim*. Barcino, 2009.

Torroella, Pere. *Obra completa*. Edited by Francisco J Rodríguez Risquete, Barcino, 2011. 2 vols.

Trens, Manuel. *María. Iconografía de la Virgen en el arte español*. Plus-Ultra, 1946.

Twomey, Lesley. *The Fabric of Marian Devotion in Isabel de Villena's Vita Christi*. Tamesis, 2013.

Ullman, Pierre L. "Juan Ruiz's Prologue." *Modern Language Notes*, vol. 82, 1967, pp. 149–70.

Valero Moreno, Juan Miguel. "Las *artes liberales* de Alonso de Cartagena: los manuscritos salmantinos y el tipo." *Modelos intelectuales, nuevos textos y nuevos lectores en el siglo XV*, edited by Pedro M. Cátedra, Seminario de Estudios Medievales y Renacentistas, 2014, pp. 135–213.

Valls Taberner, Fernando. "Los abogados de Cataluña durante la Edad Media." *Obras selectas. Vol. 2: Estudios histórico-jurídicos*, Consejo Superior de Investigaciones Científicas, 1954, pp. 281–318.

Valvassori, Mita. "Observaciones sobre el estudio y la edición de la traducción castellana antigua del *Decameron*." *Cuadernos de Filología Italiana*, Número Extraordinario, 2010, pp. 15–27.

Vasvári, Louise O. "The Novelness of the *Libro de buen amor*." *A Companion to the Libro de buen amor*, edited by Louise M. Haywood and Louise O. Vasvári, Tamesis, 2004, pp. 165–81.

Vellón Lahoz, Javier. "El proceso de ficcionalidad en la narrativa del siglo XV: la función autor/narrador y la ilusión referencial." *Rilce*, vol. 13, 1997, pp. 171–84.

Villaseñor Sebastián, Fernando. *Iconografía marginal en Castilla 1454–1492*. Consejo Superior de Investigaciones Científicas, 2009.

---. "El Libro de Horas del infante don Alfonso en el contexto de la iluminación tardogótica de la Península Ibérica." *Titivillus. International Journal of Rare Book: Revista Internacional sobre Libro Antiguo*, vol. 1, 2015, pp. 89–100.

Villena, Enrique de. "Los doce trabajos de Hércules." *Obras completas*, edited by Pedro M. Cátedra, vol. 1, Turner, 1994, pp. 1–111.

---. *Los doce trabajos de Hércules*. Edited by Pedro M. Cátedra and Paolo Cherchi, U de Cantabria, 2007. 2 vols.

---. *Obras completas*. Edited by Pedro M. Cátedra, Turner, 1994–2000. 3 vols.

Vitz, Evelyn Birge. "Desire and Causality in Medieval Narrative." *Romanic Review*, vol. 71, 1980, pp. 213–43.

---. *Medieval Narrative and Modern Narratology: Subjects and Objects of Desire*. New York UP, 1989.

Vives y Liern, Vicente. *Las casas de los estudios en Valencia*. Viuda de Emilio Pascual, 1902.

Voigt, Lisa. "La alegoría de la lectura en *Cárcel de Amor*." *La corónica*, vol. 25, 1997, pp. 123–33.

Von Richthofen, E. "Petrarca, Dante y Andreas Capellanus: fuentes inadvertidas de *La Cárcel de Amor*." *Revista Canadiense de Estudios Hispánicos*, vol. 1, 1976, pp. 30–38.

Wack, Mary Frances. *Lovesickness in the Middle Ages: The Viaticum and Its Commentaries*. U of Pennsylvania P, 1990.

Walde Moheno, Lillian von der. "Amor cortés y cultura oficial en Juan de Flores." *Heterodoxia y ortodoxia medieval (Actas de las Segundas Jornadas Medievales)*, edited by Concepción Abellán, et al., UNAM, 1992, pp. 21–28.

---. "De ejemplos y consejos en *Grimalte y Gradisa*." *La corónica*, vol. 29, 2000, pp. 193–204.

---. "La estructura retórica de la ficción sentimental." *Discursos y representaciones en la Edad Media*, UNAM-El Colegio de México, 1999, pp. 101–08.

---. "Experimentación literaria del siglo XV. A propósito de *Grimalte y Gradisa*, de Juan de Flores." *Juan de Flores: Four Studies*, edited by Joseph Gwara, Queen Mary and Westfield College, U of London, 2005, pp. 75–89.

---. "La ficción sentimental." *Medievalia*, vol. 25, 1997, pp. 1–25.

---. "La novela sentimental española." *Temas de literatura medieval española*, edited by Aurelio González and María Teresa Miaja de la Peña, UNAM, 2006, pp. 55–61.

---. "Recursos para la alienación en *Grimalte y Gradisa*, de Juan de Flores." *"De ninguna cosa es alegre posesión sin compañía." Estudios celestinescos y medievales en honor del profesor Joseph Thomas Snow*, edited by Devid Paolini, vol. 2, Hispanic Seminary of Medieval Studies, 2010, pp. 324–35.

Waley, Pamela. "Love and Honour in the Novels of San Pedro and Flores." *Bulletin of Hispanic Studies*, vol. 43, 1966, pp. 253–75.

Wardropper, Bruce W. *Historia de la poesía lírica a lo divino en la cristiandad occidental*. Revista de Occidente, 1958.

Webster, Jill R. *Els Menorets: The Franciscans in the Realms of Aragon From St. Francis to the Black Death*. Pontifical Institute of Mediaeval Studies, 1993.

Weiss, Julian. "La *Affección Poetal Virtuosa*: Petrarch's Sonnet 116 as Poetic Manifesto for Fifteenth-Century Castile." *The Modern Language Review*, vol. 86, 1991, pp. 70–78.

---. "Alvaro de Luna, Juan de Mena and the Power of Courtly Love." *Modern Language Notes*, vol. 106, 1991, pp. 241–56.

---. "Las 'fermosas e peregrinas ystorias': sobre la glosa ornamental cuatrocentista." *Revista de Literatura Medieval*, vol. 2, 1990, pp. 103–12.

---. "Juan de Mena's *Coronación*: Satire or Sátira?" *Journal of Hispanic Philology*, vol. 6, 1982, pp. 113–38.

---. "Medieval Vernacular Poetics and the Social Meaning of Form." *Atalaya*, vol. 8, 1997, pp. 171–86.

---. *The Poet's Art. Literary Theory in Castile c. 1440–60.* The Society for the Study of Medieval Languages and Literature, 1990.

---. "¿Qué demandamos de las mujeres?: Forming the Debate about Women in Late Medieval Spain (with a Baroque Response)." *Gender in Debate from the Early Middle Ages to the Renaissance*, edited by Thelma S. Fenster and Claire A. Lees, Palgrave, 2002, pp. 237–81.

---. "What Every Noblewoman Needs to Know: Cultural Literacy in Late-Medieval Spain." *Speculum*, vol. 81, 2006, pp. 1118–49.

Weissberger, Barbara F. "Authors, Characters, and Readers in Grimalte y Gradissa." *Creation and Re-Creation: Experiments in Literary Form in Early Modern Spain: Studies in Honor of Stephen Gilman*, edited by Ronald Surtz and Nora Weinerth, Juan de la Cuesta, 1983, pp. 61–76.

---. "The Gendered Taxonomy of Spanish Romance." *La corónica*, vol. 29, 2000, pp. 205–29.

---. "'Habla el *auctor*': *L'Elegia di Madonna Fiammetta* as a Source for the *Siervo libre de amor*." *Journal of Hispanic Philology*, vol. 4, 1980, pp. 203–36.

---. *Isabel Rules. Constructing Queenship, Wielding Power.* U of Minnesota P, 2004.

---. "The Politics of *Cárcel de Amor*." *Revista de Estudios Hispánicos*, vol. 26, 1992, pp. 307–26.

---. "Resisting Readers and Writers in the Sentimental Romances and the Problem of Female Literacy." *Studies on the Spanish Sentimental Romance (1440–1550). Redefining a Genre*, edited by Joseph J. Gwara and E. Michael Gerli, Tamesis, 1997, pp. 173–90.

Whetnall, Jane. "Cancioneros." *Castilian Writers, 1400–1500*, edited by Frank A. Domínguez and George D. Greenia, Gale, 2004, pp. 288–323.

---. "Isabel González of the *Cancionero de Baena* and Other Lost Voices." *La corónica*, vol. 21, 1992, pp. 59–82.

---. "Lírica femenina in the Early Manuscript Cancioneros." *What's Past Is Prologue: A Collection of Essays in Honour of L. J. Woodward*, edited by Salvador Bacarisse, et al., Scottish Academic P, 1984, pp. 138–75.

Whinnom, Keith. "*Autor* and *Tratado* in the Fifteenth Century: Semantic Latinism or Etymological Trap?" *Bulletin of Hispanic Studies*, vol. 59, 1982, pp. 211–18.

---. "Cardona, The Crucifixion, and Leriano's Last Drink." *Studies on the Spanish Sentimental Romance (1440–1550). Redefining a Genre*, edited by Joseph J. Gwara and E. Michael Gerli, Tamesis, 1997, pp. 207–15.

---. *Diego de San Pedro.* Twayne Publishers, 1974.

---. "Diego de San Pedro's Stylistic Reform." *Bulletin of Hispanic Studies*, vol. 37, 1960, pp. 1–15.

---. *La poesía amatoria en la época de los Reyes Católicos.* U of Durham P, 1981.

---. *The Spanish Sentimental Romance 1440–1550: A Critical Bibliography.* Grant & Cutler, 1983.

Wickham Legg, Leopold G., editor. *English Coronation Records.* Archibald Constable & Co., 1901.

Wieck, Roger S. *Painted Prayers: The Book of Hours in Medieval and Renaissance Art.* George Braziller and Pierpont Morgan Library, 1997.

Williamson, Beth. "Altarpieces, Liturgy, and Devotion." *Speculum*, vol. 79, 2004, pp. 341–406.

Witlin, Curt. *De la traducció literal a la creació literària: estudis filològics sobre textos antics catalans i valencians.* Institut Interuniversitari de Filologia Valenciana, 1995.

Woods, Marjorie Curry. "Performing Dido." *Public Declamations: Essays on Medieval Rhetoric, Education, and Letters in Honour of Martin Camargo.* Brepols, 2015, pp. 253–65.

---. "Rape and the Pedagogical Rhetoric of Sexual Violence." *Criticism and Dissent in the Middle Ages*, edited by Rita Copeland, Cambridge UP, 1996, pp. 56–86.

---. "Rhetoric, Gender, and the Literary Arts: Classical Speeches in the Schoolroom." *Medieval Grammar and the Literary Arts*, edited by Rita Copeland, et al., Brepols, 2009, pp. 113–32.

Yates, Frances A. *The Art of Memory*. Chicago UP, 1964.

Yarza Luaces, Joaquín. "La imagen del rey y la imagen del noble en el siglo XV castellano." *Realidad e imágenes del poder: España a fines de la edad media*, edited by Adeline Rucquoi, Ediciones Ámbito, 1988, pp. 267–91.

---. *Los Reyes Católicos. Paisaje artístico de una monarquía*. Nerea, 1993.

Ynduráin, Domingo. "Las cartas de Laureola (beber cenizas)." *Edad de Oro*, vol. 3, 1984, pp. 299–309.

---. *Humanismo y Renacimiento en España*. Cátedra, 1994.

Zaderenko, Irene. "Dante en la ficción sentimental." *Dicenda: Cuadernos de Filología Hispánica*, vol. 17, 1999, pp. 283–93.

Ziino, Francesca. "The Catalan Tradition of Boethius's *De consolatione*: A New Hypothesis." *Carmina Philosophiae: Journal of the International Boethius Society*, vol. 10, 2001, pp. 31–38.

---. "Some Vernacular Versions of Boethius's *De Consolatione Philosophiae* in Medieval Spain: Notes on their Relationship with the Commentary Tradition." *Carmina Philosophiae: Journal of the International Boethius Society*, vol. 7, 1997, pp. 37–65.

---. "Una traduzione castigliana del *De consolatione* di Boezio (MS Madrid, Biblioteca Nacional, 10193)." *Romanica Vulgaria. Quaderni*, vol. 15, 2003, pp. 257–73.

Ziolkowski, Jan. *Alan of Lille's Grammar of Sex: The Meaning of Grammar to a Twelfth-Century Intellectual*. Medieval Academy of America, 1985.

---. *Obscenity: Social Control and Artistic Creation in the European Middle Ages*. Brill, 1998.

Zumthor, Paul. "The Great Game of Rhetoric." *New Literary History*, vol. 12, 1981, pp. 493–94.

INDEX

NORTH CAROLINA STUDIES IN THE ROMANCE LANGUAGES AND LITERATURES

Recent Titles

Send orders to: University of North Carolina Press
P.O. Box 2288
Chapel Hill, NC 27515-2288
U.S.A.
www.uncpress.unc.edu
FAX: 919 966-3829

CPSIA information can be obtained
at www.ICGtesting.com
Printed in the USA
LVHW012230291119
638675LV00002B/44